Left-Hand...

his Unfortunate ... he Bag...

The Workhouse Donkey: 'Arden's masterpiece. It hit me amidships and left me feeling it was after all possible to unite passion, politics, poetry, sex and song in a living theatrical form . . . The play is not just a kaleidoscopic portrait of a living community; it also has the moral uncertainty of life itself.' *Guardian*

Armstrong's Last Goodnight: 'Arden's strongest play. Each of his thirty speakers is beautifully alive, a realised private existence integrated into a huge social canvas . . . Arden has steeped himself in the marvellous language of Dunbar and the real Lindsay, lovingly recreating it into a theatrical speech thorny with images, knotted with strength, rough and springy as an uncombed fleece.' *New Statesman*

Left-Handed Liberty: 'It is clotted with ideas . . . full of stage pictures stamped out like shots in a film.' *Observer*

The True History of Squire Jonathan and his Unfortunate Treasure: 'Rumour has it that it was once considered for inclusion in *Oh! Calcutta!*. It is certainly more erotic than anything in that show and probably ten times as literate as the sum total.' *Financial Times*
'A moral fable . . . a literary near-poetic play.' *Time Out*

The Bagman: 'A complete triumph – it was that mystical thing, pure radio . . . it was a shining piece of ingenuity as well.' *New Statesman*

John Arden was born in Barnsley, Yorkshire, in 1930. While studying architecture at Cambridge and Edinburgh universities, he began to write plays, four of which were premièred at the Royal Court Theatre: *The Waters of Babylon*, *Live Like Pigs*, *Serjeant Musgrave's Dance* and *The Happy Haven*; while a fifth, *The Workhouse Donkey*, was produced at the Festival Theatre, Chichester. For a year he held an Annual Fellowship in Playwriting at Bristol University, and Bristol Old Vic produced *Ironhand*, his free adaptation of Goethe's *Goetz von Berlichingen*. *Armstrong's Last Goodnight* was first produced at the Glasgow Citizens' Theatre and later at the National Theatre. *Left-Handed Liberty* was specially commissioned by the Corporation of London to commemorate the 750th Anniversary of Magna Carta and was produced at the Mermaid Theatre. Recent revivals of Arden's plays include *Live Like Pigs* (Royal Court Theatre, London, 1993) and *Armstrong's Last Goodnight* (Edinburgh Festival, 1994). He is married to Margaretta D'Arcy, with whom he has collaborated on many plays. Arden's first novel, *Silence Among the Weapons* (1982), was short-listed for the Booker-McConnell Prize for Fiction. His other novels are: *Books of Bale* (1988), *Cogs Tyrannic* (1991), which won the PEN 'Silver Pen' Award, and *Jack Juggler and the Emperor's Whore* (1995). He also won the V. S. Pritchett Award in 1999 for his short story 'Breach of Trust'.

JOHN ARDEN
Plays: 2

The Workhouse Donkey
Armstrong's Last Goodnight
Left-Handed Liberty
The True History of Squire Jonathan
and his Unfortunate Treasure
The Bagman

with a preface and introductory notes by the author

METHUEN CONTEMPORARY DRAMATISTS

1 3 5 7 9 10 8 6 4 2

This collection first published in Great Britain in 1994
by Methuen Drama

Reissued 2002

Methuen Publishing Ltd
215 Vauxhall Bridge Road, London SW1V 1EJ

The Workhouse Donkey first published by Methuen & Co Ltd 1964
Reprinted in the first edition of *Arden Plays: One* 1977
Copyright © 1964 by John Arden

Armstrong's Last Goodnight first published by Methuen & Co Ltd 1965
Reprinted in the first edition of *Arden Plays: One* 1977
Copyright © 1965, 1966 by John Arden

Left-Handed Liberty first published by Methuen & Co Ltd 1965
Copyright © 1965 by John Arden

The True History of Squire Jonathan and his Unfortunate Treasure and
The Bagman first published in *Two Autobiographical Plays* by
Methuen & Co Ltd 1971
Squire Jonathan copyright © 1968 by John Arden
The Bagman copyright © 1971 by John Arden

Preface to this collection copyright © 1994 by John Arden

Methuen Publishing Ltd Reg. No. 3543167

ISBN 0 413 68810 0

A CIP catalogue record for this book
is available from the British Library

The front cover shows a detail from *Der Jungbrunnen* (The Fountain of Youth) by
Lucas Cranach the Elder (1546, Gemäldegalerie, Berlin)
Photo: Archiv für Kunst und Geschichte, Berlin

Typeset by Wilmaset Ltd, Birkenhead, Wirral
Printed and bound in Great Britain by
Cox & Wyman Ltd, Reading, Berkshire

Caution

Contents

Chronology

Note: The initials '(JA/MD'A)' or '(MD'A/JA)' indicate a
collaboration between John Arden and Margaretta D'Arcy.

(JA)	*The Life of Man,* radio play, BBC radio	1956
(JA)	*The Waters of Babylon,* Royal Court Theatre, London	1957
(JA)	*When is a Door not a Door?,* Central School of Drama, London	1958
(JA)	*Live Like Pigs,* Royal Court Theatre, London	1958
(JA)	*Serjeant Musgrave's Dance,* Royal Court Theatre, London	1959
(JA)	*Soldier, Soldier,* BBC television	1960
(JA/MD'A)	*The Happy Haven,* Bristol University	1960
(JA/MD'A)	*The Business of Good Government,* Brent Knoll Church, Somerset	1960
(JA)	*Wet Fish,* BBC television	1961
(JA)	*Top Deck,* film	1961
(JA)	*The Workhouse Donkey,* Chichester Festival, Sussex	1963
(MD'A/JA)	*Ars Longa Vita Brevis,* Royal Shakespeare Company season at LAMDA Theatre Club, London	1964
(JA)	*Armstrong's Last Goodnight,* performed in Glasgow	1964
(JA)	*Left-Handed Liberty,* Mermaid Theatre, London	1965
(MD'A/JA)	*Friday's Hiding,* Royal Lyceum Theatre, Edinburgh	1966
(JA/MD'A)	*The Royal Pardon,* Beaford Arts Centre, Devon	1966
(MD'A/JA)	*Vietnam Carnival,* New York University	1967
(MD'A/JA)	*Harold Muggins is a Martyr,* performed by CAST (Cartoon Archetypical Slogan Theatre) at Unity Theatre, London	1968
(JA)	*The True History of Squire Jonathan and his Unfortunate Treasure,* Ambiance Lunch-Hour Theatre Club, London	1968
(JA/MD'A)	*The Hero Rises Up,* Roundhouse, London	1968
(JA)	*The Bagman,* BBC radio	1970

(MD'A/JA)	*The Ballygombeen Bequest*, performed by 7:84 Theatre Company at Edinburgh Festival	1972
(JA/MD'A)	*The Island of the Mighty*, in three parts, Royal Shakespeare Company at the Aldwych Theatre, London	1972
(JA/MD'A)	*Keep Those People Moving!*, schools' radio	1972
(MD'A/JA)	*Non-Stop Connolly Show*, in six parts, performed in Dublin, Ireland	1975
(MD'A/JA)	*Vandaleur's Folly*, toured by 7:84 Theatre Company	1978
(JA)	*Pearl*, BBC radio	1978
(JA)	*The Adventures of the Ingenious Gentleman Don Quixote*, BBC radio, in two parts	1980
(JA)	*The Old Man Sleeps Alone*, BBC radio	1982
(JA)	*Garland for a Hoar Head*, BBC radio	1982
(JA/MD'A)	*The Manchester Enthusiasts*, BBC radio, in two parts	1984
(JA/MD'A)	*Whose is the Kingdom?*, BBC radio series, in nine parts	1988
(JA/MD'A)	*A Suburban Suicide*, BBC radio	1994
(JA)	*The Little Novels of Wilkie Collins*, BBC radio series	1998
(JA)	*Woe Alas! The Fatal Cashbox*, BBC radio	1999

Novels by John Arden:

Silence Among the Weapons	1982
Books of Bale	1988
Cogs Tyrannic	1991
Jack Juggler and the Emperor's Whore	1995

Preface

The cover-illustration is a portion of *The Fountain of Youth*, by
Lucas Cranach the Elder (1546, painted when he was 74).
Women who have been on the edge of death arise rejuvenated
through the enchanted waters: an allegory, as I take it, of the re-
creative powers which an artist may seize again and again from
the continued process of work, a kind of magic needing no
necromantic spells but only an imagination enkindled by
mortality. Now that I am over sixty my own imagination
responds happily enough to such an idea; and a collection of
plays I wrote before I was 39 seems a suitable occasion for me to
call it to mind.

Cranach, a Lutheran of the earliest stage of the Protestant
Reformation, could not have approved of magic as such. His
'New Religion' was an expression of Hope; but his *Fountain*
would seem to contradict that Hope by evoking a Golden Age
which the Bible told him never existed except in the Garden of
Eden before the Fall. Whoever these pert little nude nymphs
may be, renewing their youth and beauty with insouciant self-
confidence, they are certainly not the companions of Adam and
Eve, and they were painted in no spirit of Christian Faith. There
was some sort of Faith indeed; but a Faith without Hope,
Cranach's Faith in his own self – in his own inconsistent dreams
– in his own aging body, which he knew (but *for the time being*
denied) was doomed very shortly to fail him altogether – and
Faith (above all) in the magic of his own mind.

A mind not so dissimilar to that of a fellow-citizen of
Wittenberg, an eccentric academic of the university there,
Luther's university; Hamlet's moreover (if we may stray, as the
picture does, from the authority of historical and theological
'truth' into fiction and legend). Dr Faust – historical personage,
legendary anti-hero, theological object-lesson in his own lifetime
– was said to have ordered up Helen of Troy from the Further

World, hiring the Christian devil to secure her; a tale which
more completely than any other encapsulates the muddled
yearnings of the Renaissance north of the Alps. Wittenberg was
quite a small place; Cranach would have known Faust; or would
surely have known others who knew him. He would have known
enough about him to understand why such tales were being told.
Was he appalled or delighted at the professor's presumption?

Faust's magic was prohibited necromancy, Cranach's the mere
fantasy of paint. Between them was a tie of desire, but a contrast
in methods of fulfilment. So too between Faust and Christopher
Marlowe. Marlowe, like Cranach, made his own magic (from
blank verse and the actors who voiced it); with an envious
fascination he *re-created* Dr Faust.

Which brings me obliquely to what I have long thought to be
one of the phenomena of the theatre: the 'necromantic' ability of
a playwright to thrust invented, or recaptured, personalities into
other persons' skins and set them walking and talking for a
public that (neither believing in it nor disbelieving) will simply
accept the circumstance for as long as the play might last.

The playwright can believe it for ever, in an ever-rejuvenating
trance of self-hallucination; as I am now discovering as I look
through these old writings of mine and remember how they were
when completed by their actors on the stage.

Cranach shows only women in his Fountain. If he did not
paint, or did not intend to paint, a companion piece of men, is it
possible that he was deterred by the need to distance himself
from his own naked male cadaver in decrepit old age? He knew
he was dreaming and *not* facing facts.

A type of evasion much employed in the theatre.

I think immediately of all those homosexual dramatists who
have felt forced by public prejudice to show love in their plays as
exclusively heterosexual, when that wasn't what they had in
mind at all. But it is not only a matter of accommodating
prejudice; prevarication is inherent in the very form of the art. A
play can never be as deeply confessional as a poem or a novel, if
only because the writer's *personae* must be given shape by
Someone Else. I do know that playwrights have been known to
perform in their own work (I've done it myself); and sometimes
very hazardously, as when the mortally-sick Molière took the
leading role in his *Malade Imaginaire*. But even in such cases, to
set up the story on a stage makes a fiction of it whether you want
it or not; the entire theatre is a material fiction; an artificial

contrivance which must always create some *distance*, however strongly the production-style may strive to close the gap.

When Faust embraced the woman who came to him amid the brazier-fumes and cabbalistic formulae of his midnight hocus-pocus, he was perfectly aware she was *not* the real Helen of Troy; he can have had no Hope that she would turn out to be other than a phantom. The gap was there and he shuddered at it.

It is a gap that I myself have spent time and energy doing my best to close, or at any rate, to *bridge*. Not in order to expose everything about my own psyche to a paying audience, which is a madhouse kind of thing even to think about – the stuff of nightmares – but to bring the subject-matter of my stories a little closer to the extra-theatrical lives of both playwright and public. The majority of these attempts have been made since 1969. The plays printed here belong before that date.* When I wrote them I was already involved with Margaretta D'Arcy in a number of projects of our own, independent of the professional managements. This creative double-life bred in me a species of schizophrenia which took years to resolve, and would probably never have come to a head if we had not had a traumatic conflict with the Royal Shakespeare Company in 1972 over our *Island of the Mighty*. For a time I thought that that extremely painful quarrel was the worst thing that had ever happened to me; then I came to see it as simply one more dip into the Fountain – only this time the water had been scarifyingly hot and some of the people on the far bank did not seem to know who I was when I got out. The banquet wasn't ready, the musicians were still tuning up, the new clothes in the dressing tent were all the wrong sizes . . .

Nevertheless, I had made it; and was eventually re-emboldened to make it again and again. At present I am writing prose-fiction. An aggressive young man in Edinburgh three years ago told me I had 'sold out' by turning away from stage-plays. I asked him why; he replied that my novels were 'crap'. I asked him, had he read them? He said no, but they had to be, because everyone had admired my plays in the days when I had an integrity. He was not very logical, being slightly foxed with drink, but he was struggling to say what he really felt. He belonged to an avant-garde theatre-group; he believed I was in

---

*For later plays, written with Margaretta D'Arcy, see the booklist at the end of this preface.

some way a deserter, a traitor to the colours. I was not at the time capable of giving him a satisfactory answer. But really, I do not think I have to. The theatre is not an army, a church, or any other sort of oath-bound vocation. It is no more and no less than a method of telling stories; a method not always suited to all story-tellers at all times of their lives. There are other methods for the choosing, with their own types of evasion built-in and tempting you, and to find them you still have to nerve yourself to cross over the pool of the Fountain and have Faith in your own Hope when you know it is hopeless.

Enough about Cranach's Fountain: a comfort to think he may have found comfort from painting it.

*　　*　　*

Some thoughts about the plays in this book:

The Workhouse Donkey

No sooner do I say goodbye to Cranach than back he comes into my mind – this play is a cross-breed between the mood of his low life satire (when he painted grotesque 'January and May' copulations) and his Golden Age erotics – my original introduction explains what I was attempting with the theatrical form – something of an impossibility, given the time and place – what, a north-of-England fertility-comedy in Chichester, in 1963, when the Home Counties stuffed-shirts were still reeling from the shock of the Profumo scandals? Too near the bone, and yet too far away from it: it fell flatly between two stools.

Two references in the original introduction need expanding, I think.

1. The play is indeed set (fantastically) in Barnsley, with Charlie Butterthwaite from *The Waters of Babylon* at the height of his hubris; but the jumping-off place for the plot was Nottingham, where a dreadful row between the Chief Constable and the city council had pushed its way onto the front pages a few years earlier. The play had originally been intended for production in Coventry (as part of a festival to celebrate the rebuilding of the cathedral); but it turned out that there had also been a dreadful row in *that* city, between the council and the church authorities, as to whether the cathedral should be rebuilt at all – 'the money should go on houses for the people!' – and *The Workhouse Donkey* was perceived as possibly hinting at this and threatening to open old wounds. The festival organisers said, 'Oh no no'. A pity;

Coventry is not in Yorkshire; but urban politics are conditioned
more by industrial conditions than geographical location; I think
Coventry audiences would have understood what I was getting at
far better than those in Chichester.

2. Mr Joseph D'Arcy of Dublin was my father-in-law. He died
of a heart-attack in 1962, the year before the play appeared.
When I wrote of his 'personality', I was thinking especially of the
way he had arrived in a taxi, for the first night of either *Live Like
Pigs* or *Musgrave* – I forget which – with a boisterous Irish
journalist – and of the hilarious counterpoint with which they
paid off the cab-driver and hurtled (rather late) into the Royal
Court foyer, asking each other which of them had the tickets,
asking the front-of-house manager was he sure it was the right
theatre, the right night, the right play – so expert a music-hall
double-act that I took some of it for the general behaviour of
Wellington Blomax, and the rest of it (metamorphosed into West
Yorkshire idiom) for the arrival of Butterthwaite and Councillors
at the Copacabana in Act One, Scene Nine.

There is another family contribution to this play, now that I
think of it: the name 'Wellington Blomax' was provided by my
two nephews, Michael and Robin Pollitt, then aged about four
and three. They had, as children will, invented for themselves an
invisible friend of that name – I could not be entirely sure who
he was and what he meant to them, for they refused to be
specific, indeed they refused any information at all and simply
giggled when I asked them – at all events, they chattered to
themselves incessantly about someone who *sounded* like
Wellington Blomax and eventually in my play *became* Wellington
Blomax. How on earth do kids catch hold of these extraordinary
verbal conjunctions? – spot-on (one says immediately) and yet
impenetrably inconsequential. . . . They are, I must suppose,
the beginnings of all poetry.

Left-Handed Liberty

My only play to have been commissioned on a particular subject
for a particular occasion – by Bernard Miles, of the Mermaid
Theatre, who was (as it were) master of the revels for the Lord
Mayor and Corporation of the City of London. All very solemn
and sober. I don't think I lived up to it.

The name of the play very nearly lost me the job. I guess, as a
Royal Court playwright, I was being looked at askance from the
beginning; and then Aldermen took '*left*-handed' to mean

Socialism and told Bernard Miles, 'Oh no no!' But he argued
them out of countenance on my behalf and the title was kept.

My worst trouble, though, was sheer lack of time; and it
shows. The essential difficulty, to lay out the history so that a
comparatively ignorant* modern audience would understand it,
and at the same time to present it so that it actually *meant*
something to the mid-twentieth century, proved insoluble
without another year's brooding over it; and that, of course, I
could not have. Margaretta said, 'Open it out before the end.' I
think she was right; and the huge direct-address monologue I
gave King John was a step towards making it right. But it
remained clumsy; and my device of Lady de Vesci sitting mute
behind him as a sort of human visual-aid was sheer cruelty to the
actress. I was afterwards told so by Margaretta in no uncertain
terms; and I have remembered it and reproached myself for it
ever since. Lady de Vesci was *needed* by the argument of the
scene, I knew it subconsciously, for all kinds of inchoate reasons
which I never had time to work out; in the end I found for her
no effective function.

To one (sober and solemn) performance of the play the Queen
and all her train arrived, with great decorum and heavy protocol.
The Mermaid's toilet facilities had to be totally rearranged for
her; apparently a mandatory accompaniment to royal visits
anywhere. Bernard Miles tried to insist I should be there, to be
'presented'. I could not bear the idea.

I hoped the play did sincerely express my political and
historical opinions; of course it accepted monarchy as a plausible
form of government for the thirteenth century; and to some
extent it tried to remove from King John some of the clots of
indiscriminate obloquy that have adhered to him over the
centuries and obscured the real importance of his struggle with
the barons and the church. (To quote the comment of a friend
when I told him what I was writing: 'Oh, John? Yes. Everyone
knows he's the villain in *Robin Hood*; apart from that – what's
there to say about him?') But I still saw no reason why this
subject-matter should oblige me to accept monarchy in 1965; so I
did not go to the royal evening. I was timid enough not to offer

---

*No more ignorant of the details of 1215 than *I* was before I began my
research. In general the British middle-class knows far less about these
cruces of history than, say, its Victorian ancestors did; I wonder what we
do know about?

any proper explanation; no denunciations or republican remonstrances; I pretended (I think) I had to do rewrites to the script – which was probably true, but an *evasion*. I hated the idea of publicity being made out of it; to me it was a simple matter of my own private choice.

Bernard Miles was exasperated, and my parents (so proud to be part of the audience that night) were sorely disappointed I was not there. Bernard's exasperation was probably mixed with relief. I heard later that while fixing details of the Occasion with a palace equerry (before he knew of my refusal) he said something like – 'Ah, the playwright; I'm sure he'll be present; but perhaps you should warn Her Majesty, he has – he has, you see, all this – *hair*.' It is true, I was unshorn in those days. So were a lot of other men. It was a style; but not yet a favoured one in 'responsible quarters'. The police in North Yorkshire, where I lived, used to stop me and question me with the utmost suspicion.

Armstrong's Last Goodnight

In 1962 Margaretta and I made our home with our young children on an island in Loch Corrib, in the west of Ireland. We had brought a load of books with us and found many more in a deserted fallen-down house on a neighbouring island. One of them was a battered volume of ballads – a shorter version of the famous Child Collection. I remember sitting in the long grass among gorse bushes and reading the *Johnie Armstrong* poem – not for the first time; it had been familiar to me for years; but with the Connemara mountains in the distance and the gray water all around me, it seemed to have a sudden immediacy. Also there were notes to it, explaining the exact circumstances of King James's punitive raid into Armstrong's country, beginning with the Anglo-Scottish conference at Berwick which was to be the first scene of my play.

With the poem all alive inside me, I took a bicycle ride into the nearest town, Oughterard, to do the week's shopping. On the way I passed the ruin of Aughnanure Castle, an early sixteenth-century stronghold of Gaelic Irish who had much the same reputation with the anglophone citizens of the nearby colony-town of Galway as had the Armstrongs with the farmers in Cumberland and Northumberland. The castle, too, was in a very similar style of architecture to that of the Border peel-towers. I stopped and walked about in the ruin. I imagined the events of the ballad emanating from there.

It was another year or two before I actually set to work on the play; but that was the germ of it; the west of Ireland combining with my own life in the 1950s in Scotland, first as a conscript-soldier and then as a student. The connection with Conor Cruise O'Brien's Katanga experience came in later, insidiously almost, as I worried over the political implications of the story. I had already read his book but had put it at the back of my mind. When I envisaged the combined Scots and English Commissioners entrusting the Armstrong negotiations to David Lindsay, I remembered the United Nations appointing Dr Cruise O'Brien for a somewhat similar job in Africa – to end the secession of Katanga just as Lindsay had to abort the *de facto* independence of the Border mosstroopers. In short, the *climate* of the tale came to me before its complete argument.

Two Autobiographical Plays
These have a preface of their own which eliminates any need for further explanation here. Except that the grotesque and erotic veins of Lucas Cranach are both present in the *Squire Jonathan* tale (the same combination, in a differently-proportioned mix, as I used for *The Workhouse Donkey*); while *The Bagman*, which was commissioned by the BBC as a modern version of Molière's *Versailles Impromptu*, turned out to owe far more to *The Pilgrim's Progress* – I suppose a very English transition. I should emphasise that if it had not been for Ed Berman's indefatigable lunch-time enterprise at the Ambience, *Squire Jonathan* would probably never have been produced. (Naked ladies taken seriously as real characters in a story caused a problem for producers, just as they do for Cranach's commentators. Were they Sex? Were they Realism? Were they Poetry? Who could say?) There was another possibility for the script, Ken Tynan's *Oh Calcutta*, then in course of preparation. But *Squire J.*, he said, was too much of a play and not enough of a revue-sketch . . . I am by no means the only playwright to owe Ed a debt of gratitude for his encouragement of the quirkier corners of our work; his contribution to the London theatre in the 60s and 70s has yet to be fully valued.

*   *   *

Collaborative texts by J. Arden and M. D'Arcy (all published by Methuen):
Arden/D'Arcy (aka *D'Arcy/Arden*), *Plays: One* (1992),
The Island of the Mighty (1974),

The Non-Stop Connolly Show (1986),

Whose is the Kingdom . . . ? (1988),

To Present the Pretence (1977): essays, including an account of the
script-and-stage history of *The Non-Stop Connolly Show*.

Awkward Corners (1988), essays etc.

Preface to an earlier version of *Arden Plays: One* (1977: in the
'Master Playwrights' series), a kind of valediction to the
established theatre.

John Arden,
Corrandulla, Co. Galway, Ireland.
May 1994.

The Workhouse Donkey

A Vulgar Melo-Drama

FOR TAMARA

This cool sweet moon (now defeated by night
    Which crossed her with raincloud and mirk)
Had, under her first rising, sent momentary light
    Through every tree in the park.
Every bush, every pool, every thicket abhorrent
Remain to my blind sight apparent:
    And I can walk yet without danger or fright.

Introductory Note

I have called this play a melo-drama: a term I intend to be understood in its original sense of a play with a musical accompaniment. In the Chichester production, Mr Addison's score provided not only settings for the several songs but also a background for much of the dialogue, and linking passages between the scenes. The band was seated on an upper balcony of the stage and remained in view of the audience throughout the action. As the play is strictly a play and not a musical or a light opera, I dare say it would be possible to present it without instrumental accompaniment, but unless economy imperatively demands it, I do not recommend that this should be done.

The Workhouse Donkey was originally commissioned for the Royal Court Theatre, and it was necessary to adapt it somewhat for the open stage at Chichester. The directions in this printed text will, it is hoped, prove applicable to any of the more usual types of auditorium. For productions within a proscenium-arch it is essential that décor be kept to a minimum and that the action be allowed to flow from one scene into the next with the least possible delay. Both costumes and settings may have a certain air of caricature: but as the play is basically accurate and realistic (indeed, a great deal of it is conscientiously historical), the limits of visual extravagance normally adhered to by the artists of seaside picture-postcards should not be exceeded.

I had considerable difficulty in preparing *The Workhouse Donkey* for the stage. My chosen subject-matter proved both labyrinthine and intractable, and I do not think I could ever have condensed it into the bounds of conventional acting time without the assistance, advice, collaboration, criticism, and frequently expressed bewilderment of:

Mr Lindsay Anderson
Mr Stuart Burge
Miss Margaretta D'Arcy
Mr George Devine
Sir Laurence Olivier
and nearly everyone employed upon or connected with the
production at Chichester.

I am, however, still uncertain how valuable our combined
efforts have been. Two-and-a-half or three hours is normally
regarded as the maximum permissible length for a new play,
and under the conditions at present prevalent in our theatres it
is not easy to dispute this. But I would have been happy had it
been possible for *The Workhouse Donkey* to have lasted, say, six
or seven or thirteen hours (excluding intervals), and for the
audience to come and go throughout the performance, assisted
perhaps by a printed synopsis of the play from which they
could deduce those scenes or episodes which would interest
them particularly, and those which they could afford to miss.
A theatre presenting such an entertainment would, of course,
need to offer rival attractions as well, and would in fact take on
some of the characteristics of a fairground or amusement park;
with restaurants, bars, sideshows, bandstands and so forth, all
grouped round a central playhouse. The design of the playhouse itself would need careful consideration, as clearly members of an audience continually moving to and from their seats
in a conventional building will cause intolerable distraction.
But I am convinced that if what we laughably call 'vital theatre'
is ever to live up to its name, some such casual or 'prom-
concert' conception must eventually be arrived at.* It will not
suit every play, and every play should not be compelled to suit
itself to it: the theatre must be catholic. But it never will be

---

* Miss Joan Littlewood has already put forward a similar and
apparently highly practicable proposition. I hope she will be enabled
to carry it out.

catholic if we do not grant pride of place to the old essential attributes of Dionysus:

> noise
> disorder
> drunkenness
> lasciviousness
> nudity
> generosity
> corruption
> fertility
> and
> ease.

The Comic Theatre was formed expressly to celebrate them: and whenever they have been forgotten our art has betrayed itself and our generally accessible and agreeable god has hidden his face.

The personality of the late Mr Joseph D'Arcy of Dublin inspired much of the play.

The personality of my native town of Barnsley also inspired a great deal of it: but I have carefully avoided the imitation of the personalities of individual inhabitants. Thus the curiosity of the malicious will go ungratified.

In view of the fact that this play was first performed in a southern county, the speeches used as prologue and epilogue were directed towards the probable audience in such a place. In productions north of the Trent these speeches should be replaced by those given on pages 130 and 131.

Some Critics said:
This Arden baffles us and makes us mad:
His play's uncouth, confused, lax, muddled, bad.

Said Arden:
Why do you accuse me and abuse me
And your polite society refuse me,
Merely because I wear no belt nor braces ?
There would be reason for the wry mouths in your faces
And reason for your uncommitted halting speeches
If you would but admit I wore no bloody breeches.

JOHN ARDEN

The Workhouse Donkey

The Workhouse Donkey was first performed at the Chichester Festival Theatre on 8 July 1963, with the following cast:

Labour

ALDERMAN BOOCOCK, the Mayor	Dudley Foster
MRS BOOCOCK, the Mayoress	Fay Compton
ALDERMAN BUTTERTHWAITE, his friend and Ex-Mayor	Frank Finlay
HOPEFAST ⎫	Peter Russell
HARDNUTT ⎬ Borough Councillors	Harry Lomax
HICKLETON ⎭	Peter O'Shaughnessy

Conservative

ALDERMAN SIR HAROLD SWEETMAN, a wealthy brewer	Martin Boddey
LADY SWEETMAN, his wife	Alison Leggatt
MAURICE SWEETMAN, his son	Jeremy Brett
F.J., his friend: Industrialist and Borough Councillor	Peter Cellier

The Police

COLONEL FENG, Chief Constable	Anthony Nicholls
SUPERINTENDENT WIPER	Robert Stephens
SERGEANT LUMBER	Robert Lang
PC LIVERSEDGE	Derek Jacobi
PC LEFTWICH, retired from active duty: Mayoral Mace-Bearer and Town Hall Factotum	Keith Marsh
TWO POLICEMEN	Terence Knapp
	Raymond Clarke

The Electorate

DR WELLINGTON BLOMAX, a physician	Norman Rossington
WELLESLEY, his daughter	Mary Miller

GLORIA, Manageress of the Copacabana Club Marion Mathie
STONE MASONS Michael Turner
Michael Rothwell
GUESTS, at the Sweetmans' Raymond Clarke,
Rowena Cooper, Marika Mann,
Jean Rogers
MAID, at the Sweetmans' Louise Purnell
LANDLORD, of the Victoria and Albert Dan Meaden
BARMAID Elizabeth Burger
ASSISTANT BAR BOY John Rogers
DRINKERS Reginald Green, Terence Knapp,
Michael Rothwell, Michael Turner
NURSE, at Dr Blomax's Rowena Cooper
DOORMAN Terence Knapp
HOSTESS Irene Sutcliffe
WAITRESSES at the Rowena Cooper,
Copacabana Club Marika Mann
DANCERS Elizabeth Burger, Rowena Cooper,
Jeanne Hepple, Louise Purnell,
Jean Rogers, Michael Rothwell
SPECIALITY Jeanette Landis
NUMBERS
JOURNALISTS Richard Hampton,
Michael Rothwell, Michael Turner
PARK ATTENDANT Reginald Green
LOVERS John Rogers, Louise Purnell
WAITRESS, in a Tea Shop Jeanne Hepple
DEMONSTRATORS Elizabeth Burger,
Reginald Green, Jeanne Hepple,
Jeanette Landis, Michael Rothwell

Produced by Stuart Burge
Music by John Addison
Décor by Roger Furse
Lighting by Richard Pilbrow
Dances arranged by Eleanor Fazan

The action of the play takes place in a Yorkshire industrial town: somewhere between Sheffield and Leeds.
The time is the present.

Act One

A building site.
Foundation stone ready in position for lowering.

    Enter BLOMAX.

BLOMAX.
    Ladies and gentlemen: let us suppose we go
    From St Pancras to Sheffield,
    To Doncaster from King's Cross:
    By either route to Leeds.

    Enter MASONS

    Not very far to go, for us or the flight of a crow
    But involving geographically an appreciable mutation,
    (I mean, in landscape, climate, odours, voices, food.)
    I put it to you that such a journey needs
    In the realm of morality an equal alteration.

    Enter WIPER, LUMBER *and* PCs *as Guard of Honour.*

    I mean, is there anything you really believe to be bad?
    If you come to the North you might well think it good.
    You might well think, as I do,
    That you should change the shape of your faces
    Or even double their number
    When you travel between two places.

    Enter civic procession. It includes BOOCOCK, MRS BOO-
    COCK (LEFTWICH *with mace preceding them*), SWEET-
    MAN, F. J., *Labour Councillors, and* BUTTERTHWAITE.
    Aldermen and Mayor in robes of office, etc. Also Conserva-
    tive Ladies and YOUNG SWEETMAN, *and several Citizens.*

The values of other people
Are not quite as you understand them.
I would not overpraise them,
I would not recommend them,
I am certainly not here to offer to condemn them.
From the beginning to the end
Each man is bound to act
According to his nature
And the nature of his land.
Their land is different from yours.
Why, it has its own music.

> *Band plays 'Ilkley Moor'.* BLOMAX *greets* WIPER, *receives a curt nod in reply, and withdraws; enter* WELLESLEY, *meets* BLOMAX *and stands with him.* WIPER *salutes the* MAYOR.

WIPER. Guard of honour present and ready for your inspection, Mr Mayor.

BOOCOCK. Good afternoon. Superintendent, it is my privilege to present to you your new chief constable, Colonel Feng. Colonel Feng, Superintendent Wiper, who has during the interregnum been very ably conducting . . .

FENG. Good afternoon, Superintendent.

WIPER. Good afternoon, sir.

FENG. Shall we have a look at the Guard of Honour, Mr Mayor ?

BOOCOCK. Right we are, sir. After you.

FENG. Superintendent . . .

> *The band plays 'Ilkley Moor' while they inspect the Constables.* BUTTERTHWAITE *detaches himself from the official group and comes down to the Masons. He holds an unlighted cigarette in an ivory holder.*

BUTTERTHWAITE. Eh, begod: the old blue marching bull. Brass bound and bloody minded. What a way to greet a lovely day. Have you got such a thing as a light, Jack?

IST MASON. Here you are, Alderman.

BUTTERTHWAITE. Alderman? You ought to know me better nor that, lad!

IST MASON. All right then, Charlie, no offence intended.

BUTTERTHWAITE. That's a bit more like.

He indicates his Alderman's robe.

We may be garnished up like the roast beef of old England, but we haven't quite forgotten all realities yet, I hope. Blimey, look at that! Left right, left right, one two three, and how long have you been in the force, my fine fellow? Jolly good. Jolly good, give that man three stripes! Eh, the police force: we can't do without 'em, but my God how we hate 'em!

The inspection is now over and the MAYOR takes his place by the stone.

Watch it: here we go!

BOOCOCK. Fellow townsmen, ladies and gentlemen, er, voters. This afternoon's little ceremony is, as you might say, a double one. Clapping as it were two birds wi't 'yah billet. Firstly, we are laying the foundation stone for our new police headquarters: and secondly, we are paying a very hearty welcome indeed to our new chief constable: Colonel Feng. Both of these innovations will no doubt impinge upon our way of life in manifold directions.

MRS BOOCOCK. Most of these, I hope, pleasant. But I also hope to some of us unpleasant. And justly so!

Laughter.

BOOCOCK. Colonel Feng comes to us by the unanimous choice of the Borough Watch Committee.

BUTTERTHWAITE (*aside*). *He* said that. *I* didn't. Why, I wasn't even there at the time.

BOOCOCK. I am happy to say that the Conservative Members of that Committee, under the respected leadership of Sir Harold Sweetman –

He and SWEETMAN *exchange bows.* BUTTERTHWAITE *grinds his teeth.*

– have concurred entirely with the opinions of us, the majority party. This being a benevolent augury, I will now request the Chief Constable to say a few words. Colonel Feng.

FENG. Mr Mayor, Madam Mayoress, Aldermen, Councillors, ladies and gentlemen. I am not, I confess, a Northern man by birth, nor yet by upbringing. I trust this will be forgiven me

Laughter.

My last post as Chief Constable was in an extremely different locality, where the prevalence of violent crime was such that only the firmest of firm hands would serve to eliminate it. It has been eliminated. We live in an age of overthrown moral standards. The criminal today is coddled and cosseted by the fantastic jargon of mountebank psychiatry. Yet I ask you, ladies and gentlemen, do these sentimental social pundits ever pause to reflect upon the agony literally suffered night after night by the women of this country who watch their menfolk go out to earn their daily bread; and they wonder (yes they do): 'Will he come home safe and sound, unbroken and unmaimed?' With God's help, ladies and gentlemen, I will put their minds at rest. Thank you.

Applause. BUTTERTHWAITE *gives a long low private whistle.*

BOOCOCK. And thank *you*, Colonel Feng. There will be many a loud hear hear to that, I dare well say . . . Now then: the laying of the stone. Who better can we ask to carry this out than the man whom I might justly call the most honoured of our leading citizens; Chairman of the Regional Branch of the Labour Party, Secretary of the local Mineworkers' Union, controlling spirit of one-hundred-and-one hard-working committees: and perhaps above all, the man who has held the office of Mayor of this borough not fewer than nine times altogether, which is, I believe, a national record!

2ND MASON (*aside to* BUTTERTHWAITE). In other words, the only man in town who really pumps the oil. Am I right, Charlie?

BUTTERTHWAITE (*aside to him*). You are.

BOOCOCK. Ladies and gentlemen, Alderman Charlie Butter-thwaite. Give him a big hand. Come on, Charlie, you've a job o' work to do here.

CHEERS. Three times three for Charlie B. Hooray, 'ray, 'ray . . .

Band plays 'See the Conquering Hero'.

BOOCOCK. By gummy. I can tell you, when I'm set up here in *these* – (*He indicates his robes.*) alongside of old Charlie, I can't help the feeling like I'm under false colours. They've all but got his name wrote on the tab at back!

Laughter.

BUTTERTHWAITE. There he is again, nicking my gags. I'll tell Colonel Feng on you for petty larceny! . . . You know, if anyone o' you had come up to me a few years ago and told me that this afternoon I'd find meself all set to trowel the mortar for a new house for t' coppers, why, I'd ha' sent him off to t'looney-bin with a good boot up his rump! But it circles, you know, it all circles round. And as far as this town goes, *we're* t' masters now. It warn't so easy to credit that in 1897 when your old uncle Charlie first saw the light of day in the lying-in ward of the Municipal Workhouse. And 1926 I call to my memory as a year of some bitterness, too. I fancy

Sir Harold Sweetman bears those days in mind. He and his confederates. They beat us at the time. But we fought and fought again, and in the end we won. And that's the end o' that. All that's left atween us now, is a few small political differences – overweighed (at least off duty) by an abiding sense of gratitude for Sir Harold's present enterprise. The Brewery Industry! Why, think of us without it! We'd be a dehydrated nation. And the frogs and the jerries, they could sweep us up like sawdust! Right: now where's this bit o' bricklaying? I've not got me union card, but I dare say we can accommodate any question o' demarcation troubles. Mortar mixed all right, Jack, is it?

1ST MASON. Aye, it's mixed.

BUTTERTHWAITE. What's your consistency?

1ST MASON. Twelve parts fine crushed stone: three parts lime putty: one part Portland cement.

BUTTERTHWAITE. Not bad at all. I like to see good workmanship. Trowel? Right. Any young lass down there want the icing smoothed over her wedding cake? She's only to say the word. I'm ready and willing for t' usual consideration.

He smacks a kiss or two towards the audience.

Nobody? All right. Here we go . . . send it down, David.

The stone is lowered on to the mortar he has spread.

It gives me great pleasure to declare this stone well and truly laid. (*He taps the corners with his trowel.*) Knock, knock, knock and it's done. Any more for any more?

BOOCOCK (*restraining him*). Wait up, Charlie. Steady . . .

All stiffen as the band breaks into the National Anthem. Then the group begins to break up and converse in knots.

LUMBER. Guard of Honour, right turn. To your duties: quick march!

He marches out with the Constables. Citizens disperse.
WIPER *bumps into* BUTTERTHWAITE.

BUTTERTHWAITE. After you, Mr Wiper.
WIPER. After you, Mr Butterthwaite.
BUTTERTHWAITE. Alderman Butterthwaite, *if* you please.

LADY SWEETMAN *and* YOUNG SWEETMAN *enter and talk with* SWEETMAN. F. J., BLOMAX *and* WELLESLEY *also come back on stage, and* BUTTERTHWAITE *sees him.*

Hello, Wellington. Is that you? I think that wor one o' my better efforts. Don't you agree?
BLOMAX. Oh, very good. Very lively, Charlie.
BUTTERTHWAITE. I'll be there at ten sharp, at the usual table.

BUTTERTHWAITE *moves away towards his Labour Councillors.*

BLOMAX. As great Bonaparte wishes . . . What he meant to say was: that this evening at ten o'clock there will be an extraordinary meeting of the working caucus committee of the Labour Party at the east end of the saloon bar of the Victoria and Albert Hotel. Alderman Butterthwaite will be in the chair. And everybody else is to hang upon his words, as is usual: as is dutiful: as is after all only convenient. Does it appear to you strange a professional man like me should hail this clown as Bonaparte? The Napoleon of the North, as we matily describe him up here? Well, professional or not, I am a corrupted individual: for every emperor needs to have his dark occult councillor: if you like, his fixer, his manipulator – me. I do it because I enjoy it. I have also in my time enjoyed the delights of carnality – a less anti-social corruption perhaps, but in my case very often a swollen carbuncle of unexpected peril. You see, I am a doctor. My name is Wellington Blomax. I have not yet been struck off the register, but as you will find, it's been a pretty close thing.

(*He introduces* WELLESLEY *to the audience.*) Here I am confronted by the fruits of my loose studenthood. This poor girl without a mother is my own daughter: Wellesley. She came back home only a day or two ago after a sufficiently long absence. She works for her living and her education (I may say: at my expense) has been regrettably incompetent. Really, we hardly know each other.

WELLESLEY *gives a short laugh. So does he.*

But I conceive it my duty to introduce her at once to the local opportunities and make up for what she's missed.

BUTTERTHWAITE (*on the way out with Labour Councillors*). I think I've told everybody, but in case I missed one out, just confirm it, will you?

BLOMAX. I'll attend to it, Charlie.

Exit BUTTERTHWAITE, *etc.*

WELLESLEY. Would you say he was one of them?

BLOMAX. One of what?

WELLESLEY. The Local Opportunities.

BLOMAX. Oh, my dearie, no. He's on my National Health, but . . . no, no, no, what *you* want, my sweetheart, is the altogether opposite aspect of this deplorable townscape.

BLOMAX *points to* SWEETMAN.

Now the heavy gentleman over there . . .

WELLESLEY. Who's the young one with him?

BLOMAX. His son and heir, my sweetheart. Sweetman's Amalgamated Brewery and Corn Products – enormous – luxurious . . .

WELLESLEY. I've already met him, thank you very much. We shared a compartment on the way down from Penrith.

YOUNG SWEETMAN *sees her and comes over.*

YOUNG SWEETMAN. Hello there.

WELLESLEY. Hello.

He leads her away from her father.

YOUNG SWEETMAN. You know, I knew perfectly well we
were going to see each other again within less than three
days. Now this time you are most definitely going to tell me
who you are and what you are doing here and what I have to
do to get to know you better . . .

The CONSERVATIVES *group together with* FENG. WELLES-
LEY *in conversation with* YOUNG SWEETMAN. *A* MAID
*brings in a tray of drinks and the group becomes a cocktail
party.*

SCENE TWO

Sweetman's House. SWEETMAN, LADY SWEETMAN, YOUNG
SWEETMAN, FENG, F. J., TWO LADIES, WELLESLEY,
MAID; BLOMAX *still on stage in foreground.*

BLOMAX.
Aha, does she not show a very pretty accomplishment ?
A long-neglectful father need not scruple to hide
The trickling down of a tear of pride ?

Exit BLOMAX.

SWEETMAN. Yes, Colonel Feng, what you saw and heard
today is by no means unusual.
F. J. He does it all the time.
SWEETMAN. Yes. He was born in the workhouse: he conducted
and ruined single-handed the General Strike: and he's everybody's Uncle Charlie and will remain so till he dies.
LADY SWEETMAN. Or until he's voted out. I'm quite sure it's
not impossible. You talk about him all the time as though he
were . . .

SWEETMAN. We are talking, my dear, about the man whose Napoleonic organization of the Socialist party machine . . .

F. J. Particularly in regard to the disposition of ward boundaries . . .

SWEETMAN. Yes, ward boundaries. It's all organized, you see. Overriding majority: organised by gerrymandering, and intended to continue. Such – Colonel Feng – is the lamentable framework into which, you will discover, you will have to accommodate yourself speedily, or else you will be . . .

1ST LADY. What do you think of it, Colonel Feng?

FENG. I have really no opinion, dear lady. I represent the force of law. I can have no opinion of political matters.

SWEETMAN. Yes. You will discover.

2ND LADY. Of course, the people do enjoy his speeches. You do have to laugh at them.

1ST LADY. Laugh at naughty children.

F. J. He rehearses it, of course.

LADY SWEETMAN. But, of course, we have to smack them.

WELLESLEY. Really have to smack? I mean, for providing entertainment? I mean, is the town really so badly misgoverned?

A pause.

YOUNG SWEETMAN. Misgoverned? Oh, it's not exactly misgoverned. It's just the wrong lot are the governors, that's all.

WELLESLEY. You see, if Colonel Feng says 'no politics' and yet he sees the town misgoverned, I mean really misgoverned . . . what do you do then, Colonel?

FENG. I rely, my dear young lady, upon the integrity of the British policeman. We live in an age of overthrown moral standards, and . . .

WELLESLEY. You said that at the ceremony.

FENG. So I did.

WELLESLEY. What about the moral standards of the British policeman? Are his overthrown as well?

LADY SWEETMAN. I suppose really the trouble is, we women, we see the personal side. While all the men all the time are looking for points of principle. But what I so dislike about people like Butterthwaite, they are not only so vulgar themselves but they expect everybody else to live at the same level. I don't see why I should. I cannot forgive them the way they deprived this town of our art gallery. It was a very nice little gallery, Colonel Feng – old masters, quite well spoken of. A genuine Titian, and there were 'Cows in a Field'. They gave it to Cuyp, but I believe it could be a Rembrandt. I have always been something of a connoisseur myself. In a small way, a collector. And so has Sir Harold.

SWEETMAN. Yes, moderns, mostly.

LADY SWEETMAN (*to* WELLESLEY). You must tell me all about yourself, my dear. My boy tells me he met you on a train . . .

SWEETMAN. Who is she?

YOUNG SWEETMAN. I met her the other day. Her father's a doctor.

SWEETMAN. And what does *she* do?

YOUNG SWEETMAN. She works in the forest.

SWEETMAN. Works in the what?

YOUNG SWEETMAN. The Forestry Commission. They plant trees in Westmorland.

SWEETMAN. A doctor, you said. Do I know him?

YOUNG SWEETMAN. I don't know. His name is Blomax.

SWEETMAN. Yes. He's a rogue and the crony of rogues. Did you ever meet her mother? She was as black as your hat.

YOUNG SWEETMAN. I don't believe you.

SWEETMAN. Yes. She was a Maltese. You will discover.

F. J. Is she one of that young crowd of yours at the Copacabana Club?

YOUNG SWEETMAN. Ha, ha. Oh no, not her.

SWEETMAN. The Copacabana? I didn't know you went there? Well, don't you go again. It's a sort of a dinner and dancing establishment, Colonel Feng. Nothing very horrifying.

F. J. Pretty tame compared to London.

SWEETMAN. Yes, and pretty trivial too . . . Of course, Colonel
Feng, you might say all forms of pleasuring are pretty trivial
when it comes down to it. All it usually comes down to in
this town is the bottom of a pint pot—

YOUNG SWEETMAN. The bottom of half a dozen pint pots.

SWEETMAN. Half a dozen? Two dozen. Three dozen. Four.
Drink themselves sick.

F. J.
And not uncommonly after licensed hours.

SWEETMAN.
An instructive experiment that you might well try
To sound the ground for your new job, I mean . . .

F. J.
Why don't you – Colonel – send a man or two
To the Victoria and Albert at half past eleven?

SWEETMAN.
Tonight perhaps.

F. J.
Tonight most suitable.

SWEETMAN.
Yes.

FENG.
A public house?

SWEETMAN.
Hotel.

YOUNG SWEETMAN.
Not one
Of ours, of course. A free house. *We* don't go there.

FENG.
You wish to lay an information, do you,
Sir Harold?

SWEETMAN.
No. Emphatically no.

We speak (in passing) of our townfolks pleasure
And – what was it she said – misgovernment?
Monopoly and party have controlled
This town for thirty years. Consider it
And consider, sir, the grave unlikelihood
That you can live and serve here and yet hold
Upon our politics no opinion, sir.

FENG.

I think, Sir Harold, I discern your working.

SWEETMAN.

Yes . . .

FENG.

Then I will tell you *mine*. I am here
To keep the law. And therefore must begin
By testing at all points the law you keep
Already, and how you keep it. Public houses
Are indeed one point. But only one. And who
Frequent such public houses, or such clubs,
Or hotels if you call them so, or what
Or where – is neither here nor there! Provided
That the law is kept. And where not kept
I should be glad of relevant information,
Or none at all. I do not know you, sir.
I do not know this people. And I must test
The whole community according to
The rigid statutes and the statutes only.
I can assure you now without vainglory
My testing will be thorough.

SWEETMAN.

Yes.

The MAID *whispers to* LADY SWEETMAN.

LADY SWEETMAN.

Dinner is served. Shall we go in ?
Colonel ?

FENG.
  Delighted, madam. After you.
YOUNG SWEETMAN (*to his father*).
  Are you quite sure he's ours?
SWEETMAN.
  What d'you mean?
  Go in to dinner . . . After you, F. J.
F. J.
• No, no, H. S. I follow after *you* . . .

  Exeunt.

SCENE THREE

Saloon bar of the Victoria and Albert.
  Enter BLOMAX *and several drinkers.*
  LANDLORD *behind his bar.*

BLOMAX. Big-hearted Arthur!
1ST DRINKER. No, no, no . . . Of course that horse is going to
  run . . .
2ND DRINKER. It's going to run at Beverley Races: there's no
  question about it . . .
3RD DRINKER. It was said very clearly . . .
BLOMAX. Big-hearted Arthur will be a non-starter! The
  information is confidential, but the oracle has delivered it.
  Alarm and despondency now spread like wildfire through
  celebrated Northern turf circles . . . Who's going to fill me?
4TH DRINKER (*handing him a glass*). Here you are, Doctor.
BLOMAX (*looking at him sharply*). Hello, hello, hello, I don't
  know you. You're not one o' my patients?
4TH DRINKER. Not exactly, no . . . but I dare say I *could* be?
1ST DRINKER. I dare say he *could* be. I'll vouch for him,
  Doctor.
BLOMAX (*clearing a space on a table, takes a pad of forms out*).

Very well then, so be it. Always carry me blank forms ready.
You see . . . Name, address and previous medical adviser?

4TH DRINKER *whispers in his ear.*

(*Writing.*) Now sign on the line, sir . . . Now then, what's
the trouble? And how can I cure it? A little matter of a
certificate perhaps? Easily arranged . . .

4TH DRINKER *whispers again.*

Aha, you were down with a runny tummy, were you, so you
couldn't possibly have been out burgling? Couldn't you? I
wonder . . . No, it won't do. I steer very clear of courts of
law, my dear sir. If it had to come up anywhere else, I would
do your documents with pleasure . . . but . . .

4TH DRINKER *shoves some money over to him.*

All right, I will consider it. But I'm very very doubtful . . .

GLORIA *enters and comes up to* BLOMAX.

GLORIA. For the sake of old times, can we have a little word?
BLOMAX. Gloria! Good gracious me! We don't expect to find
you these days slumming it in the midst of the town in this
dreary old boozing-ken! Gentlemen, you all know Gloria! –
Get her a drink! – I am surprised, my dear Gloria, that you
can tear yourself away from that expensive establishment of
yours out there on the bypass . . . (*He addresses the audience.*)
. . . known for your information as the Copacabana Club.
And this most elegant and most gorgeous lady – who was for
a space my very close friend – is now the manageress. There
you are: you all know Gloria. What you don't know – I
fancy – is where the money comes from that keeps that club
going. *I* don't know it either.
GLORIA. *I'm* not going to tell you.
BLOMAX. What *are* you going to tell me?
GLORIA. I want professional advice of a rather private nature.

Are you acquainted with Superintendent Wiper of our local police?

BLOMAX. How d'you do, in public. Not much else beyond that.

GLORIA. This isn't for in public. Let's go to the back.

> *She moves upstage.* BLOMAX *is about to follow her when* BUTTERTHWAITE, BOOCOCK *and* LABOUR COUNCILLORS *all come in.*

BLOMAX. Wait a moment, we're interrupted! The processional entrance. They need to have a tune! Charlie, Mr Mayor, how are you? How are you?

BUTTERTHWAITE. We need to have a tune. And some words to it and all. Dr Wellington, oblige.

BLOMAX (*sings*).
When Bonaparte assumed his crown
He put it on himself.
He was sole author of his power
And he piled his private wealth.
He kept his throne with sword and gun,
Dragoon and Cuirassier,
He marched with cannon at either flank
And bayonets in his rear.

BUTTERTHWAITE (*sings*).
But I am not the same as that:
I bow to the public voice.
My best endeavours are bent thereto
As befits the people's choice—

> *He sees* BLOMAX *is going out after* GLORIA.

Hey, what about the rest of it?

BLOMAX. You'll have to do it for yourself. I'm temporarily prevented. (*He joins* GLORIA.)

BUTTERTHWAITE (*shouting after him*). I wish you were temporarily prevented from one or two other activities.

BLOMAX *returns and takes* BUTTERTHWAITE *aside.*

BLOMAX. Which reminds me. Do you know what won the three-forty?

BUTTERTHWAITE. It did come to my ears. And I should like to know why, when you recommend a horse, it always develops spavins afore it reaches t'starting-gate. I gave you that money to put on for me on what you swore was a dead cert.

BLOMAX. Correction, Charlie. Twice. All you gave me was one of your promises: and as usual you chose to override my considered recommendation in favour of what you were told by some half-cock informant at the Miners' Union offices. I'm no bookie's runner, you know: but even if I was, I'd need to be paid for it.

BUTTERTHWAITE. You can't be paid today. Are you being pressed for t'cash?

BLOMAX. No, not exactly, but . . .

BUTTERTHWAITE. And what'd you expect me to do for you if you were? Burgle t'town hall?

BLOMAX. Why not? You're the great dictator, aren't you?

BUTTERTHWAITE. Get away with you, go on!

> BLOMAX *retires with* GLORIA. BUTTERTHWAITE *and party sit down round a table and the other drinkers move politely away from their vicinity. The* LANDLORD *brings their drinks.*

Barney, you have now seen the new Chief Constable. Both publicly ceremonious and privately confidential over the well-oiled social harmony of the Mayor's parlour. What do you think of him?

BOOCOCK. He's a change from t'last one, isn't he? He's got integrity; he's got energy; he's got a power of command. Of course, there won't be much for him to do.

BUTTERTHWAITE. That's just the trouble, ain't it?

HICKLETON. What do you mean?

BUTTERTHWAITE. A compendium of all the qualities Mr
Mayor has just named, if he finds himself idle he looks for a
job o' work. What I ask is: where?

BOOCOCK. I could indicate a few places. You remember what
he said about overthrown moral standards? Now, you take
that new club that's opened up on the bypass. The Coco . . .
Capoco . . . the . . . er . . .

BUTTERTHWAITE. The Cocoa-banana?

BOOCOCK. Or whatever it might be. I believe it is described as
a nightclub-cum-roadhouse. I'd call it an expense-account
brothel.

HOPEFAST. There's no proof of that, is there?

BOOCOCK. There isn't. But in my opinion that licence should
never have been issued without a few more searching questions. I've been hearing stories. There's dancing there, you
know. And a great deal of it is in the nude.

BUTTERTHWAITE. Who's in the nude?

BOOCOCK. I've been hearing stories. It's come in from London,
and it's not what we're used to.

HARDNUTT. Whose money's at back of it?

BOOCOCK. I don't know and I don't care. But young Sweetman
and his debutantey riff-raff have been frequenting it pretty
frequent. And you're not telling me *their* tastes are all in the
nature of an advanced class in metallurgy at the technical
college. I have already passed the word to Colonel Feng and
I hope he takes a look.

BUTTERTHWAITE. Ah, we don't want to interfere with the
pleasures of our gilded youth, Barney. They're an ornament
to the town.

BOOCOCK. The late-night traffic accident reports are an ornament to the town an' all – by – if I had my way I'd set some o'
them gilded youth to a couple o'years down t'pit. But then I
never do have my way. So what's the bloody odds?

GLORIA *moves towards the door*, BLOMAX *trotting behind her*.

GLORIA. All right then, I'm off. I'll waste no more time. If you won't do it, you won't.

BLOMAX. I didn't say I wouldn't.

HICKLETON (*watching her*). Oho, ho, ho!

BUTTERTHWAITE (*watching her*). Well now, I'm looking at a very privileged old divorcé indeed.

BLOMAX (*to* GLORIA). I said only what I always say. I'm promising nothing . . .

GLORIA *sweeps out*.

HICKLETON. You know who she is, don't you?

BUTTERTHWAITE. No. Who is she?

HICKLETON. What Barney wor just talking about. She runs the bloody place.

BUTTERTHWAITE. Oh! Dr Blomax, come here!

BLOMAX *obeys him*.

HICKLETON. We're all admiring your taste, lad. May we make so bold as to poke in our noses and ask . . .

BOOCOCK. We don't want to interfere, but . . .

BUTTERTHWAITE. But our attention has been drawn to what we might call the pursuits of your fair lady companion.

BOOCOCK. And I am sure you will agree with me, Doctor, that the immorality in this town has got to be very firmly checked.

BLOMAX. Mr Mayor, all I know of the lady is that she is a patient. She is under the seal of the oath of Hippocrates, which is not the same thing as the French word for hypocrites. I'm sorry, there it is.

BUTTERTHWAITE. Eh dear, we're getting ethical. We *do* stand rebuked. Come on, take a seat. Now, to return to business. We have been discussing the character of our latest public servant. And I regret to inform you our opinions are divided. When that appointment was made, I was flat on me back in

the Municipal Hospital with me mortifying gallstones. But if
I'd known they'd agreed on *him*, I'd ha' dragged meself up
and come down on that Watch Committee and vetoed the
whole bang shoot!

BOOCOCK. If you had, you'd ha' been a fool. There is not a
shadow of reason . . .

BUTTERTHWAITE (*thumping his belly*). I don't need reasons. I
know it in here!

BLOMAX. I wouldn't go so far as to say you weren't right.

BUTTERTHWAITE. Why? Have you heard summat? Come on,
what's Feng been up to?

BLOMAX. Nothing very significant. But I *have* been given the
word that tonight he is taking his dinner with His Majesty,
Lord Sweetman. Her Ladyship in attendance very gracious
over the braised lamb, and innumerable assistance provided
by members of the entourage.

BOOCOCK. Well, what's so strange about that? He's entitled to
eat his dinners where he wants, I suppose?

BUTTERTHWAITE. I wouldn't be too sure. A Chief Constable
is maintained to be a non-political office. If the first thing he
does when he comes into a town is to huddle over his grub
with a pack of roaring Tories, I claim he wants watching.
What you're going to find is an insidious partisan: And if
that's the road it turns out, *I'm* not going to dry your eyes for
you. Why couldn't you have invited him to dinner yersen?

BOOCOCK. He's welcome any time to tek a sup o'tea wi' me
and Mrs Boocock, but . . .

BUTTERTHWAITE. Oh Barney, Barney, Barney, you've no
bloody notion, have you? All right, but you'll discover, as
somebody might put it . . . Any particular problems due up
at t'next Council Sessions?

LANDLORD. Last orders, everybody. Last orders, if you please.

BOOCOCK. I'm sorry to say that it's the same old perennial.
The future of the art gallery.

BUTTERTHWAITE. Oh my gracious God.

BOOCOCK. Sweetman wants to make it an issue.

BUTTERTHWAITE. No, look, now look here! I'm sick to bloody death of that art gallery. In 1939 we took it over as an emergency annexe to the Municipal Hospital. There wor no opposition. Since then it's proved its necessity one hundred and ten per cent. Every single meeting of the Hospital Management Committee has confirmed the state of affairs. Dammit, the Chairman is my cousin's brother-in-law. I ought to know. And what about my gallstones? Wellington, bear testimony!

BLOMAX *nods agreement.*

BOOCOCK. Sweetman lays claim we could afford a new hospital and return the art gallery to its original function. What's more, he says he has some pictures of his own he wants to donate.

BUTTERTHWAITE. There is a regular diesel service on the hour every hour into Wakefield and Leeds, and good art galleries in both places. If people want pictures, let them go there. There is no demand for art in this town.

BOOCOCK. It could be an election issue.

BUTTERTHWAITE. Do you seriously imagine the ratepayers are going to stand to be plucked for a new bloody hospital? Godsake, have some common!

BOOCOCK. It ought to be considered, though.

BUTTERTHWAITE. Considered who by?

BOOCOCK. The Ways and Means Committee for a start. I've got it marked down for the agenda on Tuesday.

BUTTERTHWAITE. There's a pair o' Sweetman's pensioners w' seats on that Committee. They could use it to make trouble and hold up other business.

LANDLORD. Time, gentlemen, please.

BOOCOCK. I would like it attended to, Charlie.

BUTTERTHWAITE. All right. I'll attend to it.

LANDLORD (*putting some lights out*). Gennelmen, *if* you please. Closing time, gennelmen. Time if you please!

BOOCOCK. Right. Well, we'd best be off home. Are you coming along?

BUTTERTHWAITE. No. I've got a chap I want to see down the Pontefract Road. I'll see you tomorrow.

BOOCOCK. Goodnight to you, Charlie.

BUTTERTHWAITE. Night night, me old Barney . . .

DRINKERS (*going out*). Night, Mr Mayor . . . Night, Charlie. Night, Frank . . . (*etc.*)

> *The stage empties except for* COUNCILLORS, BUTTER-THWAITE, LANDLORD *and* BLOMAX.

BUTTERTHWAITE. Let's have another round, Frank.

LANDLORD. Wait up a minute. I've got to draw me curtains . . .

BUTTERTHWAITE. Who's on the beat tonight? PC Liversedge?

LANDLORD. Should be by rights.

BUTTERTHWAITE. Grand. We're all clear then.

> *The drinks are brought as they resume their seats round the table.*

Now look here, I'm not having it. If everybody in this Council was to dilly-dally around after Barney Boocock's formalities, nowt'd get done. Nowt. Who have we got here belonging to the Ways and Means? One, two, three. Right. There's enough for a quorum. Alderman Butterthwaite i't'chair, Councillors Hopefast, Hardnutt and Hickleton present in committee – er – Doctor Wellington Blomax, Deputy Secretary. I declare the Committee in session.

HOPEFAST. I move that the minutes of the previous meeting be taken as read.

HARDNUTT. Seconded.

BUTTERTHWAITE. Votes? All right. Passed. So the motion

before this Committee is that the time is not yet ripe for consideration of the reversal of the Municipal Hospital Annexe to its original function.

HICKLETON. Seconded.

BUTTERTHWAITE. Right. Anybody agen it? I should bloody well hope there's nobody agen it . . . All right. Very good. Motion passed, nem con. And our flash Harry Sweetman can wear that in the brim of his Anthony Eden and go to church with it . . .

Enter PC LIVERSEDGE.

LIVERSEDGE. Ha, h'm.

BUTTERTHWAITE. Evening, Liversedge. How are you? Have a pint of ale. It's on the Corporation.

LIVERSEDGE. Are you aware, sir, that it is after permitted hours?

HOPEFAST. Don't talk so daft.

LIVERSEDGE. You'll have to excuse me, Councillor. But I have my duty to perform.

BUTTERTHWAITE. You have your *what*? Look, lad. We're discussing local government business in here. You ought to be aware of that by now. What the hell d'you think you're playing at?

LIVERSEDGE. Alderman, I'm sorry, but it's very particular orders.

BUTTERTHWAITE. Orders. Whose orders?

LIVERSEDGE. There's been summat of a shake-up. You see, it . . .

Enter LUMBER *and another* PC.

LUMBER. Right, Liversedge. Who have you found? Oh! I might have guessed it.

HARDNUTT. Come on then, Sergeant. Where's the handcuffs?

LUMBER. Now, Councillor, you know it's not a matter for

handcuffs. But I *shall* have to ask you gentlemen for your names and addresses.

BUTTERTHWAITE. Oh for Godsake, flatfoot, go and get stuffed! If you don't know who we are, *I'm* not going to bloody tell you! I remember the days in 1926 I'd ha' took twelve o' you bluebottles on wi' nowt but me two boots and a twist o' barbed wire round me pick heft. What were *you* doing then?

LUMBER. When?

BUTTERTHWAITE. The General Strike 1926 I'm talking about! I know what you were doing. You warn't even wetting on your poor mother's apron. You wor nowt but a dirty thought atween your dad and his beer. . . . There's no question this is Feng! Wellington, go round to the station tomorrow and see that slimy Wiper. Find out what's happening and how serious it is. (*To the police.*) Get out o' my road.

BLOMAX (*to the police as he leaves*). Quis custodiot ipses custodias? Good night to the lot of you . . .

    Exeunt

SCENE FOUR

A street.
Enter WELLESLEY *and* YOUNG SWEETMAN.

WELLESLEY. Was I not dressed well enough to suit you?

YOUNG SWEETMAN. You were beautifully dressed.

WELLESLEY. But you say that to all the girls you bring home with you to dinner.

YOUNG SWEETMAN. I don't bring all the girls home.

WELLESLEY. Then why did you bring me? I would much rather you'd taken me out to an expensive restaurant or something.

YOUNG SWEETMAN. There *are* no expensive restaurants.

WELLESLEY. Yes, there are. In Leeds. And what about that club?

YOUNG SWEETMAN. The Copacabana? It's not really the sort of place . . .

WELLESLEY. It's very expensive.

YOUNG SWEETMAN. In any case I had to be at home this evening. Because of the Chief Constable and all the family prestige and so on. And I wasn't going to let you escape from me again like you did at the station. There's another thing, if we bring a girl home round here . . . it means that we want to . . .

WELLESLEY. To present her to the authorities as a future associate? You ought to have told me that before. You could even have proposed before. In a respectable formal fashion. Now it's too late. You tell me I didn't find favour. I wasn't dressed well enough.

YOUNG SWEETMAN. Wellesley, I have said you were beautifully dressed!

WELLESLEY. Describe me, if you please.

YOUNG SWEETMAN. Now, Wellesley, look here . . .

WELLESLEY. Go on, Maurice. Describe me. Let me hear if you still mean it.

 BLOMAX *enters. The other two do not notice him.*

YOUNG SWEETMAN.

> As I was lying on my bed
> And my eyelids blue with sleep
> I thought I saw my true love enter,
> Golden and dusty were her feet.
> Her gown of green, it let be seen
> Her shoulders white and brown,
> Her hair was tied in a high tight ribbon
> As sleek as a pool of trout
> And her earlobes like the Connemara Marble
> Moved quietly up and about.

WELLESLEY. As I breathed, I suppose?

YOUNG SWEETMAN. As you breathed, and as you were eating.
I mean, that was the impression.

WELLESLEY. Then why can't I go there again?

YOUNG SWEETMAN. Oh, Wellesley, for God's sake . . . I
have been trying to explain to you. You should have given
a different name. Your father – *you* ought to know it. For
God's sake how could *I*? They don't tell me all the scandal.
He is not persona grata, at my father's or anywhere else.

BLOMAX (*coming forward*). Indeed, and why not?

YOUNG SWEETMAN. Oh, we're overheard. I wasn't talking to
you.

BLOMAX. You were talking *about* me. I may very well be a
corrupted individual, but let me inform you I am a graduate
of Edinburgh University, which is not to be squirted at, and
I clap MD to the rear quarters of my name . . . with very
high honours. What's the matter with that?

YOUNG SWEETMAN. To put it quite bluntly, sir: You don't
have enough money. You're a resident of this town; you
don't need me to tell you the sine qua non.

BLOMAX. Ho, the 'gracilis puer perfusus liquidis odoribus sub
antro'! Don't you try and blind me with your hic haec hoc,
young man! I've heard about *you* . . . and I'm not at all sure
you're a fit companion for my beautiful daughter. (*He tries to
put his arm round* WELLESLEY, *but she shrugs him off.*) To
whom I have a manifest duty, she being in her origins an
unfortunate mistake; as was also her dear mother, now –
alas – divorced and forgotten, but traumatic in my history.

(*Sings.*)

> I married my wife because I had to
> Diddle di doo: Di doo doo-doo
> My wedding day in the month of May
> The honeymoon in flaming June
> A babe of shame of such ill fame

> All it wants is an honest name
> I married my wife because I had to
> Diddle di doo: di doo doo-doo . . .
Now sir, be off . . . before I ask you your intentions.

YOUNG SWEETMAN. Oh my God . . . Wellesley . . . I . . .

WELLESLEY. I think you'd better go. You're only making things worse.

YOUNG SWEETMAN. All right. But it's not finished.

WELLESLEY. Isn't it?

YOUNG SWEETMAN. No. I mean . . . no, it's not finished . . .

Exit YOUNG SWEETMAN.

WELLESLEY. Thank you very much. I'm sure it was well intended.

BLOMAX. All I am doing is to pursue my way of life. I put you on to him. It's up to you to hold him. If my reputation is a stumbling-block, I might very well remind you that half of that reputation is caused by what caused *you*. So why don't you go home and wipe off those tears? Go along now, whoops! I've got business in hand . . .

Exit WELLESLEY (*who has shed no tears*). BLOMAX *addresses the audience.*

Far too much business, as a matter of fact. But the Emperor has commanded: I must follow his behests.

He leaves the stage to re-enter directly.

SCENE FIVE

The Police headquarters.
Stage divided into inner and outer offices. LUMBER *and the* PCS *occupy the outer office.*

WIPER *enters the inner office (from within), takes off his coat,*

sits down, covers his face with a red handkerchief and goes to sleep.
BLOMAX *enters the outer office.*

BLOMAX. Hello, hello, hello, Sergeant Lumber, here we are again. Another day dawns and a lovely day for all.

LUMBER. Is it? I may say I'm extremely surprised to see *you* here, Dr Blomax. I've just been getting out a summons in your name. You've saved me the effort of sending a man round with it. Here you are, take it.

BLOMAX. Thank you very much . . . I'm going back by way of the Town Hall; I'll take the others as well, if you like, and save you some more effort.

LUMBER. Take what others, Dr Blomax? There's only one other – for the landlord of the Victoria and Albert, and it's already been served.

BLOMAX. Ah . . .

LUMBER. You might very well say 'Ah'.

BLOMAX (*gesturing towards the inner door*). Will he see me?

LUMBER. He won't.

BLOMAX. Ah . . . if I was to walk through, would you stop me by force?

LUMBER. I might have a try.

BLOMAX. I'm a stronger man than you are, and I can show you the proof.

He takes a banknote out of his pocket, furtively, taking care that the P Cs *cannot see it.*

LUMBER. Oh no you can't. I wor proper insulted last night and my uniform humiliated. It's not that easy forgotten.

WIPER. Lumber!

LUMBER. Sir?

WIPER. I thought I told you I wasn't to be disturbed!

BLOMAX (*sings*).

I married my wife because I had to
Diddle di doo, di doo doo-doo . . .

WIPER comes to the door.

WIPER. I've nowt to say to you. I don't know who you are.

BLOMAX (*showing him the summons*). Oh yes, you do, Alfred. Because you've written me a letter. Why, I've got it in my hand. Look.

He slips past into the inner office.

WIPER (*coming in after him*). Sergeant Lumber, will you ask the Doctor to remove himself, please.

BLOMAX. Oh no, no, Alfred. We must look at this strategically.

He shuts the door. LUMBER *and the* PCs *withdraw into their own office.*

WIPER. Well?

BLOMAX. Only two summonses, Alfred . . .

WIPER. How many more did you want?

BLOMAX. Another couple o' pair might not have been inappropriate.

WIPER. They've sent you down here to find out the odds, isn't that so? Well, I can tell you straight now: the odds is black dangerous. And it doesn't please me any more than it does you. You talk about strategy: I've been using *tactics* – at the risk of my career – to save a few faces. I've been compelled to issue that one: and the one for the landlord, as a means of a cover . . . but look how I've worked it. Who do you think's going to be on the bench when you come up afore it?

BLOMAX. I dunno, who is?

WIPER. It *could* be Sir Harold Sweetman, and then you'd be i' t' cart . . . but as it so happens it'll be Alderman Butterthwaite. You're both going to plead guilty. You'll both be let off with a conditional discharge, and no further questions. There you are, tell your pals that, and bring me back their gratitude.

BLOMAX. Oh, very good, Alfred. Very tactical indeed. But it's not quite enough. They want to know in the Town Hall how far this is going and what it portends. In other words, they know your Colonel Feng is a most intrepid pioneer, but who gave him the notion that the best place to demonstrate his sterling British pluck was the Victoria and Albert on Uncle Charlie's Committee night?

WIPER. I don't believe that anybody gave it him.

BLOMAX. Oh yes, they did. We find ourselves here, sir, at a most surgical crux. We probe into it and we cut . . .

WIPER. And all that we discover is a magnificent backbone!

BLOMAX. You mean that he's entirely impartial!

WIPER. I am very sorry to tell you he is – absolutely impartial. A pub is a pub, a man is a drunken fornicator, and an Act of Parliament is divinity!

BLOMAX. Does that make you happy?

WIPER. It does not. For one thing, although I can't call myself an enthusiastic adherent of your horny-handed gang of trade-union oligarchs, at least for some years I have managed to retain a reasonably comfortable relationship with them. That is to say, I never interfered with their evening arrangements, and they never interfered with me.

BLOMAX. Until in walked the backbone . . . eh?

(*He sings.*)

> There came a ramrod vertebrae
> And its name was Colonel Feng.
> It pointed neither left nor right
> But strictly in between,
> And like a rattling bren gun, sir,
> This song he used to sing,
> That he cared for nobody, no, not he,
> And nobody cared for him!

WIPER. Do you have to do that in here?

BLOMAX. Of course, me dear Alfred, the comfort of your relationship has not been entirely confined to the trade-union oligarchs, has it ? The word 'fornicator' was significant. What about the Copacabana Club ?

WIPER. I do not understand you.

BLOMAX. No ? If you were an honest law-man, you'd have closed that libidinous knocking-shop a long long time ago. Instead of which you've been paid to let it wriggle on. And who have you been paid by ? The manageress. And how has she paid you ? In kind, my dear Alfred. And very likely in cash. Though maybe not her own cash. It would be nice to know whose ? I'm going to do it again, same tune, different words:

(*He sings.*)

> Big Gloria is a gorgeous girl
> And keeps many more employed
> Whose gorgeous curves for gorgeous money
> Are frequently enjoyed,
> And where and how that money goes
> Is fruitless to inquire,
> For bare and fruitless ever must be
> The fruits of man's desire.

WIPER. *Don't* start on a third stanza.

BLOMAX. You see, our Gloria herself's a patient of mine. She came to me last night for an abortion. *Your abortion*, Alfred . . . if she'd read her calendar correctly. But not being unaware of me medical ethics, I refused her request . . . at least for the time being. I never act precipitately. I always prefer to know just how it all sets up.

WIPER. I'll tell you how it all sets up. I'm a married man!

BLOMAX. Oh yes, I know that . . .

WIPER. And by God, why couldn't the stupid strumpet keep her purple mouth shut!

BLOMAX. Gloria and I are very old friends. And let me inform you, Alfred, she feels badly done to. However, however, keep

your spirits hearty. It's not at all a bad thing I should know
about all this, because I fancy I can help you.

LUMBER (*looking in briefly*). Excuse me, sir. You said to warn
you, it's nearly ten to twelve.

He withdraws again.

WIPER. What! Oh, good heavens, get out of here quick! I'm
expecting the Chief Constable at dead on the hour. If he
should find you . . .

BLOMAX. No, no, no. Wait, Alfred. You and I are comfortable
men, and we don't want to be disrupted. But if Colonel Feng
is as impartial as you make out, and the Victoria and Albert
was raided last night, not to embarrass the Labour Party, but
out of pure zeal for good order: then he's not going to stop at
embarrassing his own police force, nor yet the good people
who pay for your inactivity. He's going to get you caught,
and Gloria caught, and what's more her mysterious backers –
who I'll bet are *not* disciples of Karl Marx or Keir Hardie.

WIPER. Aye, very likely. But I've not got time now. Will you
please go, before we get trapped!

BLOMAX. But supposing – now listen, I am strategical –
supposing Charlie Butterthwaite was to come to believe that
Feng is *not* impartial, but a creature of Sweetman's, that he
sent your lads to the pub to stir a political stink, then Charlie
and his comrades are going to set right about and commence
their *own* stirring. There will really be a stink, Feng will be
sacked, or else forced to resign, and all disruption will be
concluded before it touches *you*.

WIPER. It's a point, it's a point, I'll grant you it's a point . . .
but will you please . . .

BLOMAX. It's a point well worth making . . .

VOICE (*off*). Ten-shun!

FENG (*off*). Good morning. Carry on, if you please.

LUMBER. Oh my Lord, he's here. Sir, sir, he's here!

FENG *enters the outer office.*

FENG. Good morning, Sergeant. Carry on. Superintendent in?
LUMBER. Oh yessir, he's in, but . . .

FENG *passes through into the inner office.*

WIPER. Good morning, sir.
FENG. Good morning, Superintendent. I'm sorry if I'm a little early. Carry on, if you please.
WIPER. The gentleman's just going, sir.
BLOMAX (*singing to himself*).

> A babe of shame of such ill fame
> All it wants is an honest name
> Diddle di doo, di doo doo-doo . . .

He tips his hat to FENG *and goes out through the outer office.*

FENG. Who the devil's that?
WIPER. Dr Wellington Blomax.
FENG. Who?
WIPER. Dr Wellington Blomax, sir . . . A very brilliant practitioner, I believe . . . but of late years perhaps . . . er, h'm, he sometimes does our medical work for us.
FENG. Really?
WIPER. Only occasionally, of course, when the regular man's away . . .
FENG. Superintendent, what steps are you taking to control the growth of organized vice in the borough?
WIPER. Fortunately very few, sir . . . I mean there are very few to take . . . We closed down a show at the Theatre Royal last year, the odd naughty girl still tries to advertise in the newsagent's windows, but we keep a close check. By and large, it's a clean community. The North of England, you know, the old puritanical traditions . . .
FENG. Good. I have a few notions of my own that it might be as well to look into, one of these days . . . quite soon, in fact. Yes. What about next Monday?

WIPER. Next Monday, sir ? What . . . ?

FENG. Yes. Monday night. Send two or three plain clothes men to that place they call the Copacabana and find out what goes on . . . Any results of interest from your pub crawl, by the way ?

WIPER. Nothing of importance, sir, no . . . we've issued a couple of summonses . . . it is as well, however, to keep people reminded ?

FENG. It most certainly is, Superintendent. I know no attitude more corrupting to an efficient police force than that of complacency. I detect certain traces of it in your conversation; extirpate them, sir, extirpate them root and branch.

Exit FENG *through* WIPER's *inner door.*

WIPER. It can't be done, there's no time . . . besides, I don't trust that Doctor. I mean, I ask you, would *you* ? I shall have to *work* it on Monday. I shall have to work it the old way – that means by forewarning them – and it's never a safe way. I don't know what . . .

FENG (*within*). Superintendent ?

WIPER. Sir ?

FENG (*within*). Will you bring me the file upon last year's crimes of violence, please ?

WIPER. Sir, right away . . .

FENG (*within*). *And* the year before that, Superintendent, if you please . . .

Exeunt

SCENE SIX

BLOMAX's *surgery.*

Enter BLOMAX *and* GLORIA.

BLOMAX (*to audience*). I see very little reason why I should help

Alfred Wiper out of his self-created midden. Except my permanent necessity to have at least *one* copper bound to me by an obligation. And besides: I'm fond of Gloria.

(*He sings*):

The days they have been in the green of my garden
When between us was neither a 'beg your pardon'
Nor a 'stop it', nor 'give over': but 'here I am, here',
'Oh my dove and my dear', 'so close and so near'.
The days they have been, without forethought nor fear.

(*To* GLORIA.) I'm sorry to keep you waiting, but I thought it'd be better to leave it till all the other patients were finished with. Tact, you know, discretion . . .

He examines her, cursorily, while talking.

GLORIA. Well, have you changed your mind? Are you going to arrange it then?

BLOMAX. Oh dear me, no. With this unprecedented Feng a-prowling round the tent of Midian, illegal operations are very definitely *out*.

GLORIA. I see.

BLOMAX. Now look here, Gloria. Tell me truly. Who wants it? You or Wiper?

GLORIA. I thought you would ha' realized. I'm in a difficult position. I hold this job on a very tight contract and one of the clauses states that I must remain a woman of good reputation.

BLOMAX. Good reputation, in a joint like yours?

GLORIA. Of course. It's a capital investment. It's got to be safeguarded.

BLOMAX. Any more dizzy spells, by the way? Little vomitings? Any o' that?

GLORIA. No.

BLOMAX. Good girl, if you have a recurrence, take two o' these in water . . . (*He gives her some pills.*) But I just wish you could tell me whose capital it is.

GLORIA. Why?

BLOMAX. Because I think I ought to know. I need full possession of the facts. I'm trying to organize a political embranglement with the principal motive of keeping you out of jail. I tell you, Feng's prowling! The father of the son is a somewhat haunted Superintendent just at present, and he's afraid that he may not be able to give you value for your money for very much longer. He and I between us will do our level best to keep the flat feet of the law from pulverizing your terrazzo. But if we can't work it . . . be ready, and be warned.

GLORIA. You mean, I suppose, he'll have to raid the club.

BLOMAX. Something after that fashion. But no doubt he'll give you notice. All I say is: be ready.

GLORIA. Principal motive, eh? Keep me out of jail? Oh no, come clean. What is it you're after?

BLOMAX. After? But I *told* you—

GLORIA. I've known you too long. You *enjoy* your embranglements, don't you. You set them up on purpose. Just like with Charlie Butterthwaite and all them bets you let him lose, but you wouldn't dream of foreclosing. So long as all your friends are still standing under obligations to you, you've got something to live for . . . I don't want this baby. All right. What's to happen?

BLOMAX. What indeed? Oh dearie me, what indeed, indeed . . .

> It is not alone my friends
> Who stand under an obligation,
> I too have a duty, Gloria,
> In view of our past relation.
> You wish me to preserve it,
> And I will: your reputation:
> It runs tick-tock, tick-tock,
> At the core of my cogitation.

It's only a matter of days now, I have to go to Beverley to the races. Why don't you come with me?

GLORIA. I wouldn't be seen dead.

BLOMAX. At least as far as Doncaster. I can fix it up at the Office there. I know a man in the Office . . .

GLORIA. What Office ?

BLOMAX. In Doncaster. You'll find out. Oh dearie me, what a curious prescription. But legal, I think it's legal . . . Come on, cheery-up . . . and the corners of your mouth, dear, let them lift, let them lift!

He breaks into a song and forces her to dance with him. She does so unwillingly at first, but then laughs and they are gay.

> I look to the left
> And I look to the right
> I'm a dirty old devil
> Alone in the notions
>
> Of politics and progress
> And high-minded soaring
> With a little bit to drink
> And a slice of good hope
>
> For my patients
> And a smile and bright word
> And don't you go thinking
> You can call me a tortoise
>
> And a dormouse
> And a ostrich in sand
> If it ever gets too hot
> I can pull out my hand
> I can pull out my hand
> I can pull out my hand . . .

Exeunt

SCENE SEVEN

A room in the Town Hall.

LEFTWICH *enters with a loaded tea trolley and starts arranging cups and saucers.* BLOMAX *enters from the side opposite his last exit, carrying a black bag.*

BLOMAX. Good afternoon, Constable Leftwich retired.

LEFTWICH. Afternoon, Doctor.

BLOMAX. The Town Hall seems strangely empty. Is it not three o'clock yet?

LEFTWICH. Five minutes after. Town Planning Committee's in session today. As you know, His Worship takes a very close interest there, and he never were the swiftest to elucidate a technical agenda.

BLOMAX. Aye . . . How's his leg?

LEFTWICH. Nay . . .

BLOMAX. I thought so. I've brought the doings. (*He lays his bag on the trolley.*) What about Uncle Charlie? Is he at the Town Planning?

LEFTWICH. He isn't. He's down at t'Rates Office. Creating with the clerks. One of the accountants discovered a discrepancy and there's a fair foaming fury going on about it, I can tell you.

BLOMAX. That could be very timely. I'll nip down and intercept him before he cools off.

He is about to go out when he is prevented by the entrance of MRS BOOCOCK. *He makes a leg.*

Good afternoon, Madam Mayoress. Once again the sun rises upon our matutinal gloom and fog, and once again in your presence . . .

MRS BOOCOCK. Good afternoon, Dr Blomax. Herbert, where's the Mayor? Is he still wi' t'Town Planning?

Exit BLOMAX.

LEFTWICH. They should be out for a breather any time now.

MRS BOOCOCK. They'd better be. They've been stuck wi' that traffic roundabout for the best part of two months.

LEFTWICH. Here they are, they're coming . . .

Enter BOOCOCK *and* LABOUR COUNCILLORS. *They sit down, exhausted, to their tea.*

BOOCOCK. Ah . . . hello, Sarah love. How are you? Well, at last we look like coming to some sort of conclusion. But the amount o' vested interest involved in this one item . . . Oh, I do wish Charlie wor sitting in on this. *He'd* sort us out all right. What's happened to him today?

LEFTWICH. Rates Office.

BOOCOCK. Oh, that . . .

HARDNUTT. What's he got to do wi' t'Rates Office, for God-sake? It's none o' his department. He can't keep his nose out, can he?

HOPEFAST. I thought we paid a permanent staff to deal with all that.

BOOCOCK. The permanent staff are responsible to the democratic representatives.

HOPEFAST. All right, Barney, we know. But some of them representatives sometimes seem to forget that they bloody well *are* democratic.

HICKLETON. I don't think we should begrudge him his little investigations. He's only cooking up the books for his summer holidays, I dare say.

BOOCOCK. He's *what*?

HICKLETON. Just a joke . . .

BOOCOCK. Well, I don't call it funny. That's the sort of humour, fellow Councillor, that gets reported out of walls. Remember there's men in this town . . . aye, and in this building . . . if we give them so much as one crook of a

finger they will turn it back on to us like a bloody harpoon.
And that's not what we're chosen for.

> I will not have it dreamed or thought
> Or even in a whisper told
> That any man of our good men
> Can wear the shameful label:
> 'Bought and Sold'.
> We're up here to show the Tories
> How honest men can rule.
> We've a built a playground for the little children
> And a comprehensive school.
> We lead the whole West Riding
> In our public schemes of housing,
> And for the drainage of the town,
> In pre-stressed concrete firm and strong
> That not an H-bomb can ding down,
> The Borough Engineer's contrived
> A revolutionary outfall:
> And add to that we've built
> This splendid new Town Hall.

He sits down in pain.

> It comes a rugged reflection
> To a rude old man like me
> Who's had no ease to his efforts
> Nor helpful education:
> That in the hour of his honour
> And the heaping of red robes
> And gold chains of his glory
> He sets up a strong staircase
> For to stride up in his pride:
> And reaches nowt but rheumatics
> Nosing theirselves northward
> From his knee to his ribcage!

MRS BOOCOCK. He's often short of money. I've heard that for a fact.

BOOCOCK. We're all often short.

MRS BOOCOCK. Oh no, not *you*. Economically regulated, aye, but you can't say I keep you short.

BOOCOCK. That's not to the purpose. We're talking about Charlie.

MRS BOOCOCK. Aye, the famous nine-times Mayor . . . or are you sure it isn't ten?

BOOCOCK. I am the Mayor, Sarah.

MRS BOOCOCK. You wear the chain.

BOOCOCK. I hold the office!

MRS BOOCOCK. The office of what? He's selected you this season to play the centre-forward in his own private football team, but don't you imagine that gives you any control over fixture-lists, transfer-fees, or owt else o' t'manager's business!

BOOCOCK. My God, she's never been to a football match in her life.

MRS BOOCOCK. All right and I haven't. They call me Madam Mayoress and I belong in t'kitchen to mash you your tea and fry up your bacon, but happen I might wonder who really owns the belly where it lodges on its road. That's all, I say no more . . .

Enter BUTTERTHWAITE *and* BLOMAX.

BUTTERTHWAITE. I *knew* it. I knew it in here! (*He thumps his belly.*) The predictable result is this of not consulting *me*! My gallstones weren't that bad, I could ha' . . .

BLOMAX. Alfred Wiper said to me . . .

BUTTERTHWAITE. Don't you talk to me about Wiper. There's only one thing fit to be wiped off by that wedge o' greasy gammon and that's his own fat clarted . . . ha, h'm, watch our language . . .

MRS BOOCOCK. Gammon, bacon, or ham: it's time it were took off its hook. It's oversmoked and downright nasty.

Exit MRS BOOCOCK.

BUTTERTHWAITE. Have you heard what Wellington said, Barney?

BOOCOCK. No, I have not.

BUTTERTHWAITE. That business last night at the Victoria and Albert were a well-planned put-up job organized by Sweetman, for the discredit of Labour. And if it warn't for the degenerate meanderings of Superintendent Alfred Wiper, they'd ha' succeeded and all!

BOOCOCK. It sounds highly unlikely to me. Colonel Feng's only been here for nigh on . . .

BUTTERTHWAITE. What the hell does it matter how long he's been here! All that we're concerned with now is how soon he gets out!

The COUNCILLORS *suck their teeth and look doubtful.*

BOOCOCK. You know perfectly well, Charlie Butterthwaite, that you were all boozing after hours. If you got yourselves into trouble you've only yourselves to thank. I will not have aspersions cast upon an unproven public servant. He were doing nowt more nor demonstrating his efficiency, and . . .

BUTTERTHWAITE. Barney, he was striking directly at *me*. It was not only political, it was bloody well personal. And I want him done with!

BOOCOCK. I will not discuss it further. Will you take a look at my leg, Doctor; it's been acting up again.

BLOMAX *kneels and examines the leg.*

BUTTERTHWAITE. Barney, I don't think you quite understand the realities at issue. In our party and our principles, upon which we stand four-square – do we or don't we?—

COUNCILLORS. We do.

BUTTERTHWAITE. – we are confronted with a crisis upon a national scale. Is Labour, or is Labour not, to find a triumphant resurgence? I hope so. So do you.

BLOMAX. Quite a normal stiffening, I think. I'll send some more embrocation.

BUTTERTHWAITE. But no effort in Westminster is worth a damn thing by itself without a sound rammed foundation in the provincial localities. And as far as this locality is concerned if we permit the Tories to fix our police force, we're on t'first road in to mucky marsh, and your old Uncle Charlie knows it. Am I right, fellow Councillors?

COUNCILLORS. Aye . . . I dare say . . . I wouldn't dispute it. . . etc.

BUTTERTHWAITE. Mr Mayor, am I right?

BOOCOCK. It may well be as you say. But if we sack a Chief Constable on inadequate grounds the Home Secretary can withdraw the Government grant from the finances of our Watch Committee. And then who's going to pay for keeping the pavements safe from cosh-boys? You? Out of *your* winnings? Don't make me laugh. We'd best get back to Committee. Doctor, would you mind just giving me an arm as we walk down the corridor; it's not quite eased off yet. Come on, you'll be late.

Exit BOOCOCK *with* BLOMAX. *The* COUNCILLORS *move to follow him.*

BUTTERTHWAITE. If there is a police traffic-officer giving advice on that roundabout, just you treat him distant. I want them to know that I know what I know.

COUNCILLORS. Aye . . . Well . . . we'll see how it turns out . . . etc.

Exeunt COUNCILLORS.

BUTTERTHWAITE. Upon inadequate grounds. All right. Make 'em adequate . . . Lend me ten bob, will you?

LEFTWICH. What, me? Are you mad?

BUTTERTHWAITE. Constable Leftwich, it's a generation or two since you last trod the beat, but nevertheless you are wearing the uniform. Declare yourself, Leftwich! Commit your allegiance! (*He offers* LEFTWICH *a pocket flask.*)

LEFTWICH. Commit it to what?

BUTTERTHWAITE. To the Council of this town in democracy assembled or else – and I shan't take it kindly if you choose the alternative – to the oppressive bonds and authoritarian regiment of a crypto-fascist police organization! Which?

LEFTWICH. Do I have to choose either?

BUTTERTHWAITE. You do, lad, you do. Because as from this moment a state of formal war exists. Come on, now. Commit yourself.

LEFTWICH (*drinking*). I know where my bread's buttered. It's buttered in *here* . . .

BUTTERTHWAITE *takes the bottle and drinks.*

BUTTERTHWAITE. Barney won't play, and this one's too important for fiddling it behind his back. So we can't get Feng directly. What we're going to do is to employ his own tactics. Discredit him by discrediting the behaviour of his troops.

LEFTWICH. Now just you be careful. Why not leave it settle for a little while longer?

BUTTERTHWAITE. I have been struck at! Directly! In person! Herbert, I want some secrets. Who pays the top bogeys how much for keeping quiet about what?

LEFTWICH. I couldn't really say. It used to be the tarts, but since the new Act come in I've lost all me locations in *that* corner o' wickedness.

BUTTERTHWAITE. I want summat deeper. But I think we're on t'right lines . . .

LEFTWICH. Copacabana?

BUTTERTHWAITE. Naked dancing? . . . Maybe . . . but just

how rude is it ? And what evidence is there that the police are conniving at it ?

LEFTWICH. As far as I know there's none. Except that big Gloria's been to bed with Alfred Wiper.

BUTTERTHWAITE. Who told you that!

LEFTWICH. My brother-in-law's a window-cleaner, and he looks at what he sees.

BUTTERTHWAITE. I suppose he didn't look far enough to find out where t'money comes from . . . I mean, that club's new builded, it must ha' cost a lot o' brickwork.

LEFTWICH. Who were t'contractors ? 'Durable Construction', warn't it ?

BUTTERTHWAITE. Aye . . . now they also put up a new malt-house for Harry Sweetman two year sin'. It proves bloody little, but we *are* on t'right lines . . . I think it's high time I betrayed the working classes, don't you ? And patronized an entertainment that is normally above my means. (*He consults his diary.*) I've nowt on next Monday. What about Monday ? All right then, write it down, the Copacabana, Monday. And we'll see what shape of others have got nowt on on that evening. Ha, ha. You watch me conquer yet again where few will follow and none will praise me till I do it, and then they'll all fall on their knees!

He sings, with LEFTWICH *joining in the refrain.*

O Boney came from Corsica, oh hi oh,
He conquered the penisula, John Franzwo.
He went and beat the Prooshians, oh hi oh,
And then he beat the Rooshians, John Franzwo.
Boney was a General, oh hi oh,
And then he was Imperial, John Franzwo.
Boney was a warrior, oh hi oh,
Begod he was no tarrier, John Franzwo.

And so on, dancing round in a circle, drinking their whisky, then exeunt.

SCENE EIGHT

Outside the Copacabana Club.
Night.
Enter BUTTERTHWAITE *and Labour Councillors.*

BUTTERTHWAITE. A preliminary reekin-ayssance. Who'll be
the first to enter the portals of iniquity and see how the other
half lusts ?

HOPEFAST. I expect we'll have to be members.

HARDNUTT. It'll cost us at least a quid apiece, you know.

BUTTERTHWAITE. Out of the party funds, lad. It's a delegated investigation, this. And I'll answer to the secretary if
there's any questions asked . . . Lend me five bob, will you ?
We'll have to buy a beer if we're going to look natural. Come
on, lad, come on! Who paid for the taxi from the Victoria
and Albert ?

    HARDNUTT *gives him the money.*

Right, we'll go in.

    They approach the entrance and the DOORMAN *appears.*

DOORMAN. Evening, gentlemen. Members ?

BUTTERTHWAITE. We're not, but we can be. What does it
cost ?

DOORMAN. Eighty-five shillings renewable annually. Member-
ship, however, does not take effect till twenty-four hours
after payment of first subscription.

BUTTERTHWAITE. You mean we can't get in here while tomorrow night! Why, we might all be blown up first thing i'
t'morning! My lad, at this very moment the generals of the
Western world are stooping over t'map tables, the mill-wheel
of our lifetime is whirling under spate! . . . Now come off
it, sonny Jack. You know damn well if we'd just arrived in

town on a one-day business conference you'd have opened up directly.

DOORMAN. Not unless you had a sponsor, I'm afraid, sir . . .

BUTTERTHWAITE signals to HARDNUTT, *who fiddles with his wallet.*

But it's not at all impossible that something could be managed . . . Just one moment, if you please . . . (*He disappears inside.*)

BUTTERTHWAITE. See what I mean? They're breaking the law already. Note the time.

The DOORMAN *reappears.*

DOORMAN. You're fortunate, sir. A lady inside has offered to be your sponsor. So if you'll just sign the book . . .

HARDNUTT *passes money to* BUTTERTHWAITE, *who passes over tip.*

Thank you very much, sir, indeed, sir, very much . . . Now, eighty-five shillings multiplied by four, exactly seventeen pounds . . . and entrance fee five shillings each makes eighteen pounds precisely . . .

HARDNUTT *pays him.*

Thank you, gentlemen. Straight forward if you please . . . Thank you very much.

They enter the club

SCENE NINE

Inside the Copacabana Club.
Not many customers at tables. Waitresses in brief versions of Flamenco skirts. A few hostesses in evening gowns. Latin American music. A pseudo-Spanish dance-routine taking place on the small stage. YOUNG SWEETMAN (*drunk*) *at a table with a hostess.*

BUTTERTHWAITE *and* COUNCILLORS *advance into the room. They are shown to a table.*

BUTTERTHWAITE. We'll have a Guinness and a double Scotch to go with it.

WAITRESS. We don't serve Guinness, I'm afraid, sir.

BUTTERTHWAITE. You don't? Then you ought to. It'd put a bit o' blood under that nice white hide o' yourn, lass. Heh heh. What *do* you serve?

WAITRESS. Certainly whisky.

BUTTERTHWAITE. That's a bit o' good tidings, any road.

WAITRESS. But I'm afraid there's no drinks allowed without something to eat.

HARDNUTT. We don't want nowt to eat. We had us suppers already.

WAITRESS. It doesn't need more than a sandwich, you know.

HOPEFAST. All right then, four sandwiches.

HICKLETON. We don't have to have a sandwich every time we refill, do we? It's too much like hard work.

WAITRESS. Not unless you want to.

BUTTERTHWAITE. All right. And look sharp, love, won't you? We're evaporating in this heat. (WAITRESS *leaves them.*) Place seems a bit empty. They can hardly make it pay at this rate of attendance, can they?

HARDNUTT. I dare say the fancy don't come in while after midnight.

BUTTERTHWAITE. Aye, very likely.

HICKLETON (*watching a hostess*). Eh, do you reckon *she's* one on 'em?

BUTTERTHWAITE. I'd not be surprised . . . Hey up, she's coming over.

HOSTESS *approaches them.*

HOPEFAST. Now then, Charlie, watch it. We're disinterested observers.

BUTTERTHWAITE. Disinterested bloody slag-ladles. We're

full members of this joint and we're going to take advantage . . . Go on, love, have a chair. Get the weight off your thigh-bones?

She sits down at their table.

HOSTESS. I don't mind if I do.
BUTTERTHWAITE. What are you drinking?
HOSTESS. I'd like a tomato juice if you please, Alderman.
BUTTERTHWAITE. Eh, she knows who I am! There's some in this town pay proper respect where it ought to be paid. Take a bit o' note, you lot . . . but you're wanting summat warmer nor tomato juice . . . surely? Put a bit o' blood under that nice white hide, you know? Go on, love . . . have a glass o' gin.
HOSTESS. Call it a Babycham. I've got work to do.

She makes a signal to the WAITRESS.

BUTTERTHWAITE. Ho ho, have you, ducky, have you? That's what I like to hear, the craftsmanship approach, very good, eh? Ho ho, work to do . . .
HICKLETON (*watching the dancers, who are varying their routine*). Eh, Charlie, what about that?

BUTTERTHWAITE *makes a lecherous noise.*

What do you think, is she going to get 'em all ripped off?
YOUNG SWEETMAN (*lurching towards them*). What do *you* think, Councillor? Wouldn't you like to have a go at her yourself, eh?
YOUNG SWEETMAN'S HOSTESS (*restraining him*). Come on, love, behave.
YOUNG SWEETMAN. Why shouldn't I behave? I represent the standards of civilization in this paleo-paleo-paleolithicalo-lithealithic community. I've had an education.

He subsides into his HOSTESS's *lap.*

BUTTERTHWAITE. My God, you have an' all . . . I imagine, though, we have to wait while end of the evening for t'right spice o' t'show.

HOSTESS. Not tonight you don't.

HOPEFAST. Not? Why not?

HOSTESS. Haven't you heard? There's going to be a raid.

BUTTERTHWAITE. A raid? You don't mean the police?

HOSTESS. That's right.

HARDNUTT. Oh my Lord, no . . .

HOPEFAST. I say, Charlie, that's gone and torn it, hasn't it?

BUTTERTHWAITE. Has it? I'm not sure . . . How do you know there's going to be a raid?

HOSTESS. I don't know exactly. The warning just came. Gloria said she was passing it round all the members who might not want their names in the paper. Just in case something was to go wrong, you know. But you see, we were told that there'd be no danger before midnight, so there's nothing really to worry about. We're having all the popular routines now, and after twelve o'clock there'll be nothing but ordinary vocal numbers and dancing to the band and all that. We'd hoped the place would be as full as usual but a bit earlier on, but it looks like they all took fright, doesn't it?

BUTTERTHWAITE. They'd take fright in this town if a centipede ran ower t'road. Get their names i' t'papers! They think it's worse nor doing murder! Ah well, we won't worry. We're getting some o' what we paid for. We can allus come again.

HARDNUTT (*who has been given the bill*). Can we, by God? Take a look at this!

BUTTERTHWAITE. And they call this a sandwich! It's not even got a top on. (*As the* WAITRESS *is going away.*) Hey up, love! We want a Babycham for t'young lady.

HOSTESS. It's all right, she's brought it.

BUTTERTHWAITE. But I never ordered it yet.

HOSTESS. Oh, just the telegraph . . .

HARDNUTT. Damned expensive telegraph . . . fifteen and six for one Babycham, Charlie!

BUTTERTHWAITE (*watching the dance*). Shut up, lad, I'm watching summat. Use a bit of aesthetic appreciation, or else get off home. I'm here to enjoy meself. (*He cuddles the* HOSTESS.) Eh, what, me little sweetheart? Every man's entitled to his own Dolce Vita, isn't that the truth?

HOSTESS. Aye, lad, it's the truth.

BUTTERTHWAITE (*becoming uproarious*). It's the buttock-naked truth! (*He shouts to the performers, who are near the end of the act.*) Go on, tear it off, I want to see the lot!

Blackout. Lights come up. The Club stage is now empty. GLORIA *is standing beside* BUTTERTHWAITE.

GLORIA. Control yourself, Alderman, this isn't the cattle market . . . Can I join you in a whisky? Cost price for the Corporation. (*She waves to the* WAITRESS, *then points to the bill.*) Don't you pay that. You're honoured guests tonight. (*To the* HOSTESS.) Marlene, you ought to ha' warned me. I warn't to expect we'd be entertaining royalty. As a matter of fact, we warn't to expect that the royalty would be likely to find this a congenial establishment. We tend to cater for what you might call the . . .

BUTTERTHWAITE. The acquisitive and the affluent. Ah, the caterpillars o' the boss class. *I* know, I've said it all. But between what we say and what we find congenial . . .

HOPEFAST. You see, we did damn well at Beverley Races this afternoon.

HICKLETON. Did we?

BUTTERTHWAITE. We did. We made a killing. And now we're out to find ourselves some carnal satisfaction.

GLORIA. So I hope we can provide it for you. Though it's forced to be a bit curtailed tonight.

BUTTERTHWAITE. Aye, aye, she's explained already. (*Four dancing girls, one pair dressed in balloons, the other pair in little bells, appear on the club stage. Nude tableau behind. After a short dance on stage they come down among the tables.*) Hello, hello, hello, what do we do wi' these?

DANCERS. Poppety pop, pop a balloon . . . ring a ding, ding, ring a little bell.

Audience participation.

BUTTERTHWAITE. Pop.

HICKLETON. Pop.

BUTTERTHWAITE. Ding-a-ding.

HICKLETON. Ding-a-ding . . . etc.

An electric bell suddenly rings loudly. The DOORMAN comes in shouting 'Twelve o'clock Midnight'. The dancing girls hurry off. Tableau closes. BUTTERTHWAITE and the COUNCILLORS are left in the middle of the floor. The band starts to play 'The Blue Danube'. YOUNG SWEETMAN is three parts insensible and his HOSTESS tries in vain to get him to move.

GLORIA. Won't you dance, then, Alderman? (*She begins to waltz with him, and other couples follow suit.*)

BUTTERTHWAITE. Me dance . . . ho ho, dance. *I'll* give you a dance! (*To band.*) Quicken it up, lads; can't you see we're leaving you behind! (*Music changes to a Tango.*) That's a bit more like it! *One* two three four, *one* two three four, etc . . .

LUMBER *and a* PC (*in plain clothes*) *enter and sit down at a table. The dancing fades away.* BUTTERTHWAITE *points at them and leers.*

> If you ever walk down our street
> *You* will see a right pretty seet,
> All the policemen four five six
> A-knocking on the doors with big black sticks!

LUMBER. Do you think we could have half a pint of bitter beer apiece, please, miss?

WAITRESS. Oh no, I'm afraid not, you see it's after hours.

LUMBER. Yes, of course, it is, isn't it?

BUTTERTHWAITE. Go on, you give it to him. As a present, on the house! He's an agent-provocative, but so long as it's clearly understood all round no harm need be done! Isn't that so, Sarn't Lumber?

LUMBER. I think we'll have a cup of coffee. And it wouldn't be a bad idea if certain other gentlemen present were introduced to that excellent drink.

> BUTTERTHWAITE *laughs.* YOUNG SWEETMAN *rises unsteadily, and tries to walk to the door. He staggers into* WIPER, *who has just come in, and who ignores him.*

WIPER. I'm sure we would all be glad to share the joke, Alderman.

BUTTERTHWAITE. And why not indeed? Would you call it a dirty joke? Pornographic? Indecent?

WIPER. I don't think so. Why should I?

BUTTERTHWAITE. Then what are you doing here? You tell me that.

WIPER. I am acting upon an information that the entertainment provided at these premises is of a nature liable to cause offence by reason of obscenity.

GLORIA. And is it?

WIPER. Sergeant?

LUMBER. Upon our arrival here, sir, dancing was in progress in a normal fashion. Men strictly dancing with women without undue proximity. There was no display of nakedness nor other indecent exhibition.

GLORIA. And the licensing laws, Sergeant?

LUMBER. Were being properly observed. Ha h'm.

> YOUNG SWEETMAN *finally effects his departure.*

WIPER. In that case it is evident that there are no grounds whatever for the bringing of charges. May I apologize, Madam, for an unfortunate error?

GLORIA. I'm sorry you've been troubled.

BUTTERTHWAITE. Wait a moment, wait a moment . . . As a magistrate and a leading citizen, *I* desire to lay an information against the conduct of this club.

GLORIA. Why, you cunning old . . .

BUTTERTHWAITE. We have just witnessed a demonstration of the passing about among the tables of four little doxies dressed in nowt but balloons – or, in the case of two of 'em, bells – which we were invited to burst or to tingle as the case may be. I am in no doubt whatever that had it not been for the approach of midnight – liberally signalled, I may say – they would have been rendered entirely naked within the handgrasp of the customer. There were other irregularities, too, which I will detail in due course. What are you going to do about it ?

WIPER. You, er – heard what the sergeant said, Alderman. He observed no sign of . . .

BUTTERTHWAITE. Indeed he did not. Because you know and I know and our Gloria knows that the management had been forewarned.

COUNCILLORS. *And* we can corroborate it.

GLORIA. It's all a pack of lies; it's an absolute frame-up.

WIPER. This is very serious indeed, and can only be gone into in the proper manner of procedure. Please attend my office in the morning. We can then discuss it in . . .

BUTTERTHWAITE. Oho no, none o' that patter, mate!

WIPER. I wouldn't advise you to try and be too rapid. I don't think it will pay off . . . Sergeant, come along.

Exeunt police. The dancers, etc., are now all on stage more or less dressed.

BUTTERTHWAITE. Before you raging ladies come and scratch my eyesight out, I had better make one thing clear. I didn't come here to deprive you of your livelihoods. However, in the fell and calamitous grinding of two mighty opposites, someone has to go to t'wall. And them wi' fewest clothes on o' force gets squeezed hardest! Do all o' you girls belong to a union?

A GIRL. Most of us don't.

BUTTERTHWAITE. You don't? A pitiful state of affairs, which only goes to show how right I was to come here. Councillor Hopefast, will you make out a memo for the next meeting o' t'trades council, in re the possible affiliations for members of this industry. They're sweet and jetting little wildflies, and they deserve our firm attention.

>   (*He sings.*)

> When I was a young man in my prime
> Hoor ray Santy Anna
> I knocked them yeller gals two at a time
> All on the plains of Mexico!

He leads his COUNCILLORS *out, laughing grossly.*

GLORIA. All right, all out, we're closing, we're done for, clear it away, no evidence, nothing – my God that bloody old tup, but he'll get his horns curled yet!

Act Two

SCENE ONE

Sweetman's house.

Doorbell rings (off) SWEETMAN *in a dressing-gown hurries across the stage to answer it.* LADY SWEETMAN *in a dressing-gown comes in after him and stands listening.*

SWEETMAN *(off)*. Superintendent Wiper! At this time of night!

WIPER *(off)*. I'm sorry to disturb you, Sir Harold, but something very awkward . . . *(Mumble, mumble.)*

SWEETMAN *(off)*. What . . . what . . . Good God!

WIPER *(off)*. Do you think I could come in, sir? I mean it *is* rather . . .

SWEETMAN *(off)*. In? D'you mean 'in'? Just a moment, I . . . *(SWEETMAN re-enters.)* It's all right, my dear, it's nothing important . . . Would you mind going back to bed?

LADY SWEETMAN. Harold, I . . .

SWEETMAN. Bed, please. *If* you don't mind!

LADY SWEETMAN. Harold. Very well. *(She goes.)*

SWEETMAN *beckons in* WIPER.

SWEETMAN. How dare you come here, straight to this house!

WIPER. I had no alternative. I'm getting meself into a right pitchy mess-up looking after your interests.

SWEETMAN. My what did you say?

WIPER. We have never dealt together personally on this matter before, but the Copacabana is your private investment. And don't you try and deny it.

SWEETMAN. I most emphatically do deny . . .

WIPER. No, it won't do. You know perfectly well what goes on there, and who's been getting paid for keeping it protected. The time has now arrived for *you* to protect *me*. You're an Alderman and a magistrate, so use it to some purpose!

SWEETMAN. Yes . . . How much does Butterthwaite know?

WIPER. He knows that the police raid was established with collusion . . . Good God, he was told it straight by one o' those half-wit tarts! But I don't think he knows details and I don't think he knows about *your* concern, specific.

SWEETMAN. Was he drunk, by any chance?

WIPER. Drunk? I smelt a pong off all four of 'em like a streetful of breweries!

SWEETMAN. Breweries? Yes.

WIPER. Yes, well . . .

SWEETMAN. What was he doing? Precisely?

WIPER. Dancing the tango.

SWEETMAN. Wildly?

WIPER. Uproariously.

SWEETMAN. Then we'd better tell the Chief Constable. (*He goes towards the telephone.*) No. Wait. Have they been charged? I mean, for drunkenness, or the like?

WIPER. Not yet, no . . .

SWEETMAN. Then see that they are not. The accusations they have brought are, ha-hm, very wild indeed, and we are in considerable danger here of a first-class political row. Men of that type who have been in absolute power for over thirty years, why, they'd stick at nothing. We don't want to see a responsible public servant like Colonel Feng turned into a political shuttlecock. Do we? Get hold of all the other customers who were in the club this evening and get sworn affidavits as to the innocence of the show, and also, if you like, the hooliganism of Butterthwaite. Impress Colonel Feng with the hooliganism of Butterthwaite.

WIPER. What about the club itself?

SWEETMAN. Yes . . . I'll have to think of something. I may turn it to advantage . . . Yes. Good night, Superintendent.

As he shows him out, LADY SWEETMAN *re-enters.*
YOUNG SWEETMAN *enters and meets* WIPER.

YOUNG SWEETMAN. Oh my God, not here as well. Oh God, I'm off. (*He goes out again.*)

SWEETMAN. Maurice! You come back here, boy!

WIPER. I'm sorry about this, Sir Harold. I suppose you won't want me to take an affidavit off of *him*?

SWEETMAN. Was he there, too? . . . Good heavens . . . No, we can't risk exceptions, take his statement with the rest – in the morning. There are five steps to the front door. *Don't* miss your footing. Good night.

WIPER *goes out.* SWEETMAN *calls:*
Maurice!

Re-enter YOUNG SWEETMAN.

It's all right, he's gone. Now then: who were you there with? Blomax's girl?

YOUNG SWEETMAN. No.

SWEETMAN. Oh, weren't you? Astonishing . . . Has she not got you caught yet, then?

YOUNG SWEETMAN. Caught? Do you mean . . . ?

SWEETMAN. Yes, I damn well *do* mean it! Now I give you a fair choice, boy, leave her alone, or get out of my brewery. There's a great deal of villainy turning itself round in this town that you know nowt about. And think yourself lucky the police have done nothing more than warn me about you.

YOUNG SWEETMAN *goes in.*

Do you know what the time is?

LADY SWEETMAN. What did he want?

SWEETMAN. Who?

LADY SWEETMAN. The Superintendent.

SWEETMAN. Maurice. The boy was drunk.

LADY SWEETMAN. So I see . . . Can they send you to prison ?

SWEETMAN. What . . . !

LADY SWEETMAN. I couldn't help overhearing. How deeply are you mixed up in it, Harold ? Have you been bribing the police, have you been . . .

SWEETMAN. No. Emphatically! No. I have not! Now will you please go back to bed!

LADY SWEETMAN. I wish you weren't so bad-tempered. I'm only trying to . . .

SWEETMAN. I'm sorry. I didn't mean to be. No . . . but, er, it's just a return of the old bother, it makes me a bit edgy . . . (*He mimes a pain in his heart.*) I'll take a drop of medicine and come to bed when it settles . . . Go on, now. Happy dreams . . .

She goes, avoiding his embrace.

Happy dreams and sweet awakenings . . .
    It has been argued and by no less a voice
    Than that of the Prime Minister, that today
    Class-struggle is concluded. All can rise
    Or fall according to desire or merits
    Or (it may be) according to finance.
    I am as rich as any man in Yorkshire,
    I brew good beer and drink my own good product.
    I fabricate perfected breakfast food
    And crunch it with my family round my table.
    Both beer and breakfast food are drunk and crunched
    By simultaneous millions through the land.
    So Sweetman should have risen, so he has,
    But to what eminence ? Financial, yes.
    And social: yes indeed. My wife has mink,
    My daughters, jewels and suitors: My three tall sons
    Inhabit, or have inhabited, public schools.
    They grow to love the world I set them in,
    And, loving it, become it as they walk.

I am a prince, I am a baron, sirs!
And yet I have no sovereignty, no.
For what is power of gold when politics
At every turn deceive my high aspiring?
The election lights on Butterthwaite – not once
But three times three, or nine times nine, I fear.
No national trend, nor local, gives me hope
Of an improvement. Yet Butterthwaite must fall
And fall so low that not the whole ineptitude
And hopelessness of Tory forecasts can
Reverse his long-delayed catastrophe.
He has himself prepared his own trap-door
And greased his easy hinge. Tonight, he did it!
All it needs now, cagy play and watch
For luck to rock the lock and heave the lever:
And he's down! Prison? . . . No, I do not think so . . .
I am too expert. And in their good time
I turn to the electorate and they turn
In *my* good time, to me! And turn for ever! Yes . . .

Exit

SCENE TWO

A room in the Town Hall.

Enter BOOCOCK, BUTTERTHWAITE *and* LABOUR COUN-
CILLORS.

BOOCOCK. This is very troublesome altogether, Charlie. I hope
you haven't gone too far.

BUTTERTHWAITE. I haven't, Barney.

BOOCOCK. Just how sozzled were you at the Copacabana,
Charlie?

BUTTERTHWAITE. At the Copacabana, Barney, I was as sober
as a chief constable. Isn't that the truth?

COUNCILLORS. Aye, it's the truth.

BUTTERTHWAITE. The buttock-naked truth!

BOOCOCK. I have no desire whatever to make a statement to the Press.

BUTTERTHWAITE. If you don't, I will.

BOOCOCK. I am quite sure that you will . . .

Enter JOURNALISTS.

Gentlemen, good morning. I am sorry you have been brought here. I have remarkably little to say. Except that it does appear that all is not well with the borough police force.

1ST JOURNALIST. Is it true, Mr Mayor, that the Copacabana Club . . . ?

BOOCOCK. I am naming no names.

2ND JOURNALIST. Have you discussed it with the Chief Constable ?

1ST JOURNALIST. It is arguable, is it not, that the Chief Constable has the right to conduct his *own* investigation into matters concerning the . . .

BUTTERTHWAITE. I'll answer that, Barney. Now look here, young man. The police are public servants and responsible to the public!

1ST JOURNALIST. But surely the Home Secretary . . .

BUTTERTHWAITE. The Home Secretary's nowt to do wi' it! The Home Secretary's a Tory and he lives in bloody London! The Government here is *us*, and we're not satisfied. Mister Feng's police force is putrid with corruption and if he don't take a long-handled dung fork to it pretty damn quick, I want his resignation! What's more, I'm going to get it. He has wrapped himself up, neck and navel, to an unscrupulous political minority. I am preparing a full exposure. (*He flourishes a document.*) On this piece o' paper I've got half the facts I'm seeking. When the list is complete, I shall broadcast it out before the voters o' this borough! They'll know what to do! . . . *And* he won't get his first-class travelling expenses neither, I can tell you.

BOOCOCK. I, er, I hope, gentlemen, you won't try and build this up into too much of a sensation . . . er . . . thank you very much . . .

Exeunt all save JOURNALISTS.

JOURNALISTS. Thank you, Mr Mayor.

1ST JOURNALIST. Right. Number one demonstration of prejudice and bias. Now for number two.

2ND JOURNALIST. Boots polished, trousers pressed, anybody need a haircut? Very good. Shall we take our places?

They move round the stage

SCENE THREE

The Police headquarters.

JOURNALISTS *still on stage. Enter* FENG, WIPER *and a* PC.

FENG. Gentlemen, I am exceedingly sorry that Alderman Butterthwaite has chosen to publish these allegations. There is, of course, *no* political influence behind the conduct of the police. What else do you expect me to say?

2ND JOURNALIST. Would you be willing to talk matters over with His Worship the Mayor, if . . .

FENG. His Worship the Mayor has apparently taken as gospel everything Alderman Butterthwaite has seen fit to tell him! So what is there left to talk about, pray? Personally I would welcome an inquiry. An independent inquiry, conducted by the Home Office. And none other! That is all. I thank you. Good morning.

JOURNALISTS. Good morning, Colonel. Thank you very much . . .

The PC *shows them out and then stands well aside.*

FENG. Now tell me, Superintendent. What am I to think?

Both you and Sir Harold have given me the benefit of your no doubt independent analyses of this miserable affair, and certainly the public attitude of our Socialist friends would appear to bear you out. But supposing behind their demagogic antics there were in fact some truth? This sergeant you sent round to the club . . . what's his name? Lumber?

WIPER. Yessir. Sarnt Lumber.

FENG. What's his record?

WIPER. An exceedingly good one, sir. I would personally stand very fast indeed behind Sergeant Lumber . . . We could, of course, suspend him until the matter has been cleared up?

FENG. No. They would tell us, would they not, that there is no smoke without fire. But you will investigate, Superintendent, both deeply and confidentially, and I shall be investigating your investigation, and I shall be investigating *you*, sir.

WIPER. Oh . . . in that case, Colonel Feng, I must ask you to accept my resignation.

FENG. No. If you have done your duty, you will indeed feel your honour impugned. But it is not only *your* honour, it is the honour of the entire force, it is *my* honour, sir, *mine*, that is being dragged like a dead dog through the egalitarian garbage of these streets!

WIPER. You're quite right, sir, quite right. I withdraw my resignation.

FENG. I am glad to find your reaction so extremely correct . . . Now above all, Superintendent, let us not get rattled. Cool nerves, keen brains, no statements to the Press. We will soon defeat these unworthy attempts. They are a symptom of the age, I have met them before. It is not difficult to prevail against them. I look forward to your report.

Exit WIPER. PC *helps* FENG *into coat and hat and umbrella and goes.*

I am a man under authority. Having soldiers under me, or at least constables, and I say to this man 'go' and he goeth, and

to another 'come' and he cometh, and to my servant 'do this'
and he doeth it . . .
Not difficult to prevail but difficult indeed
To live and hold that prevalence, yet live
A social and communicating creature.
The law by nature is civilian,
But it can only work through mode of warfare.
So, we, like soldiers through the English streets,
They fear us while they look to us for strength.
The violence of authority seems to grow
In face of growing violence of crime,
Wrying the neck of our disturbed profession.
They call me Colonel, but by courtesy,
I command and serve, and which is which ? Who knows ?
I tell you, I do not. We used to wear
Top hats and sober clothes like sober tradesmen
But where top hats were worn the heads were broke,
So, military helmets. And the tunics,
Once frock-coats, breed badges and bright buttons,
Confirming in their cut to use of war.
We are not armed. I fear we shall be soon.
I hope we must be. There are too many dead.
Yet then how can we say we only serve
Civilian purposes ? The pay is low
So nobody will join. Then raise the pay
And bad recruits will join for money only ?
I have no hope and therefore walk alone:
Only alone can I know I am right.

SCENE FOUR

A public park.

FENG, *on stage still, walks about in meditation, then sits down
wearily on a seat, which a* PARK ATTENDANT *brings him.*

WELLESLEY *comes in, depressed. She walks about, too, then sits down as well and pays the* ATTENDANT *for her seat.*

FENG. Er h'm . . . Miss Blomax, is it not?

WELLESLEY. H'm? . . . Oh yes. Good morning.

FENG. I – er – I think we have had the pleasure. Er – Feng – how do you do?

WELLESLEY. We met at the Sweetmans'.

FENG. We did. At the Sweetmans'.

WELLESLEY. Are you all by yourself, then – or—?

FENG. Oh, yes: quite as usual, all by myself. A short turn in the park during the luncheon-break. Companions, of course, invidious, to a man in my position. As it were, the ship's captain.

WELLESLEY. Ship's—?

FENG. Oh yes. Private quarters under the quarter-deck and so forth: unwise to be too general, a necessary loneliness, I am sure you will understand me, you being also known in these curious parts as an enemy alien, are you not, Miss Blomax?

WELLESLEY. A what?

FENG. I mean, from the South?

WELLESLEY. Oh no, I live in Westmorland.

FENG. Oh yes. Of course. The forests . . . Your father is a native here?

WELLESLEY. I think he was born in Twickenham.

FENG. Ah? Ah yes, the South . . .

They sit for a while. FENG *acknowledges the salute of a passing* PC.

You made, I recollect, at Sir Harold's table, a few remarks about the government of the town, which struck me at the time as, er – somewhat penetrating, Miss Blomax. You will no doubt forgive me if I appeared to have dismissed them. I have now, however, reason to believe you may have spoken more shrewdly than you realized.

WELLESLEY. Oh, I realized very well. You can tell all you

want to know about the climate of the town by the arrangement and the trimming of the trees in this park.

FENG. Ah yes, the trees. I quite agree with you. Barbarous. No
notion how to plant. No notions at all. Borough engineering.
A tee-square and a compass and lop off every branch that
refuses to conform. Barbarous!

WELLESLEY. I wouldn't have thought you'd have had that
much sympathy for a nonconformist tree.

FENG. Trees are not people. They are a gentle entertainment
provided by our Creator for ourselves and for Himself. It is
churlish to abuse them. We must educate our society and
prevent such abuse.

WELLESLEY. Educate? . . . Oh, I'm so glad I didn't go to
school here. I've got my father to thank for that if for nothing
else. The day that you leave school here you're expected to
reach the age of forty in about three hours and that's all. If
you won't do it, you know what you get? Hump of the old
shoulders and the old grunt comes out at you!

> Too young, too tall, and your eyes too bright,
> You look too near and you look too hard,
> You dream too deep in the deep of the night,
> And you walk too long in my backyard.
> You stand and ask for your white bread
> And you stand and you ask for your brown,
> But what you will get is a good horse whip
> To drive you out of town.

How old are you, as a matter of interest?

FENG. Oh? Oh, sufficiently old. No longer irresponsible. Rigid,
you might say. Hardened arteries, young lady, unsympathetic
and crumbling. Hardness, however, is nothing if not necessary. It derives from my post and my years in the Colonial
Service and the necessity therein for unwavering powers of
decision. And so I *have* decided. Quite suddenly. Unexpec-
tedly. I am, alone, not sufficient, in fact I am bewildered.
Particularly now, surrounded as I am by a confusion of

democracy and alien loyalties, for support I turn – where? Of necessity to another alien. I would like you to become my wife . . . Or do you not perhaps share my belief in the similarity of our predicaments? I have within me – I mean as a man, not a policeman – an extraordinary humanity, of necessity concealed. Improbable longings, attempts at self-betrayal, I think I can crush them, by this improbable method. I would be glad of your opinion.

WELLESLEY. Oh dear . . . Oh no . . . I don't think it's very likely. I mean, I don't think –

FENG. Perhaps it is not. It would have been easier for me to have forgotten my impulse and to have continued our conversation upon a more usual subject. As it might be, the trees. Perhaps it is not too late for me yet to forget it . . . or, I observe you are a pedestrian. I always prefer to talk to pedestrians, at least of our milieu . . . They are the less likely – you see – to bear a grudge against my occupation . . . but I have a car around the corner. Do you think I could possibly offer you a lift anywhere?

WELLESLEY. I was just sitting in the park. There is nowhere I want to go to, really . . .

FENG. Yes. By all means. I wish I could sit with you further. But duty, alas . . . Good day to you, Miss Blomax. I, er, I would look forward very much to meeting you again, some time? . . . Good day . . .

Exit FENG.
She sits for a while, then YOUNG SWEETMAN *enters.*

YOUNG SWEETMAN. Wellesley . . . hello . . . Wellesley.

WELLESLEY. . . . . I suppose you've come to tell me that they have told you that you must never see me again?

YOUNG SWEETMAN. Well, as a matter of fact . . .

WELLESLEY. All the old grey heads are breaking one another's blood out, because of who saw what of what girl below the waist, when we all know very well they would *all* love to see it. And why shouldn't they? It's a free country. Have you seen it?

YOUNG SWEETMAN. What?

WELLESLEY. At the Copacabana, Maurice. Have you seen it?

YOUNG SWEETMAN. As a matter of fact, yes.

WELLESLEY. And who tells the truth about it? You tell me that, the Reds or the Fascists?

YOUNG SWEETMAN. Neither, of course.

WELLESLEY. So there you are. Yet those are the people who claim they can regulate your life and my life, and make our unwavering decisions. Not for what they think of us, but for what they think of each other. We have no obligation to them. Only to ourselves; we ought to fight for what we want. What do *you* want, Maurice?

YOUNG SWEETMAN. You.

WELLESLEY. Do you? – I wish I knew what *I* did . . . I have a father and he calls himself a stumbling-block. If only there was someone to show me the way to turn him into a stepping-stone . . .

> *She goes out.* YOUNG SWEETMAN *follows after her calling 'Wellesley . . . Wellesley . . .'*
> *Enter* BLOMAX *with a brown paper parcel.*

BLOMAX. Oh dear, oh dear . . . Beverley Races, what a performance! Ben Jonson's Delight was pulled by his jock and I lost a cool fifty. What's more, I wasn't warned. I don't know why the stewards don't enforce these things better. Something's gone very queer with my sources of advance information. And not only at Beverley. What have I come back to! Well, you've seen it more than I have. *I* don't know where it's going to conclude . . . I suppose it would be strategical to have a word with Gloria? I last left her at Doncaster, very astonished. On such a beautiful evening – now that club of hers is apparently closed – she will no doubt be found supine in her back garden, enjoying a drink of tea . . .

SCENE FIVE

The back garden of GLORIA's *house.*

BLOMAX *remains on stage.* GLORIA *and* WIPER *enter for sunbathing in the garden with a crate of beer.* WIPER *is playing an accordion. They do not notice* BLOMAX *at first.*

BLOMAX. Oh well, more or less . . . Somebody's sense of crisis isn't very highly developed. I suppose you could call it the good old British phlegm . . .

WIPER (*singing*).

> The lady's walls are large and high
> The lady's grass is green and dry
> The lady herself is green and blooming
> And big fat Alfred, he's consuming . . .

Here, have another . . . (*He passes a bottle.*)

GLORIA (*to* WIPER). I hope you know what you're doing, sprawling here in broad daylight. I don't call it safe.

WIPER. Of course it's bloody safe. I came in the back gate, I go out the ditto, and we're not overlooked . . .

BLOMAX. Cock-a-doodle-doo . . .

They both leap up in alarm.

WIPER. Good God, how did *you* get in here?

BLOMAX. I carry a key in my little fob pocket.

WIPER. Oh you do, do you? And might I ask you why?

BLOMAX. And might I ask *you* why you've abandoned Mrs Wiper in such very hot weather with all the washing-up in a stuffy little kitchen?

WIPER. Leave my wife out of it.

BLOMAX. All right then, you leave *mine*.

WIPER. What? What's that!

He whips round on GLORIA, *who nods her head.*

GLORIA. Doncaster Registry Office. Monday morning. On his way to the races. It seemed the safest notion. But that gives you no cause to come barging in here as if you owned the bloody place . . .

BLOMAX. Now then, my dear, don't let's get edgy. A woman in your condition . . .

WIPER. But why didn't you tell me?

GLORIA. I didn't want to spoil things.

WIPER. You didn't want to spoil things . . . !

Knocking on the garden gate.

GLORIA. Oh my Lord, who's that! (*She calls out.*) No thank you, not today; I never buy at the gate!

Knocking continues.

I'd better open, I suppose. Keep out of sight. We don't know *who* it might be.

She hurriedly pulls on a housecoat over her bikini. WIPER *thrusts himself into his trousers and gathers up his shirt, tunic, etc.* BLOMAX *runs into the house.* GLORIA *opens the gate.* LADY SWEETMAN *enters.*

Lady Sweetman! How do you do?

LADY SWEETMAN. I am not very well. I have a migraine headache. Do you think I could come in a minute?

GLORIA has to let her in the gate.

Sir Harold Sweetman, Sir Harold, I may tell you, Sir Harold is extremely upset.

GLORIA. Aye, I can believe you . . .

WIPER, *who has not quite finished doing up his buttons, is caught.*

LADY SWEETMAN. Superintendent Wiper?

WIPER (*adjusting his buttons*). Good evening, Lady Sweetman.

LADY SWEETMAN. I know what you are here for, Superintendent. I know all about it.

WIPER. You do?

LADY SWEETMAN. And may I say I am appalled. You see, Sir
Harold is a sick man. He has a coronary condition. All these
cabals, these distasteful intrigues, I may tell you, are killing
him. (*She sniffs at her camphor.*)

GLORIA. A very jolly deathbed and all by the look of his com-
plexion.

LADY SWEETMAN. Coronary trouble expresses itself in an
unhealthy heightened colour.

GLORIA. Aye . . .

LADY SWEETMAN. However, we have no course but to be
practical. I came here to find out what my husband refuses
to tell me. How deeply is he involved in this unpleasant affair
at the Copacabana?

WIPER. Up to t' lug-oyles.

LADY SWEETMAN. Oh . . . He is most confident, you understand, that he will be able to extricate himself, and even, I
think, use it to political advantage.

WIPER. I'm delighted to hear that, Lady Sweetman. It really
does me good.

LADY SWEETMAN. But is his confidence justified?

WIPER. It all depends on Colonel Feng and how deep he
decides to delve. He could burn our bottoms yet, could
Colonel Feng.

GLORIA. Never mind about Feng. What about Butterthwaite?

LADY SWEETMAN. Has he made a definite accusation?

GLORIA. No, but he soon will.

LADY SWEETMAN. And if so, can he prove it?

GLORIA. That chap can prove anything if he's left alone with
it long enough. It's up to us to get in first and on a field of
our own choosing. Do him down through summat else.

LADY SWEETMAN. Not politics. It mustn't be politics. Think
of my husband's heart.

GLORIA. All right then. We'll keep it personal. But what?

LADY SWEETMAN. I think we should consider Mr Butter-thwaite's character. Such outrageous vulgarity must be there for a purpose, you know. Nobody could behave like that naturally.

WIPER. Oh, I don't know, Lady Sweetman. An astonishing great deal comes very naturally to some of us. (*He offers her a beer.*) Here – have a wet. The old family firm, you know.

LADY SWEETMAN. No, thank you . . . No, it is deliberate. He is concealing a social weakness. Of course, he is bound to feel inferior in many respects.

GLORIA. I can tell you one respect where he not only *feels* but he very definitely *is*.

LADY SWEETMAN. Oh. And what is that?

GLORIA. The gee-gees.

LADY SWEETMAN. The—

WIPER. She's not wrong, you know, she's right. If he tried to fix the ballot boxes as crafty as he fixes the tote, there'd be no Labour Party left.

LADY SWEETMAN. Tote, Superintendent? Gee-gees? I don't quite . . .

GLORIA. The races, Lady Sweetman. He loses his bets.

LADY SWEETMAN. Ah . . . Oh well, that makes it much easier. We must expose him, of course.

WIPER. How? He never bounced any cheques so far as I know . . .

GLORIA. He never *used* any cheques. But there must be a couple o' hundred quid at least queuing up in his IOU's.

LADY SWEETMAN. You see? It's all quite easy. We must find out who his creditors are and, er, assemble what my husband calls a Pressure Group. Sir Harold will be so grateful, you know. He never will believe that we women have a place in public life, but—

GLORIA. It's assembled already, the Pressure Group. It consists of one creditor only and his name is Wellington Blomax.

LADY SWEETMAN. Oh – Dr Blomax!

GLORIA. You know him? Well, he's just acquired a highly intelligent new wife.

LADY SWEETMAN. Oh, I'm so glad. I've always said that poor child of his needs a properly organized home, and I don't think she's been getting it.

GLORIA. No . . .

LADY SWEETMAN. Well, we must approach Mrs Blomax and make her understand – as I am sure that she will, being a woman – that her husband has a manifest duty to the community—

BLOMAX (*inside*). Wellesley, I'm warning you, you'll not be welcome out there—

GLORIA. Hey up – who's in the house!

Enter WELLESLEY.

WELLESLEY. He's just told me you're his wife!

LADY SWEETMAN. *You* are!

GLORIA. I dare say it does come as a bit of a surprise . . . Lady Sweetman, my – er – my stepdaughter, I suppose . . . It's the first time we've met.

LADY SWEETMAN. How very convenient. So we can keep it all in our own little circle and save so much unpleasantness. Now, Wellesley . . .

GLORIA. Superintendent, it's time you were off. Your recreation's over. Get back to Mrs Wiper.

WIPER. What? Why? Hey—

GLORIA. I don't want you to know too much. You'll only muck it up again if you do. But it is very unwise to fall asleep too soon in the shade of so dangerous an orchard. Keep hold on the fruit-basket – watch out for what drops.

WIPER. What drops? Where?

GLORIA. Butterthwaite. He's ripe enough . . . Go on, get off with you.

WIPER. Oh, oh, very well . . . Good evening, Lady Sweetman.

   Exit.

LADY SWEETMAN. Good evening, Superintendent . . . Quite
   a nice man – when you get to know him better.

GLORIA. Nice ? Oh aye . . .

WELLESLEY (*takes beer*). Do you mind, I feel thirsty . . . He
   left one of his little notes on his surgery door to say where he
   was for the benefit of his patients. It'd just serve you right to
   get six kids with measles and a couple of polio subjects inter-
   rupting the honeymoon. (*To* LADY SWEETMAN.) I suppose
   you've come to see my father to complain about me and
   Maurice and all the rest of that ?

LADY SWEETMAN. Complain ? Oh my dear child, I'm not
   going to complain. Do you *want* to marry Maurice ? He wants
   to marry *you*, you know.

WELLESLEY. I have had other offers. I have not yet made a
   choice. All that I want is my right to do so, unprejudiced,
   when I want, do you see ? I want it and I'll fight for it.

   BLOMAX *enters, behind, listening.*

LADY SWEETMAN. Oh, you young people – so noisy about
   your *rights*. But what about your responsibilities, Wellesley ?
   I don't know whether you will understand this, my dear,
   because, of course, you're not entirely English, are you ? But
   I am afraid that you yourself must to some extent be held
   responsible for your father.

WELLESLEY. Responsible ? Me ? Are you out of your mind ?

LADY SWEETMAN. I have always been told he is a very good
   doctor – at least for his panel patients. But as a professional
   man, he must know very well he is known by his friends.

WELLESLEY. His friends aren't *my* friends.

LADY SWEETMAN. Yes, my dear, I know. And *you* must make
   yourself responsible for seeing they are no longer *his*. I am
   going to be quite strict about this, Wellesley, and I'm going

to apply pressure. He must be made to understand the folly
of his conduct. And then we shall *all* be happy. You will, *and*
Maurice. Yes . . . Good-bye, Mrs er – Blomax, I leave it all
in your hands . . . Oh dear, my poor head . . . In your
hands, Mrs Blomax. I do hope I can trust you . . .

> *Exit*
> BLOMAX *comes forward.*

GLORIA. So you overheard us, did you ? . . . Pressure. You'd
do well to prepare yourself.

BLOMAX. I don't know what you are talking about. Wellesley,
my dove, I bought two pair o' kippers. Not much, but they're
protein. You see, I had a bad day.

GLORIA. The news may not have filtered through to you at the
Beverley Grandstand, but Alfred Wiper and your flash companions from the Victoria and Albert have grown somewhat
incompatible.

BLOMAX. Flash companions indeed! They are very old friends
of mine.

GLORIA. That's the trouble. You realize what's happened to
Alfred ? He is lined up with Sweetman. And your daughter,
as it happens, has a taste and fancy also to line up with
Sweetman . . .

WELLESLEY. Wait a minute . . .

GLORIA. You just keep quiet, love. All I want *you* to do is to
stand over there and look pathetic. (*To* BLOMAX *again.*)
You'd be well advised to take example and to line yourself up
likewise. I mean, get rid of Butterthwaite, and join your own
class of people. Don't you want her to stand in the favour of
her chosen new in-laws ? And besides, your own position in
regard to the police isn't all that it might be. Suppose they
were to hear about what you've been prescribing for certain
other of your female patients ?

BLOMAX. An issue of mercy, their condition demanded it . . .

GLORIA. Yes . . .

BLOMAX. Yes . . . of course, I do acknowledge a definite duty towards my neglected little daughter . . . But *I* don't know . . . Charlie Butterthwaite? What do you expect me to *do* about him, Gloria?

GLORIA. Tell him where you stand and tell him who you are! Be decisive. Insult him. Press him for your debts. You'll be done with him *then*. Don't tell me you've got qualms?

WELLESLEY. How can he have qualms? He's an old rotten rascal and he'_ given me no good ever. I want what I want and I'm going to break his head for it. Are we to have these for supper?

She takes the kippers into the house.

BLOMAX. You'd better go and help her. She'll turn those kippers into charcoal if you give her half a chance.

GLORIA. We want an answer from you before you go to bed.

BLOMAX. Bed?

GLORIA. Aye, bed . . .

> And the shape of your answer
> Will doubtless decide
> Whether that bed
> Will be narrow or wide! – hubby!

She goes into the house.

BLOMAX. Well, whether it's one or whether it's the other, I still seem to have invited into it the east wind and the west and they're scrapping like two catamounts between my skin and my pyjamas . . .

He picks up the empty bottles, pours out the dregs into one bottle, and drinks it.

Fact of the matter is, I *have* been betraying my class. Wellesley *is* entitled to the natural advantages of her place in society, the snooty little bitch. I am, after all, a comfortable man: and

I don't want to be disrupted. When all is said and done, this town is run by an ignorant overweening yobbo: and it's time I stood up firm to him and accepted the responsibilities of my superior education . . . Furthermore, he owes me money.

He goes into the house

SCENE SIX

A room in the Town Hall.

Enter BOOCOCK, LEFTWICH *and* HOPEFAST.

HOPEFAST.
>He came and asked for thirty quid,
>I said I hadn't got it.
>I said I wasn't made o' brass,
>He said he bloody knew it.

BOOCOCK.
>I can't imagine Charlie
>Running really short o' money.
>He hasn't said a word to me.

HOPEFAST.
>I think there's summat funny.

LEFTWICH.
>He's lost it on the horses.

Enter HARDNUTT.

HARDNUTT.
>I think there's summat funny.
>Did you hear Charlie Butterthwaite
>Wor trying to borrow money?

BOOCOCK.
>He never said a word to me.
>I've been often pleased to lend him

> The odd quid here and there,
> I gave it him, he gave it back,
> All fair and no one wondered.

LEFTWICH.

> He's lost it on the horses.

BOOCOCK.

> He can't have done.

HARDNUTT.

> He did.

HOPEFAST.

> He did.

HARDNUTT.

> It sounds to me like Balaclava bugles,
> This day some clown has blundered.

BOOCOCK.

> We all know Charlie Butterthwaite,
> And know him without turpitude,
> Nine times he's held the rank of Mayor,
> And now the peoples' gratitude.
> With all the battles he has fought
> In all his loyal rectitude
> If he should be in trouble
> We should grant him our support.

Enter HICKLETON.

HICKLETON.

> What's up with our old Charlie,
> Asking everyone for money ?
> I mean to say he's often short . . .

BOOCOCK.

> We all of us are often short.

HICKLETON.

> He asked me for one hundred quid!
> And coming at a time like this,
> The day we've all but clapped the lid

On Feng and Sweetman and the Tories . . .
I think there's summat funny,
And I hear there's funny stories
Have been spread around about.

HARDNUTT.

His face wor red and white
And his eyes wor poking out.

HICKLETON.

And asking me for five score quid.

HOPEFAST.

He rang me up i' t'midst o' t'night,
First in a chuckle, then in a shout.

HICKLETON.

And then he came to my front door.
I said, o'course, I hadn't got it.

HICKLETON ⎞
HOPEFAST ⎠

I said I wasn't made o'brass.

ALL 3 COUNCILLORS.

He said he bloody knew it!

Enter BUTTERTHWAITE.

BUTTERTHWAITE. Hello! I know. I've got red ears . . . All
right, I don't come twice to a sold-out chip-oyle, t'subject's
done with. Now, Mr Mayor, there's a delegate outside from
the Forces of Reaction. Are you going to talk to him?

BOOCOCK. I am. And this time, Charlie, you keep your oar out.
I am highly concerned for our reputation abroad. Have you
seen the *Yorkshire Post* today?

BUTTERTHWAITE. Aye, it were good reading. I tell you,
they're getting frightened.

BOOCOCK. I don't call it good reading. We're in the London
Telegraph an' all, let alone that two-faced *Herald*. The time
has now come for appropriate negotiations.

BUTTERTHWAITE. Appropriate? All right, but Feng has got to go.

BOOCOCK. Eh dear . . . I don't know . . . Herbert, let him in.

LEFTWICH *ushers in* F. J.

F. J. Good evening, Mr Mayor. May I take it you are speaking for the Labour Party as I in my turn am speaking for the Conservatives?

SWEETMAN *comes in and stands at the back.*

BUTTERTHWAITE (*pointing to* SWEETMAN). I see him, over there!

BOOCOCK. Charlie, do you mind?

F. J. Bearing in mind the unsettling effect of such a dispute and particularly in regard to the criminal element of the town . . .

BOOCOCK. Granted.

F. J. I beg your pardon?

BOOCOCK. Granted.

F. J. Mr Mayor, I beg you, please moderate your attitude. The police should be above party recrimination.

BOOCOCK. Granted.

F. J. Sir Harold is thinking in terms of an independent inquiry. He has authorized me to . . .

BOOCOCK. Alderman Butterthwaite has laid a definite information. It is the duty of the Chief Constable to either prosecute the Copacabana or to give adequate reasons for refusing to prosecute. If he should finally determine to refuse, then I imagine an inquiry would be mandatory. But until then, certainly not.

F. J. But, Mr Mayor . . .

BOOCOCK. And let alone the whole question of corruption in his ranks!

F. J. If you will not agree to a Home Office inquiry, Sir Harold is fully prepared to lay the facts at his disposal in front of the electorate. And they are not entirely synonymous with those presented by Alderman Butterthwaite.

BOOCOCK. Who has presented *no* facts! Sub judice evidence cannot be publicly brought forward.

F. J. Not brought forward. Slid.

BOOCOCK. I beg your pardon?

F. J. Granted. I said 'slid'. Rumours deliberately insinuated. We may be reactionaries, Barney, but we're not complete idiots. There's plenty of personal dirt we can throw into the next election. We don't like it, we've never done it, but if we have to, we will!

BOOCOCK. I'm sure your hearts will bleed.

F. J. Oh, and by the way, the art gallery. You may not believe it, but there are certain people who regard it as important.

BOOCOCK. *I* regard it as important. What the hell are you talking about?

SWEETMAN. It has been shuffled once too often. I am now making it my personal concern.

Exeunt SWEETMAN *and* F. J.

BOOCOCK. Well, you all heard him. An independent inquiry! Now that's a very big concession. I think we ought to take it.

COUNCILLORS *murmur agreement.*

BUTTERTHWAITE. Oh, no, no, no . . . I'm not being fobbed off wi' no cocoa-and-water compromises. I want my gullet stuffed wi' the good fat roast goose to the point of a vomit, *and* I'm getting it an' all.

BOOCOCK. Ah . . . What do you think he meant about the art gallery, Charlie?

BUTTERTHWAITE. The art gallery's been attended to.

BOOCOCK. And after what manner attended to, Charlie?

BUTTERTHWAITE. It's all in the Committee Minutes if you care to look it up. A unanimous decision was taken against any further discussion of the point.

BOOCOCK. Two Conservatives on that Committee. Which way did they vote?

BUTTERTHWAITE. They were unavoidably absent.

BOOCOCK. Oh, they were, were they? By, Charlie Butter-thwaite, if I wor a younger man I'd put my bloody booit into thee! Who do you think you are, going behind my back like that!

BUTTERTHWAITE. I'll tell you who I am.

> I'm the King of this Castle, Barney,
> And that by right of conquest,
> Elected for main engagement
> In each and every issue
> Our party has pursued
> Throughout perilous generations.
> I turned tramcars over
> In the turmoil of twenty-six,
> I marched in the hungry mutiny
> From the north to the metropolis,
> I carried the broken banner.
> When hungry bellies bore no bread,
> I dreamed of my dinner
> In the wasted line of dole,
> And by fundamental force of strength
> I fetched my people through it.
> Call it the Red Sea, call it
> The boundaries of Canaan,
> I carried them over,
> My care, my calculation
> Lived as a loyal Englishman
> Through long-suffering and through languishment,
> I chiefly did, and I chiefly deserved.
> Can you deny it?

BOOCOCK. No. Chiefly is true. But party is party We cannot call it 'King'.

BUTTERTHWAITE. I spoke by way of metaphor.

BOOCOCK. We cannot call it 'King'.

BUTTERTHWAITE. Ah, Barney, Barney, Barney . . . Constable Leftwich, look at us both! Which one's the King?

LEFTWICH. Neither. I'd say Mrs Boocock.

They all laugh.

BUTTERTHWAITE. How *is* the missus, Barney?

BOOCOCK. Sarah continues robust.

BUTTERTHWAITE (*taking him aside*). And I suppose she still holds the old Boocock cheque-book, eh?

BOOCOCK. Ah . . . I wondered when you were going to pluck up face and come to me about it. How much is the total?

BUTTERTHWAITE. She'd never let you have it.

BOOCOCK. Three figures, they wor telling me . . . I'm afraid that she wouldn't. I'm afraid there's not a chance. Now a tenner or a fiver.

BUTTERTHWAITE. Nay, I'd not take it.

BOOCOCK. All right, I'll not force you . . . It's time we were off home. You can be locking up, Herbert; the office staff will all have gone.

LEFTWICH. Goodnight, Mr Mayor.

BOOCOCK (*turning back on the way out*). Now, Charlie, this inquiry, think it over very careful. I believe we should agree to it. . .

BOOCOCK AND COUNCILLORS. Night, Charlie, night Charlie . . *etc.*

Exeunt all save BUTTERTHWAITE *and* LEFTWICH.

BUTTERTHWAITE. Go and lock up. I won't be half an hour. I've got some letters to attend to.

LEFTWICH. I say, Charlie, is it that bad?

BUTTERTHWAITE. There's nowt that bad, Herbert, as can't be made better with a bit o' pride of achievement in some other field. All I want to do is get rid o' Feng. If I can manage that, I don't give a bastard's egg if I spend the rest o' my life i' t'workhouse!

LEFTWICH. Well, you were born i' t'bloody place, worn't you?

Exit LEFTWICH.

BUTTERTHWAITE. Wellington! Wellington! You scarlet intestine-rummaging dun, where ha' you got to?

Enter BLOMAX.

BLOMAX. Are you alone yet?

BUTTERTHWAITE. I am.

BLOMAX. Have you got it?

BUTTERTHWAITE. I have not.

BLOMAX. I am sorry to do this, Charlie! I've got to have that money!

BUTTERTHWAITE. Five hundred bloody nicker . . .

BLOMAX. Charlie, you're a cheat. You're a chiseller. You're rotten. You are not a loyal friend.

BUTTERTHWAITE. What!

BLOMAX. I mean to quarrel with you, Charlie. I am forced to cast you off . . .

BUTTERTHWAITE. Wellington . . . if you weren't in bad trouble, you would never use such words. Come on, lad, what is it? Are you being blackmailed?

BLOMAX. Oh, Charlie, I am! You see, it's been like this. I'm going to be frank with you, Charlie. I – I er don't know how to put it . . . it's a question of – a – question of – all right, professional reputation. Yes. Now here is the truth! Overindulgent prescriptions! Suppose I put it that way? . . . I only regarded it as an extension of a normal bedside manner. But it looks like coming up at a coroner's inquest, so I've got to pay up or hic haec hoc, I'm done!

BUTTERTHWAITE. Are you telling me the truth?

BLOMAX. The absolute and clear-starched verity! I'm always being half blackmailed, but this time it's dead serious. Oh,

Charlie, I've done you a power of services up and down this town as a general intelligencer, and if ever you've found me of any use at all . . .

BUTTERTHWAITE. It has never been said that Charlie Butterthwaite was the man to watch his mates fall under. Gratitude wi' Charlie for services rendered is the king-post of his roof-tree:

> It holds the tiles above his house-place
> The smoke-hole for his fire
> It overhangs his weighty table
> And the bed of his desire!

Wellington, you'll have your money, but out o' *my* bank-balance ? Oh dear . . . How are we going to manage ?

BLOMAX. I don't know. How are we ?

BUTTERTHWAITE. Burgle t'Town Hall.

BLOMAX. It's all right *laughing* . . .

BUTTERTHWAITE. Wellington, I'm not laughing . . . Did I ever tell you I was born in the workhouse ? Well I was, and it was horrible. Oh, they've not got me back there yet, not a carrot nor a stick can compel this bloody donkey where he doesn't want to go! (*He sings, with a little dance.*)

> In the workhouse I was born
> On one Christmas day
> Two long ears and four short feet
> And all I ate was hay.

> Hay for breakfast, hay for dinner
> Lovely hay for tea,
> I thanked my benefactors thus
> Hee-haw hee-haw *hee* !

Now then, it's none so very difficult. All you need to know is the right key to t'safe. I've got it on me watchchain. We make a quick glance around in the interests of security, good, they've all gone home to their teas, we open it up . . . (*He opens the safe.*) And . . . the Borough Treasurer's petty cash!

(*He sings.*)

> When I was grown as tall as this
> I asked if I might go
> Into the world, the lovely world,
> I saw it through the window!

Aye, and they gave me permission and all:

> Get out, they said, you dirty brute,
> You've grown up quite disgusting.
> The world is welcome to your stink
> And to your horrid lusting.
> I thanked my benefactors thus . . . !

BLOMAX. Charlie, I say, Charlie, is this the real issue? I mean to say, there's no real hurry – it's not really that urgent . . .

BUTTERTHWAITE. Of course it's the real issue, you consequential fathead! There's nigh on a thousand in here. I don't know how many times I've had to tell these skiving clerks this is *not* the Barclays Bank!

BLOMAX. But surely they'll have made a note of the numbers?

BUTTERTHWAITE. Not on your life they haven't! Ho, there's some heads going to roll in this office tomorrow morning. (*He is counting out packets of banknotes.*) There's your five hundred. Put it in your pocket! Go on, put it in!

(*He sings.*)

> I thanked my benefactors thus
> Hee-haw hee-haw haw.
> I could not understand, you see,
> Just how it was they thought of me
> Or what it was they saw!

What am I going to do wi' t'rest? I might keep it. But I won't. It'll only draw attention . . . I know . . .

He sings, and as he does so he scatters money about the stage.

> I travelled out into that world
> With never a backward glance,
> The street was full of folk, they said,
> He's got two ears upon his head
> He's got four feet upon his legs
> He's got . . . My God, look what he's got,
> They cried, Get back to France!

I said, what do you mean, France? I've never been to France in my life! I wor born in the workhouse. I never set foot over the doorstone while this morning!

> They cried, Get back to France!

Oh my God, it makes me tired . . .

> I could not think what I had done
> That I was so derided
> For Nature gives no donkey less
> Than what I was provided.

You see what I'm doing? We scatter it around, thereby indicating a similitude of ludicrous panic . . . as though disturbed in the act we have fled from the scene in terrified disorder.

> I said – hee-haw – you're very rude
> I do the best I can.
> You couldn't treat me worse, I said,
> If I was a human man!

(*He begins wiping fingerprints away.*) And the minute I said that they all fled away. Not a soul in sight in the whole of that long city . . . starved and hungry, there I stood, Wellington, Ooer and a rumble-oh, in my poor thin belly. All the pubs were shut, aye, and the chip-oyles an' all . . . I walked along slowly by a pawnbroker's window, and as it chanced, I saw my reflection in a gilt-framed ormulo mirror . . .

> O what a shock, I nearly died,
> I saw my ears as small as these,
> Two feet, two hands, a pair of knees,
> My eyeballs jumped from side to side,
> I jumped right round, I bawled out loud,
> You lousy liars, I've found you out!
> I know now why you're fleeing . . .
> I am no donkey, never was,
> I'm a naked human being!

You know, after that, it was easy . . . all I had to do was to buy a suit of clothes . . . they came back, they came back, me boy, and there I prospered, there I grew . . . and you look at me now!

BLOMAX. But how are we going to cover all this up?

BUTTERTHWAITE. Do you mean to tell me you haven't been listening to a word I was singing? I have just given you my entire and lamentable autobiography and all you can say is 'How do we cover it up?' . . . ! All right then, I'll tell you. It is now eight o'clock as near as makes no difference, and by reason of the inclemency of the weather, it is all but dark outside. I am going to proceed home at a normal pace. On entering my garden gate at approximately eight-twenty-five, I am going to be struck on the head by a blunt instrument, wielded by an unknown criminal, who then secures my bunch of keys, leaps into his motor-car, and drives to the Town Hall. He gains entry through a side door, passes through the administrative offices, and opens the safe. On his departure, he leaves the keys i' t'lock-oyle.

BLOMAX. What about the night-watchman?

BUTTERTHWAITE. Do you mean Herbert Leftwich? We gave him the telly in his room six months ago, and he never stirs out of it while eleven o'clock at earliest . . . Now I'll tell you *your* part! You go straight off home, too. And you'll wait beside your blower till about a quarter-to-nine when my landlady (or concubine or whatever you call her) rings you up with an urgent call for assistance. On arrival, you examine my person, and discern a serious contusion on the top of me nut. All right, I'll have to provide one. But I don't want to kill meself. I rely on your diagnosis to make it appear sufficiently brutal. And don't you turn up with all that hot paper stuck inside your wallet. Take it out and bury it. And any rate, don't spend it all at once. But you don't want to spend it, you're being blackmailed – my God, they could trace it back to you if you hand it all over in one lump to some villain.

BLOMAX. I think I could hold out on him for a few days longer, but—

BUTTERTHWAITE. I think you'd better had. Our job's to fox the police, not to assist them . . . Fox the police. By God, it *will* fox 'em and all. Feng – we've got him diddled! Corruption they can live with, but incompetence – ho ho! Leftwich will have bolted the front door by now. You go out the side way, and see you leave it open. I'm going down by Leftwich's office to establish my time of departure. He'll let me out the main door and return straightaway to warming his old frustrations in front o' the juke-box jury . . . So there we are, get home with you! And no bloody dawdling, Wellington, or I promise you I'll twist your windpipe out!

Exeunt.

After a pause, enter LEFTWICH. *He is on his rounds, with a torch. He sees a banknote on the stage, picks it up with a 'Tut-tut', sees another, picks it up, sees another, and so on, casually, until he is led by his paper-chase up to the unlocked safe. He puts the money in, and turns away.*

LEFTWICH. I never knew a more careless lot in all my born

days. The place could have been robbed ten times over. (*Double-take. He rushes back to the safe, opens it, looks in, shuts it, and turns wildly round.*) Hey! Stop thief!

LEFTWICH *rushes to the side of the stage and presses a button. Alarm bells ring, all round the theatre.*
Police cars, gongs and engines heard. Uniformed PCS *run in, look at the safe, run out again, run in again, take up positions.*

LUMBER *and* WIPER, *in plain clothes, run in. Fingerprint man and police photographer set about their work.* LEFTWICH, *hurriedly replacing the money on the stage where he has found it, avoids being seen by the others, and succeeds in pocketing at least one banknote.* BOOCOCK *comes in, registers horror, collides with* WIPER *on the staircase: general confusion.* JOURNALISTS *come in with flash cameras. They take a series of photographs, illustrating:*

(1) WIPER *and* LUMBER *examining evidence.*
(2) BOOCOCK *ditto.*
(3) WIPER *and* LUMBER *taking statement from* LEFTWICH.
(4) BOOCOCK *taking statement from* LEFTWICH.
(5) WIPER *and* LUMBER *taking statement from* BOOCOCK.
(6) WIPER, LUMBER, BOOCOCK *and* LEFTWICH *taking statements from four* LABOUR COUNCILLORS, *who enter in disarray.*
(7) SWEETMAN *and* F. J. *examining evidence on their entry.*
(8) *The entry of* FENG.

FENG, *entered last, quickly examines the situation, while everyone else stands back.*

FENG (*to* WIPER, *confidentially*). Probably an inside job, Superintendent. But difficult to establish, I dare say. However, carry on.

Exeunt.

Act Three

SCENE ONE

A tea garden in the park.

Enter BLOMAX *carrying a folded newspaper.*

BLOMAX. I never thought it would work. I let myself be hypnotized by the magic of his personality . . . him and his contusion . . . sufficiently brutal . . . *my* diagnosis . . . It wouldn't have knocked out a three-days-old baby, what I found on his top! And they're playing cat-and-mouse with me now . . . for over a week it's been going on!

A plain-clothes PC *enters, reading a newspaper.*

That's a great big purring tom over there, with official-issue boots on, and he's looking at me through a little hole in the fold of his *Sheffield Star*. Of course, I can do the same. (*He opens his paper and makes a hole in it with his finger, through which he watches the* CONSTABLE.) But where does it get me? I think I'll have a cup o' tea. There's surely no danger in that?

A PARK ATTENDANT *arranges tables and a* WAITRESS *lays them.*

BLOMAX sits down at a table which is laid ready, pours himself a large cup of tea and swallows it noisily. Takes aspirins. The PC also sits down at an opposite table and continues watching from behind his paper.

A man who has sat at a table at the rear of the stage turns round and is seen to be FENG. *Noticing* BLOMAX, *he half gets up, indecisively.* BLOMAX *recognizes him and chokes into his tea-cup.*

Oh . . . it's got extremely stuffy sitting down all of a sudden

. . . I think I'll take a turn in the park . . . (*To the* WAIT-RESS.) Don't bother with the change, miss. You can buy yourself a . . . a knick-knack! (*He gives her a pound note and hurries out.*)

The PC *gets up to follow, but is intercepted by* FENG.

FENG. What was he doing here?
PC. Third teaplace he's visited since dinnertime, sir. A large pot o' tea and a couple of aspirins in each one. I fancy he's getting nervous.
FENG. So I observe. A change of tactics, Constable. Go after him now and take him down to the station. Tell the Superintendent to see if he can persuade him to reconsider his original statement. I think he might be ready to.
PC. Very good, sir . . . (*To the* WAITRESS.) I've left it on the table. (*Exit* PC.)

The WAITRESS *approaches* FENG.

WAITRESS. The usual, sir?
FENG. If you please. A variety of cakes. I thank you . . . Ah . . .

WELLESLEY *enters.* FENG *holds a chair back and she sits down with him.*

Miss Blomax . . . I'm so glad you could come. I have ordered the tea . . . I do not think, Miss Blomax, that you ought to have come . . . I do not think I should have asked you.
WELLESLEY. Go on, tell me why.
FENG. It is not possible.
WELLESLEY. Of course it is . . . I'm going to have one of these with the toothpaste in. (*She takes an éclair.*) Why don't you have one yourself? And drive off the black bull from the top of your tongue.

FENG.
>It is not possible that I should tell you why.
>I have not known you very long.
>For right or wrong
>Except when authorized for formal public utterance
>I must endure perpetual public silence.
>And so, for private purposes, I find
>My words are of necessity muted.
>You have not seemed to mind.
>You have drunk tea,
>Eaten cakes and toasted bread
>And jam, and you yourself have talked to me
>And I have been transported.
>Did you know it?

WELLESLEY. Oh yes, I knew it.

FENG. But did you share it? . . . No.

WELLESLEY. It's not my job to share it. It's your job to be courageous, I suppose, and nasty when you have to . . . Sometimes you can be quite gentle, and, of course, you're sentimental . . . But I don't approve of you, you know. I think I should make that clear because you seem to be working up to a renewal of your proposal.

FENG.
>No! It is not so. It cannot be.
>It is not possible. I am destroyed in you.
>Do you not see,
>By my official bond I am destroyed
>And you yourself in me.
>I cannot talk or think proposals, either way or none.
>Not now. I cannot recognize your company. Not now!
>Although in one sense, I suppose, the damage has been done.

WELLESLEY. Because of my father.

FENG. I did not say so.

WELLESLEY. You don't believe what he told you about the attack on the Alderman. If you want to marry me, you're in a

difficult position . . . I don't know what to say. I don't want
my father to go to prison. I don't want to make things any
worse for you . . . you're the only one of the old grey heads
I have any respect for. I don't want to hurt you, though I
don't care if I *have* to . . . And after a fashion I'm engaged
to Maurice Sweetman, and I don't really know whether I like
him at all. In a way I'd prefer you. You *are* some sort of *man.*

FENG. Do you mean that?

WELLESLEY. Why not? But I mean it, *provided* . . . I wish
you would change your job. Or at least become a bit human
at it and leave my father alone.

FENG. I can't hear what you say . . .

WELLESLEY. I said, leave him alone. He's a damned twisting
idiot, but he never did serious hurt.

FENG. No, no, I can't hear! Please leave me alone! . . . Or
rather, I'll leave you . . . We might be seen together, we
have been seen together, *heard* together, look! There is the
waitress! (*He shoves some coins on the table.*) Here you are.
See. It should include the tea, all the cakes I dare say; you
want to eat them, in *my* mouth they are sawdust . . .

WELLESLEY *goes. He tries in vain to stop her.*

No, don't you go . . . It is *I* that should be leaving *you.* (*He
collides with the* WAITRESS.)

WAITRESS. How many cakes did you have, sir?

FENG. Cakes? Have? What . . . ?

Enter BOOCOCK.

BOOCOCK. I've been seeking you all afternoon. You may not
care for what I stand for, but I *am* Chief Magistrate and I'd
say it was up to you to show yourself available for once!

FENG. Mr Mayor, I . . .

BOOCOCK. Five hundred pound and upward burgled out o' my
Town Hall, near fifteen days gone by and who's arrested?
No one! There are professional thieves living in this town;

they keep their wives and families by it; it's your job to know their names. All right then, bring 'em in!

FENG. Bring in *whom*, sir?

BOOCOCK. The lot in, one by one, till you find out the man! Instead o' which to choose to doubt the open word of an alderman and a doctor, honest and reputed, doubt their word and watch their houses, tread upon their heels i' t'street . . .

FENG. Mr Mayor, I cannot hear you!

Enter LABOUR COUNCILLORS.

HOPEFAST. Call your traps off Charlie Butterthwaite, Feng.

HICKLETON. Call 'em off. We want your resignation.

HARDNUTT. We want your resignation!

BOOCOCK. My mind is changed toward you, you've now gone over t'mark.

BOOCOCK AND COUNCILLORS. We want your resignation!

WAITRESS. Order your teas or else get out. We don't have brawling here. Do you want me to call the police!

FENG. I told you, sir, I cannot hear one word that you have said to me!

Exit FENG.

BOOCOCK. There is no further question of reproachment or conciliation. This is deadlock.

HOPEFAST. Done.

HICKLETON. And capped.

HARDNUTT. And outright ended.

Exeunt

SCENE TWO

The Police headquarters.

PCS *in outer office, ignoring* BUTTERTHWAITE, *who is walking about with a bandage round his head. He is unshaven and appears to have taken few pains about the order of his clothes.*

BUTTERTHWAITE (*to the audience*). Will you all take note of what I am about to say. I have been called to this police station by Superintendent Wiper. I have been waiting here for five or six hours, and not one o' these incontinent coppers has taken a blind bit o' notice!

> WIPER *enters his inner office from within. He holds a type-script.*

WIPER. Sarnt Lumber!
LUMBER (*off*). Sir?
WIPER. Time?
LUMBER. Half-twelve, sir. All fixed.

> LUMBER *enters the outer office.* WIPER *comes through to it also.*

WIPER. Afternoon, Alderman. How's the head?
BUTTERTHWAITE. Aches.
WIPER. Oh, dear me. Now to go through your statement just once again, if you don't mind the trouble . . . just a few points . . . (*Refers to typescript.*) On passing through your garden gate, two masked figures rose from behind the privet hedge, one at either gatepost, you were stood betwixt 'em . . . so?

> *He and* LUMBER *at either side of* BUTTERTHWAITE.

Which one hit you?
BUTTERTHWAITE. You did!
WIPER. Sure? It couldn't have been the sergeant?
BUTTERTHWAITE. It could not.
WIPER. But here's the contusion.
BUTTERTHWAITE. Ow, don't touch that bandage!
WIPER. We've had ballistics research in on this. No conceivable injury could from this angle cause even the most temporary failure of the faculties.

BUTTERTHWAITE. You can't catch me. *I've* read me Sexton Blake. I was turned the other way. (*He turns round.*)

WIPER. Are you in the habit, Alderman, of entering your garden backwards?

BUTTERTHWAITE. In the moment of alarm I instinctively swung round to face the open street. What's wrong wi' that?

WIPER. Aha, we're there before you. We photographed your footprints. Quite right, you *were* turned round. Now then, which one hit you?

He and LUMBER *change places.*

BUTTERTHWAITE. You did, you!

WIPER. Me?

BUTTERTHWAITE. No, not you, you booby! *Him.*

WIPER. I see. And from the rear. Now ballistics research has conclusively established . . .

BUTTERTHWAITE. Spare me the Jack Hawkins, will you! The fact remains that I got coshed and here's the wound to prove it. Now get around that if you can.

WIPER. We've got.

BUTTERTHWAITE. You've what?

WIPER. Constable, let's be having him!

Two PCs *bring in* BLOMAX, *rather the worse for wear and holding a mug of tea.*

BUTTERTHWAITE. Wellington! Have they been roughing you up? Oh . . .

WIPER. Dr Blomax, your original statement diagnosing concussion and lesions of the brain has not been borne out by further medical opinion. Do you wish to modify that statement?

LUMBER (*taking a typescript from a* PC). He does, sir.

WIPER. Let's hear it.

BUTTERTHWAITE (*as* LUMBER *is about to read*). I want to telephone my solicitor.

WIPER. All in good time.

BLOMAX. Hey, so do I.

WIPER. If you're going Queen's Evidence you don't require a solicitor.

BLOMAX. Oh, Charlie, it's not my fault – they've had me in here all night; I wasn't able to withstand them!

BUTTERTHWAITE. I don't suppose you were. As I have frequently had cause to preach, you can't by individuality hold up props against the overtippling world. By solid class defence and action of the mass alone can we hew out and line with timbered strength a gallery of self-respect beneath the faulted rock above the subsidence of water! Alfred ·Wiper, you watch out. I bear a name that still commands proud worship in these parts!

Enter FENG, *into the outer office.*

FENG. Has the Doctor reconsidered his testimony?

WIPER. He has, sir. Here we are.

FENG *goes into the inner office and* WIPER *follows with* BLOMAX's *statement.*

FENG. I see. It is unusable, I'm afraid.

WIPER. But, sir . . .

FENG. There are reasons, Superintendent, relating to my personal honour, names which might be coupled. I cannot permit this particular man to have the advantage of Queen's Evidence. He must stand his trial with the other.

WIPER. We can't do that! He's submitted this voluntarily – we've no choice but to take it. It'll look very queer indeed if—

FENG. Queer?

WIPER. I mean to say, sir, your personal honour . . . Well, folk are going to wonder if it hasn't already become a bit bent.

FENG. That's quite enough of that. You must find out your

own evidence by correct detective measures. I have no more to say.

FENG *goes out through the inner door.* WIPER *returns to the outer office.*

WIPER. Sarnt Lumber, a change of tactic. There is more hard work entailed than we in our innocence had imagined. So send the gentlemen home.

He goes back through the inner office and exits that way.

LUMBER. All right. You heard him. Go home.

BLOMAX. Oh, my dearie me, what an amazing metamorphosis . . . (*He scurries out.*)

BUTTERTHWAITE. Well, well, well, Sergeant. Are you sure it's worth the effort ?

LUMBER. The results of human striving are very rarely worth the effort. For instance, did you hear that after all your worthy struggle the Copacabana Club has closed its doors for the last time, only to re-open on the first day of May as the 'Sweetman Memorial Art Gallery' ? What about that for the artistic interests of the town ?

BUTTERTHWAITE. Why warn't I informed!

LUMBER. You *have* been informed.

BUTTERTHWAITE. In a very irregular manner . . . So he did own that joint all the bloody while, did he ?

LUMBER. I wouldn't know. According to the story, he acquired it last week. *I* wouldn't care to come up with a contradiction. And I don't suppose *you* would . . . under the circumstances.

BUTTERTHWAITE. Get out o' my road!

Exit BUTTERTHWAITE.

LUMBER (*calls after him*). Alderman, be careful, we're not done wi' you yet!

Exeunt

SCENE THREE

The Victoria and Albert.

> *Enter* LABOUR COUNCILLORS, *a few* DRINKERS, LAND-
> LORD *behind bar.*

The COUNCILLORS *sit down at a table.*

HICKLETON. Why hasn't Feng resigned? There's been a
formal council vote of no confidence and yet he's still here!

HOPEFAST. The last I heard o' Charlie, they pulled him in this
morning afore he'd even had his breakfast.

A DRINKER (*sings.*)
O where are the people for to give their voice to glory?
They stand before the altar on the elbow of the Tory . . . !

> *Other* DRINKERS *join in the song and repeat it.*

HARDNUTT. If we can't be private we can take our money elsewhere!

LANDLORD (*hurrying over to them*). I'll sort it out . . . (*To the*
DRINKERS.) Now come on, gents, have some decency while
a funeral's in progress!

> *He puts a screen round their table which conceals them from*
> *the rest of the room.*

But they're not wrong, you know, they're right. There's been
a definite trend in the general talk. (*He goes back to the bar.*)

HOPEFAST. When all is said and done, the image of our party
must not be distorted.

> MRS BOOCOCK *comes in and joins them behind the screen.*

MRS BOOCOCK. Have any o' you seen Barney?

COUNCILLORS. Why, Sarah, sit down, have a chair, love, it's a
surprise to see you here. What are you drinking? *etc.* . .

MRS BOOCOCK. That doctor's gone Queen's Evidence. Start

with the Ways and Means Committee. Have we a quorum?

HARDNUTT. We have.

MRS BOOCOCK. We've not got time to waste. Come on . . . Councillor Hopefast i' t'chair, Councillor Hardnutt and Hickleton present in Committee, Mayoress Mrs Boocock as deputy secretary.

HOPEFAST. I declare the Committee in session.

HARDNUTT. Minutes of the previous meeting regarded as read . . . Come on . . . Come on . . .

HICKLETON. Seconded.

HOPEFAST. Passed. Motion before the Committee, temporary absence of Alderman Butterthwaite necessitates reconstruction of Committee. Who's to replace him?

HICKLETON. I move that Councillor Hathersage be deputed to do so.

HARDNUTT. Seconded.

HOPEFAST. Passed . . . Now then, Borough Education. I declare the Committee in session, have we a quorum?

MRS BOOCOCK. I'm in on this one.

HOPEFAST. Councillor Hickleton deputy secretary, change about places . . . Councillor Hardnutt i' t'chair . . .

HARDNUTT. Minutes of previous meeting . . .

ALL. Etcetera etcetera . . .

HARDNUTT. Motion before . . . etcetera etcetera . . . Who's to replace him?

MRS BOOCOCK. I move that Councillor Hartwright be deputed to do so.

HARDNUTT. Seconded. Passed . . . Parks Playgrounds and Public Baths Committee.

HICKLETON. Councillor Hickleton i' t'chair, Mayoress Mrs Boocock again deputy secretary.

ALL. Etcetera etcetera . . .

HARDNUTT. Who's to replace him?

HOPEFAST. I move that Councillor Hampole . . .

ALL. Seconded, passed!

HOPEFAST. Any more for any more, we've got no time to waste!

BOOCOCK comes in and joins them. He carries a letter.

MRS BOOCOCK. Barney, where have you been?
BOOCOCK. What are you doing here?
MRS BOOCOCK. I'm having a drink.
BOOCOCK. That's most unwonted, ent it? . . . The Home Secretary in person has sent us a letter. He does not like the name our township is achieving. Indeed, he is so disturbed by it that he has threatened to go so far as to withdraw the government subsidy for our local police. Well, all I say is – *this!*

He tears the letter and crumples it and grinds it underfoot.

We are a self-governing Socialist community with Dearne and Don and Calder for our inviolate boundaries, and we will continue to press for the resignation of Feng!
HOPEFAST. Barney, did you hear that they've arrested Charlie?
BOOCOCK. Indeed, I did hear it. Why else have I done this?

He points to the remains of the letter.

MRS BOOCOCK. Our party cannot afford to be associated with thieves.
BOOCOCK. Sarah!
MRS BOOCOCK. Action has been taken, Barney. Tell him.
HOPEFAST. The natural suspicion attaching to a criminal charge has rendered inexpedient the retention of Alderman Butterthwaite on various committees. Of course, we don't rule out the eventual possibility of rehabilitation.
BOOCOCK. You . . . you can't just vote him out! There aren't sufficient present.
HOPEFAST. Provisionally we can do. The rest can be arranged.
MRS BOOCOCK. It will be arranged. I'm off to see to it now.

Barney, my dear, as usual, you have arrived a bit too tardy. (*She goes out.*)

HARDNUTT. This is a party issue, Barney. You can't stand independent. (*He goes out.*)

HICKLETON. None of us wanted it. None of us like it. (*He goes out.*)

HOPEFAST. Bear in mind, Barney, he *was* short of money. (*He goes out.*)

BOOCOCK (*stamping with frustration*). His Worship the Mayor. His Honour and His Worship. His Grace and His Majesty and His Worship the Mayor . . . Oh, oh, my leg . . .

He staggers and falls, knocking the screen over. BUTTER-THWAITE *is standing at the bar. He is much as in the police station, but wearing a ragged old muffler, and a woollen tam o'shanter over his bandage.*

BUTTERTHWAITE. Aye aye, me old Barney. I heard what was said.

BOOCOCK. Charlie! You're out of jail! They couldn't pin nowt on you! Thank God for that! I believe in you, Charlie. I'm going to combat this sordid betrayal. I will not permit . . .

BUTTERTHWAITE. You can't prevent. The wheel of years is now rotating. I'm voted out. This afternoon, I'm drinking.

BOOCOCK. *I'll* show you my loyalty.

BUTTERTHWAITE *laughs and* BOOCOCK *goes out.*

BUTTERTHWAITE. Who's drinking with me? Why, is there nobody?

A DRINKER. You gave us the appearance of wanting to be on your own.

BUTTERTHWAITE. Appearances are deceptive. Frank, here you are! You can serve us i' t'back. (*He throws a handful of money on the bar.*) I don't want to see anybody bahn off to their dinners until this is drunk up. But afore you make your choices, which gentlemen present take an interest in fine arts?

General giggles.

A DRINKER. If you mean dirty postcards . . .

BUTTERTHWAITE. Not precisely dirty postcards . . . This good brass I am expending here is the last of all my petty savings – the dregs of a lifetime of service to the community. Look, here's me Post Office book – 'Account Closed', do you see it? . . . Community? What's community? *You?* 'Oh no,' you said, 'not me,' you said – and rightly said, by Judas – 'leave it to the mugs,' you said, *'we're* lousy.' Well, Charlie's lousy too: and Charlie bears in mind that the first day of May is not only a day of Socialist congratulation but also a day of traditional debauchment in the base of a blossoming hedge-row . . . *I* pay for the drink, *you* sup it up, and in return you're going to do what I request – least-roads, I *hope* you are, for any lad as tries to finkle *me*, by gor, I'll finkle *him* till his eyes are looking out through the cleft of his armpit . . . Come on into t'back bar; I'm not calling you twice . . . (*He leads them all into the inner room.*)

SCENE FOUR

Inside the Copacabana Club . . . now an art gallery.

Artistic screens hung with paintings occupy the upper part of the stage. The front stage area is a sort of foyer laid out for a reception. One table covered with green baize holds catalogues, etc. Another table set out as a buffet with champagne and sandwiches. Paperchains from the roof. A white ribbon tied across the back of the foyer, as a formal barrier preventing access to the pictures.

GLORIA (*in a very demure dress*) *superintending buffet and catalogues,* LADY SWEETMAN *and* YOUNG SWEETMAN *hurrying about making last-minute alterations.*

Enter BLOMAX (*he is not noticed by the others on the stage*).

BLOMAX (*to the audience*).
And so we lead on, to the final cruel conclusion
Compounded of corruption and unresolved confusion.
I think the time has come to resolve it, if I can.
Here I stand alone, an embrangled English man
Nerving myself up in the torment of my duty.
The first day of May is the day of Art and Beauty,
The dust of Sweetman thrust into the eye-balls of you all
For to wash you white and whiter than the whitewash on the
   wall.
But out in the dark back lane
The great grey cat still waits by the mouse's hole.
You'll observe the general sense of bygones being bygones
. . . (*He points to* GLORIA.) Who'd recognize her now, stood
ready to draw out the corks for the nobility and gentry? Who
indeed would recognize the premises themselves, where the
only indication of what's under the underwear is on a canvas
by Titian . . . or at least William Etty? Titillation, if you
like, but in a form that even Lady Sweetman regards as
desirable.

   The room begins to fill.

   SWEETMAN *with wife and son.* FENG, WELLESLEY,
   CONSERVATIVE LADIES, F. J., BOOCOCK, COUNCIL-
   LORS *are present.*

   BOOCOCK *wears his chain, but no robes.*

SWEETMAN. Ha-h'm. The opening of a new art gallery is, or
   should be, a pleasurable labour, for the benefit of thousands.
   Therefore, I will not remind you that works of art – no less
   magnificent than those from my collection which already
   hang here – are lying at this moment in the cellars of the
   Municipal Hospital, unthought-of and unenjoyed . . . but
   not, may I hope, for ever? It gives me enormous pleasure to

detect one sign of reconciliation – His Worship the Mayor is with us today, and also many of his . . .

BOOCOCK. Not to be construed as an official occasion but purely as a social courtesy in recognition of cultural attainment.

MRS BOOCOCK. Sir Harold Sweetman, Lady Sweetman, ladies and gentlemen, we feel in the Labour Party that the provision of an art gallery, albeit a worthy objective, does not warrant the expenditure of public money upon what is, after all, a luxury amenity. So all the more do we of the Labour Party welcome the initiative of private enterprise upon this issue. I would like to say . . . 'thank you', Sir Harold. And thank you also, Lady Sweetman; you have done us all a proud and worthy service.

Applause.

SWEETMAN. Yes. Madam Mayoress, thank *you*. Now it only remains that I request my dear wife to formally inaugurate the Gallery.

LADY SWEETMAN. Let me tell you first about the dedication of this Gallery. It is called the 'Sweetman Memorial Gallery', not in memory of Sir Harold, who is still very much with us . . .

BLOMAX *picks up a glass of champagne.*

GLORIA. Hey . . .

BLOMAX. Morituro te salutant!

GLORIA. You get out of here at once!

BLOMAX. No. Dulce et decorum est pro filia pulcherrima incarceri in vinculis. Wellesley, let go of me; you'll undermine me resolution.

LADY SWEETMAN (*trying to ignore his interruption*). . . . but in memory of his father, the late Mr. Fortunatus Sweetman, whose enterprise and industry brought wealth and fortune to us all . . .

BLOMAX. I want to talk to Colonel Feng!

FENG (*to* SWEETMAN). Had you invited Mr Blomax here, sir?

SWEETMAN. Indeed I had not. Are you aware, Doctor, that this is a private function?

BLOMAX. Colonel Feng, observe my daughter. She requires a new father, and behold, here he is! I am washing myself in public with the detergent of self-sacrifice. Five hundred pounds. Take it, Mr Mayor. You know where it comes from.

(*He hands the money to* BOOCOCK.)

BOOCOCK. We all thought you'd been exonerated.

BLOMAX. No, no, I am confessing. And the extraordinary thing is, I had already confessed. I offered Queen's Evidence! Why was it refused?

SWEETMAN. Was it, Colonel? Why?

FENG. Queen's Evidence, albeit dramatic, is not necessarily sufficient. Or even true. You surely know that, sir.

LADY SWEETMAN (*in desperation*). So it gives me great pleasure to declare the 'Sweetman Memorial Art Gallery' open for all time to the people of this town.

She takes a little pair of scissors and cuts the tape.
Applause.

Now I hope you will all enjoy yourselves and don't go home till you've seen everything.

She and her husband contrive to move the guests up among the pictures. BLOMAX, BOOCOCK *and* FENG *remain in the foyer.* SWEETMAN *returns to them.*

BLOMAX. In any case, I can tell you, my Queen's Evidence was highly sufficient – and every word of it was true. I am very sorely afraid I have been deliberately victimized. So I am making my appeal to the high society of the town.

BOOCOCK. This is very very shocking indeed, Wellington. But, Colonel Feng, Dr Blomax has been my medical adviser for a great many years. I think it would show a more humane spirit if you accepted his plea. After all, he *has* returned the money.

SWEETMAN. Yes. Colonel, surely we don't need to press this matter now in regard to Dr Blomax? That is, if he *can* give us all the full details of everything that happened . . .

YOUNG SWEETMAN. That's the voice of two magistrates, Colonel. You can't entirely neglect it.

SWEETMAN. Speak when you're spoken to.

FENG. The decision is *mine*. It is nobody else's. This man is an accomplice, but the thief himself is still at large: and until he is apprehended you must permit me to handle it as best I know how.

WELLESLEY. And handle it inevitably so that my father goes to jail? And he going to jail will leave your conscience clear enough for you to marry me.

BLOMAX. Marry? Him? You? . . . But what about Maurice? I confessed because of *him!*

WELLESLEY. And Colonel Feng confessed. He confessed he was in love with me. So I naturally asked him to destroy his integrity and make it easier for you.

FENG. Naturally.

WELLESLEY. And equally naturally he has been unable to do it. I have often dreamed I would be the beautiful destruction of the strength of a good man. It has turned out to be more comfortable to deal only with feeble ones. What about you, Maurice, how are you for integrity?

YOUNG SWEETMAN. *Me?*

WELLESLEY. Don't worry, I will marry you: because I don't have to respect you and I don't have to continually involve myself in the curls and contortions of an extraordinary code of ethics. Have you even seen a boa-constrictor that strangled itself with itself? . . . Oh dear, I feel so miserable.

The GUESTS *have drifted away from the pictures and the last few speeches have been heard by everyone.*

SWEETMAN. Colonel Feng, is this true? I mean, *have* you proposed to her?

FENG. Yes, sir, it is true, as a matter of observable fact. I will not humiliate myself, Sir Harold, by explaining my motives. But I take it that as a gentleman you will not dispute my word when I inform you most solemnly that my professional integrity has in no whit been compromised by whatever mis-construction this young woman puts upon it, *deliberately* puts upon it. She has *not* destroyed me, no . . . She does not influence me, sir, in one way or the other; my private life is private . . . It appears I am confounded, sir, by endeavour-ing to preserve it so, but . . .

SWEETMAN. But in fact you're telling me that if it wasn't for this little half-dago doxy that bloody robber Butterthwaite would have been behind bars a week since!

F. J. Precisely what side do you imagine you're on!

FENG. Side, do you say, sir, side! I am not, sir, aware of it. I am aware that my *own* side, my private side, Sir Harold, may well indeed be for derision, humiliated and confounded, but, sir, I am not destroyed, sir . . . I am not yet aware of *side !*

BLOMAX. In that case, Colonel Feng, you're the only man present that isn't!

FENG. You! You are not to speak further. I cannot bear it further!

BLOMAX. *I've* had to bear more than *you've* had to bear! I've had to commit myself, and as a result without intention I have dropped my poor friend Charlie where I cannot believe he will ever get out of. I thought when I determined to return the five hundred we could call it a closed book . . . but I see that we can't. Alas, the British police, with their well-known impartiality and their zeal for adamantine truth and justice, are clearly going to triumph yet again. So I now have no choice but to deliver my second preparation – all typed out in quadruplicate. (*He produces some sheets of typescript.*) Oh, Gloria, I beg your pardon, for you this is catastrophe, I have stripped us all fair frozen, with not one obligation left honoured.

He distributes his papers.

Mr Mayor, here's your copy – Chief Constable, yours! Sir Harold, here's yours! The unexpurgated history, gentlemen, of the Copacabana Club that was and Superintendent Wiper that still is, with all his little relationships that even Charlie didn't find out. And by and large the entire question of the bracing and the strutting of your backbone, Colonel Feng!

SWEETMAN (*throwing his paper on the floor*). You will not of course, Colonel, attach any credence to . . .

BOOCOCK. Colonel Feng, you are holding that piece of paper upside down. Permit me to . . .

FENG *turns his back and walks away among the pictures.*
Enter WIPER *in a hurry.*

WIPER. Where's the Chief Constable? . . . Hello, what's going on?

BLOMAX *gives* WIPER *the fourth copy.*

BLOMAX. Mr Mayor, do *you* believe what I've written down on these?

BOOCOCK. I must say I am afraid it is only too plausible . . . Go on, read it, Superintendent. We would like to hear your comments!

WIPER. You jerked-up Jack-in-office, do you not realize what's happening! My comments can wait. I've got a job to do! Sir Harold, I must ask you to close down your gallery.

SWEETMAN. What . . . whatever for?

WIPER. A matter of public order. A quarter of an hour ago Alderman Butterthwaite removed himself from the Victoria and Albert with the entire mid-morning congregation of that celebrated resort, and at this present moment he is on his way out here . . . with half a hundred others, of the lowest type in town, layabouts, tearaways, every man of 'em half-seas over!

LADY SWEETMAN. But what does he want!

WIPER. I think he wants to wreck your gallery. We've only just found out, but it appears he's been working this up for over a week.

SWEETMAN. Why haven't you stopped him?

WIPER. In the middle of the town? How much open scandal do you really want to have? Up here we can contain them – I've given orders for a cordon, but . . .

SWEETMAN. Chief Constable!

F. J. Where is he?

FENG *comes back into the main stage.*

SWEETMAN. Chief Constable, come here. I am holding you responsible if there is violence or damage, entirely responsible!

FENG.
        Violence, damage . . . done already, done,
        All violence perpetrated, broken down
        In violence, brickwork cracked and fallen, damage,
        Responsibility . . . whose? Not long ago
        In this elected Council there was in violence
        Raised a violent demand I should resign.
        I did not notice it. I said that I
        Derived authority for my high office not
        From the jerk and whirl of irrelevant faction –
        You, sir, and you, your democratic Punch and Judy –
        But from the Law, being abstract, extant, placed,
        Proclaimed 'I am'! But, as you say, sir, now,
        Violence and damage, I *do* resign, sir, now.
        Good day to you, Superintendent. Law and Order?

Here is your confidence, your credence, *here*
Is your impartial service. *I* resign,
Continue, Mr Wiper . . . Preserve the peace.

*While he is speaking there is a growing clamour outside which
resolves itself into shouts of 'three times three for Charlie B',
etc. . . . and a ragged singing of 'Ilkley Moor'.*
Enter LUMBER *in a hurry, and several* PCs.

LUMBER. Colonel Feng, sir . . .
FENG (*waves him towards* WIPER). No, no, to *him* . . .

FENG *goes upstairs.*

LUMBER (*looking from one to the other*). Er . . . sir ?
WIPER. Well ?
LUMBER. It's not going too well; we were took by surprise
across the lunch hour; you see, they've all piled on the buses
. . . I'm afraid they'll be in here before I can get a full
cordon. I've three radio cars up already, but one of the lorries
has developed magneto trouble . . . I've ordered out the
mounted squad . . . what about the dogs ?

The noise grows.

They're forcing the cordon now! It's sheer weight of numbers! I've got all the PCs lined up on the steps but . . .
WIPER. Get these men to the doors! You, you, you, you –
there, there, there, there!

The PCs *rush off, at his direction, down the aisles to hold the
auditorium doors, which are being forced. Sounds of struggle
from the foyers. Some demonstrators break in. They are
carrying bottles, and placards with such slogans as 'All fine
art is a hearty fart', 'Paint me, paint my dog', 'You can't gild
a mucky lily', 'If the people scrawl, put glazed tiles on the
wall', and so on. Some placards have drawings on them of
women's bodies, etc.*

The PCs *pursue them and succeed, after fighting in the aisles
or on the stage, in chasing or dragging them out. The doors are
finally held, but only by the utmost efforts of the police.
During the commotion* BUTTERTHWAITE *has come in at the
rear of the stage. He sweeps some plates off the buffet and sits
on the table cross-legged. He helps himself to champagne and
a hunk of iced cake.*

BUTTERTHWAITE. If you've got in mind to rax me off this
table, you can have another think. There's more uses nor one
to a bottle o' bubbly, and I'm proficient in 'em all.

He sings.

As it fell out upon a day, rich Dives he made a feast,
And he invited all his friends and gentry of the best,
But Lazarus he sat down and down and down at Dives' door,
Some meat, some drink, brother Dives, he said, bestow unto
    the poor!

FENG. Now, Mr Wiper, what's your next move?
WIPER. *I'm* handling this.
FENG. I know. I am highly entertained, sir.
WIPER. Sergeant . . .

LUMBER *makes a move towards* BUTTERTHWAITE, *who
poises his bottle menacingly. A little* DEMONSTRATOR
breaks through one of the doors, slips past the PCs *trying to
prevent him, and scuttles on to the stage as though for sanctuary. He squats down at* BUTTERTHWAITE'S *feet, and the*
PC *pursuing him gives up indecisively.*
FENG *turns his back and affects interest in the pictures.*

BUTTERTHWAITE. Now then, Brother Boocock, are you holding up all right, are you? With all them prime Sheffield
knifeblades I've inserted in your shoulder bones.
BOOCOCK. I am still in great part vertical. Which is more than
can be said for you, Charlie. I don't know why you've done

this, but your last remaining friends can do nowt for you now. You have pulled your own self down.

BUTTERTHWAITE. Aye. But there's others aside from me have had their hands on t'ropes, though . . . haven't they, me old Wellington?

BLOMAX. Charlie, I've been pulling on all the ropes round here. Not only on yours.

BUTTERTHWAITE. Go on? Who else is done for?

BLOMAX *makes a gesture towards* FENG.

Oh no, not Colonel Feng! You've not got rid of Feng! Not *you* . . . Oh God, *you!* The subsidence of water . . . After all my subtle skirmishes, my cannonadings, my outflankings . . .

BLOMAX. You yourself were outflanked, Charlie. Although you didn't know it, at the crux of the campaign I was fighting for the Prussians. This unhappy Chief Constable was never at war at all.

BUTTERTHWAITE. Oh, but he was, though . . . he was in treaty with Sweetman.

BLOMAX. You've always enjoyed my little bits o' patter, Charlie. But you should never ha' believed 'em.

BUTTERTHWAITE. So that's how it was . . . the beloved physician . . . Colonel, I say Colonel, I'm talking to *you!* I give you no apology. You're a strong-backboned man and you chose of your own free will to do our dirty work. And if it's turned out a sight dirtier than might have been foretold, I am sure that you will find yourself an occupational philosophy, and remain like Barney Boocock in great part still vertical. Oh, oh, oh, I have lived. I have controlled, I have redistributed. The Commonwealth has gained. The tables have been spread. Not with bread and marge, you know, like they used to in the workhouse, but with a summation of largesse demanding for its attendance soup-spoons in their rank, fish-knives and forks, flesh-knives and forks, spoons

for the pudding, gravy and cruet, caper sauce and mayon-
naise . . . and I by my virtue stood the President of the
feast! . . . All right, you've got the belly-ache, and so I've
got to go. But I don't take it kindly. Philosophy be damned.
There's a foul wind blows over t'moor-top on this cold Mayday morning. The peoples of the world are marching and
rejoicing alongside the saluting-bases, but here I've called to
action a detachment of forces that have never heard a bugle!
My army today is a terrible shambles. Look at 'em, fellow
Councillors; you ruled 'em, *I* ruled 'em, and we never knew
who they were! I'll tell you who they were; they drank and
slept and skived and never punched a bloody clock when
clocks was for the asking. We piped to them and they did not
dance, we sang them our songs and they spat into t'gutter.
(*He pats the little* DEMONSTRATOR's *head.*) I was the grand
commander of the whole of my universe. Now all that's left
me is the generalship of these. I need to assume a different
order o' raiment. (*He pulls the baize tablecloth to him and
arranges it like a shawl.*) Three times three, but all that's left
is paper.

He pulls down a paper chain and hangs it round his neck.

Three times three is nine, but the old cocked hat's bashed in.
So here's a replacement.

*He picks up a ring of flowers that has been garnishing the
buffet and puts it on his head.*

. . . In my rejection I have spoken to this people. I will
rejoice despite them. I will divide Dewsbury and mete out
the valley of Bradford; Pudsey is mine, Huddersfield is mine,
Rotherham also is the strength of my head, Osset is my law-
giver, Black Barnsley is my washpot, over Wakefield will I
cast out my shoe, over Halifax will I triumph. Who will bring
me into the strong city, who will lead me into the boundaries

of Leeds? Wilt not thou, oh my deceitful people, who hast
cast me off? And wilt not thou go forth with Charlie?

LITTLE DEMONSTRATOR. Hey ey, we're going, we're all
going forth together!

BUTTERTHWAITE. No. Oh no. Oh no, you aren't. The only
place you're going is into t'black maria.

Police car noises from offstage and voices giving orders.

LUMBER (*to* WIPER). Sir, it's the reinforcements . . .

WIPER. Right, Mr Butterthwaite, we'd like a word with you
outside.

The PCs *drag out the* DEMONSTRATOR, *and then come for*
BUTTERTHWAITE, *who lets himself go limp. As* BUTTER-
THWAITE *is removed up the aisle, he sings:*

BUTTERTHWAITE.
> Out he goes the poor old donkey
> Out he goes in rain and snow,
> For to make the house-place whiter
> Who will be the next to go?

> Clean the kitchen and the parlour,
> Scrub the wall and scrub the floor,
> Clean the hoofmarks off the lino
> And the smears from off the door.

> Climb a ladder and wipe the windows,
> Swill the roof with water clear,
> Pour your soap suds down the chimney
> Till none can tell what beast was here.

> When all is washed and all is scoured
> And all is garnished bright as paint,
> Who will come with his six companions
> And a stink to make you faint?

*The song is taken up by those outside the theatre, and con-
cludes (if time allows) with a fortissimo reprise of the first
stanza.*

SWEETMAN. Thank you, Superintendent. Most commendably
accomplished, sir.

BOOCOCK. There is still a very great deal to be gone into and
sorted out. Nothing of what has happened redounds to anyone's credit. So who's going to make a start and establish a
fair inquiry?

BLOMAX. Oh it's not so bad as all that. The start has already
been made. Our accumulated garbage has all been carted out
and there's nothing more to do now but to polish the sides of
the dustbin a bit and keep away the horse-flies. The Conservative Party, on balance, will find the whole business . . .

SWEETMAN. The whole business should, on balance, weigh
slightly to our advantage.

F. J. I think it should.

SWEETMAN. Yes.

BLOMAX. While the Labour Party, on the other hand . . .

HARDNUTT AND HICKLETON. We prefer to defer comment
upon this unsavoury episode.

HOPEFAST AND MRS BOOCOCK. But we wish nevertheless to
publicly dissociate ourselves from it.

ALL THE COUNCILLORS AND MRS BOOCOCK. We lay the
matter with confidence before the good sense of the electorate.

BLOMAX. The Superintendent will resign . . .

WIPER. Of my own free will, please note, no questions asked,
and I get a pension.

BLOMAX. My darling daughter Wellesley will marry her
fiancé . . . Go on, go on, give him a kiss.

WELLESLEY *does so.*

And in consideration of my future tact and silence on all

public occasions, I, her useless father, shall be liberally accepted into the bosom of his family. (*He shakes* SWEETMAN *by the hand.*) How d'you do, sir ?

SWEETMAN. How d'you do ?

BLOMAX. Lady Sweetman . . . ?

LADY SWEETMAN. My dear Doctor . . .

BLOMAX. May I present my dear wife ?

LADY SWEETMAN. I would be delighted, Doctor. My dear Mrs Blomax . . .

BLOMAX. It's really so much tidier and altogether less awkward. I have made arrangements for a private maternity ward in Leeds . . .

WIPER. To be, of course, defrayed from the aforementioned pension.

BLOMAX. Wellesley, my darling, why don't you kiss him again ? No one's going to interfere.

She does so.

ALL AS CHORUS (*except* FENG).

No one's going to *dare* to interfere.

FENG. I am very sorry, Miss Blomax, to have exposed you to the imperfections of your person at so unseasonable a time. I trust that it will not be long before you regain your equilibrium. Gentlemen, I am going to London. I shall inform the Home Secretary how much I have appreciated the efficiency and speed with which the Superintendent dealt with this . . . Gangway, if you please, I'm coming through . . . (*He leaves.*)

ALL.

We stand all alone to the north of the Trent
You leave us alone and we'll leave you alone
We take no offence where none has been meant
But you hit us with your fist, we'll bash *you* with a stone!
Withdraw those quivering nostrils

We smell as we think decent
If we tell you we've cleaned our armpits
You'd best believe we've cleaned 'em recent.
We have washed them white and whiter
Than the whitewash on the wall
And if for THE WORKHOUSE DONKEY
We should let one tear down fall
Don't think by that he's coming back . . .
The old sod's   gone for good and all!

THE END

ALTERNATIVE SPEECHES FOR PROLOGUE AND EPILOGUE

(1) BLOMAX' *opening speech* (*Act One*):

Ladies and gentlemen, I am a native
Of the Greater London conurbation.
I found at first your northern parts not very conducive
To what was perhaps my more courtly mode of deportment:
But having arrived here I soon made the adjustment,
Involving geographically an appreciable mutation,
(I mean, in landscape, climate, odours, voices, food).
I put it to you that such a journey needs
In the realm of morality an equal alteration.
I mean, is there anything you really believe to be bad?
If you lived in the south you might well think it good.
You might well think, as I do,
That you should change the shape of your faces,
Or even double their number
When you travel between two places.
The values of other people
Are not quite as you understand them.
I would not overpraise them,
I would not recommend them,
I am certainly not here in order to condemn them.
From the beginning to the end
Each man is bound to act
According to his nature
And the nature of his land.
Your land is different from theirs.
Why, (county by county*) it has its own music.

      *   *   *

(2) *Concluding* CHORUS (*Act Three*):

We stand all alone to the north of the Trent
Let them leave us alone and we'll leave them alone
We take no offence where none has been meant
But they hit us with their fist, we'll bash 'em back with a stone!
They can pull up their damn nostrils,
We smell as we think decent.
If we tell them we've cleaned our armpits
They'd best believe we've cleaned them recent.
We have washed them white and whiter
Than the whitewash on the wall
And if for the WORKHOUSE DONKEY
We should let one tear down fall . . .
Don't think by that he's coming back:
The old sod's gone for good and all!

     ★   ★   ★

★ Words in parenthesis to be omitted in the West Riding of Yorkshire.

Armstrong's Last Goodnight

An Exercise in Diplomacy

TO CONOR CRUISE O'BRIEN

who (to quote John Skelton) wrote

' . . . of Sovereignty a noble pamphelet;
And of Magnificence a notable matter,
How Counterfeit Countenance of the new jet
With Crafty Conveyance doth smatter and
    flatter,
And Cloaked Collusion is brought in to clatter
With Courtly Abusion; who printeth it well in
    mind
Much doubleness of the worlde therein he may
    find.'

And not only did he write it but he was also not
ashamed to act upon his observations.

Introductory Notes

This play is founded upon history: but it is not to be read as an accurate chronicle. The biggest liberty I have taken with the known historical facts is in connecting Sir David Lindsay with the events leading up to the execution of Johnny Armstrong in 1530. But these events must have involved considerable political and diplomatic manœuvring, and it is known that Lindsay was not only the author of *The Three Estates* and Lord Lyon King of Arms but also regularly employed upon diplomatic missions for the Scottish Crown. His own views upon the Armstrong business may be partly deduced from the lines in *The Three Estates*, where he makes his crooked Pardoner offer for sale as a blessed relic –

> . . . ane cord, baith gret and lang,
> *Quhilk hangit Johne the Armistrang*
> *Of gude hemp, soft and sound;*
> *Gude, halie pepill I stand for'd*
> *Quha ever beis hangit with this cord*
> *Neidis never to be dround.*

Also, in *Complaint of the Common-weal of Scotland* he says, of the state of the Border counties:

> *In to the South, allace! I was neir slane;*
> *Ouer all the land I culd fynd no relief:*
> *Almost betuix the Mers and Lowmabane*
> *I culd nocht knaw ane leill man be ane theif.*
> *To schaw thair reif, thift, murthour, and mischief,*
> *And vicious workis, it wald infect the air:*
> *And as langsum to me, for tyll declair.*

From which we may guess that (a) he was able some years later to regard the celebrated hanging with sardonic and perhaps complacent detachment, and that (b) he by no means approved of the violent activities of the Border freebooters, who have in succeeding centuries found their own romantic advocates.

It is only fair to state, however, that there is – as far as I can discover – no evidence at all that Lindsay had anything whatever to do with James the Fifth's punitive expedition of 1530.

I have also made rather free with the date of the Reformation. English heresy was not likely to have been worrying the Church in Scotland at this date, and I doubt if any forerunners of John Knox were wandering the Ettrick Forest. But Lindsay himself took what might perhaps be called a non-Fundamentalist view upon religious questions: and certain modern parallels prompted me to introduce these views into the play and to present a more extreme philosophy in the person of the Evangelist.

I have no idea whether or not Lindsay had a mistress.

In writing this play I have been somewhat influenced by Conor Cruise O'Brien's book *To Katanga and Back:* but I would not have it thought that I have in any way composed a 'Roman à clef'. The characters and episodes in the play are not based upon originals from the Congo conflict; all I have done is to suggest here and there a basic similarity of moral, rather than political, economic or racial problems.

The language of the play offered certain difficulties. It would clearly be silly to reconstruct the exact Scots speech of the period – as quoted in the two passages from Lindsay's work given above. But on the other hand, Scots was at this time a quite distinct dialect, if not a different language, and to write the play in 'English' would be to lose the flavour of the age. The Scots employed by modern poets such as MacDiarmid and Goodsir Smith owes a great deal to Lindsay, Dunbar, Henryson and the other writers of the late Middle Ages and early Renaissance: but it is also a language for the expression of twentieth-century concepts. In the end I have put together a sort of Babylonish dialect that will, I hope, prove practical on the stage and will yet suggest the sixteenth century. My model in this was Arthur Miller's adaptation of early American speech in *The Crucible*.

Note on Sets and Costumes

The play is intended to be played within the medieval convention of 'simultaneous mansions'. These are three in number and represent the Castle (for the Armstrongs), the Palace (for the Court) and the Forest (for the wild land of the Borders). The Castle and the Palace are practicable buildings, one on either side of the stage, each with a roof from which actors may speak. They need not be more than porches or tabernacles: but their style should be definite and suggestive. The Castle is a rough stone building, with battlements and a defended gate or doorway: the Palace is a more elaborate structure in the

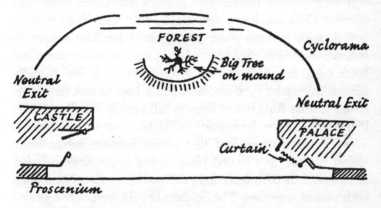

SKETCH PLAN OF SUGGESTED STAGE ARRANGEMENT

The Forest may be painted all round the Cyclorama: or else only in the centre, and the sides of the stage surround painted a neutral colour. Wherever in the course of the play a character enters or leaves the stage without it being specified that he does so via one of the three 'mansions', the Neutral Exits shewn on the sketch are intended to be employed. If there is room, space may be left between the Castle and the Palace, and the inner side of the Proscenium Arch, and this space used for entrances and exits via these two 'mansions' when several characters are involved and there is risk of overcrowding the doors of the 'buildings'. As the 'simultaneous' staging is a medieval device, and extremely formal in its conception, a formality of style should be adopted in the painting and design of the 'mansions'. If they are too naturalistic, the production will appear incongruous and peculiar.

fanciful Scots manner of Linlithgow Palace or Roslyn Chapel, painted and gilded, and topped with pretty finials. The entry is closed with a curtain, which should be painted to resemble tapestry. The Forest, which occupies the central upstage area, is basically a clump of trees. These should be dense enough to afford at least two concealed entrances for the actors: and one large tree (which should be practicable) stands in front, to the centre, and can be raised on a small mound.

The costumes should be 'working dress' – that is to say, each of the characters should be immediately recognizable as a member of his respective social class, rather than as a picturesque element in a colourful historical pageant. The borderers will wear mostly leather and hodden grey: the Politicians (Clerks, Commissioners, Secretaries, etc.) will be in subfusc gowns, with perhaps some use of small heraldic badges to indicate their local alignments. Lindsay wears a non-committal black suit, and adds to this at different times his herald's tabard, his scarlet robe of office, and a leather coat like Armstrong's. The King is first seen in full regalia like an old MS. illumination. Later he appears in Highland dress for hunting. This Highland dress (and that of the Soldiers in the same scene) belongs to a period prior to the introduction of clan tartans, and its basis is the long saffron shirt – sometimes worn with a short waistcoat. The Soldiers should have bare legs and bare heads, and are armed with claymores and targets: the King could be more 'civilized' and wear hose, embroidery upon his waistcoat, and a plain bonnet. When Gilnockie dresses up in the last act he puts on an assortment of clothes obtained in raids, and they do not necessarily agree very well with each other. But his general appearance must be extremely gaudy and peacock-like. The Evangelist should wear a very plain suit of cheap material, becoming threadbare. The Cardinal's Secretary has the Dominican habit of black and white.

The bagpipes are, of course, lowland pipes, which were not a specifically Scots instrument at this time, but played fairly generally throughout Western Europe – c.f. the paintings of Dürer and Breughel.

Notes on the Characters

THE KING   He is only seventeen, and small. He appears young for his age, and when dressed in his regalia looks like a sacred doll.

LINDSAY   In his late forties, but quick and athletic in his movements, and sprightly in his speech.

MCGLASS   Young, ardent, and handsome.

THE LADY   Aged about thirty-five: strong, sensual, and humorous.

THE MAID   Like her mistress, but slighter in body and fifteen years younger.

GILNOCKIE   A great bull, or lion, of a man: he has difficulty in talking coherently, a congenital defect like an exaggerated stammer that he is only able to overcome when extremely excited or when he sings. Full of a certain innocence of spirit. Aged about forty.

GILNOCKIE'S WIFE   A nervous, chaste lady, in great fear both of and for her husband.

THE ARMSTRONGS   Tough loyal clansmen, devoted to their Laird. The GIRLS are their younger relatives and do the work in the house and fields. (Gentry, not peasants.)

STOBS   A bitter, hard, rigid, cruel man.

YOUNG STOBS   As harsh as his father, but more impulsive.

MEG   Throughout the play she is shocked with grief; but before the death of her lover she has been warm, gentle, and quiet.

WAMPHRAY A foolish handsome man, middle-aged, tough and rude-mannered.

THE EVANGELIST Aged about thirty, prematurely grey hair: a converted sensualist, his rigidity derives as much from inward doubt as from strength of character.

THE COMMISSIONERS Experienced political gentlemen, whose emotional public remarks bear little relation to their real feelings.

THE CLERKS They appear to be both older and wiser than their Commissioners: but, in fact, the two types are designed to work together as a team.

THE SECRETARIES These men are really responsible for the political decisions and policies of their masters, and know it.

THE PORTER A pompous mouthpiece, and that is all we know of him.

THE HIGHLAND CAPTAIN Speaks with the unexpected politeness and gentleness of the Gaelic soldier. He and his men look, and no doubt fight, like wild animals.

Notes on the Casting

There are thirty parts in this play, but it may be played by a company of sixteen, if seven of the actors take more than one part, as follows:

I FIRST SCOTS COMMISSIONER
  SECOND ARMSTRONG
  CARDINAL'S SECRETARY
II FIRST HIGHLAND SOLDIER
  SECOND SCOTS COMMISSIONER
  STOBS
  LORD JOHNSTONE'S SECRETARY

III FIRST ENGLISH COMMISSIONER
     FIRST ARMSTRONG
IV   SECOND ENGLISH COMMISSIONER
     THIRD ARMSTRONG
     LORD MAXWELL'S SECRETARY
V   SCOTS CLERK
     YOUNG STOBS
     PORTER
     HIGHLAND CAPTAIN
VI   ENGLISH CLERK
     KING
VII WAMPHRAY
     EVANGELIST
     SECOND HIGHLAND SOLDIER

The remaining roles (including all the female parts) cannot conveniently be doubled. At a pinch, the GIRLS could be omitted entirely. The parts of the KING and the THIRD ARMSTRONG perhaps present problems if the respective actors have other parts to play: because it may be thought that the KING should, in order to produce a better effect in the last act, be as it were isolated: and I have suggested that the THIRD ARMSTRONG should be the Piper: in which case he may be a specialist and not necessarily a versatile actor. But this is a matter for local circumstances and taste to determine.

PS. Also at a pinch, but may I hope only a very sharp one, two of the COMMISSIONERS may also be omitted – one from each country.

Note on Production

For the production of this play by the National Theatre at the Old Vic (1965) it was found useful to begin Act One with Scenes Three and Four, followed by Scenes One, Two and

Five. This was done in order to make an English audience familiar with the language before the more complex exposition of the plot had to be embarked upon. (Wamphray's death is an episode which more or less explains itself in visual terms, whereas the conference scene has to be *verbally* understood or it makes no sense.) I think this readjustment of scenes justified itself, and producers who wish to use it may do so: but from the point of view of the overall shape of the play, I prefer my original arrangement, which is accordingly printed here.

John Arden

Armstrong's Last Goodnight was first performed at the Glasgow Citizens' Theatre on 5 May 1964, with the following cast:

JAMES THE FIFTH OF SCOTLAND	Hamish Wilson
SIR DAVID LINDSAY OF THE MOUNT	Leonard Maguire
ALEXANDER MCGLASS, his Secretary	John Cairney
A LADY, Lindsay's Mistress	Lisa Daniely
HER MAID	Hannah Gordon
FIRST SCOTS COMMISSIONER	Phil McCall
SECOND SCOTS COMMISSIONER	Ian McNaughton
FIRST ENGLISH COMMISSIONER	Brian Ellis
SECOND ENGLISH COMMISSIONER	Glen Williams
CLERK TO THE SCOTS COMMISSIONERS	Alec Monteath
CLERK TO THE ENGLISH COMMISSIONERS	
	Stephen MacDonald
THE POLITICAL SECRETARY TO LORD JOHNSTONE	
	Phil McCall
THE POLITICAL SECRETARY TO LORD MAXWELL	
	Brown Derby
THE POLITICAL SECRETARY TO THE CARDINAL OF ST ANDREWS	Glenn Williams
PORTER TO THE ROYAL HOUSEHOLD	Alec Monteath
CAPTAIN OF THE HIGHLAND INFANTRY	
	Stephen MacDonald
SOLDIERS	Bill Henderson
	Peter Gordon Smith
	Brian Ellis
	James McCreadie, Jnr.
	David Gloag
	Ian Sharp
	Thomas McNamara
JOHN ARMSTRONG OF GILNOCKIE	Iain Cuthbertson
HIS WIFE	Janet Michael
WILLIE ARMSTRONG	William McAllister
TAM ARMSTRONG	Alex McCrindle
ARCHIE ARMSTRONG	Alistair Colledge
FIRST GIRL OF GILNOCKIE'S HOUSEHOLD	Bonita Beach

SECOND GIRL OF GILNOCKIE'S HOUSEHOLD	
	Aileen Salmon
THIRD GIRL OF GILNOCKIE'S HOUSEHOLD	
	Wieslawa Kwasniewska
PIPER	Jimmy Wilson
GILBERT ELIOT OF STOBS	Harry Walker
MARTIN ELIOT, his son	Bill Henderson
MEG ELIOT, Stobs's Daughter	Anne Kristen
JAMES JOHNSTONE OF WAMPHRAY	Brown Derby
A PROTESTANT EVANGELIST	Ian McNaughton

Directed by Denis Carey
Designed by Juanita Waterson

The action of the play takes place in Scotland, early in the
second quarter of the sixteenth century.

Act One

SCENE ONE

[LINDSAY, ENGLISH *and* SCOTS COMMISSIONERS, *their* CLERKS.]

A trestle table in the middle of the stage, arranged with papers and ink etc., and stools placed for a conference.
LINDSAY (*in his herald's tabard*) *enters.*

LINDSAY. There was held, at Berwick-upon-Tweed, in the fifteenth year of the reign of James the Fift, by the Grace of God King of Scotland, and in the nineteenth year of Henry the Eight, by the Grace of God King of England, ane grave conference and consultation betwixt Lords Commissioner frae baith the realms, anent the lang peril of warfare that trublit they twa sovereigns and the leige peoples thereunto appertainen. The intent bean, to conclude this said peril and to secure ane certain time of peace, prosperity, and bliss on ilk side of the Border. I am Lord Lyon King of Arms, Chief Herald of the Kingdom of Scotland. It is my function in this place to attend upon the deliberations of the Scots Commissioners and to fulfil their sage purposes with obedience and dispatch. As ye will observe: when peace is under consideration, there is but little equability of discourse. The conference this day bean in the third week of its proceeden.

LINDSAY retires into the Palace, and immediately appears upon the roof, from which he watches the rest of the scene.
The two SCOTS COMMISSIONERS *enter from the Palace* (LINDSAY *stands aside and bows to let them pass*) *and take their seats. With them is their* CLERK.
There is a pause.

Then the ENGLISH CLERK *comes in, bows to the* SCOTS, *and takes his seat. He is followed by the* FIRST ENGLISH COMMISSIONER, *who bows and takes his seat.*
Another pause.
Enter SECOND ENGLISH COMMISSIONER; *he bows, sits, and then stands.*

SECOND ENGLISH COMMISSIONER. My lords: many weighty questions have been brought these weeks beneath discussion, and I think I may say that at least a partial agreement has been arrived at. The line of succession to the Scottish royal house; excise due upon merchandise imported or exported; claims arising from damages inflicted during previous hostilities – all these are satisfactorily settled.

FIRST ENGLISH COMMISSIONER. Heresy—

SECOND ENGLISH COMMISSIONER. Yes. The prevention and deterrence of subversive transportation of professors of alleged heresy between the realms. In the present disturbed state of Christendom, clearly we must—

FIRST SCOTS COMMISSIONER. The religious intentions of King Henry are as yet some whit ambiguous. Can he offer ane precise definition of what he means by heresy? The Court of Consistory at Sanct Andrews will desire—

FIRST ENGLISH COMMISSIONER. We have an annotation in the margin to that effect, sir. In God's Name let us not confound our business in the quagmires of theological dialectic.

SECOND SCOTS COMMISSIONER. We'll be here while neist year's harvest else. Gang forwarts, gif ye please, sir.

SECOND ENGLISH COMMISSIONER. Very well, we now come to a crucial and exceedingly delicate matter, which both parties have, I believe, agreed to leave until the last. I mean, the Security of the Borders. Or rather, their present in-security. Indeed, lords, their present state of bleeding anarchy and murderous rapine – to use no stronger words. I do not wish to revive bitter memories of past destruction. But I must remind you, lords, that the very accession to the throne of His Grace King James was consequent upon—

SECOND SCOTS COMMISSIONER. It was consequent upon the death of his father at the Field of Flodden, sir: and we're all very weel acquent with it.

SECOND ENGLISH COMMISSIONER. And how terrible was that battle. It appears to me that Scotland is not yet recovered from it. And no man here can desire its repetition.

SECOND SCOTS COMMISSIONER. Were it repeatit, it could weel find ane different conclusion. Scotland was ane dis-unitit kingdom that unlucky tide.

FIRST SCOTS COMMISSIONER. I think we have little need of historical recapitulation here. Sir, I will anticipate your argument. Ye are about to denounce the raiden and ridens of our bold Scots borderers, are ye nocht? Ye hae lost upon the English side ower mony cattle, horses, sheep, pigs, roof-trees, byres, kirk-ornaments, tableware, personal jewellery, and the maidenheids of women. Very good. We will acknowledge these circumstances as regrettable. But you are here for peace – ye have tellt us so yourself.

SECOND ENGLISH COMMISSIONER. It is imperative for peace that there be no more masterless raids from Scotland into England in search of booty. Or if there be, the offenders must be punished, at the hand of Scotland's Grace, and he be seen to punish them. This has not happened, has it? There is more than a suspicion that outrages of recent years have been openly encouraged, indeed in origin set on, by great men in your kingdom—

SECOND SCOTS COMMISSIONER. Sir—

SECOND ENGLISH COMMISSIONER. And great men, sir, who stand too close to Scotland's throne.

SECOND SCOTS COMMISSIONER. I want to hear their names!

SECOND ENGLISH COMMISSIONER. It were better not, I think.

SECOND SCOTS COMMISSIONER. Aha, why nocht?

SECOND ENGLISH COMMISSIONER. I do not care to rub it deeper, sir, but—

SECOND SCOTS COMMISSIONER. There's been nae riden without good reason. For every heid of cattle the Scots hae grippit, your English carls took twelve. I have a paper here—

SECOND ENGLISH COMMISSIONER. We too are furnished, sir, with papers—

FIRST ENGLISH COMMISSIONER. Permit me for one moment.

He reads from a paper:

December the 21st, last; John Armstrong of Gilnockie and his brother Armstrong of Mangerton harried twenty miles within the English ground and burned and killed their way from Bewcastle to Haltwhistle.

January the 15th: the men of Liddesdale and Eskdale rode further yet, to Hexham, and there obtained by force five score horned beasts and drove them home under moonlight, led on this occasion by John Armstrong of Gilnockie and Gilbert Eliot of Stobs. The same John Armstrong and another Eliot – I think a Martin Eliot—

FIRST SCOTS COMMISSIONER. Aye, he's the son of Gilbert – ye seem to be correct thus far.

FIRST ENGLISH COMMISSIONER. I thank you. Martin Eliot. They set their ambush on the road between Carlisle and Brampton and held to ransom no less a traveller than the Lord Abbot of Monkwearmouth and two brethren of his cloister, threatening these holy men with abominable indignities if payment were delayed.

SECOND SCOTS COMMISSIONER. And was it?

FIRST ENGLISH COMMISSIONER. Foolishly, perhaps, it was not. Two months after that the same Armstrong of Gilnockie in confederation with – with a man called James Johnstone of Wamphray—

FIRST SCOTS COMMISSIONER. Na na, ye are in error there,

sirs: Wamphray and Gilnockie are at feud. Confederation betwixt 'em's inconceivable. Look for ane other name.

SECOND ENGLISH COMMISSIONER. The name may well be mistaken. The offence took place. Has there been offered compensation? Indeed no, there has not. Why not? I reiterate: there are great men who wink at this, and England's Grace has said it is intolerable.

FIRST ENGLISH COMMISSIONER. His very word. Be warned by it. He is an angry King.

SECOND SCOTS COMMISSIONER. God: what ane turbulence of lyen janglers is this same warld we dwell in! Ye have held this business till the end, lords, gullen us and lullen us three weeks ane front of peace, of friendship, amiable words, nae threats, nae rage, nae conflict. And now it comes! I have speirt of myself ilk day, is England turnen Christian at last? Ha, ha, we have our answer! Forbye, it craves ane starker man than you are to put this Commission in dreid. We tell you, lords – in maist severe and potent voice: nae Scottish borderer receives his chastisement until sic time as we observe ane good reciprocation. Ye nourish your ain limmer thieves in Redesdale and in Tynedale – see them hangit first, and then we'll deal with ours! There is nae mair to say. Ye are deliberately provocative, and ye intend to break this Council!

FIRST ENGLISH COMMISSIONER. Indeed sir, we do not.

SECOND SCOTS COMMISSIONER. Intend it or no, then it has had that effect. Negotiation is concludit. Be reason of your intransigence. You can tell that to England's Grace, when ye gang back barren to Windsor or to Westminster. Be sure we'll tell it plain eneuch in the Palace of Halyrood.

SECOND SCOTS COMMISSIONER *goes out, into the Palace.*

SECOND ENGLISH COMMISSIONER. I warn you, this is most unwise.

FIRST ENGLISH COMMISSIONER. England's Grace has set his heart upon this treaty. Should he find himself balked therein, we cannot answer for the consequence.

FIRST SCOTS COMMISSIONER. Aye, ye won Flodden. But ye didna win the kingdom. Nor will ye win it, by ane second cast, nor third, nor fourth, against it. We are forwarnit of your malice, lords, and we ken but owerweel whaur the blame of further war will lodge.

> FIRST SCOTS COMMISSIONER *goes out into Palace.*
> The ENGLISH COMMISSIONERS *go out.*
> LINDSAY *retires from the roof of the Palace.*

SCENE TWO

[LINDSAY, ENGLISH *and* SCOTS CLERKS.]

The CLERKS *are left behind, assembling their papers and clearing away the tables and stools.*

SCOTS CLERK. Permit me, sir, ane short and private word with you.

ENGLISH CLERK. With pleasure, sir.

SCOTS CLERK. We have heard, sir, the necessair defiances deliverit in public and publicly receivit. Now sir, for the inwart verity of the business, the whilk is writ upon nae record, but I trust will rin to England's ear directly. Are ye with me, sir?

ENGLISH CLERK. I am.

SCOTS CLERK. The matter of the unruly borderers is in nae guise easy to conclude. Their depredations in truth are as muckle towards Scotland as they are towart England, and the Liddesdale and Eskdale men are sae weel entrenchit in their hills, in their strang towers of defence, that they are nocht to be howkit therefrom without grave danger to the

State and expense upon the Treasury. There are, indeed, as has been said, great men in Court at Halyrood that will assume the borderers' part against all injury, and yet upon their power King James is forcit to lean, whatever be his ain opinion of their lealty. He is ane young, but prudent King, and kens his peril. Therefore, the binden and controllen of these Armstrangs, Eliots, Maxwells, and the lave, maun find itself by sure and slow advancement; and gif God will, through policy, nocht force. Are ye with me?

ENGLISH CLERK. Can it be done? And if it can, how long will it take? King Henry is impatient.

SCOTS CLERK. King Henry maun contain his patience Christ-like, sir, and virtuous, as is his wont. But the matter is in hand. The maist ferocious of these thieves, and – I will admit to ye – the hardest to suppress, is John Armstrang of Gilnockie. King James has in his grace and wisdom ordainit ane confidential emmissair to treat furthwith with Armstrang, seek some fair means of agreement, and in the end secure baith the lealty and obedience of this dangerous free-booter.

ENGLISH CLERK. Do you think that it is possible?

SCOTS CLERK. Here is the emmissair.

LINDSAY *enters from the Palace.*

Sir David Lindsay of the Mount. If he canna dae it, there is nae man that can. Sir David, d'ye see, is ane very subtle practiser, he has been tutor to the King, is now his herald, ane very pleasurable contriver, too, of farces, ballads, allegories, and the like delights of poetry. He has wit, ye ken, music, ane man of rhetoric and discreet humanity. Do I flatter ye, Sir David, or are ye indeed serpent eneuch to entwine the Armstrangs in your coil?

LINDSAY (*to* ENGLISH CLERK). Come here, sir, here . . . Whilk man of us twae is the better dressit, d'ye think?

ENGLISH CLERK. Dressed?

LINDSAY. Aye, dressit.

ENGLISH CLERK. I scarcely understand you, sir. But if you intend a sense of correctness and decency of apparel, I do not think myself in any way at fault. My clothes express my function: unassuming, cleanly, subfusc. You, of necessity, wear your official livery, which is, of necessity, both splendid and delightful, and suited to the pageantry of state. Is that what you would have me say?

LINDSAY. Aye, it'll serve. Splendid and delightful. As it were, ane ornament for a Mayday foolery or ane heathenish idol dedicate to blood-sacrifice. I will remove it, d'you mark? There is ane man under it, and remove what's left upon him, and there's naething for ye but nakedness. What can we dae wi' that in the service of diplomacy?

> The rags and robes that we do wear
> Express the function of our life
> But the bawdy body that we bear
> Beneath them carries nocht
> But shame and greed and strife.
> It is pleisand to naebody
> Of its hairy sweat and nudity;
> Save belike to ane cruel tormentor
> Whaur his whip will leave the better bloody mark,
> Or save belike to our ain rejoict Creator,
> Whaur he walks through the green glade
> Of his fair garden and his fencit park,
> Or save belike to ane infatuate tender woman:
> And then best in the dark.
> Yet here I stand and maun contrive
> With this sole body and the brain within him
> To set myself upon ane man alive
> And turn his purposes and utterly win him.
> That coat is irrelevant:
> I will wear it nae further
> Till Armstrang be brocht

Intil the King's peace and order.
I will gang towart his house
As ane man against ane man,
And through my craft and my humanity
I will save the realm frae butchery
Gif I can, good sir, but gif I can.

ENGLISH CLERK. Is there not, however, a more certain way than that? Your Commissioner mentioned a feud between the Armstrongs of Gilnockie and, er, and—

SCOTS CLERK. Wamphray. James Johnstone of Wamphray. Aye, they are at feud.

ENGLISH CLERK. Then why not offer Wamphray, from the hand of the King, some sort of emolument – I mean, in short, give a bribe to one ruffian to do away with the other?

SCOTS CLERK. M'm, we did consider it. And Johnstone was agreeable. But the man is a greit-heidit fool: he's no killt Armstrang yet, and I canna believe he ever will. It was sheer waste of hard-gathert taxes.

LINDSAY. Mair than taxes, man – humanity. To murder ane murderer is a'thegither waste, and bad waste at that. Like silly wee childer that pick up a caterpillar – they crush it in their fingers, and then ye find them greeten ower the dearth of butterflies in summer. Besides, it's no sae simple. This caterpillar is protectit. He is the vassal of Lord Maxwell.

SCOTS CLERK (to ENGLISH CLERK). Ane tyrannous and malignant peer at the Court and ane constant threatener of rebellion. Nae Armstrang rides against England outwith his implicit permission.

LINDSAY. Or indeed occult command. The nobility of this land, sir, are mair treacherous and insensate than ony gang of thieves in Christendom . . . I wad never condemn ane proposition to murder Lord Maxwell. There are mony good poison mushrumps grow in the Ettrick forest – on my road to Gilnockie I could gather ye a wee bag, eh? Will I dae it? Wad ye like it?

SCOTS CLERK (*gives an embarrassed giggle*). Just so, Sir David, just so . . . When do you intend to ride?

LINDSAY. To Gilnockie? Directly.

SCOTS CLERK. And what people will ye bring?

LINDSAY. Aye well, there will be the lady—

SCOTS CLERK. The lady? Your wife.

LINDSAY. Did I say that? She is ane paramour, sir – aha, ye do mislike it?

SCOTS CLERK. Ah na na . . . But when all is said and done, sir, do you find her presence ane absolute necessity?

LINDSAY. Absolute. At unpredictable intervals: but absolute. (*To* ENGLISH CLERK.) Do ye remember the story of the Gordian knot?

ENGLISH CLERK. I think that I may recollect—

LINDSAY. Aye weel, there was ane emperour, and he went with ane sword and cut it. He thocht he was ane god, walken. Why in God's Name could he no be a human man instead and sit down and unravel it?

SCOTS CLERK. You yourself, Sir David, are to show him the way there, I take it.

He takes him out of earshot of the ENGLISH CLERK.

And shew him it with speed, as ye hope for your salvation! Scotland can nocht sustain ane other war with England. The conference is broke, the urgency is merciless—

LINDSAY. Aye, aye, we ken . . . (*To* ENGLISH CLERK.) He says it is ane urgency. Well, Lindsay's urgent, too. Observe him: he's awa'. (*Exit into Palace.*)

ENGLISH CLERK. I will report to the Grace of England what I have been told: and I will pray for your success. Good day, sir, fare you well. (*Exit.*)

The SCOTS CLERK *stands hesitating for an instant and then goes into the Palace.*

SCENE THREE

[GILNOCKIE, WAMPHRAY, ARMSTRONGS.]

Hunting horns, sounds of hounds and horses.
   Enter, through the Forest, GILNOCKIE *and his men, dressed for the chase.*
   WAMPHRAY *comes with them, arm in arm with* GILNOCKIE.

WAMPHRAY (*to audience*).
   To the hunten ho, cried Johnny Armstrang
   And to the hunten he has gaen
   And the man that seeks his life, James Johnstone,
   Alang with him he has him taen.
FIRST ARMSTRONG.
   To the hunten ho, cried Johnny Armstrang,
   The morning sun is on the dew,
   The cauler breeze frae aff the fells
   Will lead the dogs to the quarry true.
SECOND ARMSTRONG.
   They huntit hie, they hunted law,
   They huntit up, they huntit down,
   Until the day was past the prime
   And it grew late in the afternoon.
   They huntit hie by the Millstane Edge
   Whenas the sun was sinken law—
GILNOCKIE. Ca aff the dogs!

   This cry is taken up offstage and horns blow again.

SECOND ARMSTRONG.
   Says Johnny then, ca aff the dogs
   We'll bait our steeds and hamewart go.

   They sit down to rest.

THIRD ARMSTRONG.
   They lightit hie at the Ewes Water Heid

Between the brown and benty ground
They rested them but a little wee while:
Tak tent then lest ye sleep too sound.

FIRST ARMSTRONG. We hae gien ye but poor hunten,
Wamphray. The dun deer of Eskdale had word ye were
comen, I think. They're awa beyond into Teviotdale to
bide on their lane there until we show them our backs.

GILNOCKIE (*passing a flask*). Tak a drink while we rest. Let
the huntsmen earn their meat. Sit ye down for God's sake.

WAMPHRAY. It was ane gentlemanlike and honourable action
for ye, Gilnockie, to celebrate the reconciliation betwixt our
houses with this day's sport, howsoever frustratit, and a
bottle of good usquebaugh. Gie ye lang life and fruitful riden.

FIRST ARMSTRONG. And the Grace of God betide us all
intil ane time of peace and friendship.

GILNOCKIE. We have but few years left us, James.

FIRST ARMSTRONG. And then we maun gang to our graves.
The Laird of Gilnockie wad tell ye, forbye, this reconciliation
requires some formal handfast and ane apparent declaren
before witnesses.

GILNOCKIE. You men, are ye with me, hear it, all you men!
Your hand!

He clasps hands with WAMPHRAY *in a ceremonious fashion.*

FIRST ARMSTRONG. Neither Armstrang nor Johnstone frae
this day furth shall pursue their ancient enmity. All plots,
devices, ambuscades or manslauchters, either to t'ither,
conceivit, intendit, or made in time past are hereby void,
forgotten, and entirely outwith the consideration of our
lives. In their stead stands friendship, britherhood, and ane
certain protection and assistance against all heinous attempts.
Is that weel spoken? Gilnockie wad be glad of your agreement.

WAMPHRAY. Under witness of God, Jesus His hangit Son,
and the Haly Ghaist in Trinity, I call it weel spoken.

Johnny, God help me, I could desire ane equal word frae
Gilbert Eliot of Stobs. You are yet close confederate with
him; could ye no mak his people turn towart me in peace in
like manner with your ain?

GILNOCKIE. Gilbert Eliot? The man has ane dochter.

FIRST ARMSTRONG. It wad be nae matter of difficulty,
Wamphray, gif there were little mair than driven kye or
broken byres in dispute betwixt the Eliots and yourself. But
Gilbert believes ye hae lain wi his dochter.

GILNOCKIE. Against her will, he tells me.

WAMPHRAY. Ah na, na, na, against her will is ridiculous.

GILNOCKIE. But ye did swyve the lassie?

WAMPHRAY. Aye, that I did.

FIRST ARMSTRONG. Ye are ane free widower, however.
Gilnockie wad speir what prevents ye frae marriage.

THIRD ARMSTRONG. Ye will mind that Gilnockie's ain wife
is the sister of Stobs: ane alliance betwixt the three houses
wad be gey convenient, Wamphray.

GILNOCKIE. Convenient. Wad be honourable. Tak ye ane
other drink!

WAMPHRAY. Alliance, marriage, are ye out of your senses?
Gif I called Meg Eliot my kirkfast marriet wife, within less
than a year my ain greeten wean'd call the pigman of
Wamphray by the name of bloody uncle! Ach God, she is
ane gat-leggit strumpet, Johnny, and I tell you I kent it the
first half-hour after!

GILNOCKIE. After? What after?

WAMPHRAY. Heh heh, what d'ye think?

FIRST ARMSTRONG. Ye'll no tell that to Stobs.

WAMPHRAY. I seek nae opportunity to tell anything to Stobs.
He can find it for himself.

FIRST ARMSTRONG. Gif he finds *you*, sir, you will be finishit.
His castle is nae mair than ten miles awa frae here. Suppose
that *he* should hae chosen to hunt these fells the day? What
wad ye do?

WAMPHRAY. I wad call upon my host for assistance and protection in accordance with his word.

FIRST ARMSTRONG. Aye. Gilbert nor his sons wad never do you violence gif you were standen with the Armstrangs: there's nae question o' that. Forbye he is ane sudden man with his weapon, Gilbert; he has three and twenty notches cut in his hilt for the lives he has taen of men that were in search of his. I mind that he said to the Laird: I ha never yet heard of the laddie that wad kill me, he said, but what I was forewarnit of it and dealt him ane quick vengeance before he could sae mickle as graith up his brand.

GILNOCKIE. Speir at him what wad he do—

FIRST ARMSTRONG. He says what wad ye do, what action wad ye set afoot, gif ye heard there was ane complot made by your enemies to brenn your house aboon your heid and you in your nakit bed with your wife and your bairn, sleepen?

WAMPHRAY. Gif I heard that, I wad – I wad first demand matter of proof of it, Gilnockie.

GILNOCKIE. Aye, aha, aye?

FIRST ARMSTRONG. There was ane trustless word abroad that sic ane black design was in process upon Gilnockie, upon the safety of our castle, upon Janet the Laird's wife, upon his bairn within the cradle, upon the good men in his hall – is this the truth?

WAMPHRAY. Gilnockie, he said trustless. Trustless is true. Nae circumstance else.

GILNOCKIE. Wad ye tak aith upon that?

WAMPHRAY. What?

FIRST ARMSTRONG (*producing a book from his pouch*). Wad ye swear upon the Gospel? Ye are aware of nae plot by fire or by steel to destroy John o'Gilnockie while he sleeps?

GILNOCKIE. There's the Book, there.

FIRST ARMSTRONG. Are ye preparit to swear it, sir?

WAMPHRAY. I hae gien ye already ane handfast of friendship.

GILNOCKIE. Aye: mak it siccar. Tak aith upon the Book.

WAMPHRAY. Gilnockie. Ye do wrang. Indeed, ye do me wrang to insist upon this thing.

GILNOCKIE. Insist? Jamie, I wad never.

FIRST ARMSTRONG. Your word, sir, is your honour, and it's no to be disputit. Sit ye down with the Laird, you are his good friend. But ye ken very weel, upon this Border, a man maun look keen to his ain proper safety.

GILNOCKIE (*sings*).

There's nane may lean on a rotten staff
But him that risks to get a fall:
There's nane that may in a traitor trust
Yet trustit men may be traitors all.

FIRST ARMSTRONG. I assure ye, sir, they may.

GILNOCKIE. Toom the bottle, Jamie, we're nane of us fou yet.

WAMPHRAY. Nor like to be neither, on the edge-hills of Teviot. Good luck then and good horsemanship to auld Gibby of Stobs, and the reeken breeks of his dochter! He-hech—

(*He sings.*)

And when he came to the hie castle yett
He beat upon that door
Oh where are you, my lily-white love,
Where are you, you dirty whoor!

He gives a drunken laugh and lies back. The others do likewise, and all appear to fall asleep. When WAMPHRAY *is clearly snoring heavily, the* ARMSTRONGS *sit cautiously up.*
GILNOCKIE *signs to the* FIRST ARMSTRONG, *who slips off into the Forest.*

GILNOCKIE. Brand. Get his brand. Tangle it up.

The SECOND ARMSTRONG *takes* WAMPHRAY'S *sword and wraps twine about the hilt, tying it to the scabbard.*

Let's hae his gully-knife.

> *The* SECOND ARMSTRONG *passes over to him* WAM-PHRAY'S *knife.*

You the gun.

> *The* THIRD ARMSTRONG *picks up* WAMPHRAY'S *hand-gun.*

THIRD ARMSTRONG. Load it.

GILNOCKIE. Aye. Water.

THIRD ARMSTRONG. We've nae water here. Do ye want me to—

GILNOCKIE. Then pour in bloody usquebaugh and ask nae mair fool questions.

THIRD ARMSTRONG (*pouring whisky down the barrel*). This is no a very provident method, Gilnockie. I doubt—

GILNOCKIE. Do it.

THIRD ARMSTRONG. Aye.

GILNOCKIE (*looking at the sword*). He'll yet pull that out. See. Mak it siccar.

> *He improves the knots at the sword-hilt. The* FIRST ARMSTRONG *returns, holding a bridle.*

FIRST ARMSTRONG. Here's his bridle.

GILNOCKIE. What hae ye done wi' the horse?

FIRST ARMSTRONG. I've whippit him hame to bloody mither.

GILNOCKIE. Good. He's still asleep.

> *He puts back the sword.*

SECOND ARMSTRONG. Gilnockie. Are you entirely clear that this affair is in consonance with your—

GILNOCKIE. With my what?

SECOND ARMSTRONG. With your – with your honour, Gilnockie?

GILNOCKIE. What's your name?

SECOND ARMSTRONG. My name is Armstrong.

GILNOCKIE. Aye, I thocht it wad be. Then you see that you keep it.

They stand around waiting, and looking into the distance.

FIRST ARMSTRONG. A quarter hour frae now and the red sun's drappit under. Whaur to hell are the Eliots?

A horn in the distance.

Ah: here they are. It should be Gilbert the Laird and his eldest son, aye riden like a pair of wildwood bogles! (*He speaks to the sleeping* WAMPHRAY.) James Johnstone of Wamphray, ye are ane sackless murderit man.

GILNOCKIE. Wake him up: wi' that.

The THIRD ARMSTRONG *blows a horn in* WAMPHRAY'S *ear.*

WAMPHRAY (*starts up*). Eh, who, what—

FIRST ARMSTRONG. Wamphray, we're trappit. There's fifteen of the Eliots riden ower the north rigg. Mount your steed, man, and gang!

WAMPHRAY. Eh, what, gang whaur?

FIRST ARMSTRONG. Back to Gilnockie's castle; they are riden at feud!

GILNOCKIE. Get to your horses!

His men run out into the Forest.

Come on, man, awa—

WAMPHRAY. Johnny, whaur's my horse?

GILNOCKIE runs out after his men.

FIRST ARMSTRONG (*off*). Awa hame to bloody mither!

THIRD ARMSTRONG (*off*). Wamphray, ye are ane forsworn traitor, and ye maun bide there for what comes after ye!

Their laughter is heard receding, off.

SCENE FOUR

[WAMPHRAY, STOBS, YOUNG STOBS, MEG.]

WAMPHRAY *looks around him in despair.*

WAMPHRAY. Bide here for what – fifteen men, fifteen Eliots, on their horses, at feud— (*He tries to draw his sword.*) The kindless bastard! (*He looks around and picks up his gun.*) And what's he done to the gun? Sodden, sodden weet and cloggit wi' usquebaugh – why, the gun's fou! Jamie's fou, too . . . Gully, gully, he's not even left me my gully-knife, gin he'd left me but that I could cut free my brand—

He sits down helplessly, tugging at the knots on his hilt.

STOBS (*off*). Johnstone?

YOUNG STOBS (*off*). Johnstone of Wamphray.

STOBS (*off*). Are ye there, my mannie, are ye there?

YOUNG STOBS (*off*). We're here.

STOBS (*off*). We want ye.

> STOBS *and* YOUNG STOBS *enter from the Forest. They carry hunting spears.*

Wamphray. Ye ken our names and ye ken our quarrel. There is auld feud betwixt us lang syne, Wamphray, and this month it is augmentit. Ye hae lain leg across my dochter and we're here to kill ye for it. Will ye stand to your death like a man, or will ye squat upon your hurdies like a wee doggie wi' the worms?

> *He pricks him with his spear and* WAMPHRAY *jumps up and back. He holds his scabbarded sword on guard in front of him.*

YOUNG STOBS. That brand's little good to ye, gif Gilnockie kent his business.

> WAMPHRAY *fights them hopelessly, using his sword as though it were a cudgel, but they force him back to the big tree, and pin him to it with their spears.*

WAMPHRAY. When ye neist gratify your wame at Johnny
Armstrang's table, speir at him frae me, what betidit with
his honour?

He dies.

STOBS. I do nocht regard this as a relevant question. Gilnockie
has certain proof that this thing we hae pit down, here, was
collaborate with ane undiscoverit enemy to oerthrow Gilnockie's people. And, with his people, ours. He will remain
here on this fellside for the better nourishment of the corbies.
Ride.

The two ELIOTS *go out through the Forest, leaving the
spears in the body.*
MEG *enters at another side of the Forest. After a pause:*

MEG. Jamie? . . . Jamie? . . . Ah, they hae finisht their
wark with ye, Jamie, they hae finisht it gey complete. There
are nae better butchers in the land.

*She pulls out the spears. The body slumps down and she
kneels beside it.*

In twa minutes they hae turnit ye intil ane auld man; ye
werena that last week.
These lips that were sae red and fat
Will snarl across your chaps for ever
Like the grin of a dirty rat:
The yellow hair sae sleek and fine,
That did illuminate your hard hasty skull
And the deep secret dale here of your chine,
In twa minutes has revertit
To the draff-black bristles of a wild-wood swine.
James, ye cruel drunken lecher James,
Whaur is now departit
Your thrust and tender carelessness of lust?
And in what unkent bed do ye scatter

Your barren seéd this nicht ? Aye, totter,
Stagger, stumble intil sleep:
Nae Matthew, Mark, nor Luke, nor John, will keep
Their watch oer you—
To baith your woman and your godly faith
Ye were untrue.
Are ye comen, my wearie dearie,
Are ye comen, my lovely hinnie,
I will find ye a wee bracken bush
To keep the north wind frae aff your ancient body.

She drags the corpse out into the Forest.

SCENE FIVE

[LINDSAY, MCGLASS.]

LINDSAY *enters from the Palace.*

LINDSAY (*to audience*). The grief of this woman is the grief of
the Common-weal of Scotland. Naebody to hear it, and but
few to comprehend it, gif they did. And of those few, how
mony could comprehend the means of consolation ? Where
is my secretair ? Alexander ? Mr McGlass!

Enter MCGLASS *from the Palace.*

MCGLASS. Are ye ready for the road, Sir David ? We had best
lose nae time setten furth. God kens what could happen
upon the South-West Border before we get there. They tell
me there is ane manslauchter within ten mile of Carlisle
every third day.

LINDSAY. I wait, Mr Alexander, for my wanton and unpunctual lady. Whaur is she, d'ye ken ?

MCGLASS She was to hae left Linlithgow in good time to hae
met with us on the road, but this day I have ane letter frae

Jedburgh to say that she is held there by the ill condition of
the weather and that she will proceed to Gilnockie's castle
on her ain when there is better chance of travel.

LINDSAY. I am of opinion, Mr Alexander, that the lady's love
and inclination towart me is somewhat fainter than it did
use to be. Do you imagine she will hae fand ane better man
for her pastime?

MCGLASS. Better man than Lindsay? Better for what? The
poetry of love or the wicked deed itself? Either gate, I think
it were scarce possible.

LINDSAY. Ye have ane gey feeble notion then of the bounds of
possibility. Will ye no sing ane sang as we travel?

MCGLASS. Gaelic or Scots?

LINDSAY. Scots, man: we're in the Lawlands. And mak it
ane sang of the unkindness of womankind.

MCGLASS (*sings as they march with* LINDSAY *joining in the
refrains.*)

> When I cam hame frae riden out
> I fand my love in bed.
> A minstrel harp hung on the rail
> And a coat of the scarlet red.
> 'What man was here?' I speirt at her
> And this is what she said –
>   'Oh a dree dree dradie drumtie dree.

> 'My brither cam at mirk midnicht
> He was sae cauld and weet
> That I maun fetch him intil bed
> And warm his frozen feet.
> Indeed his feet are warm eneuch
> And his instrument sae sweet
>   Plays a dree dree dradie drumtie dree.'

LINDSAY. Aye, and it's now time to hear a bit out o' *your*
instrument. Here is the castle of Gilnockie: we stand before
his yetts: gie him ane blaw of the wee trump.

MCGLASS, *who carries a bugle horn, blows a blast.*

Blood and wounds, are they all deaf in there? Blaw again.

MCGLASS *blows a second call.*

SCENE SIX

[LINDSAY, MCGLASS, GILNOCKIE, *his* WIFE, ARM-STRONGS.]

GILNOCKIE'S WIFE *appears on top of the Castle.*

GILNOCKIE'S WIFE. Who are ye? What's your business? Frae what place d'ye come here? This is John o'Gilnockie's castle and the Laird has nae desire for strangers. Declare yourselves directly.

LINDSAY. Madam: I am sent here by the King.

FIRST ARMSTRONG *appears at the Castle gate.*

FIRST ARMSTRONG. And whatten King wad that be?

MCGLASS. King James of Scotland: what King d'ye think else?

FIRST ARMSTRONG. King of Scotland? King of bloody Lothian. That's the best name he carries here.

GILNOCKIE'S WIFE. Willie, Tam, Archie – here are men frae the King—

Two more ARMSTRONGS *emerge from the Castle, with weapons.*

Fasten their hands. They hae come here to wark us ane treason.

The men seize LINDSAY *and* MCGLASS *and tie their hands behind their backs, and take away their swords.*

FIRST ARMSTRONG. Blawen your damn trumpets before the yetts of Gilnockie. The Laird'll hae ye hangit.

MCGLASS. Hangit!

LINDSAY. Hangit? For what indeed?

MCGLASS. We are servants of the King—

FIRST ARMSTRONG. There's but ae King in Eskdale, my mannie, and he's King John the Armstrang. We hae them fast bandit, mistress.

> GILNOCKIE'S WIFE *has left the top of the Castle and now comes out of the gate, below.*

Will we pit them in the black hole?

GILNOCKIE'S WIFE. Na, na, no yet. The Laird'll want to see them when he is risen frae his meat.

THIRD ARMSTRONG. He'll no want to see them stood like ornament statues within the width of his yard, mistress. They maun gang beneath the trap-hatches, quick.

> *The* FIRST ARMSTRONG *begins to hustle them.*

GILNOCKIE'S WIFE. Willie, let them be. I'll speak a word wi' them first.

FIRST ARMSTRONG. The Laird'll no be pleast at it.

GILNOCKIE'S WIFE. Willie.

FIRST ARMSTRONG. Whatever ye say, mistress: ye are the Laird's lady.

GILNOCKIE'S WIFE (*to the* ARMSTRONGS). Stand a bit back, sirs; remember your places.

> *They withdraw, rather sulkily.*

Tam, will ye fetch me my chair? Tam, my chair, gif ye please!

> *The* SECOND ARMSTRONG *goes into the Castle and brings out a chair.*

FIRST ARMSTRONG (*aside*). I had best to tell Gilnockie what has chancit within his house.

THIRD ARMSTRONG (*aside*). Tak tent, he will be angry.

FIRST ARMSTRONG. I had best tell him.

The FIRST ARMSTRONG *goes into the Castle.*

GILNOCKIE'S WIFE (*sitting down on the chair*). The Laird will be angry. Ye are aware, are ye no? that the King has had him proclaimit outlaw and rebel at Edinboro Cross and that he in return has proclaimit the King nae King ower Eskdale but ane traitor to his people. Frae what cause do ye come to this border but to bring tyranny and coercion to the inhabitours thereof? I tell ye, Gilnockie will be angry, and when he is angry he is ane man to consider with. In God's Name, he is ane devil, sirs – and you yourselves are ane pair of equal devils, ye are Mephistophilis and Beelzebub, to stir up mair warfare when there is but peace and truce here and community in Christ.

LINDSAY. In Christ, madam? Is that the verity? Community with the English? The English are Christian men.

GILNOCKIE'S WIFE. The Laird and his people have sufferit mickle wrang frae the English. Ower generation and generation the English hae warkit destruction frae Carlisle to the Ettrick Forest and frae the forest to the sea-coast, and alang the sea-coast intil Forth. The Laird has his purposes – they are strang purposes for defence. He has aye been courageous in their difficult fulfilment, and what hae ye to tell him that will serve him ony advantage, but rather cruel hurt to his peace, and disadvantage to his people, sirs; for the Laird *is* his people, and his people were ance the King's, but now they are naebody's. Gilnockie is their ae protection. They maun starf outwith his hand. What are your names?

LINDSAY. I am David Lindsay of the Mount. Ye will hae heard of me, I guess?

GILNOCKIE'S WIFE. Fore God, ye are the King's Herald?

LINDSAY. I am. And this gentleman is Mr Alexander McGlass, my servant and my writer.

MCGLASS. Madam, I am maist honourit to offer ye ane salutation.

GILNOCKIE'S WIFE. What? What? What honour to mock at me in the very house of my good man, ane puir terrifyit woman, haven ane bitter weird of violence aye thrawn within my spirit, sir? Gilnockie will be angry. What soldiers have ye brocht here?

LINDSAY. Nae soldiers at a', madam.

SCENE SEVEN

[LINDSAY, MCGLASS, GILNOCKIE, *his* WIFE, ARMSTRONGS *and* GIRLS.]

GILNOCKIE *enters with* FIRST ARMSTRONG *from the Castle. His* WIFE *gets up from the chair and he takes her place. He looks keenly at the two prisoners.*

GILNOCKIE. Their names.

SECOND ARMSTRONG. Lindsay, McGlass.

GILNOCKIE. Mac – Mac – Mac – Glass? Ane Hielandman? He wears breeks.

SECOND ARMSTRONG. He spak to us in good Scots.

GILNOCKIE. Better than that – me – the Gaelic, me. Ha ha, how's this? Hechna, hochna, hochna, hoo! Ha ha ha—

FIRST ARMSTRONG. There is an exposition of versatility for ye, mister; what d'ye think o' that for ane good Lawland mou full of dirty Erse?

GILNOCKIE. Lindsay. That is ane name: I heard it. Delamont: Lindsay of the Mount. David Lindsay Delamont. Sir.

GILNOCKIE'S WIFE. Aye, that is correct, Gilnockie, ane kent man: Sir David Lindsay of the Mount, he is the Herald of the King.

GILNOCKIE. Herald, King? Herald, Herod, King, the wee childer. Ilk ane o' them murderit. Cut oot their throats.

Jesus Christ escapit. King Herod was ane King: and he doubtless had ane Herald.

FIRST ARMSTRONG. The Laird intends to tell ye, sir, that him that ye serve is but ane prodigious tyrant, like—

GILNOCKIE. Will be. God he is ane bloody wean yet.

FIRST ARMSTRONG. The Laird tells ye furthermair—

LINDSAY. The Laird can tell me himself. He has ane tongue of his ain, has he no? What for does he talk to me through varlets?

GILNOCKIE *roars.*

GILNOCKIE'S WIFE. Sir, ye had best apprehend—

FIRST ARMSTRONG. Ye had best apprehend, sir, that the Laird has had ane impediment in his speech syne the day of his nativity. He receives his interpretation through the words of his leal gentlemen.

GILNOCKIE'S WIFE. You are discourteous to remark upon it, Sir David.

GILNOCKIE. Gentlemen. That's no the women. Haud your damn't whist.

GILNOCKIE'S WIFE. I crave pardon, indeed, John, for the interruption of your discourse—

He glares at her and she is silent.

GILNOCKIE (*fingering* LINDSAY'*s clothes*). Silk, Satin. Velvet. Gowd – is it gowd?

LINDSAY. It's gilt-siller, Gilnockie. I'm no yet ane Marquess.

GILNOCKIE. Aye? No yet's Johnny.

MCGLASS. Ye could be, could ye no?

GILNOCKIE (*showing his own clothes*). See. Linsey-woolsey. Buft leather. Steel. Hackit steel. Hackit flesh. Here is ane brand. (*He draws his sword.*) She gies ye answer to her name. Tell him.

FIRST ARMSTRONG. He calls his brand Kings' Dreid,

Delamont. Because that is her manner of life. Compare them.

He measures GILNOCKIE'S *sword against* LINDSAY'S.

GILNOCKIE. Langer, braider, heavier. Nae King whatever—
FIRST ARMSTRONG. Nae King whatever has had the might to put down Armstrang. Jamie Stuart the Fourth sent against us ane officer, and horsemen forbye. And hear ye what sang was made by his people – the Laird wi' his ain hand slew—
GILNOCKIE (*sings*).

> I slew the King's Lieutenant
> And garr'd his troopers flee
> My name is Johnny the Armstrang
> And wha daur meddle wi' me?

The ARMSTRONGS *pick up the refrain and repeat it.*

LINDSAY. Wha daur? David Lindsay daur. King Johnny of Eskdale indeed! King Curlew of the barren fell. King Paddock of the wowsie mosses. Ye squat on your blood-sodden molehill and ye hoot, Johnny: and naebody in Scotland considers ye mair than a wet leaf blawn against the eyeball on a day of September wind. So ye slew the King's Lieutenant, hey? And whatten reck d'ye imagine the King made of that? What hour or what wee minute was reft out of the Royal sleep, what disturbit instant was thrust in for you betwixt James Stuart and his concubine when he heard word of the peril of Gilnockie in the corner of his border? Fore God, ye have ane precellent conceit of your power, Mr Armstrang!

GILNOCKIE *growls*.

Ye are ane inconvenience, I will grant ye. Ye are ane tedious nuisance to the realm. Ye are indeed cause for ane itchy paragraph or twae in some paper of state. But were ye the great man of danger and subversion that ye fain, sir, wad think yourself, can ye credit then the King's Herald wad hae come to your house wi' nae footmen nor horse, nae pikemen nor archers, nae bombardiers nor pioneers – wi' nocht in God's Name but ane demi-priestling writer and sax inches of bent brass bugle! I crave your pardon, Sandy, I had nae intent to disparage ye, but the noise that ye mak on your instrument can scarcely be callit the clangour of warfare.

GILNOCKIE. Armstrang. Mr Armstrang. *Mister—*

FIRST ARMSTRONG. The Laird has his proper entitlement of style. He's no ashamit to use it, nor yet to hear it usit. *Gilnockie,* gif ye please, when ye open your mou to the Laird!

LINDSAY. Gilnockie, gif ye will. He draws his rent frae the local middens, by all means let us concede him the flattery of their name.

> GILNOCKIE *leaps forward and grips* LINDSAY *by the throat, shaking him in rage.*

FIRST ARMSTRONG. Will we hang him, Gilnockie?

SECOND ARMSTRONG. Cut his heid off?

THIRD ARMSTRONG. I'll dae it – this minute!

GILNOCKIE (*throwing* LINDSAY *down*). Na . . . Ane precellent conceit. Nocht, in God's Name, but ane writer and ane bugle. To stand against me. Johnny. For what?

FIRST ARMSTRONG. Aye, tell him; for what?

GILNOCKIE. Willie, search his purpose.

FIRST ARMSTRONG (*hauling* LINDSAY *upright again*). You are ane courageous man, Delamont, to heave up your undefendit face intil the face of Gilnockie. Gif you're no here for coercion, ye maun hae brocht with ye ane offer of terms. Do I pursue the passage of your mind correctly, Gilnockie?

GILNOCKIE. Aye.

FIRST ARMSTRONG. Declare to the Laird, then, first, what does the King want?

LINDSAY. He wants to prevent ane English conquest of the kingdom. For what else is he King?

GILNOCKIE (*laughs*). And is the riden – Gilnockie, Stobs, or paddock of the mosses – ride intil England, and prick them, prick them – can we – hey?

FIRST ARMSTRONG. The Laird means, Delamont, that when he and his good-brither Eliot mak ane raid intil England, the whilk ye hae just tellt us is ane insignificant provocation at the hands of unregardit men, then what way can this insignificance gar the great King of England set abroach ane formal war? Can we prick King Henry's quarters indeed thus sharply – when our lances are sae blunt, and short, and pitiable?

LINDSAY. I had nae sort of intent towart sic ane implication. Your raidens and ridens are naething of import whatever. But English policy *is*: and English policy, continual sin the time of heroic Wallace, is the domination of Scotland and the destruction of her rulers. True, or untrue?

GILNOCKIE. True.

LINDSAY. Aha, we progress. Now let us bear our minds back, a wee space intil history. I could bear mine the mair freely gif my hands were to be loosit – gesticulation, whiles, is ane useful stimulant to the deftness of the tongue—

GILNOCKIE. Na.

LINDSAY. Ah . . . Intil history. Bannockburn. Ane victory. Wha won it?

GILNOCKIE. We did.

LINDSAY. You. And the Bruce?

GILNOCKIE. The Bruce? He was nocht, was nae place, was but deid but for gentlemen. Armstrang. In that battle. There was he. Aye and Eliot. Otterburn alsweel. It was Armstrang did mak prisoner Hotspur Percy. Of this aye house the bonny gentlemen.

LINDSAY. Precise. Ane veritable conception of history indeed. It was upon sic perilous occasions that the Lawland gentlemen alane did create the defence of this realm: when baith monarchy and nobility were shook with internecine faction like the bell-ropes in the tower of Giles's Kirk!

MCGLASS. At Bannockburn— The Bruce—?

LINDSAY. Sandy: I am in ane spate of words – be silent. Gif Henry of England, as he plans, as I ken weel he plans, should turn his calculation, sir, towart ane second Flodden – King James bean young and oer-tormentit by a wheen sorry intriguers at his Court – whaur will then reside the protection for our people?

GILNOCKIE. Here.

LINDSAY (*walking round each of the* ARMSTRONGS). Here . . . here: here: here. And the King is conscious of it, sir, and for that reason he doth pray you pardon his prior intransigence against the valour of your clan. He has sent me to tell you that gif you will render him ane true and leal obedience hencefurth, he will put his Royal trust in you, and look to you and yours to keep his historic Crown for ever integrate, and Scots! There is ane specific offer—

GILNOCKIE. Specific: aye.

LINDSAY. Ane specific offer of Royal privilege I am commandit to present to ye. I will ask Mr Alexander to expound it now – he is weel versit indeed in the legalities and practicalities. Sandy?

MCGLASS. The King's offer is maist bountiful, ane preclair, majestical, and unprecedentit offer – I hope ye will agree. Upon receipt of ane true assurance frae John, Laird of Gilnockie, that he will follow the course of war ahint nae other banner than that of King James of Scotland, King James has determinit to create and dispone for him ane office of mickle dignity and honour: to wit, Warden of Eskdale and Free Lieutenant of the King; permitten the said John, upon occasion of fray, the sole right and privilege within Eskdale, Liddesdale, and Teviotdale, of defence, command, and levy. I wad add to that, forbye, that ony passage of theft across the borders of England in time of peace or truce is maist strictly to be renouncit. Renunciation receivit, King James will then rescind the decrees of outlawry and rebellion heretofore postit against John of Gilnockie, and will issue free pardon for all offences committit by the said John or any of his people in time past . . . There ye are!

GILNOCKIE. Nae theft; nae feeden. Then whaur?

FIRST ARMSTRONG. Then whaur, says the Laird, will we obtain our sustenance?

LINDSAY. Ane land unburdenit with the fear of war contains within its ain acres mickle sustenance, and growth of sustenance, Gilnockie: sheep, nolt, swine, fish, fowl of the air, corn upon your hillside fields – and merchants in your towns – ye'll prosper, sir: ye maun attempt it – do ye daur?

GILNOCKIE. Daur? Gilnockie daur a'thing . . . Whaur's auctority?

MCGLASS. Auctority? Aye, sir, we have that. But it's here in my pouch. I canna get at it wi' my hands bandit.

GILNOCKIE. Tam.

The SECOND ARMSTRONG *takes a letter out of* MCGLASS'S *satchel. He gives it to* GILNOCKIE, *who looks at it wisely.*

Seal of the King. Good.

LINDSAY. Will ye no read the letter?

FIRST ARMSTRONG. Do ye think the Laird is ane shave-pate eunuch bible-clerk? Read it yersel.

LINDSAY. Is there naebody here can read? It is writ in good English. Gif I were to read it ye, or Sandy here, ye wad hae but little reason to credit us, I think. Bear in mind we are politicians.

GILNOCKIE'S WIFE. I can read the letter.

LINDSAY. Will ye no let the lady read it to ye, sir? It were best ye should hear it.

GILNOCKIE (*giving the letter to his wife*). Read.

GILNOCKIE'S WIFE. It is ane extraordinair brief letter, Gilnockie.

GILNOCKIE. Read.

GILNOCKIE'S WIFE. It says but these words: 'Sir David Lindsay of the Mount is the King's tongue and the King's ear. Hear him and speak, and the King will baith speak and listen.'

LINDSAY. Precise and laconical. The King has had good tutors in the disposition of his rhetoric. Weel, sir, his ear is herewith presentit you.

GILNOCKIE. Loose.

The men release their wrists.

Warden of Eskdale. Lieutenant. Ane Officer of the King!

LINDSAY. It suits ye exceeden fitly, Gilnockie. Ye seem a larger man for it already.

GILNOCKIE. Maxwell.

LINDSAY. Ah! the Lord Maxwell. Belike ye do suspect that ye wad do wrang to cleave to the King outwith Lord Maxwell's permission – he bean your suzerain, and you in your turn—

GILNOCKIE. Pay him his rents.

LINDSAY. And divide with him your booty?

GILNOCKIE *laughs.*

SECOND ARMSTRONG. When he hears of it.

THIRD ARMSTRONG. Grip the sark frae aff your back, wad Maxwell.

MCGLASS. Do ye hauld him then ungenerous?

GILNOCKIE. Ane mansion-house in Linlithgae. Sups his broo wi' creish Kirk-Prelates. On his chaumer flair is ane carpet. Ane carpet. They did sell it him out of – out of—

THIRD ARMSTRONG. Persia. Wad ye credit that? Ane carpet out of Persia.

FIRST ARMSTRONG. But notwithstanding this: towart Lord Maxwell the Laird has sworn ane ancient lealty.

GILNOCKIE'S WIFE. Aye, aye, lealty. It has to be considerit.

LINDSAY. Gilnockie: for mony years I had care of the King's education. And I did instruct him in a' that was necessair in the government of his realm. Gif he be unable at his present age to compel to his obedience ane lord that lives as saft as do the votaries of Mahomet: God help the kingdom!

GILNOCKIE. Aye, ha ha, God help it . . . Your wame, I heard it nicker.

LINDSAY. Wame? Nicker?

FIRST ARMSTRONG. The Laird wad speir, Sir David, whether or no ye've eaten the day?

LINDSAY. It is maist courteous of the Laird. We havena.

GILNOCKIE'S WIFE. Archie.

The THIRD ARMSTRONG *goes into the Castle.*

The Laird has just come frae his dinner. But meat and drink will be providit ye, Sir David.

GILNOCKIE. Break it with ye. Bread: salt. Ye are the King's Herald: ye bring the offer of the King. Acceptit! I am his Officer. Ye are ane good man. Gilnockie's roof-tree renders welcome. Welcome, sir.

He shakes LINDSAY'S *hand with ceremony.*

Mr Hieland Pen-and-Ink, your hand. Ye are ane good man.

He shakes MCGLASS'S *hand.*

SECOND ARMSTRONG. When ye shake Gilnockie's hand, ye shake the hand of honour, sir.

LINDSAY. Indeed, I am full sensible of it.

The THIRD ARMSTRONG *comes out of the Castle, followed by* GIRLS *carrying trays of food – brown bread and red wine. This is handed to* LINDSAY *and* MCGLASS.

GILNOCKIE *shares it with them in a token but solemn fashion.*

(*To* GILNOCKIE'S WIFE, *who seems disapproving.*) There is ever ane sair question, madam, when a man sees his ancient life upon the brink of complete reversal. Reversal belike of lealty, aye: but of enmity alsweel. (*To* GILNOCKIE.) Maxwell will be your friend yet: and what about Johnstone?

GILNOCKIE (*choking over his refreshment*). What – whilk?

LINDSAY. Whilk? Whilk Johnstone? The Lord or the Laird? I had in mind the baith of them. Ye are at feud with the Laird of Wamphray, and Lord Maxwell is at feud with Lord Johnstone, who is Wamphray's kinsman and suzerain. There is here ane opportunity to put ane end to this sad quarrel; for the Johnstones lang syne hae been the King's servants, while you are now his Officer. Ane meritable wark, the conclusion of truce. Will ye dae it?

GILNOCKIE *laughs.*

FIRST ARMSTRONG (*aside*). What will we tell him, Gilnockie?

SECOND ARMSTRONG (*aside*). Tell him it's made, what else?

FIRST ARMSTRONG. The Laird says it's made. Wamphray is now in condition of peace, with ilk ane of the Armstrangs, and with a' men other. The Laird and himsel hae ridden in amity thegither in pursuit of the wild deer. They were accordit good sport thereat, and they drank as companions upon the side of the fell.

THIRD ARMSTRONG. They claspit their hands forbye as ane true earnest for evermair.

MCGLASS. Is this indeed the truth?

GILNOCKIE. For why nocht? I am ane Christian.

LINDSAY. I'll tell ye nae lie, Gilnockie: this was indeed un-lookit for. Howbeit, it is maist pleisand and agreeable to hear, and God be thankit for it.

GILNOCKIE. Paps o' the Virgin, how delightsome it is to be at peace with auld enemies! Peace! Whaur's my piper ? Whaur's music ?

FIRST ARMSTRONG. Whaur's reid wine for the gentlemen ? The bottle is toom, begod!

SECOND ARMSTRONG. Gilnockie cries for his music.

The THIRD ARMSTRONG *goes and fetches bagpipe.*

GILNOCKIE. Let's hae the bloody piper. Delamont, ye will dance with her. (*Indicates his wife.*) All the maids and men of Armstrang, let them set their feet to it, let them sing and gaily dance!

They dance and sing:

> Oh merry blooms the hawthorn tree
> And merry blooms the brier
> And merry blooms the bracken bush
> Whaur my true-love doth appear:
> He maks his bed and waits therein
> And when I walk beside
> He will rise up like a laverock
> And his arms will open wide—
>
> Oh start up and leap, man:
> And never fall and weep, man:
> Quick quick and rin, man:
> The game will just begin, man—

SCENE EIGHT

[LINDSAY, MCGLASS, GILNOCKIE, *his* WIFE, ARM- STRONGS, GIRLS, EVANGELIST.]

The EVANGELIST *enters from the Forest, carrying a pack on his back. He walks into the middle of the dancers, who fall apart from him and the music stops.*

EVANGELIST. Good people. Scotland is my native realm: but I am ane traveller, I am ane pedlar out of distant lands. In specific, the lands of Germany.

He opens his pack which contains a number of household articles, pots, napkins, wooden trenchers, etc.

And here in my kist I hae brocht hame for your advantage wark of craft and beauty, Almayne wark in wood, clay, claith – paintit and weel-corven, delightsome to your een, ane ornament for humanity, ane gaud for the material body of man. Wha'll buy it, wha'll buy it?

The WOMEN *gather round and look at his goods.*

GILNOCKIE'S WIFE (*taking a Bible out of the bottom of the pack*). What's this?

EVANGELIST. Aye, madam, d'ye look deeper? Why, what is it but ane book?

LINDSAY. Ye'll dae little good wi' books here, master. We live by blood and booty here – it'd serve ye far better to gang to Sanct Andrews.

EVANGELIST. Sanct Andrews, do ye tell me – Sanct Andrews of the Cardinal, the Doctors, the Prelates – this book to Sanct Andrews? Why, they wad cast me incontinent intil the fire of the Inquisitours for this. Brethren, this book is the undisputit Word of God. It is the Haly Scripture, sirs—

LINDSAY. In English?

EVANGELIST. Aye.

LINDSAY. Aha.

GILNOCKIE. English.

SECOND ARMSTRONG. Show it to the Laird.

EVANGELIST. The Laird. You are John Armstrang.

GILNOCKIE. English. Is ane heresy?

LINDSAY. Precise.

GILNOCKIE. Name? The name: Luther? Why?

FIRST ARMSTRONG. He says, for why d'ye bring ane German

heresy here intil Scotland? We ken little about it here, though we hae heard of the man Luther. Expound it. To the Laird.

EVANGELIST. Here, in this forest, they tell me, there are gentlemen that are dividit against their Princes, and brook nocht their commandments. The Prelates of the Kirk are in like manner this day with the Princes of the State. They are forgotten by God because God is forgotten of them. They are outwith His benevolence, for they wadna feed their sheep when their sheep were an-hungerit. John Armstrang – ye are ane mickle hornit ram – are ye weel-fed by your shepherds – spiritual, temporal? I trow nocht. I trow nocht.

LINDSAY. And I trow somewhat different, master. The wame of this Laird nickers nae langer. Why, he is—

GILNOCKIE. I am the King's Officer! God's tripes, I am distendit!

EVANGELIST. Your flesh is distendit. And what of your conscience, sir?

LINDSAY. Aye, what of it? I never yet heard that Martin Luther did enjoin disobedience to the King.

EVANGELIST. Obedience, he doth enjoin, to the commandments of God: and the commandments of God are ane voice that is in ilk ear present. In my puir mortal ear, or in yours, or in—

GILNOCKIE. Here. Set him, here. You are ane heretic. For your conscience, ye wad brenn, in the het fire indeed, courageous?

He smacks the EVANGELIST *in the face.*

EVANGELIST. Struck with the blaws of martyrdom, I yet maintain to you the other cheek, as is commandit me by Jesus Christ. And notwithstanding, bear I furth my testimony.

MCGLASS. There's nae Inquisitour whatever upon these borders here. Ye maun send him awa north to the correct process of the Kirk – will ye do that for him, Gilnockie, and

manifest in public your true responsibility to this Christian
Kingdom?

GILNOCKIE'S WIFE. To see him brennt in agony for nocht
but his conscience; it wad be ane unco cruelty.

GILNOCKIE. Aye, cruelty. Delamont: *his* conscience: *mine:*
what about *yours*?

LINDSAY. Wad ye speir my opinion, Mr Lieutenant? I'm
nae ecclesiast. But see, this good man, he is but, as he saith,
ane pedlar, his merchandise is tawdry, the wark of some
Almayne boor, it's naething at a' – we mak pots as good as
this in Scotland. The book alane is notable. Master, I will
purchase this, I think. (*He takes the Bible and hands over a
coin.*) Here ye are – tak it! Now then, Gilnockie, what will
ye dae with him?

MCGLASS. Without his book there's nae evidence. Sure ye
wad never brenn a man without evidence.

GILNOCKIE. No gien the Lieutenantship to roast mens' flesh
for Cardinals. Fidelity, he hath. Fidelity, maist admirable.
Godsake, let the carl gang!

The men who have been holding the EVANGELIST *release
him, and he gathers up his goods.*

LINDSAY. And hear ye this, Evangelist, as ye tak your good
leave of us. Consider what is writ in this book I hae obtainit
of ye. I will gie ye ane text to mind – Sanct Paul to the
Ephesians, chapter sax, verse five: 'Servants, be obedient to
them that are your masters.' For treason, ye will hang. Tak
tent on't – ye will.

EVANGELIST. Aye, Ephesians: same chapter, verse twelve.
'For we wrastle against the rulers of the darkness of this
warld, against spiritual wickedness in hie places.' I think ye
are ane man that kens weel that wickedness, but by reason of
the comfort of your slothful existence, ye wad prefer to
oerlook it and thereby to condone it. Within the House of
Rimmon is your habitation, and very weel ve may hang me

there: but you yoursel will taste damnation. The Lord our God is never moderate.

Exit into the Forest.

LINDSAY. I will now to the King, sir, and inform him furth-with of what has passed betwixt us. I will return in good season and bring you the confirmation of your office. Lieutenant and Warden, John Armstrang, for this time, I bid you fare-weel.

GILNOCKIE'S WIFE. Sir, fare ye weel and may God's grace gang with you. You are ane mild and virtuous envoy.

LINDSAY *gives her the Bible.*

GILNOCKIE. Salutation – wi' your bonnets aff, stand!

The MEN *line up bareheaded.*
The WOMEN *curtsey. The* PIPER *plays and leads them all back into the Castle.*

SCENE NINE

[LINDSAY, MCGLASS.]

They walk about the stage.

LINDSAY. Aye, Sandy, salutation. Tak your bonnet aff, stand!

MCGLASS. Did he kill Wamphray with his ain hands?

LINDSAY. Him or ane other. Of course, there is nae proof of it yet.

MCGLASS. Aye, but he will hae done it. And he receives his reward. 'Howbeit', I heard ye say, 'It is ane pleisand and agreeable thing to hear ye are at peace with Wamphray.' Man, what like of peace is ane treacherous murder, for I'll wager it was little else?

LINDSAY. Sandy, ye are gey direct. But it's no the path of wisdom. Now, consider it this fashion: The King set

Wamphray on to kill Armstrang, gif he could. But he couldna, you see, and frae the day it became clear that he cọuldna, he was nae langer the King's man. Armstrang taks his place, because Armstrang has murderit Wamphray. *Because*, no in spite of!

MCGLASS. And what way do you intend to ensure that this belovit murderer will keep his promises?

LINDSAY. His promises will be broke, Sandy, for Lord Maxwell will encourage it. I believe indeed Lord Maxwell is paid to encourage it by the English Ambassador.

MCGLASS. Unproven.

LINDSAY. Unproven, but gey probable. Though Gilnockie couldna conceivably credit it. The man's ancestors won Bannockburn for God's sake! Single-handit. Did ye never read it in the Chronicles? . . . Now: because our Lord Maxwell is paid by the English to prepare provocation for ane English invasion – *because*, no in spite of – he maun receive ane better bribe than even Armstrang.

MCGLASS. He has a taste for luxury, it seems. What like of bribe wad suit him?

LINDSAY. The destruction of his enemy? Lord Johnstone intil prison: what about that?

MCGLASS. Johnstone is ane leal subject. He is innocent of treason, Sir David.

LINDSAY. It is ane axiom of state that nae Baron is ever innocent. When Lord Johnstone hears of the death of his man Wamphray—

MCGLASS. Unproven.

LINDSAY. Aye, aye, unproven— When he hears of the death he will mak ane feud of vengeance: therefore for the better preservation of the safety of the King and the realm and the—

MCGLASS. Sir: I do nocht like this policy. It is the exaltation of blind flattery and dishonour—

LINDSAY. Blind. We *are* blind: we grope on a rocky road wi' sticks too short to reach our feet. What was it I said:

> To set myself upon ane man alive
> And turn his purposes and utterly win him?

I've no turnit them at all, Sandy. Johnny Armstrang's purposes remain precisely the samen as ever they had been – violent, proud, and abominable selfish.

MCGLASS. He is ane terrible Gogmagog, he is ane wild Cyclops of the mountain: begod he has baith his een – but hauf a tongue in the man's heid . . . Did ye listen to his Gaelic? I think we need to cut his throat.

LINDSAY. Ye ranten feuden Hieland Gallowglass – cut his throat! Cut Armstrang's, cut Eliot's, cut Maxwell's, cut Johnstone's – whaur do we stop? Na, na, but gang ane circuit – indirect, undermine the nobility; and we begin with the furthest distant, Johnstone. Set them a' to wonder what in the de'il's name we're playen at. I think our wee King will enjoy this business, Sandy. He was aye ane devious clever knave in the schoolroom. But no courageous. That's pity. We're at his palace. Blaw your horn.

MCGLASS *blows his bugle at the Palace.*

SCENE TEN

[LINDSAY, MCGLASS, PORTER.]

The PORTER *appears on the roof of the Palace.*

PORTER. Wha is it blaws his trump before King James's yett? Stand whaur ye are and show furth your business.

MCGLASS. Sir David Lindsay of the Mount, Lord Lyon King of Arms, craves ane audience with His Royal Grace upon matter of state and policy.

PORTER. His Grace is at all times attentive to the good services of Lord Lyon. Ye will be admittit upon the instant, sirs.

He descends from the roof.

LINDSAY. We maun dress oursel correctly, Sandy. A robe and a collar of gowd upon us to furnish counsel to the King.

The PORTER *comes out to them carrying* LINDSAY'S *robes of office.*

Aha, here we are: weel attirit for ane work of politic discretion.

He dresses himself.

MCGLASS. Sir David, ye hae forgot.

LINDSAY. Forgot what?

MCGLASS. Forgot the lady.

LINDSAY. Ah na, na. She is in Jeddart, ye tellt me.

MCGLASS. Aye, but she was to proceed to Gilnockie – she will be—

LINDSAY. She will be snug in ane house in Jeddart till we're done here and can send her word. Is the King at his leisure?

PORTER. He is, sir.

LINDSAY. Then we'll enter the presence, Mr McGlass.

MCGLASS. Sir David, at your hand.

They go off into the Palace.

Act Two

SCENE ONE

[EVANGELIST, MEG, LADY.]

The LADY *comes out of the Forest and walks about a little as though waiting for someone. She wears a travelling-cloak with a hood over her low-cut gown.*

MEG *comes running out of the Forest. She does not see the* LADY, *who withdraws behind a tree.* MEG's *clothes are all ragged and stained and her feet are bare.*

MEG. Whaur is he? Whaur are ye gaen, master? Come here, here. Aye, aye, we're alane here. It is ane richt solitaire place, here. And I will tell you ane secret.

The EVANGELIST *comes out of the Forest after her.*

EVANGELIST. What are ye, woman? Are ye ane gipsy? There are godless gipsies in Scotland in sair need of Jesu Christ, and I mysel am Christ's ain gipsy sent to exalt the sauls of the outcast folk and rebellious men of this forest. What gars ye look at me like that?

MEG. I am in dreid that ye will ravish me.

EVANGELIST. Ravish? Aye, I could. But no the fleshy body. Na, na, the immortal ghaist within it. I carry upon my worthless tongue twa words or three that will maist suddenly arrest and clarify the misconstruction of your life. Now hear this, woman. God did mak man in the image of His glory: therefore ilk ane of us is as it were ane God: but no yet manifest – our flame is as yet hid aneath the warldly bushel of expediency. Ye need nae wealth nor gifts of Princes for to cast it aff. Stand furth upon your ain, and brenn! The gipsies are God's people nae less than are the gentlemen –

let us begin with the gipsies and by the mercy of their conversion gar fire of glory rin thraeout the land—

MEG.

> Glory? Whatten glory? I think I will be sick.
> Master, ye carry ane muckle strang stick.
> It was ane stranger than that
> They did drive it far in
> For to harry the life
> Of the black corbie's nest.
> The puir corbie had ane wife.
> For to lig on her bare breist
> Was it her glory or his sin?
> She kens weel, she kens weel,
> He'll ne'er tread her again.

EVANGELIST. Why, certain you are nae gipsy. I think you maun be gentry. But distractit – forsaken? And what's this about the corbie? About bare breists, and – and – glory? I trow that you did yield yoursel up to ane unchaste lust and now ye feel the torment for it. Is that the truth, ye were concupiscent! Before we can expound the reformit faith here, we maun pray, woman, pray, for ane deep and grave repentance. Glory – nae glory of foul flesh. Cleanse it first, cleanse it; there will be nae atonement else—

LADY (*coming forward*). By what ordination of the Kirk are you appointit to be her confessor?

EVANGELIST (*whirling round*). By nae ordination but by common humanity. I am in dreid for this woman of the conflagrations of Satan.

The LADY's *cloak has fallen open, revealing her décolletage.*

Aye, and for you, too. Ye bear the appearance of ane frantic courtly vanity. Belike you are yet chaste and Christian: but in these wild woods, madam, the exposition of your secret parts is neither congruent nor godly. Are ye Rahab or Delilah that ye stand thus flamboyant in your lust?

LADY. Forgie me, sir, indeed. I had nae thocht to provoke you. Though ye seem gey provokable for ane man I had ne'er met till this aye minute. I am upon a journey that went astray in the bad weather, and I seek for the castle of the Armstrangs in Eskdale.

> MEG *gives a sudden cry and backs away, rolling and groaning* 'Armstrang, John Armstrang'. *The* LADY *goes to her and makes some effort to comfort her.*

What ails the lassie?

EVANGELIST. She suffers appropriate pain for her sin, that is all. I wad prefer ye no to speak to her. You are contaminate, like ane filthy honeypot.

MEG.

> John the Armstrang is to the hunten gaen
> Wi' his braid sword at his side
> And there he did meet with a nakit man
> Alane on the green hillside.
> And John John John he killt neither hart nor hind
> At the end of the day he hameward rade
> And never a drap of blood did fall
> Frae the tip of his nakit blade.

They had stroken it instead aboon the lintel of the house of Stobs. And that's whaur I did dwell – ance. But now it is whaurever I can find— Aye, gang ye to the Armstrangs, honeypot, and tell them that ye met me, whaurever. That's the word, is the word, whaurever . . .

> *She runs into the Forest.*

EVANGELIST. I will follow her.

LADY. Aye, I doubt ye will.

EVANGELIST. It is not meet she be without companion.

LADY. I think you are ane lecher.

EVANGELIST. Na, madam, na—

LADY. But ane lecher without carnality. Can ye no see the

improvement of her saul maun wait upon the strength of her body ? What do ye carry in your bottle ?

EVANGELIST. Sma' beer.

LADY. Then administer it, with charity. Bring her intil shelter and look that I hear ye do her nae scaith. I am of import in this kingdom, master, and I wadna care to see ye brocht before the Inquisitours. Awa' wi' ye, catch the lassie.

The EVANGELIST *runs off into the Forest after* MEG.

SCENE TWO

[LADY, MAID, FIRST ARMSTRONG.]

The LADY *walks about impatiently.*

LADY. Am I to haver in this forest until the dark comes over me ? Whaur are ye, burd – here!

Enter MAID, *breathless.*

MAID. Your pardon, madam, I had a' but lost my way. The lave of your people have gane forwart to the castle.

LADY. And nae message left in Jeddart – Sir David, in Jeddart, he left me nae message ?

MAID. Nae word at a', madam. He has travellit direct to the King, they tell me.

LADY. Then we hae little alternative but to seek Gilnockie's hospitality. For what it is worth. I doubt it will be barbarous.

They approach the Castle. The FIRST ARMSTRONG *appears at the gate.*

You are John o' Gilnockie's man ?

FIRST ARMSTRONG. Aye.

MAID. We hae come to his castle after Sir David Lindsay.

FIRST ARMSTRONG. He's nae here, but ye may enter. We're expecten him back within the month. Ye can bide till he comes. The Laird is hospitable, to the friends of his good friend.

LADY. I thank ye, sir, you are richt courteous.

She goes into the Castle.

FIRST ARMSTRONG. And what's *her* business wi' the King's Herald, hey?

MAID. She wad like fine to dance wi' him.

FIRST ARMSTRONG. Dance?

MAID. D'ye no jig to that like o' music here on the Border?

FIRST ARMSTRONG (*sings*). Och aye—

> She met wi' him in the kitchen
> Wi' the strae strewn on the flair,
> Beside the fire he laid her down
> His fingers in her hair.

MAID (*sings*).

> And first he pu'd the emerauds aff
> And then the diamonds bricht
> That hing upon her lovely halse:
> He didna need their licht!

They both laugh.

FIRST ARMSTRONG. That'll be an action to be seen in Gilnockie's kitchen, I can tell ye – come awa ben, my wee chanten burdie, there's good meat turns on the spit.

They enter the Castle, familiarly.

SCENE THREE

[LORD JOHNSTONE'S SECRETARY, LORD MAXWELL'S SECRETARY.]

LORD JOHNSTONE'S SECRETARY *enters from the Palace.*

LORD JOHNSTONE'S SECRETARY (*to audience*). I am the privy secretair to the Lord Johnstone of Johnstone. Here is ane evil time for all good men of nobility and lineage. My master has been wardit intil the Tolbooth prison at the order of the King: and nae good reason given.

LORD MAXWELL'S SECRETARY *enters from the Palace and stands by the door.*

That man there – I see him, he sees me – that man there, sirs, is the secretair of Lord Maxwell. Betwixt the houses of Maxwell and of Johnstone there has lang time been feud, but here today is true enormity. Sir!

LORD MAXWELL'S SECRETARY. Good day, sir. Ye are of Johnstone, are ye nocht?

LORD JOHNSTONE'S SECRETARY. As ye weel ken, sir. And you're of Maxwell.

LORD MAXWELL'S SECRETARY. My master commands me to tell ye, sir, that he has great grief at his heart for what has befell the Lord Johnstone this day; it is maist terrible to hear of.

LORD JOHNSTONE'S SECRETARY. God's Haly Cross, but are ye nocht ane hypocrite? It was at the device of your Lord Maxwell that my master has been wardit; it is bootless to pretend other. Can ye deny, sir, but that there is news frae the Border that Lord Johnstone's vassal and kinsman, Johnstone of Wamphray, rade to the hunten and nocht but his horse cam hame? And what man was it killt him?

LORD MAXWELL'S SECRETARY. Belike ane Armstrang or ane Eliot. He was at feud with baith of them, it matters little whilk.

LORD JOHNSTONE'S SECRETARY. Ye do admit it?

LORD MAXWELL'S SECRETARY. Why nocht? It is apparent. But ye do Lord Maxwell wrang, to credit that he condones sic murder at the hands of his vassals.

LORD JOHNSTONE'S SECRETARY. Then why is my Lord in the Tolbooth? Because the King has determinit, by the advice of David Lindsay, to concede to Johnny Armstrang a'thing that he demands: and that includes protection frae the just vengeancy of the Johnstones anent his wicked murder. Armstrang is Maxwell's man: and there is occult collusion here betwixt Lindsay and Maxwell. Maxwell craves ane absolute auctority ower every laird upon the South-West Border—

LORD MAXWELL'S SECRETARY. And what does Lindsay crave?

LORD JOHNSTONE'S SECRETARY. Aye, ane good question. I have nae clearness whatever about the motivations of Lindsay.

LORD MAXWELL'S SECRETARY. And neither has Lord Maxwell. Lindsay has persuadit His Royal Grace that your master is a danger to the kingdom.

LORD JOHNSTONE'S SECRETARY. I had rather say a danger to the Armstrangs.

LORD MAXWELL'S SECRETARY. Ah. Ye havena heard?

LORD JOHNSTONE'S SECRETARY. Heard what?

LORD MAXWELL'S SECRETARY. Why, man, the Armstrangs *are* the kingdom! Lindsay has had Gilnockie made Lieutenant of the Border and sole Warden of Eskdale!

LORD JOHNSTONE'S SECRETARY. He has had him made—

LORD MAXWELL'S SECRETARY. Aye! He is an Officer, ane Officer of sae strang ane title that it rins directly counter, sir, to the hereditary privileges of Maxwell his Lord.

LORD JOHNSTONE'S SECRETARY. But – but what is Lindsay's purpose, sir, what d'ye think can be his—

SCENE FOUR

[LORD JOHNSTONE'S SECRETARY, LORD MAXWELL'S SECRETARY, *the* CARDINAL'S SECRETARY.]

The CARDINAL'S SECRETARY *enters from the Palace. He is a Dominican Friar.*

CARDINAL'S SECRETARY. I will expound to ye his purpose, gentlemen. The Blessen of God be upon ye baith, and the Haly Sancts of Heaven assist your deliberations. I represent the Cardinal Archbishop of Sanct Andrews. I will declare to ye for your recollection some portion of that severe and solemn curse late set by His Grace the Archbishop of Glasgow upon the common traitors and thieves that wad break the peace of the Border. The Lord Archbishop said: 'I curse their heid and all the hairs of their heid: I curse their face, their een, their mouth, their neise, their tongue, their teeth, their crag, their shoulders, their breist, their heart, their wame, before and behind, within and without. I curse them gangen, I curse them riden, I curse them standen, I curse them sitten, and finally I condemn them perpetually to the deep pit of hell, there to remain, with Lucifeir and all his fellaws.' For of necessity, gentlemen, peace between Christian realms is mair than mere expedience: it is commandit by the Kirk on peril of your salvation. And how, sirs, do we obtain that peace? Assuredly, by maken strang the kingdom, by placen trust in the hereditary Lords that administer the lands upon the marches – your master, sir, and yours: trust that they will refuse all temptation to ride in quest of private booty, trust that they will refrain frae murderous feud baith among themselves and their vassals: and last, but dearest to the hearts of all religious men, trust that they will stand ever ane firm and constant bastion against the spread of devilish heresy.

LORD MAXWELL'S SECRETARY. Heresy, sir?

LORD JOHNSTONE'S SECRETARY. Heresy? Ach, this is plain irrelevance – the man is ane fanatic meddler; let us leave him for God's sake—

CARDINAL'S SECRETARY. Gentlemen, gif ye please! I represent the Cardinal. And I was about to speak of Lindsay.

LORD MAXWELL'S SECRETARY. Aye, sir, what of Lindsay?

CARDINAL'S SECRETARY. First, he is ane adulterer. He hath

ane open paramour. I believe he even sent for her to accompany him on his embassage to the Armstrangs.

LORD JOHNSTONE'S SECRETARY. There is nae man in the Court that hasna had a paramour ae time or anither – why, the King himsel—

CARDINAL'S SECRETARY. Wait. Sir David Lindsay is alsweel ane man of maist remarkable intellect. He is ane clever makar of libidinous poetry, he has writ baith plays and pungent satires: and they are, in great part, contrair the excellence and supremacy of the Kirk. Ye were aware of this?

LORD MAXWELL'S SECRETARY. Of course.

CARDINAL'S SECRETARY. And this is the man the King has sent to safeguard the English Border? What wark does King Henry Tudor pursue within that Border at this present? I will tell ye, sirs: he does defy our Haly Father the Pape – and upon ane matter of adultery forbye.

LORD JOHNSTONE'S SECRETARY. Do ye mean to imply then that Lindsay is ane heretic? Do ye put the name of Luther on him, sir?

CARDINAL'S SECRETARY. Na, na, I wadna speak sae strang as that. Were he indeed ane Luther, the Cardinal wad barely have sufferit his extent the length he has. Na, na, we think he is but moderate. He is nae Luther yet. Likewise we think the King of England is, as yet, nae Luther: but ane sair misguidit bairn of Christ, whose cruel procedures in his realm can some day lead to Luther unless they be preventit.

LORD MAXWELL'S SECRETARY. What ye wad say, I think, sir, is in effect this: ane English aspect of religion and ane Scots aspect of policy are scarce compatible, even in a man of sae subtle a mind as Lindsay.

CARDINAL'S SECRETARY. Scarce compatible. Ane just word for it. Scarce. I wadna put it nearer than that, but—

LORD JOHNSTONE'S SECRETARY. Ye wadna? Then *I* wad. Gif Lindsay is ane heretic, by God he is ane traitor. His intentions are manifest – to mak feeble the defences of the

Border by the irruption of feud and disharmony amangst the noblemen that protect it. Hence Lord Johnstone in the Tolbooth, and after him, Lord Maxwell – whaur? The gallows? There sticks in my mind ane thing alsweel. Flodden. That dolorous field wad ne'er hae been lost had our last King James fand mair support amang his ministers. He had ane flock of faint-heart croakers at his back when he set furth to battle, and Lindsay was their principal.

LORD MAXWELL'S SECRETARY. And James the Fift, his son is but ane schoolboy still and still in dreid his umwhile tutor will command him bend his hurdies for the tawse.

LORD JOHNSTONE'S SECRETARY. He maun stand like a man, and stand like a King, with his hinder parts decently coverit, and defer his policy to naebody.

CARDINAL'S SECRETARY. Excepten ever to the Haly Kirk of Christ. Sir David Lindsay, they tell us, is maist zealous in his quality as Lyon King of Arms. Weel, sae that's his function. Let him keep to it.

A trumpet off and cries of 'Long live the King!'

The King gaes to the Abbey Kirk to hear Mass. We had best attend our masters.

LORD JOHNSTONE'S SECRETARY. Attend our masters. For me, I find but small security of employment while this new abundant tyranny of the King obtains towart his barons. Howbeit, sirs, we are agreed upon our policy. Maxwell and Johnstone are nae longer at ane enmity.

He shakes hands with LORD MAXWELL'S SECRETARY.

LORD MAXWELL'S SECRETARY. Ane blessit and Christlike conclusion. What do you say to it, sir?

CARDINAL'S SECRETARY. What should I say? I represent the Cardinal. Amen, therefore, and Benedicite.

LORD MAXWELL'S SECRETARY *and* CARDINAL'S SECRETARY *go off.*

SCENE FIVE

[LORD JOHNSTONE'S SECRETARY, LINDSAY, MCGLASS, *the* KING *and* ATTENDANTS.]

LINDSAY *and* MCGLASS *come out of the Palace.*

LORD JOHNSTONE'S SECRETARY. Sir David: Lord Maxwell and my master are nae langer at enmity.

LINDSAY. Hoho? . . . The cause of it nae doubt is the great grief Lord Maxwell feels for the misfortune of Lord Johnstone.

LORD JOHNSTONE'S SECRETARY. They tell me he is maist easily moved to tears for his fellow men in tribulation.

LORD JOHNSTONE'S SECRETARY *goes into Palace.*

LINDSAY. And nae news yet frae Jeddart? God, gif I had her here, I wad set her to lie with Maxwell. For how else can we bribe him now? This means he doth oppose Gilnockie's Lieutenantship. The King is in dreid of him and will undertake what he demands. Gilnockie will repudiate the agreement he has made with us. I think we had best advise the King to put Maxwell intil prison, on the ground of his suspectit intercourse with the English Ambassador, and thereby discredit his honour as a Scot. Sure, after that, Gilnockie wad consider him a'thegither unworthy his continuit obedience.

MCGLASS. Maxwell has ower-mony strang confederates – Bothwell, Buccleuch, the Douglases – the King wad never daur to ward him, Sir David.

LINDSAY. Wad he no? Belike. But we will yet find ane answer. Gif we canna destroy the mickle lords, we maun build up the lesser. As for example, the victor of Bannockburn . . . God, gif I had her here, I wad lie with her this minute. Sandy, we will be late for Mass.

The KING *is carried across the stage in a palanquin. He wears his full regalia and is followed by the* SECRETARIES *from the previous scene (and any other extras available).* LINDSAY *and* MCGLASS *join the procession and exeunt. Cries of* 'Long live the King!'

SCENE SIX

[LADY, MAID.]

LADY *and* MAID *enter from the Castle.*

LADY. And nae word yet frae Lindsay?

MAID. Nane at a', madam.

LADY. And for how long does he expect me to wait his leisure here? It seems that he regards me as his luggage, ane marriet burgess-wife, nae less: and yet he puts upon himself the style of poet.

MAID. He is alsweel ane politician, madam. The King's business is gey exigent and nae doubt requires great courage.

LADY. Impertinent. Ye are forbid to mak mock of his courage, burd. He has that in good measure – it's no his courage, it's his love. I'm nae jimp and rose-wand lassie ony langer – I'm hauf-gate on to be ane auld wrunkled carline, laithsome to the sicht of his een and the caress of his fingers – aye, and the snuff of his nostrils alsweel, I wadna wonder.

MAID. The snuff of his nostrils?

LADY. What else wad ye expect? I hae been dwellen all these weeks in the castle of Gilnockie. I canna describe it as the maist salubrious hall in Scotland. We're a' fair stinkards now, burd: me, you, and every servant I've got left. We're as nasty as the Armstrangs.

MAID. What for will ye no gang back to Edinburgh, madam?

LADY. What for? For David Lindsay, that's what for. Meet me, says he, upon the door-stane of John Armstrang. And

that's whaur I am – and by God I will abide here. Ach, he'll
come back, he'll mind whaur he's left me – he canna dae
without me. When all's told, the chief purpose of the man's
life is naething less than me. Lindsay is ane poet. His lady is
his existence. He has sworn it to me, burd, ane unremittit
aith, wi' the tears upon his cheek-bane.

GILNOCKIE'S WIFE *comes out of the Castle.*

Here's our good hostess. Slender she is, pale, discontentit:
why? She has ane man in her bed like a lion, and eneuch
English beer and beef in her storehouse to fill her as fat as
Potiphar's wife. Good day to ye, lady.

SCENE SEVEN

[LADY, MAID, GILNOCKIE'S WIFE.]

GILNOCKIE'S WIFE. Good day to ye, madam. Hae ye heard
word yet frae Sir David Lindsay? Is he to come again
presently to Eskdale?
LADY. Is he indeed? The King's business is gey exigent.
GILNOCKIE'S WIFE. Aye, but the confirmation of Gilnockie's
title? Gilnockie wad speir gif the title of Lieutenant be truly
his or no. Sir David gave his promise.
LADY. Then the King will surely keep it for him.
GILNOCKIE'S WIFE. Aye, but ye see, Gilnockie doesna
entirely trust the King. For why should he? He was five
times postit rebel: and officers sent against him: he has had
embargo made upon his land and goods – are you yoursel
acquent with the King, madam?
LADY. I was weel acquent with his father.
GILNOCKIE'S WIFE. His father?
LADY. Begod I slept in his bed.

GILNOCKIE'S WIFE. His bed? You did that?

LADY. I was but fifteen years auld at the time: but it was a kind of glory for me.

GILNOCKIE'S WIFE. How lang hae ye been the paramour of Lindsay?

LADY. Lang eneuch, madam, for what I've gotten out of it.

GILNOCKIE'S WIFE. He hath ane wife.

LADY. He hath.

GILNOCKIE'S WIFE. And what like of woman is she?

LADY. She did aspire in the warld at the same time that he did. She was ane seamstress of the Court, and obscure – as he too was obscure, bean but ane schoolmaster to the bairns of the nobility. They havena dwelt thegither for ane lang lang time. Sir David had a taste for mair wantonness in a wife than she could provide, and less stateliness of social port. She wad walk like ane Archdeacon up the length of the Canongate frae the palace to the kirk, and she was as dour and rectilinear as the stanes she set her feet on.

MAID. Mickle feet forbye.

LADY. Hauld yer whist, burd: I tellt ye, ye are impertinent.

GILNOCKIE'S WIFE. Madam, amang the ladies of Edinboro and Linlithgow, are there mony like yoursel?

LADY. And how d'ye mean, *like*?

GILNOCKIE'S WIFE. I mean, with nae reck of the vows of marriage – nae shame to be keepit mistress by a man that was weddit in kirk till ane other. I crave your pardon, madam, I intend nae offence. It is indeed strange for us here in the rural places to be told of these things. Gif I were to be fause to Gilnockie, I think that he wad kill me.

LADY. And gif he were fause to you?

GILNOCKIE'S WIFE. Aye, gif he were . . . Whiles, madam, he *is*. But wi' the lasses frae the tenant farms, or the tinker women upon the moss, or when he brenns ane house of the English. He wad never swyve a lady. Haly Peter, it is inconceivable. But you yoursel, madam, you are ane manifest lady, ye've had ane good education – I doubt you are capable of baith the Latin and the French—

MAID. Aye – and Greek and Gaelic.

GILNOCKIE'S WIFE. There was a strange man cam hither thrae the forest, he spak to us of Jesus Christ and the Testament, and of the New Religions in Germany: how the priests of our ain Kirk are the foretold Anti-Christ and how by penitence and martyrdom we can yet again recapture that liberty of God and of virtue that has lang syne departit frae the warld. Gilnockie said he was ane heretic: but Sir David gave him counsel it were better he should loose him and let him gang.

LADY. I ken the man ye mean.

GILNOCKIE'S WIFE. Madam, it was my opinion that he is ane godly pastor and he has indeed been grantit ane vision of divinity.

LADY. Aye – belike, belike, but—

GILNOCKIE'S WIFE. And I trow he would look gey unkindly upon the adultery you keep with Lindsay Delamont. I will tell ye this, madam, there was a lassie upon this border, she lay with a man outwith the bond of wedlock – and what befell her then?

LADY. What did befall her, madam?

GILNOCKIE'S WIFE. She was casten out by her folk: they did sparr up their yetts against her: and the strength of her body was broke by the cruel blaws of her father's whip. It was ane just chastisement: she had brocht shame upon his house. Forebye the shame was mine alsweel: Her father was my ain brither, madam.

LADY. What was her name?

GILNOCKIE'S WIFE. She was the dochter of the Laird of Stobs. And whaur is now the man that had her? I said whaur is he now? He sprawls beneath a bracken bush and there will be ane sair vengeance for him yet upon the heid of Gilnockie because of this murder. Here is Gilnockie.

SCENE EIGHT

[GILNOCKIE, *his* WIFE, LADY, MAID, *the* FIRST ARM-STRONG.]

Enter GILNOCKIE *from the Castle. He is wearing a new collar of gold links.*

GILNOCKIE. Murder.

GILNOCKIE'S WIFE. Gilnockie, I didna tell her. I wadna hae said to her, I wad never hae—

GILNOCKIE. What murder?

LADY. Your good wife, sir, was maintainen her discourse upon the great respect ye hauld in these parts for the virginity of your young women. And upon the bitter punition accordit to the seducers thereof. Is there ocht wrang in that, sir?

GILNOCKIE. Punition no wrang. Aye: bitter. Ye are ane courteous whoor. Extradinair. Lindsay's. When does he come?

LADY. That, sir, I canna tell ye.

GILNOCKIE. I should be Officer. Lieutenant! I hae pit up the title. Had made to me the chain. Whaur's confirmation?

GILNOCKIE'S WIFE. Surely, John, it will be sent soon. Lindsay is ane trustable man.

GILNOCKIE. Lindsay? To trust him? Ach, he did trust Johnny. Because that I said I had made peace with Wamphray. Murder. What murder?

LADY. It was but in general talk, sir.

GILNOCKIE (*indicating his wife*). Na. I heard her greet.

He jerks his thumb towards the Castle.

Ben.

GILNOCKIE'S WIFE. Gilnockie.

GILNOCKIE. Ben. Or I'll spin your blood.

GILNOCKIE'S WIFE *goes into the Castle.*

LADY. Sir, you're no wise to be sae ungentle to your wife. She doth love ye, sir, and gif she be timorous it is for your ain safety.

GILNOCKIE. Wha's ungentle? (*To the* MAID.) You. You're wantit within. Willie wants ye.

MAID. I fail to understand ye, sir.

GILNOCKIE. Understand me damn weel. Willie.

The FIRST ARMSTRONG *appears at the Castle gate.*

Tak her ben and steer her. Gif that's what she wants. She has, I guess, sufferit it at your hands hereto – heretofore.

MAID. Gilnockie, I am in attendance here upon my lady. I'm no to be matit at your will to ony man in your service.

GILNOCKIE. Then ye needna be bloody matit. But get out of this place. Willie: I'm on my lane!

FIRST ARMSTRONG. I hear ye, Gilnockie. Come awa, lassie. Sharp. The Laird wad be private.

He takes the MAID *into the Castle.*

SCENE NINE

[GILNOCKIE, LADY.]

GILNOCKIE. Gey private. Tak your claithes aff.

LADY. What?

GILNOCKIE. Here. I want to see your flesh. Aye, and maintain it with infusion of mine. Johnny's the man. They never refuse to Johnny. Tak 'em aff.

She draws a little penknife and points it at him as he tries to embrace her. She is laughing, and he laughs, too, as he disengages himself.

Aha, ha. But you *are* ane whoor?

LADY. I'm no *your* whoor.

GILNOCKIE. But whoor, it is common. Is for a' men. Is for me.

He advances upon her again, more menacingly.

I could. I could violate.

LADY. In your ain castle, Johnny? I belang to the King's Herald: why, man, it wad be treason. And d'ye imagine he wad bring ye the Officership after that?

GILNOCKIE. He wad kill for ye? Lindsay? Mak ane murder? Wad he?

LADY. I canna tell ye that. I've never kent he had cause for it.

GILNOCKIE. For, gif he wad. He is maist honourable. For honour of ane whoor to kill ane gentleman. Honour of ane poet's whoor. Ane Herald-of-the-King's whoor. As ye micht say it, he wad comprehend his obligation. Obligation of honour is the thrust of ane pike, herein, here— (*He touches his heart.*) David Lindsay is ane Herald. He wad therefore comprehend.

LADY. Ah, Johnny, Johnny, my strang and beautiful Johnny, you are observit. And with great disappointment, sir. I trowit that ye had conceivit ane instant desire of love towart me, or lust if nae better, and even lust wad flatter me. You are ane lovely lion to roar and leap, and sure wad rarely gratify all submissive ladies beneath the rampancy of your posture. You are indeed heraldic, sir. Emblazonit braid in flesh and blood, whereas David Lindsay can but do it with pen and pencil upon his slender parchment. I did deny ye your demand this minute because ye were baith rude and rapid: but had ye thereupon attemptit ane mair gradual kindlen of my body, ye micht damn weel hae had me, sir, beneath this very tree.

GILNOCKIE. Aha . . .

LADY. But, Gilnockie. Ye hae been observit. Rude and rapid, aye, but devious alsweel. What ye desirit was never in principle me, it was the proof of the jealousy of Lindsay. For gif Lindsay were to hauld the possession of his paramour, ane manifest harlot, as matter for gravest honour: then what way could he condemn you for the murder of – of Wamphray, is the name? Whilk murder, as I guess, bean to avenge ane lost chastity. But ye are in dreid it has been discoverit, and ye willna get your Royal Pardon.

GILNOCKIE. Pardon! John the Armstrang in dreid for ane Pardon!

LADY. And for why nocht? Ye wadna hae me credit ye attach sae mickle import to the wearen of a gilt collar and the title of Lieutenant—

GILNOCKIE. Whist! You mak an abominable roaring with your mou! Clap it close. Like that.

He closes her lips with his fingers. He lets them remain there longer than would seem needful, to which she does not object. Then he stands back a pace sharply: and unhooks his sword-belt.

Here is ane brand. Aff.

He drops belt and sword on the stage.

Here's a gilt collar and ane title. Aff.

He throws his collar down.

Here is ane buft jacket of defence. Aff.

He strips off his buff coat.

Here is my gully. Out.

He pulls his knife out of the top of his trunk-hose and drops it.

I'm in my sark and my breeks wi' nae soldiers, nae horses. As there were nae soldiers wi' David Lindsay, when he stood before my yett. Am accoutrit convenient for ane passage of love. Or for execution. Or for what else? Ane Pardon? Gif the King himsel were here I wad never beg his Pardon. I wad demand: bot defence, bot threatenens, bot alliances: I wad

demand he saw me as ane man, that he wad accord me
recognition thereas, and that he wad give me as ane man
a'thing he could conceive that it were possible I did deserve.
And what do I deserve? Ye have ane answer. Speak it.
Speak.

LADY. John, ye do deserve to be ane equal man with ony King
in Christianity.

GILNOCKIE. In Eskdale. Nae place else. I am maist moderate.
I'm nane of your presumptuous Lothian-men, ye ken. Eskdale and Liddesdale alane, that appertain towards John
Armstrang; they are my kingdom, and I content therein my
people with the justice of my government. And my government in this small region is ane bastion for the hale of Scotland. The man that strives to pit down Armstrang is the man
that means to bring in England, whether his name be
Johnstone or Lindsay or even Stuart. They do presume to
bribe my honour with their pardons and their titles: and then
they do delay – d'ye note – in the fulfilment of their fearful
bribes. And they do justify this delay by scandalous talk of
unproven murder. They wad gain ane better service out of
Armstrang gif they were to cease to demand it as ane service:
and instead to request it – d'ye hear the word, request – to
request it in humility as ane collaborate act of good friendship and fraternal warmth!

LADY. Why, Johnny, whaur's your lockit tongue? Ye do
deliver me these maist clear words as vehement as ane mill-
wheel, Johnny. This is the first ae time ye hae been heard to
utter without ane weir of tree-trunks across your teeth. And
what has causit it, sir?

GILNOCKIE. You.

LADY. Aye, me—
    When I stand in the full direction of your force
    Ye need nae wife nor carl to stand
    Alsweel beside ye and interpret.
    There is in me ane knowledge, potent, secret,

That I can set to rin ane sure concourse
Of bodily and ghaistly strength betwixt the blood
Of me and of the starkest man alive. My speed
Hangs twin with yours: and starts ane double flood:
Will you with me initiate the deed
And saturatit consequence thereof—?
Crack aff with your great club
The barrel-hoops of love
And let it pour
Like the enchantit quern that boils red-herring broo
Until it gars upswim the goodman's table and his door
While all his house and yard and street
Swill reeken, greasy, het, oer-drownit sax-foot fou—

GILNOCKIE. Red-herring broo—

LADY. In the pot. On the fire. All the warm sliden fishes,
Johnny, out of the deep of the sea, guttit and filletit and weel-
rubbit with sharp onion and the rasp of black pepper . . .

*He leads her into the Forest. As they walk he unbuttons and
casts off her mantle, her scarf, and the tire from her head.*

SCENE TEN

[LINDSAY, MAID, MCGLASS.]

LINDSAY *appears on the roof of the Palace.*

LINDSAY. I wad never claim that I had in ony way foreseen or
contrivit this particular development. Gif I had, I wad hae
been ane pandar.

The MAID *comes out of the Castle, humming a tune.*

To the base lusts and deficiencies of humanity. The material
of my craft, in fact. Accept them, mak use of them, for
God's sake enjoy them – here is a wee maid that expresses

her enjoyment in the music of ane sang. She is betrothit to my secretair: she has just been coverit by Armstrang's man: and Armstrang himsel at this moment is coveren— Ach, the deil wi' it!

MAID (*sings*).

> It was upon a day of spring
> Before the leaves were green and fair
> They led me frae my mither's house
> And bad me serve them evermair.
> Beneath the sun that in summer did shine
> And amang the rows of the harvest corn
> The young men took me in their rankit line
> Ilk ane of them of a woman born.

She begins to pick up the various articles of dress and other gear left on the stage by GILNOCKIE *and the* LADY, *and puts them in two piles.*

> Till autumn cam in grief and pain
> And the leaves fell down across the lea:
> There was naething left for me to fulfil,
> But to gather them up maist diligently
> Intil their piles like kirkyard graves –
> The snaws of December, the frost and the gloom
> Will utterly bury them after their pride,
> Deep-buried and frozen, and endit their bloom.

MCGLASS *comes out of the Palace.*

LINDSAY. Mr McGlass, ye maun gang on your lane to Eskdale. I canna leave the Court at this stage of the business.

MCGLASS. Will the King arrest Maxwell?

LINDSAY *shakes his head.*

Your circuit was a yard or twae ower-large belike. A wee King needs but a wee circuit to confine him. We wad dae better to serve the King of England.

LINDSAY. McGlass, ye talk treason.

MCGLASS. Aye. And what am I to talk to Gilnockie?

LINDSAY. Ye are to talk of the increase of Armstrang for the better reduction of Maxwell. And talk of it with tact. Forget ye are ane Hielandman. Jacob, Sandy, never Esau – let Gilnockie be your Esau. God gang with ye.

LINDSAY *retires.* MCGLASS *comes across the stage to the* MAID.

SCENE ELEVEN

[MAID, MCGLASS.]

MCGLASS. *Mo ghaol, Mo ghràdh, mo thasgaidh*[1] – Sir David sends ye his gallant salutation.

MAID. Belatit.

MCGLASS. Whaur's the lady?

MAID. It is ane question.

MCGLASS (*looking at the piles of clothes*). Aha. She wadna bide in Jedburgh. There were nae men there sufficient large for her capacity? Gilnockie's brand. And his coat forbye. Whaur's his breeks?

MAID. I doubt they are nae langer on his shanks.

MCGLASS. And your shanks? Sin ye arrivit in this place I canna believe that they've seen nae service as ane saft nakit ladder for the ascent of some strange venturer? Ah weel, it was to be expectit, was it no? The King did require Lindsay to win Gilnockie's purposes – belike the lady will succeed whaur the politician fails.

MAID. Fails?

MCGLASS. Aye. There is nae office whatever now for the decoration of John Armstrang – this collar here will signify him naething while Maxwell and Lindsay stand at ilk side of

[1] My sweet sparrow, my love, my delight.

the King's Grace, aye tuggen at his lugs, left hand and richt hand, till the sacred Crown of Scotland is near to tumble like a – like a ninepin. Howbeit, as I said, maybe, out of this . . . (*He twirls the* LADY'*s head-tire in his fingers.*) . . . will we contrive some mair sanguine conclusion. For what reason does she lie with him? For lust, for generosity, for admiration of his strength – or for ane dutiful and politic assistance of Sir David? Gif it were the last—

MAID. Gif it were the last, she were ane true harlot, Sandy, ane prostitute of state: and nae mair worthy of your master's devotion than the bitter wife he had already. My lady is awa with Armstrong because Armstrang is what he is. Gif that be sufficient for her, ye should crave no further reason. Ye decline to speir ower-closely intil *my* behaviour in this castle: it was, ye said – expectit. Let Sir David accord ane equal trust towart her, and she will wark him nae treason. She hath her ain honour.

MCGLASS. As hath Gilnockie. Ha, here be gentlemen.

SCENE TWELVE

[STOBS, YOUNG STOBS, MCGLASS, MAID.]

The two ELIOTS *enter through the Forest. Their hands are on their sword-hilts.*

MCGLASS. Good day to ye, sirs.

STOBS. Good day.

MCGLASS. Ye seek Gilnockie?

YOUNG STOBS. Aye.

MCGLASS. He's no here at the present.

YOUNG STOBS. We'll bide his arrival. What's your name?

MCGLASS. McGlass.

STOBS. Ye are ane Hielandman. A King's rat. I'll put my foot upon ye, ratten. Whae's the burd? She's yours?

MAID. She's naebody's but her ain. Ye have the tongue of a
carl and ane auld carl forbye. Learn some courtesy, gif ye
can; ye are dressit like a gentleman, but your manners are
scarce concomitant.

STOBS. They are the manners of the country, lassie, and the
country's no yours. Sae adapt yoursel with speed, or else
haud your whist.

YOUNG STOBS. Will I clap her across the mou and haud it
for her, father?

STOBS. Ye will nocht. We are within Gilnockie's boundaries
and we'll leave her to him.

YOUNG STOBS. Frae what I hear, Gilnockie's dislike of
vermin in his house is no sae strang as it used to be.

STOBS. That's eneuch o' that, boy. Gilnockie is wed to my
sister. He has benefit of our good opinion until sic time as
it is proven misplacit. When does the Laird come back? I'm
talking to you!

MCGLASS. I'm no in his confidence. He will be back when he
comes.

MAID. He will be back directly, sir . . . he's here.

SCENE THIRTEEN

[GILNOCKIE, LADY, MAID, MCGLASS, STOBS, YOUNG
STOBS.]

GILNOCKIE *and the* LADY *come out of the Forest, walking
amorously, unbraced and dishevelled. When he sees the*
ELIOTS, GILNOCKIE *lets go of her. The* MAID *hands her her
clothes, etc.*

GILNOCKIE. Ah. Gilbert.

STOBS. Aye. It's Gilbert.

GILNOCKIE. Martin. (*To the women.*) Ben the house. I'll call
for ye. You, sir, gang your gate within.

MCGLASS. I will attend you, sir.

LADY (*aside to* MCGLASS). Whaur's Lindsay?

MCGLASS (*aside*). Edinburgh.

LADY. Ah . . .

Exeunt the LADY, *her* MAID, *and* MCGLASS *into the Castle.*

SCENE FOURTEEN

[GILNOCKIE, STOBS, YOUNG STOBS.]

GILNOCKIE. Gilbert—

STOBS. John.

GILNOCKIE. There is ane matter here. Is delicate.

STOBS. Aye. The day we put our blades in Wamphray he did croak ane word towarts me. He said, 'Speir at Johnny Armstrang, what betidit with his honour?' Ye are Lieutenant, are ye no? Ye are King's Warden, are ye no? And what Royal rank, then, is accordit to the Eliots? Can ye gie us the answer to that, Johnny? I wad like fine to hear ye try.

GILNOCKIE. The King of Scotland, Gibby, daurna fecht wi' me. Nor wi' you, neither. He daurna fecht wi' Eskdale: nor Liddesdale: nor Teviot. Is that agreed?

STOBS. Gif James Stuart were to levy war against us, it wad be ane sair war for the realm, and he kens that, aye, his generals ken it, and his captains: his soldiers wadna march. Our castles upon this border are impregnable, and we dwell here, and we hae dwelt, and we will dwell for ay in our ain strang integrity. Therefore, John, what's this?

He has picked up the collar.

Good brother, ye maun justify to me.

YOUNG STOBS. Aye and to me.

STOBS. Martin: I said be silent. Here is matter for the chiefs. Ye maun justify. Can ye dae it?

GILNOCKIE. We grant us then impregnable. But whilk is better: impregnable as ane outlaw – baith back to the Scots and front to the English to fecht? Or as ane friend of Scotland, be impregnable: against English alane? Gibby, we can wear the King's collar. Can tell to the King, we do serve his banner. Are nae subjects, but Officers. Ane like collar for the Eliots alsweel. And yet we fecht the English. Yet we can ride: derive our prey out of England: defend the realm: is glory, Gibby. Is greater glory than here – than hereto – heretofore.

YOUNG STOBS. Nae subjects, but Officers. I canna tell the difference. Ane officer maun obey commandment; when did ye ever hear of ane Eliot that wad obey?

STOBS. At this aye minute: or I'll split your crag, boy. Gif we are the King's Officers, we maun obey him: will he pay for that obedience?

GILNOCKIE. Is possible. Ane honourable pension—

STOBS. Aye. But he may default on it. What when we need mair kye? There's good kye across in England, we canna grip them because of the King's word. But suppose the English were to start ane war themselves? Suppose they were to brenn a goodman's house in Liddesdale? What then?

GILNOCKIE. We can then ride. Defence of the Realm. Ane just reprisal for enormity.

STOBS. Ane English provocation and ane necessair response thereto. The braw Lieutenant levies mèn, and fills his byres forbye. Martin, expound to the Laird what we have in our mind this day.

YOUNG STOBS. The neist full moon, Gilnockie, it's three nichts beyont the present Sabbath. We can bring ye five and twenty riders— To the south of Carlisle there is a kirk and a wee town o' the name of Salkeld.

GILNOCKIE. Salkeld. I'm no familiar. We will require ane guide.

YOUNG STOBS. We have a rogue at Stobs this minute wad

tell us the Cumberland trackways – aye and conduct us thereacross. Does it seem to you practicable, Gilnockie?

GILNOCKIE. Practicable.

STOBS. Then ye will ride?

GILNOCKIE. Whaur's the provocation?

STOBS. Ah, d'ye hear him, Martin, the Lieutenant has his conscience. Weel: Mickle Sim of the Mains hasna paid me his blackmail this twelvemonth past. So neist week he wakes at midnicht and finds his roof on fire. Wha's brent it? A dozen hoodit riders wi' English badges on their coats: and there's your provocation. Sufficient for ye, Johnny?

GILNOCKIE. Ach, ha: I canna tell. Is delicate. Ane sort of cruelty belike. To brenn a Scotsman's roof, and lay the wyte of it on the English. In time past he has, has Mickle Sim, rade bravely at our backs. Consonant. Can we call it consonant?

STOBS. Consonant wi' what?

GILNOCKIE. With honour, Stobs. There is in this –

He takes hold of the collar.

– ane honour. Howsoe'er we may regard it. Gey delicate. I canna tell.

STOBS. John: we are auld companions, and Janet Eliot is your wife. Stobs and Gilnockie thegither: aye, sin we were bairns. What consonancy of honour was it laid ye in the arms of that harlot of the Court before the barbican of your ain castle, and my sister within it? I did peer with my good steel into the red wame of Wamphray for what he did to my dochter. It is but for ancient friendship alane I hae sparit your life this day. And ye haver with me now upon resumption of that friendship? Ye hae but the ae choice, Johnny: ride wi' the Eliots, or die like a Johnstone. I will in and see my sister: I will mak nae mention in her presence of ony ither woman: and when ye hae decidit, inform me of your will. Ye ca' this matter delicate. Aye, it *is* delicate – it is as delicate indeed as the hale reputation of your name. Armstrang is ane name I wad be richt laith to forget.

He and his son enter the Castle.

SCENE FIFTEEN

[GILNOCKIE, MCGLASS.]

GILNOCKIE *stands for a moment, toying with the collar. Then* MCGLASS *enters on the roof of the Castle. They look at each other.*

GILNOCKIE. Whaur's Lindsay? He said he wad come back. That he wad bring me confirmation. I've had made me the chain. Confirmation: hae ye brocht it?

MCGLASS. I hae brocht ye ane tidings that will emancipate your joy: Lord Johnstone is in prison.

GILNOCKIE. For what?

MCGLASS. For prevention of feud in pursuance of the death of Wamphray.

GILNOCKIE. What death? Wha killt him? Wamphray? When? Obscure, ye are obscure . . . Lord Johnstone to the black corbies: in the face of Lord Johnstone I spew. Am I Lieutenant or no!

MCGLASS. No.

GILNOCKIE. Come down here.

MCGLASS *retires from the roof.* GILNOCKIE *puts the collar on the end of his sword blade. When* MCGLASS *comes out of the Castle he holds this out at him.*

Young man, will ye tak it. For me, I've nae entitlement. Tak it: and tak the risk of what gangs with it.

He holds the sword in a threatening manner. MCGLASS *looks at him nervously, but carefully: walks slowly towards him, puts the sword aside and at the same time slides the collar up the blade till it hangs round* GILNOCKIE'S *wrist.*

MCGLASS. Gilnockie, it's no wise to attempt to be precipitate. There is ane reason for the refusal of the King to accord you this title.

GILNOCKIE. Wamphray?

MCGLASS. Wamphray?

GILNOCKIE. Na?

MCGLASS. Ye hae just said yersel that the matter of Wamphray was – obscure. Let us consider rather the relation betwixt ane vassal laird and his superior. Lord Maxwell is—

GILNOCKIE. Jealous! He is jealous of my merit! He has consortit with the English: there can be nae other explanation. Fornication of the Magdalene, but I will render him ane sufficient cause to feel ane jealousy of me!

MCGLASS. Ye will, sir? And what cause? For Sir David Lindsay alsweel has his merit and his honour struck at in this. Mind ye, he made you his promise—

GILNOCKIE. God, but he did! And he never meant to keep it!

MCGLASS. Sir!

GILNOCKIE. Sir, sir, sir – and whatten wass she cause offence then whateffer to the shentlemen of Rannoch Moor? Tell me for why he has no pit Maxwell intil prison!

MCGLASS. Because Maxwell had ane dangerous faction – there is Bothwell, there is Buccleuch, there is even the Cardinal—

GILNOCKIE. And what about the Hielandmen?

MCGLASS. The Hielandmen?

GILNOCKIE. They are alsweel ane faction, ane bare-leggit bloody faction. Fetch them in.

MCGLASS. I will tell you directly about the Hielandmen, Gilnockie: they combine within their character ane precellent and personal lealty with ane mislike of ignorant insult whether in their ain glens or at the Court, or – na, na, here is Jacob, never Esau, Jacob, Jacob, Jacob . . .

GILNOCKIE. I tell ye, fetch them in, mak ane balance: ane equal – equal—

MCGLASS. Equilibrium? The Hielandmen and Armstrang against the lave of all the Lawlands? Original, indeed, ane new and sophisticate policy: but credit me, Gilnockie, it wad never serve just yet. The Hielandmen are—

GILNOCKIE. Geld the bloody Hielandmen. Pluck aff their sporrans and geld them! I repudiate Lord Maxwell and am his man nae langer. The decision of my conduct, for peace or for war, belangs to me and to nane other!

He calls toward the Castle.

Whaur's that woman?

SCENE SIXTEEN

[GILNOCKIE, *his* WIFE, LADY, MAID, MCGLASS, STOBS, YOUNG STOBS, ARMSTRONGS, GIRLS.]

GILNOCKIE'S WIFE, LADY, *and* MAID *come out of the Castle.*

LADY. Here's three women.

GILNOCKIE. I want the splendid harlot of the Court – you! Ye do speak French?

LADY. I do.

GILNOCKIE. What word in Scots wad ye call Lieutenant?

LADY. Lieutenant – '*Le Lieutenant*' – the man that haulds ane place. As, the place of his master.

GILNOCKIE. Master: is no Maxwell. Master is ane King. And to hauld the King's place craves ane honour of equality. Tell the King his Lieutenant is Armstrang. And as his Lieutenant I demand ane absolute latitude and discretion for my governance of this territory. And tell this alsweel: Johnstone

of Wamphray – I do desire reversal of that traitor's property
and lands. He did conspire against my life. I am a King's
Officer. That's treason. If the lands are no grantit me, ye can
tell the King I will grip them!

MCGLASS. But this is enormous, sir: it is inordinate: it is—

GILNOCKIE. It's what I want. Ensure I get it. Awa with ye,
the three of ye.

> MCGLASS, *the* LADY, *and her* MAID, *obedient to* GIL-
> NOCKIE'S *peremptory gesture, retire upstage among the
> trees. They confer together.*

GILNOCKIE'S WIFE (*brings her husband downstage*). John, ye
will never succeed.

GILNOCKIE. No?

GILNOCKIE'S WIFE. The King will never brook it, John. It is
too insolent.

GILNOCKIE. Impregnable. I canna understand why I didna
tell it to Lindsay at first. Whaur are ye, whaur are ye –
Armstrang, Stobs, whaur are ye?

> *The* ELIOTS *come out of the Castle with* ARMSTRONGS
> *and* GIRLS.
> MCGLASS *and the two women walk out into the Forest. And
> thence into the Palace.*

Gilbert, the neist full moon. Order your men. Gilnockie and
Stobs. Companions. Nae further word and nae need of
provocation. Gilbert, we will ride.

> *There is a general cheer.* YOUNG STOBS *kisses the two
> GIRLS in his excitement.* STOBS *grips both of* GILNOCKIE'S
> *hands in his own. The* FIRST ARMSTRONG *begins to sing,
> and the others all take it up:*

> Some speaks of Lords, some speaks of Lairds,
> And sic like men of hie degree:
> Of a gentleman I sing a sang

Sometime called Laird of Gilnockie.
He aye wad save his country dear
Frae the Englishman. Nane are sae bauld
While Johnny doth ride on the border-side
Nane of them daur come near his hauld!

Exeunt – the men into the Forest: the women into the Castle.

Act Three

SCENE ONE

[LINDSAY, MCGLASS, LADY, MAID.]

LINDSAY, *still wearing the robe he assumed in Act One, Scene two, is reclining with the* LADY, *and* MCGLASS *with the* MAID, *enjoying the pleasures of love.*[1]

MCGLASS (*improvising verse*).

> This news was brocht to Edinbugh
> Whaur Scotland's King then dwelt
> That John the Armstrang on the border
> His ain state yet upheld.

LADY (*in the same manner*).

> Riever and rebel he was before
> But now ane starker style outsprings:
> He is ane Emperour complete
> Betwixt twa petty Kings.

LINDSAY. Well, ye can baith cap verses with some truth of prosody. It is evident that companionship with the King's makar has to this extent brocht furth its fruit. But for the content of the said verses? Ane Emperour? Hardly that, I think.

LADY. In his ain een he is ane Emperour.

LINDSAY. Aye, and in his ain codpiece, I daur weel hazard. For that's whaur it began. Gif we are at wark upon the improvisation of occasional stanzas, here is ane rhyme of Lindsay's – mark:

> Lady, the love I hae maintaint
> For you nine year—

---

[1] If there is no curtain to provide a discovery here, the characters enter from the Palace.

LADY. Ten.

LINDSAY. For you ten year with nae complaint
    Should for your treason wax full faint,
    Maist shamefully expire.
    But you are ane Ashtaroth of outrage,
    Ane gowden sepulchre, ane stage
    Whaur I play out the tale of my gray age
    Aye for the increase and never the assuage
    Of venereal desire.

LADY. Jeddart is a weet and a nasty town, David. Ye left me in ane tavern there with green wood upon the fire and great gaps in the roof. And ye trippit oer the back-ankle of your ain metre in the last three lines of your – your—

LINDSAY. Doggerel? It is but doggerel. There's nae astringency left. I tell ye, I'm flatulent.

MAID. That's a puir recommendation to my lady of your venereal increase, Sir David. I think that ye should—

LINDSAY (*walking about in agitation*). I think I should postpone baith venery and poetry and set my wits to wark on policy. Lord Maxwell is richt violent angerit against us. The man's been repudiate by his vassal. Gif what he will tell the King is creditit by the King, there will be ane rope around this halse in less than two weeks.

MCGLASS. Ane noosit rope, lady. This is nae game.

MAID. Sandy, we ken that.

MCGLASS. Aye? But to her it *was* game. She did embolden John Armstrang to the extent they will impeach Lindsay!

LADY. Mr Alexander, the King will never credit Maxwell. The King hates Maxwell. He will require his Lindsay yet, the man that did divert his puberty nocht alane with the Latin Grammar, but alsweel with the bawdy satires of Petronius. My misbehaviour ye did satirize as the wark of ane Ashtaroth – ane carnal goddess, David – then accept the goddess's gift and build your policy upon it. To begin: surely Maxwell repudiate is ane benefit to the realm?

LINDSAY. Ane benefit to the Lairds on yon side of the English Border. John of Gilnockie, with nae suzerain to control him, wad be ane honest man to deal with, wad he no? For his treacheries derive frae the occult procuration of dark men that movit ahint of him: and they're gane. Sandy – what's the adage: 'The English of the North and the Border Scot'?

MCGLASS.

The English of the North and the Border Scot
Are ilk ane like the ither:
Their tongue is the same and their life is the same
Ilk man is as puir as his brither.

LINDSAY. Precise. Now: ane free confederacy of the borderers of either nation, ane alliance of mutual poverty, with their ain Parliament, gif ye will, under the leadership of – why nocht Armstrang? In the manner of the mountain cantons of the Switzers as I hae observit them on my travels. Nae hereditaire nobility, nae theft, nae feuden, and gif they lust yet for battle – ane mercenary service in the army of the Pape, or the Emperour, or the King of France. What's wrang wi' it?

MAID. England.

MCGLASS. It is ridiculous and unpractical. England wad never consent to it – why, it wad mean peace!

LINDSAY. King Henry has preoccupations. Religious, financial, amorous. I trow that he craves for peace – sincerely.

MCGLASS. He craves for the execution of Gilnockie and I think that we hae nae choice but to gie it him.

LINDSAY. What way, man? Whaur's your army, whae's your hangman – you? Wad ye mak your name ane byword for tyranny and coercion, and – and—

LADY. David, recollect yoursel – ye hae the reputation of ane man of placidity.

LINDSAY. Mak me placid, then. Love me.

She does so.

McGlass, what I hae tellt ye is practicable, and it is honourable. I hae writ indeed ane letter about it – ane treasonable
letter, to the English Ambassador.

LADY. David, that is dangerous!

LINDSAY. Agreeable danger. I did ever tak pleisure in ane
devious activity. God help me, I'm as bad as Maxwell.

SCENE TWO

[LINDSAY, MCGLASS, LADY, MAID, *the three* SECRETARIES.]

The three SECRETARIES *enter from the Palace.*

LORD MAXWELL'S SECRETARY. What do ye mean, as bad?
My master will oerwhelm you yet—

CARDINAL'S SECRETARY. Sir David Lindsay, the Blessen of
God upon you, sir; and may He in His inestimable mercy
oerlook your transgressions.

LINDSAY. What transgressions? Specify. Her, do ye mean?
Lady, will ye strip your body, stand up before them like
Phryne before the Judges of Athens, and ilk ane of them
will return ye ane similar acquittal. Though I doubt they
wad expect ye to pay for it in kind. These are gentlemen of
commerce – they buy their love and sell it: love of women
and love of country. Weel, what's the news?

LORD JOHNSTONE'S SECRETARY. What's the news, the
man demands—

LORD MAXWELL'S SECRETARY. Why, ye arrant Machiavell,
here is the news—

CARDINAL'S SECRETARY. John the Armstrang, Thomas his
brother, the Eliots of Stobs, and other of their gang, hae
ridden intil Cumberland. The town of Salkeld is brennt. The
Laird of Salkeld is slain within his ain fold-yard: and the
Lord Warden at Carlisle has ordainit ane general muster of
his levies: for revenge. That, sir, is the news. You and your

slee dalliance amang the heresies of England – ye hae brocht war upon your native Catholic land!

LINDSAY. And are ye nocht blithe to hear it? Ye smile, the three of ye smile! By God, I blaw my neise at ye.

He blows his nose at them.

LORD MAXWELL'S SECRETARY. The King will cut your heid aff.

CARDINAL'S SECRETARY. The Cardinal will brenn ye.

LORD JOHNSTONE'S SECRETARY. Traitor—

CARDINAL'S SECRETARY. Satirist—

LORD MAXWELL'S SECRETARY. Englishman—

CARDINAL'S SECRETARY. There is nae mair to say.

The SECRETARIES *go off into the Palace.*

SCENE THREE

[LINDSAY, MCGLASS, LADY, MAID, ENGLISH CLERK.]

LINDSAY. There is a great deal mair forbye. But we maun wait for it – out of England. Placidity, and patience . . . *Retournons-nous à nos fesses.*

LADY. *Mais c'est une situation très grave, mon chéri: il nous faut penser à notre propre sécurité: pas de fesses et pas de tétins aujourd'hui – par dieu, c'est terrible!*

LINDSAY. *Non, ce n'est que ridicule – une connerie inévitable, et c'est une connerie de ton con – tu as tourné le monde entier tout à fait de haut en bas . . Tais-toi, et baise-moi . . .* Aha, here he is: I thocht he wad come soon.

Enter the ENGLISH CLERK, *with a letter.*

ENGLISH CLERK. Sir David, we can prevent open war, and we must prevent it – now. The English Ambassador has sent me to tell you—

LINDSAY. Did he read my letter yet?

ENGLISH CLERK. He did: I have it here. A very cunning letter, Sir David; you have not even signed it. But nobody could doubt that it came from your hand.

LINDSAY. Absence of doubt is nae presence of proof.

ENGLISH CLERK (*laughs a little*). Your curious proposals, for the establishment of what amounts to an independent sanctuary for outlaws and masterless men between England and Scotland, have been examined with a more sympathetic attention than perhaps you will give credit for. . . . Why not go back to Eskdale and put your ideas to Armstrong? We can do the same to our own rude gentlemen in Cumberland and Northumberland. But we must have assurances that they will remain content within their own boundaries. Your Maxwells and your Douglases will certainly endeavour to stir up disharmony. Will they be controlled, Sir David? This is absolutely cardinal.

LINDSAY. Ach, I canna tell ye: but I'll dae the best I can: creep in and creep out and tangle them whaure'er it's possible. I doubt I'm a wee bit discreditit at the Court here at present.

ENGLISH CLERK. Yes, we have heard so . . .

He goes out.

LINDSAY (*calling after him*). Hey – hey – brenn that letter!

SCENE FOUR

[LINDSAY, MCGLASS, LADY, MAID, PORTER.]

LINDSAY. Aha, they've heard it, have they? Mr McGlass, we maun put it tae the proof. Blaw your horn, we're gangen in.

MCGLASS. Ye'll no be permittit.

LINDSAY. Blaw it.

MCGLASS *blows the bugle. The* PORTER *appears on the Palace roof.*

PORTER. The King's Grace regrets that he is unable this day to find occasion to speak with Lord Lyon.

The PORTER *retires.*

SCENE FIVE

[LINDSAY, MCGLASS, LADY, MAID.]

MCGLASS. Sure it was inevitable that he wad become ane adult.

LINDSAY. God, McGlass, he's nae adult yet. He has acquirit ane different dominie, but he's still *in statu pupillari.* And it is for you and me to pull him out of it this minute. We will accept the advice of our consequential English friend, and gang direct to Eskdale. I intend to bring Gilnockie to a *de facto* truce and handfast with the lairds beyond the border. That includes the Salkeld men: ane strang immediate torniquet before the wound bleeds further. I ken very weel what is in John Armstrang's mind—

MCGLASS. There is naething in his mind but the enjoyment of manslauchter.

LINDSAY. Na, na, the man desires – he yearns in his mirk bowels, Sandy, for ane practicable rational alternative: and I trow we can provide it him. He is ane potential magnificent ruler of his people – he did steer *you* to your muckle pleisure; you tell us what ye think of him!

LADY. Potential, true indeed: but unpredictable, David. Whiles he is generous and intelligent, ane lion, gif ye will – but when he turns intil ane wolf . . . Besides, ye will be rebel; ye will be against your ain King for this.

LINDSAY. Rebel? I am already traitor, it wad seem. Certain it is ane risk. I am about to set ane absolute trust upon King James. This is ane test for him, ane preçise temptation: he kens my value, gif he will bethink him: let him see my purposes, and let him see the purposes of Lord Maxwell and the lave: and mak ane clear choice betwixt them. There was a time when his father was your lover. Explain to the son then, what it is I intend.

LADY. I will do what I can, David.

LINDSAY. Gif he be at last ane man, he will discern what David Lindsay means, and then there will be nae mair talk of rebel or of traitor. But gif he prefer to remain for ever the schoolboy that he has been, he will put himself for ever outwith all hope of stringent kingly government. It is ane act of faith to trust him: Sandy, will ye come?

MCGLASS. *Amadain, tha thu clis is cearr ach tha mise leat agus thig mi.*[1] I will come.

LINDSAY. Ladies, this wark is yours. Begun within the wames of women: now it maun be carryit through, at the hands and brains of men, tormentible, destructible men. Accord us your bitter blessen and get within your doors.

LADY. There are ower-mony brands and lang guns in the forests of Eskdale. Gif ye shouldna return hame—

LINDSAY. Ye may get intil the King's bed. He is of ane age for it, I think.

MCGLASS (*to* MAID). I shall return: in whatever shape they bring me, ye wad never withauld me welcome?

MAID. *Tha thu ro óg airson a'bhàis.*[2]

MCGLASS. *Na creid facal dheth.*[3] Lindsay, are ye ready? Then let's gang: and the de'il gang wi' us, for I doubt that naebody else will.

The women kiss them and go into the Palace.

[1]'Stupid, impulsive, a miscalculation, but I am your man and I must come.'

[2] 'You are too beautiful to die.'

[3] 'Never believe it.'

SCENE SIX

[LINDSAY, MCGLASS, GILNOCKIE, *his* WIFE, ARMSTRONGS,
MEN, GIRLS, EVANGELIST.]

LINDSAY *takes off his robe and puts on a buff coat. He and*
MCGLASS *walk across the stage, and call out at the Castle gate.*

LINDSAY. Now then, for Eskdale . . . Gilnockie, are ye
there?

MCGLASS. Mr Armstrang!

LINDSAY. Johnny!

GILNOCKIE *comes out of the Forest.*

GILNOCKIE. Here.

LINDSAY. Ah, out of the wynds of the forest, as befits a rank
reiver that recks little of King or Baron but uphaulds for a'
time the standard of his ain strength. Sir, I do salute you:
you are lord entire within your boundaries.

GILNOCKIE. And what are you?

LINDSAY. The salamander of sanity, belike, betwixt the
gleeds of your het fire.

The EVANGELIST *and all* GILNOCKIE'S *household come
out of the Forest behind him.*

EVANGELIST. Sanity or sanctity, Sir David?

LINDSAY. Ah? Gilnockie, the English are preparen war. I have
come to preserve your manhood and your liberty in the face
of either nation.

EVANGELIST. You do interrupt with your feckless brawlen the
service of the Lord God. The Laird of Gilnockie has
declarit himself at last amang the congregation of the Elect.
We were about to sing ane haly sang of praise.

*He leads them all in a hymn, speaking each line, which is then
sung by the congregation:*

ALL.   Lord God of Wrath, our arms mak strang
              To deal the right and hale down wrang

              Thy people are but few and faint
              And Thou wilt hear their just complaint.

              Our native land, O Lord doth bleed:
              Assist us to fulfil her need.

              We praise Thee and adore Thy rage:
              Thy words are writ upon our page.

              We praise Thee and adore Thy love:
              O cause, O cause our hearts to move.

EVANGELIST. Again, again, brethren, assail the ears of God!

ALL. O cause, O cause our hearts to move!

The EVANGELIST *launches into an ecstatic homily, while the congregation, moved to excess, interject cries of religious passion.*

EVANGELIST. Let them move indeed, let them pursue Thy impeccable purpose notwithstanding fear and feebleness of spirit—

ALL. We are but few and faint—

EVANGELIST. —until that we can at the last within this barren land of Anti-Christ and corruption declare to the uttermaist—

ALL. Lord, Lord, declare it—

EVANGELIST. —and out of ane hale and sanctifyit mind give furth with pregnant voice the fervent utterance of Thy glory—

ALL. Glory, glory, glory—

EVANGELIST. —and thereupon erect Thy temple—

ALL. Lord, Lord, Thy true resplendent temple—

EVANGELIST. —upon the banks and braes of Eskdale!

ALL (*including* EVANGELIST). Glory, glory, glory, Lord, Lord, whaur is Thy temple?

MCGLASS. And is this what ye want the Lady to tell the King was your intention – to set up ane temple?

LINDSAY. Never.

MCGLASS. It wad hae been better to hae deliverit up this Evangelist to the fires of the Cardinal, as prescribit in the law, and never mind in what tongue is writ the orthodox Gospel.

LINDSAY. Na, na, Alexander – never that neither! God, I am at my wits' end. I had come to maintain Gilnockie by ane argument to his ain self-interest – but this is nae self-interest: this is ane coercive zeal for martyrdom and fanatic excess that I am scarce able to credit.

MCGLASS. Ye trow that our Johnny isna sincere?

LINDSAY. I trow that he isna godly. The man is exceeden politic: mair politic than me. I will ask him ane question.

During the above dialogue the drone of devotion has been continuing, but more subdued. Now the EVANGELIST *cries again in full strength.*

EVANGELIST. For the sins and the errors of our past life, we maun shew furth our sober penitence. John, are ye indeed washit white in the Blood of the Lamb?

GILNOCKIE. White, washit, clean, pure. Glory to God for that I did sin with ane carnal and abominable sin, but glory, glory, glory—

ALL. Glory, glory, glory—

GILNOCKIE. But all is turnit now towart election and salvation—

EVANGELIST. This brand that ye do bear—

GILNOCKIE (*draws sword*). Is the Lord's brand and consecrate—

ALL. Glory, glory, glory—

GILNOCKIE. For the execution of God's enemies and the renovation of His Kingdom!

ALL. Glory, glory, glory. Hallelujah upon Mount Sion . . .
etcetera.

The religious orgasm fades away: GILNOCKIE *comes down to*
LINDSAY.

GILNOCKIE. Delamont, ye are ane vanity. Ye are ane warldly
infection with your collars and vile titles. I am naebody's man
but God's.

LINDSAY (*takes him aside*). There is nae credibility in this,
Johnny, and I think nae practicality—

GILNOCKIE. Ah. Practicality. Hear ye this, Lindsay – your
wee man Evangelist there – ye canna ca' him unpractical.
We intend to extend the Kingdom of Christ—

LINDSAY. Northwarts, or south?

GILNOCKIE. Whilkever direction can ensure me the best
wealth and food for my people. There are monasteries in the
Scots Lawlands. They tell that in Germany Martin Luther
has made free the nuns and monks. And why nocht alsweel
in Scotland? And Johnny will prove ane gey furious
fechter, new-washit as ye see him, white in the Blood of the
Lamb!

SCENE SEVEN

[LINDSAY, MCGLASS, EVANGELIST, GILNOCKIE, *his*
WIFE, ARMSTRONGS, MEG.]

MEG *comes out of the Forest.*

MEG. Lamb's blood or man's blood, it was never white, but
mirk, thick, blue-red, and it dries upon the bleachit linen
stiff as ane parchment.

EVANGELIST. Be silent.

MEG. I wad speak like yoursel the day, master, I wad speak the
prophetic tongue. I was possessit twa year by the fury of

Lucifer: he drave me like a packmare intil the moss and mire of iniquity: in the fleshly beds I did roll and I did wallow.

GILNOCKIE'S WIFE. Haud fast your gapen slot, cousin, ye incontinent wee carline – did ye no hear the good preacher—

MEG. —but there is mair shame than mine craves absolution here. Aye and chastisement forbye. For ane secret murder done on the riggs of the moor – what chastisement for that, master – punition, revenge, ane heavenly correction – I cry, I cry, I cry: Glory, glory, glory, Lord God amend all, strike down the men of blood, strike down Armstrang, strike down Eliot. Glory, glory, Lord—

GILNOCKIE. She's runnen mad—

GILNOCKIE'S WIFE. Ye will no hear her further; she brings scandal upon the conventicle—

GILNOCKIE. It is the fiend speaks within her. Or witchcraft—

GILNOCKIE'S WIFE. Aye, witchcraft—

EVANGELIST. I did trow she wad be penitent . . .

GILNOCKIE. Penitent. *I'm* your penitent here. Wamphray was slain for ane lustful confederacy against me and against the Eliots, and *she* was part of it! Gif she in truth be penitent, God's throat, she should be *glad*! Ben the house, cast her awa, she is ane withcraft adversary – ben!

He leads his WIFE *and people into the Castle.*

SCENE EIGHT

[LINDSAY, MCGLASS, EVANGELIST, MEG.]

MEG (*sings*).

Fall, Sword of God, upon his heid
And bite intil his brain
For he slew the lovely lover of me
That will ne'er love me again.

EVANGELIST. I did trow that she was penitent.

MCGLASS. Ha, but she is, master. She is your child and your disciple – a wee bit difficult to control, whatever, but yours – observe her, sir, she hath ane strange passion for you. Is it no reciprocate in your ain body? It is indeed, consider: maist certain ye do feel ane risen lust within you! She hath hauld upon your garment – look!

EVANGELIST (*withdrawing his skirts from the kneeling woman*). This is filthy and incomprehensible.

MCGLASS. Then attempt to comprehend it! The cause of her distraction is John Armstrang, that did kill her man. And ye hae sanctifyit that murderer in all verity with the words of the Gospel? Whilk of these twa penitents of yours will ye accept or reject? Ye canna credit the baith of them? They canna be baith guests at the same Christian marriage table.

LINDSAY. McGlass, that's sufficient.

MCGLASS. Na, na—

LINDSAY. It is! Ye will confound all my policy with this fool's talk of marriage tables. McGlass, ye maun tak tent—

MCGLASS. Aye, aye, and gang ane circuit! You put temptation upon the King, very weel – I put it in this minute upon this Evangelist: whaur is conscience and humanity, master – with this tormentit lassie, or with Gilnockie and his brand? Whaur is your conscience – whaur is Christ, this minute!

EVANGELIST. Here, Satan, here—

He snatches the knife out of MCGLASS's *belt and stabs him with it.*

The flesh prevails ever. The Lord hath hid his face. Within three days I could hae biggit the temple in Eskdale. Oh, ye mountains of Gilboa: cover me, cover me frae the abundant wrath of God—

He runs out into the Forest.

MEG. Never forsake me now, master, I will despair; never forsake me, master—

She follows him, crying.

SCENE NINE

[LINDSAY, MCGLASS.]

MCGLASS *has sunk down at the edge of the stage, so that he is half-seated, half-propped against the wall. The knife is still in the wound. He laughs.*

LINDSAY. Sandy, did he wound you? What's sae damn droll, man? Here is nocht but bloody frenzy. Maintain your manly dignity, stand upon your feet – Sandy, do ye hear me?

MCGLASS. Sir David, there is ane gully-knife sticks out at my side. Look. Whaurever we gang now there is ever ane gully-knife, or ane brand, or ane lang rope, Sir David. Nae circuit nae langer: finish it, sir, finish it.

LINDSAY. I will bring ye intil the castle—

MCGLASS. Na, na: finish it. Edinburgh. Finish it.

LINDSAY (*helping him up*). Finish it? Finish it what way?

MCGLASS. The way of the Cyclops, or Gogmagog or whatever. He has deliverit himself, has Johnny, intil the hands of Evangelists: and in the hands of Evangelists there are red reeken gullies. Ye did tak pride in your recognition of the fallibility of man. Recognize your ain, then, Lindsay: ye have ane certain weakness, ye can never accept the gravity of ane other man's violence. For you yourself hae never been grave in the hale of your life!

LINDSAY. That is entirely untrue—

MCGLASS. Na, na, it is utter verity. But John Armstrang is ane gey serious boy: and gif he claims to be ane Luther – he may

nocht be sincere in it – but I tell ye, I tell ye, he will be as
dangerous – and as lunatic – as the maist promiscuous
Evangelist that ever held a book. Now get me intil Edinburgh.

LINDSAY. Ye canna mak the journey in that condition,
Sandy—

MCGLASS. I can. Observe me, sir: I'm maken it. Observe, I'm
upon the road.

He staggers round the stage, supported by LINDSAY. *As he
goes, he sings:*

O lang was the way and dreary was the way
And they wept every mile they trod
And ever he did bear his afflictit comrade dear.
A heavy and a needless load.
A heavy and a needless load.

Ye should hae heard me at the first – your rationality and
practicality has broke itself to pieces, because ye wad never
muster the needful gravity, to gar it stand as strang, as
Gilnockie's fury . . . There is naething for you now but to
match that same fury, and with reason and intelligence, sae
that this time you will win.

LINDSAY. Will win and win damnation.

MCGLASS. Aye, man, ye'll win and be damned . . . Do ye
mind what ye said to Gilnockie the first time ye met him?
'There is ever ain sair question when a man sees his ancient
life upon the brink of complete reversal!' For my sake, Sir
David, will you reverse your life for me? Show to the King
the gully in my side: and tell him to act: and first he maun
put intil prison: Johnstone – he's there already: Maxwell:
Bothwell: Buccleuch: ony man else? I canna mind . . . But
let them all be lockit up, upon the same hour, of the same
day, and let the King, alane, ken in what prison, they are
keepit. Then let him come to the conclusion of Gilnockie . . .

A heavy and a needless load . . .

SCENE TEN

[MCGLASS, LINDSAY, MAID, LADY, PORTER.]

They have come to the entrance of the Palace. The LADY *and the* MAID *look over the walls and see them: the* MAID *gives a cry: and they come down and receive them at the doorway.*

LADY. David, what's to happen now? Ye wad never kill Gilnockie – David, he was my lover, David—

MAID. Can ye find ane policy to gang ane circuit around this?

LADY. Hauld your tongue, burd: Sir David makes his ain decision here.

LINDSAY. McGlass, ye do disgrace your master. Ye bring the gully in your side for ane nakit witness against me.

MAID. How lang is there left of him of life?

MCGLASS. Burd: I'm a deid man before my dinner. Will ye show it to the King! *Greas ort, greas ort, iarr air an righ Gilnockie a mharbhadh. O mo gheol ghadl bhithinn sona gu bràth na d'aclais.*[1]

LINDSAY. The King will hear me: I will nocht brook prevention. Whaur's his Porter? Whaur?

The PORTER *appears on the Palace roof.*

The King shall hear me: the King shall see this: the King shall! Let me in!

PORTER. Lord Lyon, please to wait in patience, sir. I will inquire.

He retires from the roof. MEG *is keening.*

LADY. David, you are ane new man. I am unable to recognize you, David.

LINDSAY (*indicates* MCGLASS). Can ye recognize him?

LADY. I am talken about you. I tellt ye, I am unable.

[1] 'Quick, quick, and tell the King to kill Gilnockie. O my lovely girl, I would have lived within your arms for ever.'

The PORTER *beckons them into the Palace.*

Belike the King will fare better. Ye may divert wi' this his manhood as ance ye did his puberty. Indeed, it is provocative of comedy and mirth.

They carry in MCGLASS'S *unconscious body to the Palace.*

SCENE ELEVEN

[GILNOCKIE, *his* WIFE, ARMSTRONGS.]

GILNOCKIE *appears on the roof of the Castle.*

GILNOCKIE. Whaur's he gane? Whaur's the Evangelist? He's no within the Castle – gang out and find him. Whaur did ye leave him?

The ARMSTRONGS *come out of the Castle gate.*

I tell ye, that man, he is the word of Jehovah God, he is the good fortune of Gilnockie, he is the luck of Johnny's house.

GILNOCKIE'S WIFE (*appearing also on the roof*). Be patient, Gilnockie; he will return in his ain good time. Belike he has stayit to pray.

GILNOCKIE. Pray, woman? What? What's it, pray? Find him, bring him in—

The men run into the Forest.

SCENE TWELVE

[LINDSAY, GILNOCKIE, *his* WIFE.]

LINDSAY *comes out of the Palace. He is wearing his herald's tabard, and carries a scroll.*

LINDSAY (*to audience*).
> I did swear a great aith
> I wad wear this coat nae further
> Till Armstrang be brocht
> Intil the King's peace and order.
> To gang against his house
> As ane man against ane man,
> Through craft and through humanity –
> Alas, and mortal vanity,
> We are but back whaur we began.
> A like coat had on the Greekish Emperour
> When he rase up his brand like a butcher's cleaver:
> There was the knot and he did cut it.
> Ane deed of gravity. Wha daur dispute it?

He walks across the stage to the Castle.

John, I have ane letter. It is ane letter of love frae the hand of the King. Will ye come down and read it? Or will ye let your lady read it? Or will *I* read it, John? I wear my Herald's coat the day: it is ane surety of Royal honour that there will be nae deception.

GILNOCKIE. Read.

LINDSAY (*reading*). 'We, James, by the Grace of God,' and so furth and so furth, 'to our weel-belovit—'

GILNOCKIE. Our weel-belovit subject?

LINDSAY. Subject? Na, na, I canna see it writ here . . . 'To our weel belovit John of Gilnockie,' that's what he says, 'Our weel-belovit John of Gilnockie, Warden and Lieutenant . . . we do hereby send our Royal greeten. We intend to mak ane sportive progress for the improvement of our health and for the pursuit of the wild deer, throughout the lands of the Border. Gif John of Gilnockie, and sae mony of his people as do desire to come with him, will attend our person and household at the place callit Carlanrigg: he may there be assurit of ane richt cordial and fraternal welcome.'

GILNOCKIE. Fraternal?

LINDSAY. Fraternal.

GILNOCKIE. That means he calls me his brither. He wad call King Henry brither?

LINDSAY. Listen to the lave of it. 'This letter will serve the recipient baith as ane Free Pardon and as ane Safe Conduct upon his arrival at Carlanrigg.' The signature 'Jacobus Rex', and the seal appendit. Ye will recognize the seal.

GILNOCKIE'S WIFE. And we are to trust to this letter?

LINDSAY. Safe Conduct, Free Pardon, the King's seal, the Herald's coat upon me? Remember the words of Virgil Mantuan, madam: '*Timeo Danaos et dona ferentes!*' – 'The gifts of your enemies are e'en sweeter to the taste than those of your friends!' The King hath said 'fraternal'. Do ye mean to reject him?

GILNOCKIE. Lord Maxwell?

LINDSAY. He is in prison.

GILNOCKIE. Bothwell?

LINDSAY. In prison.

GILNOCKIE. Buccleuch?

LINDSAY. Prison.

GILNOCKIE. The hale gang of them. I'll no believe it.

LINDSAY. John, ye had best. The King has become ane adult man this day. Ride out, sir, and bid him welcome to your lands. At last, at last, Gilnockie, he has listent to my advice!

GILNOCKIE. It is necessair, this matter should, with earnest deliberation, be embracit.

He and his WIFE *descend from the roof. They come out of the Castle.*

It is necessair, ane good preclair appearance: as in dress, and plumage. Whaur's the men?

GILNOCKIE'S WIFE. Ye sent them to the wood, for the Evangelist.

GILNOCKIE. Evangelist? What's an Evangelist? Call 'em
back! Whaur's the women? Armstrang! Armstrang!

SCENE THIRTEEN

[LINDSAY, GILNOCKIE, *his* WIFE, ARMSTRONGS, GIRLS.]

His MEN *reappear from the Forest, and the* GIRLS *come out of
the castle.*

GILNOCKIE. The King has callit me brither! My gaudiest
garments, ilk ane of them, a' the claiths of gowd and siller,
silk apparel, satin, ilk ane I hae grippit in time past out of
England. Fetch 'em here.

The GIRLS *bring out a chest which they open and take out
rich clothes.*

Lindsay Delamont: tak tent: ye see Gilnockie's putten on
his raiment. It is the ceremony: John the Armstrang's pride
and state.

*He looks at the garments presented him, and strips off his
buff coat, and under-tunic.*

Here, this yin, that yin – no that, carl's claithing – rags and
tatters – that: ane coat of glory for ane glorious King to
hauld the hand of his brither! The King has callit me brither!
GILNOCKIE'S WIFE. He did call ye Lieutenant alsweel.
GILNOCKIE. Lieutenant? What's Lieutenant? Forgotten:
subordinate, nocht . . . (*He is now dressed in a fine cloth-of-
gold tunic and accessories.*) Aha: and now a bonnet.
FIRST ARMSTRONG. The Laird wants his bonnets.

A GIRL *fetches a number of hats.*

GILNOCKIE (*looking through them*). Na, na, for ane cattle-
drover, that . . . ane Carlisle bloody burgess, that . . .

belike, but whaur's the feathers? . . . Aha, ye've brocht it.
This did belang to the Lord Warden of the English side; I
dang it aff his heid wi' my fist at the conclusion of ane parley.
Mair of these targets; pin 'em in. (*As an afterthought he puts
on the Lieutenant's collar.*)

FIRST ARMSTRONG. Mair targets, pin 'em in.

*The hat he has selected has a wide brim turned up over the
forehead, with one or two jewelled badges pinned on the
underside. The* GIRLS *now fetch out a box with more badges
in it, and they set to work to add these to the hat.*

GILNOCKIE. On the road to Carlanrigg, Johnny Armstrang
requires his music. Whaur's the piper?

FIRST ARMSTRONG. Whaur's the piper?

THIRD ARMSTRONG (*fetching the pipes*). Whatten air d'ye
want me to play, Gilnockie?

GILNOCKIE. Ane new-made air: I made it mysel': ye havena
blawn it before. It rins in my heid these twa-three days – nae
words to it yet, but they'll come – wait, I'll gie you the line
of the melody.

He hums a tune, carefully.

Can ye follow it?

The PIPER *tries it out.*

THIRD ARMSTRONG. Aye, belike.

GILNOCKIE. Play . . . Set onwards then, we march.

The PIPER *plays the tune, and they start to march about the
stage. They form a little procession, first the* PIPER, *then*
GILNOCKIE, *then the other* ARMSTRONGS, *and* LINDSAY
bringing up the rear. GILNOCKIE *carries his sword drawn,
and holds the scroll, which* LINDSAY *has given him, in his
other hand. His two men carry hunting spears.* GILNOCKIE'S
WIFE *has gone up to the roof of the Castle, and the* GIRLS
have gone inside.

GILNOCKIE'S WIFE (*calling from the roof as they march*).
John – John – God send ye safe, John: remember the King
is—

GILNOCKIE (*stops briefly to reply*). The King is what? The
King's fraternal!

GILNOCKIE'S WIFE. God send ye safe.

She retires from the roof.

SCENE FOURTEEN

[GILNOCKIE, LINDSAY, ARMSTRONGS, HIGHLAND
SOLDIERS, *the* KING.]

A HIGHLAND CAPTAIN *comes out from the Forest. He
intercepts the procession, with his drawn claymore.*

HIGHLAND CAPTAIN. Stand whaur ye are. Declare your
name and business, sir, gif ye please.

GILNOCKIE. Wha's this?

LINDSAY. It is the Captain of the King's Guard. Show him
your paper.

GILNOCKIE. Ane draff-black bare-arse Hielandman, the
Captain of his Guard – when he rides intil the Lawlands!
Hechna hochna hochna hoo – it is a'thegither inconsiderable.
Gang past him: blaw your pipe!

More HIGHLAND SOLDIERS *have entered and taken up
positions behind the* CAPTAIN.

HIGHLAND CAPTAIN. Sir, I said stand. Gif you be indeed ane
gentleman that hath business with the King's Grace, you
will have papers thereto anent: and it is to myself that you
maun shew them, gif you please.

The KING *is standing among the* SOLDIERS, *but he is
inconspicuous in a plain Highland dress.*

GILNOCKIE (*jeering at the* CAPTAIN). Loók at the legs of him, the puir ignorant cateran – I ken a whin bush in Eskdale that'd wark some damage there, gin ye daur to trample through it!

LINDSAY (*to the* CAPTAIN). Captain MacFadyan, this is Mister John Armstrang of Gilnockie, and here is his Safe Conduct.

He takes the scroll from GILNOCKIE *and gives it to the* CAPTAIN.

KING. *Am bheil fios aige gum feum iad an armachd fhagail an seo? Thu fhein a dh'iarr sin a dheanamh, nach tu, Shir Daibhidh?*[1]

LINDSAY. *Innsidh mise sin dha.*[2]

HIGHLAND CAPTAIN. *Faodaidh tu imse dha cuideachd e nas lugha mhimhodh a nochdadh do Ghaidheil an righ.*[3]

LINDSAY. *O tuigidh e sin an uine gun bhi fada.*[4] It is the King's desire, Gilnockie, that baith you and your men remove your weapons and leave them here.

GILNOCKIE. What? Na—

LINDSAY. Peace, good fellowship, fraternity. Wad ye spite the King's intention?

GILNOCKIE (*to his men*). Aye. Did ye hear him? Spears down, gullies out.

FIRST ARMSTRONG. Dangerous.

GILNOCKIE. Peaceable. Obey it. We are here upon ane trust.

The weapons are piled, and one of the SOLDIERS *carries them away.*

Now then, whaur's the King?

[1] 'Does he know that they must remove their weapons and lay them down here? Your own instructions, Sir David, were they not?'

[2] 'I will tell him, sire.'

[3] 'Perhaps, sir, you would also tell him to restrain himself from insults to the King's Gaelic subjects.'

[4] 'He will understand in good time.'

KING. Sir, I will conduct you to His Grace.

He leads GILNOCKIE *downstage.*

GILNOCKIE. And what are you?

LINDSAY. Ane Officer of his Household, Gilnockie.

KING. Will ye please to come this way.

As they walk across the front of the stage, GILNOCKIE'S *men behind them are silently taken away by the* SOLDIERS.

GILNOCKIE. They tell't me it was ane progress of sport, against the wild deer of the forest. Wherefore soldiers? Wherefore bloody Ersemen, here?

KING. As it were, ane time of solace and recreation for the King's dependents: the Border lands are weel notit for the joy of the chase. Ye wad never wish to withhauld your hospitality frae men of sic gallantry? Will ye tak a wee dram with me, Gilnockie, before we see His Grace?

He offers a flask.

GILNOCKIE. Aha, boy, I will that. (*He drinks.*) Ersemen or Norsemen, Spaniards or heathen English, they're free and welcome here, every man, every bonny fechter! Gilnockie bids ye welcome. It's Gilnockie's land: it's no the King's, mind that. Gilnockie's land and God's. We are reformit, here, sir: we have ane true religion here; aye, aye, the verity of the Gospels . . . Whaur's the King?

KING. Aye. Whaur is he?

GILNOCKIE. Hey – what?

KING. There is ane richt curious circumstance, Gilnockie, doth attend the King of Scotland. When he stands within ane company, he will be the anely man present wi' a hat on his heid.

GILNOCKIE. Aye? (*He looks round and realizes that he and the* KING *alone wear hats. He laughs – a little uncertainly.*) Aye: nae doubt he will: then it's either you or me, boy.

KING. It's no you, I'll tell ye that! Ye are ane strang traitor. The hale of your life ye have set at nocht the laws and commandments of the kingdom: ye have made mock of our person and the Crown and the Throne of Scotland: ye have embroilit and embranglit us with England the common enemy: and by dint of malignant faction ye have a' but split the realm! What in the Name of God gars ye believe I wad pardon ye now? Gilnockie, ye maun be hangit: furthwith, direct, nae process of law: our word in this place is sufficient. Hang him up.

The KING *turns his back abruptly. The* SOLDIERS *close in upon* GILNOCKIE.

GILNOCKIE. Hang? Hang me up? But ye sent me ane letter – ane letter of Safe Conduct—

KING (*without turning round*). Whaur is it then?

GILNOCKIE. Lindsay, I gave it to—

LINDSAY (*deadpan*). What?

GILNOCKIE. Whaur hae ye taken my men? Ane letter. Delamont. The King's letter. The King's honour, the Royal seal – but nae man can say a word against *my* honour: the elect, the godly, me: washit white in the Blood of the Lamb! Whaur are my men, my leal people? Delamont, they are my kinsmen. Delamont, d'ye hear me? What hae they done with my piper?

LINDSAY. What good's your piper now?

GILNOCKIE. For music, what else? Johnny wants his music. He has fand him words to his new air. Nae piper: nae music: Johnny maun sing on his lane.

(*Sings.*)

> To seek het water beneath cauld ice
> Surely it is ane great follie
> I hae socht grace at a graceless face
> And there is nane for my men and me.

KING (*stamping his foot*). I said to you to hang him up. For what do you wait?

The SOLDIERS *lay hold of* GILNOCKIE *with considerable violence: he struggles: they rip the fine clothes off his back, and wrap ropes around him: they force him on to his knees and drag him with the ropes upstage to the big tree. Throughout this he tries to complete his song.*

GILNOCKIE (*singing*).
> But had I wist ere I cam frae hame
> How thou unkind wadst be to me
> I wad hae keepit the border side
> In spite of all thy men and thee—

The words of the song are all broken up in the struggle. They stand him under the tree, throw a rope over the bough, place the noosed end round his neck.

For God's sake let me finish my sang! I am ane gentleman of land and lineage – and ane Armstrang for ever was the protection of this realm—

They hang him.

SCENE FIFTEEN

[LINDSAY, KING, HIGHLAND CAPTAIN, *and* SOLDIERS.]

The KING *picks up* GILNOCKIE'S *coat and hat and other articles of his adornment.*

KING. Will ye look at what the man was wearen? Gif we were to set ane crown upon the carl, he wad be nae less splendid than ourself. The noblemen that we hae wardit intil prison may be releasit upon surety of good behaviour. The good behaviour of Lord Maxwell in particular will carry with it ane grant of the lands heretofore held by the late Armstrong of Gilnockie – thereby we may hope to secure his further lealty to our person. Ane message direct to the English Ambassador – ye will attend to it, Sir David – recount to him briefly the course of our Royal justice here at Carlanrigg: and express our trust in the eternal friendship of King Henry his master. What mair – can ye think?

LINDSAY. Naething mair, sire. The man is deid, there will be nae war with England: this year. There will be but small turbulence upon the Border: this year. And what we hae done is no likely to be forgotten: this year, the neist year, and mony year after that. Sire, you are King of Scotland.

KING. We do think we are indeed. Henceforwart, we require nae tutor, Sir David. But we have ever ane lust for good makars and faithful heralds. Continue to serve us in either capacity. Our gratitude is as mickle as our state can contain. Gentlemen: we will ride to kill the deer.

A horn blows. Exeunt all, save LINDSAY, *into the Forest.*

SCENE SIXTEEN

[LINDSAY, GILNOCKIE'S WIFE, *the* ARMSTRONG GIRLS, LADY, MAID.]

The LADY *and her* MAID *appear on the roof of the Palace.* GILNOCKIE'S WIFE *and the* GIRLS *appear on the roof of the Castle.*

LINDSAY. There was ane trustless tale grew out of this conclusion—

GILNOCKIE'S WIFE. That the tree upon whilk he was hangit spread neither leaf nor blossom—

LADY. Nor bloom of fruit nor sap within its branches—

LINDSAY. Frae this time furth and for evermair. It did fail and it did wither upon the hill of Carlanrigg, as ane dry exemplar to the warld: here may ye read the varieties of dishonour, and determine in your mind how best ye can avoid whilk ane of them, and when. Remember: King James the Fift, though but seventeen years of age, did become ane adult man, and learnt to rule his kingdom. He had been weel instructit in the necessities of state by that poet that was his tutor.

If there is a curtain it falls upon this tableau.
If not, LINDSAY *concludes his speech with a bow to the audience, and turns away. Other members of the cast immediately re-enter and* GILNOCKIE'S *body is lowered and released before they all make their bows and then exeunt.*

Glossary of old Scots terms

Certain regular usages should be noted:

gh becomes ch: as	'brocht' for 'brought'.
o becomes a: as	'haly' for 'holy'.
ea becomes ei: as	'heid' for 'head'.

also read:

'money' for 'many'.	'no' or 'nocht' for 'not'.
'hae' for 'have'.	awa' for 'away'.
'nae' for 'no'.	'deil' for 'devil', etc.

o (long) becomes ai: as 'baith' for 'both'.

The past tense ends 'it' instead of 'ed' thus: 'defendit' for 'defended'.

'ing' becomes 'en' or 'an' as: 'riden', 'sleepen', etc.

Aboon	Above
Alsweel	As well
Ane	A, An, One
Anent	Concerning
Ben	In
Brand	Sword
Brenn	Burn
Bot	Without
Broo	Soup
Buft	Untanned leather
Burd	Girl
Carl	Person of the lower classes
Complot	Plot
Corbie	Crow (a bird)
Chaumer	Chamber
Crag	Neck
Creish	Fat

Dang	Knocked (past tense)
Daur	Dare
Dominie	Schoolmaster
Draff	Rubbish (a technical term from brewing, I think)
Dram	Drink
Eneuch	Enough
Erse	Gaelic
Fecht	Fight
Flair	Floor
Forbye	Moreover
Fou	Drunk (literally, Full)
Gate	Way
Gat-leggit	With legs outspread
Gey	Very
Gif	If
Gleed	Hot coal
Gin	If
Gully	Dagger
Graith	Girth
Greet	Weep
Halse	Neck
Hinnie	Darling (literally, Honey)
Howkit	Hooked
Jeddart	Jedburgh (a town)
Kirkfast	(of a wedding) made in church
Lave	Remainder
Laverock	Skylark
Lealty	Loyalty
Makar	Poet
Mickle	Big
Muckle	Much
Mou	Mouth
Mushrump	Mushroom
Neise	Nose

Nicker	Neigh (like a horse)
Nolt	Cattle
Paddock	Toad
Quern	Hand-mill
Ratten	Rat
Reeken	Smoking
Riever	Thief
Rigg	Ridge
Sackless	Helpless
Sark	Shirt
Siccar	Secure
Slee	Sly
Speir	Ask
Steer	Have sexual intercourse with
Strae	Straw
Swyve	Have sexual intercourse with
Tawse	Strap (used to whip schoolboys)
Target	Jewelled badge in a cap
Thrawn	Twisted
Toom	Empty
Umwhile	Sometime
Usquebaugh	Whisky
Wame	Stomach or Womb
Wean	Child
Weird	Destiny
Wha	Who
Whae?	Who?
Wheen	Few
Whilk	Which
Weet	Wet
Whoor	Whore
Wynd	Path or passage
Yett	Gate

Left-Handed Liberty

A Play about Magna Carta

Introductory Notes

JOHN   Aged forty-eight in 1215, but seems older. Corpulent, short, with dark hair turning to grey and going bald, well-trimmed beard, a grinning wolfish mouth full of bad teeth. Very energetic but out of condition. His moods fluctuate unnervingly. Terrifying in his anger, but can also be jovial and generous – not always in order to deceive.

ISABELLE   The ladies in this play are dimly-glimpsed, but the subject makes this difficult to avoid. The Queen is in her late twenties, of a delicate beauty, a warm and dreamy personality.

ELEANOR   Eighty-two years old, which is very old indeed by the standards of the time. Has been a fascinating dark Mediterranean beauty who has introduced into Western thought and poetry the concept of chivalry in the service of romantic love.

HENRY   He does not have to speak: but is a doll-like royal child who takes more after his mother than his father.

ARCHBISHOP   In late middle age – intellectual, strong-minded, passionate in pursuit of what he conceives to be right. What would now be called a 'progressive' churchman, in contrast to –

PANDULPH   who is dogmatic, sly, politically tough, but despising politics. An elderly man whose spiritual life is as deep as his worldly involvements are dubious. Not a man to make fun of, whatever one may think of his ideas.

MARSHAL   Over seventy – a great age for an active soldier and statesman. Handsome, unimaginative, a paragon of the conservative virtues.

YOUNG MARSHAL In his twenties. Much like his father –
chivalrous and earnest though not so easily shocked.

FITZWALTER A bull-necked fighter in the prime of life,
unscrupulous and insensitively cynical.

DE VESCI Like Fitzwalter, but with a neurotic edge to him,
particularly where his personal concerns are in question, and
rather more intelligent.

LADY DE VESCI Late twenties, a strong young woman with
a sense of satire and not easily humiliated. A reserved
disposition.

THE MAYOR OF LONDON A serious-minded businessman,
who is a little cowed by the responsibilities he has taken on
and the company he finds himself in: but determined none
the less to stand up for himself and his city.

THE CLERK Although in Holy Orders he has the job of a civil
servant and his professional mannerisms do not differ
greatly from those to be found in Whitehall today. Aged
about thirty.

PHILIP Seen only as a political persona – a walking statue of
Kingship, with no personal idiosyncracies to blur the picture.

LOUIS As his father: but in a state of aspiration rather than
fulfilment.

BLANCHE A cold icon of a great lady, and unfortunately the
exigencies of the plot prevent any further understanding of
her.

THE GIRLS Strident in dress, coarse in voice. The blonde
one is fat – otherwise they are mainly distinguished one
from the other by the colours of their hair, which should be
clearly artificial – wigs or violent dyes. All three are very
young. The DARK and RED-HAIRED GIRLS, who have to
appear in Act III as street entertainers, should dress for this

part of their rôles in a gipsified fashion – all ribbons and trinkets.

GOLDSMITH   A thin mean bilious man, late forties, dressed in good clothes which have been worn threadbare.

GOLDSMITH'S WIFE Early twenties, foolish, amorous; domesticated and demure despite her equivocal way of life.

PARSON   A well-built rubicund, Friar-Tuck sort of fellow – the fool of the family put into the Church.

BARONS in general   These have nothing much to say but should give the impression of resolute soldierly competence unspoilt by much refinement.

OFFICERS AND SOLDIERS   These are John's brutal Flemings – battle-scarred professionals of immense aptitude at their trade.

Author's Notes

There is very little in this play which cannot be justified historically. I have had to sandwich events here and there and transpose a few episodes, but I have only invented – as far as I can be sure – Pandulph's correspondence on behalf of the King with the Flemish recruiting agent; Young Marshal's love for Lady de Vesci; the episode at Dover with the Goldsmith and his Wife; and Lady de Vesci's relationship with John. The latter intrigue is supposed to have taken place at an earlier date in John's reign, and in fact to have been foiled by the substitution of a woman of the lower orders, in the manner of a folk-tale. But John was often accused of seducing the wives of his nobility – he is also said to have violated Fitzwalter's daughter – and the story is convenient for the play, so I put it in. Pandulph's correspondence certainly took place at the hands of somebody, and the role of the Papal Legate was sufficiently partisan at this time for my version to be plausible. Young Marshal may or may not have fallen in love with another Baron's wife – such behaviour was regarded as a necessary part of a young knight's emotional development. The King's Justice at Dover is a fictional but not untypical example of John's high-handed and humorous way of handling such situations. The tension I have suggested between the Barons and the City of London is not actually described in history, though Roger of Wendover (a baronial partisan) does accuse the leaders of the 'Army of God' of 'playing at damnable dice, selecting for themselves the best wine for drinking, and practising who knows what besides'. If this was so, it is probable that their relations with the City Fathers would not have been of the best.

The above notes refer to the *facts* contained in the play. The *opinions* are perhaps less historical. It is difficult to know exactly what thirteenth century statesmen and clerics were thinking about most of the time – the chronicles of the period are usually bald and prejudiced. John himself was very roughly handled by their compilers, largely because he had quarrelled with the Church in the earlier part of his reign: and even though, by the time of the Charter, the Pope and he were reconciled, the English clergy continued to vilify him. It seems unlikely, however, that any of the men concerned with drawing up the Great Charter had any conception of the reputation the document would have for future generations. They no doubt believed that they were defining an uncertain and disputed frontier between the rights of the king and those of his subjects; and any idea that they were preparing 'the cornerstone of English liberty' must have been far from their minds. Indeed it was far from the minds of any Englishmen until about the end of the sixteenth century. The great lawyer Coke, in the reign of James I, used the Charter as an authority for his attacks upon the royal prerogative: and during the disputes between Charles I and Parliament it was frequently referred to and acclaimed as a general statement of libertarian principle – not always very honestly – but any stick is good enough to beat a tyrant with, it might well have been thought. Since then, this view of the Charter has obtained, though modern historians have done their best to correct it. But most people remember little of mediaeval history from their school-days, and the picturesque image of the villainous king, brought to bay upon the banks of the Thames one sunny day in June, sticks in the minds of many who in their own lives would not dream of adopting so unsophisticated an attitude towards political reform.

Nevertheless, the 'cornerstone' theory has something to be said for it. If Coke and the seventeenth century parliamentarians were able to 'misuse' the Charter so effectively, they gave to it an importance which is not diminished by being shewn to be unthought-of in the days of John. Of course, much of the document is now entirely out of date. Clauses relating to the minutiae of feudal service and such purely local grievances as fish-weirs in the Thames have dropped out of the national memory. The general principles of 'no imprisonment without judgement by one's peers' and 'no denial or sale of justice' may not have meant in 1215 quite what we take them to mean today – indeed, they were not *principles* at all in 1215: but have since been elevated to that status. This is due, no doubt, to the very convenient generality of the language in which they are expressed. I have in the play allowed King John to claim this as his own inspiration – there is no evidence that it was: but on the other hand no evidence that it was not. The form of the Charter was decided upon after considerable negotiation with the king: and no doubt he did succeed in getting the wording changed here and there. Perhaps I view his character and motives too favourably. It is difficult, however, to resist the rather weird charm of any of the Plantagenets when one comes to examine their personalities at close range. Even the worst of them – and it is hard to find any other category for John, with the best will in the world – seem to have stood head and shoulders above most of their contemporaries, at least in the political field.

When I accepted this commission, I knew little more about the Charter than what I had been taught at the age of fourteen. It was a considerable surprise for me to discover how soon the agreement between John and the Barons was repudiated, and how unfortunate his reconciliation with the Pope had proved for the Baronial party. This apparent complete failure of the Charter struck me as a more fruitful theme for a play than the more obvious one of the events leading up to Runnymede. If this play has any direct message – and I am not normally an enthusiast for didactic drama – I suppose it is that an agreement on paper is worth nothing to anybody unless it has taken place in their minds as well: and that if we want liberty we have to make quite sure that

(a) We know what sort of liberty we are fighting for:

(b) Our methods of fighting are not such as to render that liberty invalid before we even attain it:

(c) We understand that we are in more danger of losing it once we have attained it than if we had never had it.

A final point: the City of London. This play has been commissioned by the descendants of the City Fathers of King John's day. I hope that they will not be disappointed by the not very glorious rôle played by the Lord Mayor of that time. I cannot however do anything about this. He was associated with the Barons in a subordinate capacity and as this was the first time that the commercial middle class took an active part in English politics it is to be expected that its attitude would have been fairly tentative. The unattractive portrayal of the Baronial leaders is fully justified by history: fortunately idealism was present on their side in the person of Archbishop Langton. I have tried to make the Mayor more akin to the Archbishop than to Fitzwalter: which is the best I can do for him, as he is not known to have initiated any active deeds or policy.

The Language of the Play. Most of the characters would have conversed in Norman French or (in the case of Pandulph, for example, who was an Italian) in Latin. The lower and middle class people would have spoken old English. I have no idea what tongue would be employed in a conversation, say, between Lord de Vesci and a prostitute in London. Probably Londoners were nearly all able to manage a little French, and most nobles who lived away from the Court could at least summon up a few words of English for agricultural, military or sexual purposes.

Therefore I have tried to write a kind of dialogue which has the straightforwardness of mediaeval speech – more florid for courtly scenes and more colloquial for other episodes, but generally without regional colouring. De Vesci was a Northumbrian lord, and quite possibly spoke his French with an accent different from that of the King, whose contacts were as much with France as England – but it is no doubt safer to ignore this. Similarly the Mayor of London and the three Girls should not be allowed to be too cockney, nor should the people of Dover become involved with a Kentish burr. Certainly Pandulph must not be a stage-Italian, and Lady de Vesci – although Scots by birth – belongs like her husband to the prevailing Norman culture.

Details of Staging. I do not think much scenery is involved or should be involved. The main requirements are a chair for Pandulph at the front of the stage, right in one corner (where he can sit throughout certain scenes without being too obvious: and yet the audience must be aware that he is there) and a frame or easel in the corresponding position on the opposite side of the stage where the emblems for each act (chart, parchment, and map of England) are hung. These emblems should be as large as is convenient, and drawn or written, in a plausible mediaeval style. The chair is similar to a bishop's throne in a cathedral, with a Gothic canopy and a reading desk. The desk can serve to conceal the various props that Pandulph needs while he is there, and when he has nothing else to do – particularly during John's long speech in Act III – he should be busy with books and papers upon it.

In the centre of the main stage is an area curtained-off, which is to be used for the discovery of persons and furniture where necessary. This area should project forward into the acting area, and be surrounded on three sides by drapes which might well be of a rich tapestry-material, appropriate to the period. There is no need for these drapes to be taller than, say, eight or nine feet. Above them, and in the same plane, is suspended a screen for the projection of the scene-emblems – the views of Runnymede, London river etc. These pictures I imagine drawn in the style of thirteenth century MS illuminations. Certainly they must not be realistic. If real pictures of the period are available, so much the better.

Otherwise the stage is to be bare, and the furniture should be kept to an absolute minimum.

J.A.

Left-Handed Liberty was commissioned by the Corporation of the City of London to commemorate the 750th Anniversary of the sealing of Magna Carta.

The first public performance was given on Monday, 14th June, 1965, at the Mermaid Theatre, Puddle Dock, London, following its presentation to invited audiences under the auspices of the Corporation during the week 7th to 12th June, 1965. The cast was as follows:

KING JOHN	Patrick Wymark
ISABELLE his Wife	Jennifer Clulow
ELEANOR OF AQUITAINE his Mother	Sonia Dresdel
PRINCE HENRY his Son	Roy Hills
STEPHEN LANGTON, Archbishop of Canterbury	
	Bernard Miles
PANDULPH the Papal Legate	Robert Eddison
WILLIAM MARSHAL, Earl of Pembroke	Esmond Knight
YOUNG MARSHAL his Son	Eric Allan
ROBERT FITZWALTER } Leaders of the	Freddie Jones
EUSTACE DE VESCI } Baronial Party	Timothy Bateson
LADY DE VESCI	Barbara Mitchell
MAYOR OF LONDON	Redmond Phillips
PHILIP, King of France	Colin Ellis
LOUIS his Son	Jeremy Rowe
BLANCHE, Wife of Louis	Liane Aukin
THREE WHORES	Sally Miles
	Denise Coffey
	Janet Gahan
A GOLDSMITH	Frederick Hall
His WIFE	Denise Coffey
A PARSON	Ronald Herdman
A CLERK of the Royal Household	Colin Ellis

Barons, Clerks, Servants, Ladies in Waiting, Officers, etc.

Terry Adams	Ronald Cunliffe	Ronald Herdman
Edward Argent	Robert Gillespie	Douglas Milvain
Roger Bizley	Michael Gleave	Adrian Reynolds
John Bloomfield	Christina Greatrex	Georgina Simpson

Directed by David William
Designed by Adrian Vaux
Costumes designed by Robin Pidcock

Act One

A chart opposite PANDULPH's *chair shewing the world and the heavenly bodies. House lights still up.*

Enter PANDULPH.

PANDULPH. Let me explain very briefly that progress in the affairs of this world has ceased to exist. That is to say, there has been progress: there have been certain cardinal events. Eve in Eden ate her fruit and then she fell and her man fell, and they discovered how naked they were. Later the Deluge, God promised it would not occur again and it did not, and after that . . . well, you may read your Bibles, it is all there. So, after many degenerate and bewildered generations, the Master of the Vineyard sent His Son to inspect the work. The disaffected workmen nailed Him up, upon the trellis of their own neglected vines, and were astonished when He was not dead. God, who had moved throughout human history, moved out at last for ever – no, not for ever. He will come once more, one day, when? I do not know. Maybe tomorrow morning, before you even reach your places of work; but in the meantime He is not here. He has left His representative, the Church. The Church is central to human life, as the world itself is central to the organization of the universe –

He refers to the chart:

There is the world; the moon, and the planets, revolve in their spheres – there is the exterior sphere upon the inner surface of which the myriad stars are painted or embossed or perhaps are but little openings pricked out by God's finger to let in the light of Heaven. And here is Heaven. Hell: Purgatory: Limbo. Very good.

Now, as the world is the centre of the whole created system, so Jerusalem, God's Holy City, is the centre of the world – but Jerusalem, as you know, is held by the infidel. The late King Richard Lionheart endeavoured to relieve it, but failed. Therefore the temporary or acting centre of the world may be taken to be Rome, which is appropriate because of the prior example of the Caesars – and the nations of Christendom revolve around the Roman citadel of Christ's own Vicar, just as these outer planets, here, revolve around the world.

As we can expect in our affairs no further direct intervention of Divinity until the Second Coming, and as, without Divinity, man is little more than meat bones and water on the slab of a butcher's shop, it must therefore be clear that no alteration, no betterment, no human improvement, no progress is going to be possible: unless it comes through the Church or the Saints of the Church. Which would be intervention indeed, but indirect and inevitably spiritual rather than material. If the Church were to concern Herself with material circumstances She would be usurping the prerogative of God's own directness, fabricating illegitimately a second Deluge perhaps, or rewriting the Ten Commandments, already divinely and immutably engraved, or occupying Herself with a new tidal wave in an unauthorized Red Sea.

So therefore we concern ourselves only with the sins and repentance of individual men, and, instructed by Our Lord, take no thought for the morrow, what raiment we should put on or what food we should consume, or how we should organize the government of nations. John, King of England, Lord of Ireland, Duke of Normandy, born Anno Domini 1167, is an anointed King and therefore requires the obedience of his subjects. That is all the Church has to say upon the matter. His widowed mother, of course, being of a subordinate yet blessed sex, may choose to say more, but

remember the words of Jesus: 'Woman, what have I to do with thee? My hour is not yet come'.
A Castle in Aquitaine, 1204.

He resumes his seat.

Act One

SCENE ONE

A figure of the Virgin and Child.

ELEANOR *discovered on a throne, wrapped in furs.* JOHN *enters and makes obeisance.*

ELEANOR. Our son was late. Very late. Two hours late.

JOHN. I have already apologized, mother, with (I thought) a very fair address of courtesy. Matters of state, matters of alarm of state, detained me, and the roads were extremely bad. (*He calls to someone offstage.*) Tell my Clerk of Works it is time they were attended to! But I have arrived in your hall, I was not too late for the consumption of wine and spices.

ELEANOR. No. And with a very fair address of courtesy. Queens are susceptible to it. Stone walls have never heard of it. For our son has been late elsewhere, has he not? He failed to save his castle from the enemy. Saucy Castle on the borders of Normandy. The King of France flies banners from the roof. We in Aquitaine have heard that news already. Normandy tomorrow will belong to France. Our son, who was the Duke of it, our son who is the King, was late. Landless John, his father called him, because he gave him no portion when he was born. Now that he has inherited to the full the portions of all those other sons who came into the world before him, and who left it before him in their time and in the time of God, he should be no longer landless. Yet we have heard there are some who still describe him so. They name him Bluntsword also, King Softblade, is it not?

JOHN. Or even King Slapstick – that is one way I have heard it put. Very funny. Malicious. But I would not call it true. The military circumstances are –

ELEANOR. Our husband King Henry could have been the greatest king that the English ever had. King William the Bastard, for all his cruelty, was not a greater than he. Because William was but self-sufficient, by himself alone he conquered himself his kingdom: he ruled it by himself for fifteen years until the King of France one day laughed at his huge belly and called him a pregnant woman. William, being by himself, had nobody to laugh with when France chose to laugh *at* him, and in his impotent and childish anger he burst his poor huge belly and that was the end of him. Sufficient in the end for nothing but a mortal loss of temper. He should have had a wife.

JOHN. His children were legitimate – he did have a wife.

ELEANOR. He should have had a wife to laugh with him and to laugh at him instead of that unfortunate lady who spoke two words to him once, and having incontinently been dragged by the hair of her head at the tail of his horse from one end of the city to the other, preferred ever after to remain silent.

JOHN. He did have a wife. *I* have a wife.

ELEANOR. Did you speak?

JOHN. I said I have a wife, mother.

ELEANOR. Your father had a wife. He was about to have been the greatest king the English had ever heard of, but he decided to be self-sufficient, and he dispensed with his wife. Why, he put her into prison. He divided by force the twin flesh that had been made one, and the sons of her poor huge belly turned upon him with their adolescent chaos, and it burst his own belly for him and that was the end of him. John.

JOHN. Yes, mother: I am attentive, mother.

ELEANOR. John. I am very old. And I am sitting so un-naturally still and so upright because if I were to move I think I should fall down. I am waiting for someone to come and take me away. When he comes he must find me elegant, in the manner of my youth.

He will break down the door –

JOHN (*calling to someone offstage*). The Queen is ill, she requires attendance –

ELEANOR.

He will break down the door.

He must not find me lying on the floor.

He is the only one

Who is sufficient. He is alone.

You are alone, my landless bluntsword son.

The disciple whom Jesus loved, they called him John.

Into his care walked the Lady Mary slowly

Slow, easy, secret, so arrogant she seemed so lowly,

She went around where he breaks in.

He will break in and I will go with him.

Slowly and gently and he will be ashamed of his breaking.

What way will you go?

After what manner are you making?

JOHN.

I am making what I want to make

In the manner I want to make it.

The English are mine

And what I want I shall take it,

Or provide it, when I want,

In the manner of my father.

ELEANOR.

The manner of your mother

Is always much better.

Hide behind the corner

Dictate a polite letter.

So if it has to be done, do it easily and quietly,

Afterwards deny it.

No-one need know it.

Sometimes for my lover

Sometimes for my poet

Always I kept the back door unlocked

Never for the King:
He could beat at the great gate
Until the hinges rocked.
John. John. On your left hand
Wear your most beautiful ring
And do not let it show.
The military circumstances
Enforce you to be slow
But you must never be late.

Where is my visitor? I was expecting him . . . It is discourteous to be so unpunctual when an old lady is waiting . . .
ELEANOR *is hidden from view.*
Next scene to follow immediately.

SCENE TWO

The Papal Arms.
JOHN *comes downstage.*
JOHN. My mother, Queen Eleanor of Aquitaine, received her tardy visitor upon April the first, 1204 – they call it All Fools' Day in England. And we buried her at Fontrevault. She was eighty-two years old. However rudely death came in unto her, and however directly he attempted to force her to walk, I have no doubt but that she remembered the name of the day and made a fool of him in the passage. Not on the first of April, but on the nineteenth of June, some eleven years later, there came together a large number of my subjects to try to make a fool of me – being, as I was, the son of a meandering mother, and for that matter, the son of my father, who would never be governed, never –
PANDULPH. Your Grace, you have omitted something.
JOHN. Am I corrected? Does someone dare? Ah, Master Pandulph: The Legate of the Pope. (*He looks at* PANDULPH'S *chart.*) I mistrust these geometrical figures, Pandulph. They are altogether too pat. If one of these

circles here were to have a little kink in it, thus – you would find perhaps Mars banging into Venus at a vulnerable and tender point and your entirely perfect mechanism would be wrecked by eccentricity.

PANDULPH. Exactly so. *If* there were a kink. But a kink would be a falsehood, and a falsehood in the geometry of God is inconceivable. But you are not the geometry of God, Your Grace, you are a mortal man and very prone to falsehood. As I said, you have omitted something. In your account of your stewardship of the remote English vineyard, you failed to mention, did you not, that for six whole years you yourself were excommunicate and your kingdom laid under Interdict. You chose to defy the Pope –

JOHN. Over a technical matter –

PANDULPH. The appointment of an Archbishop. Technical? Perhaps. But in the end, you were governed. You were compelled to submit.

JOHN. I chose to submit. I viewed the matter in a larger perspective. I never make the mistake of elevating small disputes into questions of principle. Besides, I had to deal with Baronial discontent and a danger of invasion from France.

PANDULPH. Nevertheless, you surrendered your crown to the Pope and received it back, upon terms. Here it is. (*He holds up the crown.*)

JOHN. I am glad to get it back. All my jewels are beautiful, this more beautiful than most, quite apart from its significance. You haven't abstracted any of the decorations, have you? No: that is just as well.

PANDULPH (*withdrawing crown from* JOHN's *reach*). Kneel, my son, and acknowledge your fault.

JOHN. Under pressure, and with all due calculation, I will kneel. (*He does so.*)
Having offended God and our Mother the Holy Church in many things, and hence being in great need of the Divine

Mercy, we offer and freely yield to God and to the Lord Pope Innocent III and his catholic successors, the whole kingdom of England for the remission of our sins, so that from henceforth we hold it from him and from the Holy Roman Church our Mother, as a sworn vassal. And let this Charter of Obligation remain for ever valid.

PANDULPH. Come then, exalted Prince, fulfil the promises given and confirm the concessions offered, so that God Almighty may ever fulfil any righteous desire of yours, enabling you so to walk amid temporal blessings as not to fail of winning the eternal.

He places the crown on JOHN's *head.*

JOHN (*standing up*). And furthermore I swear that as soon as I have the means and opportunity I will lead an army to the Holy Land and redeem from the Paynim Turk, by force, the Blessed Sepulchre of Christ.

PANDULPH (*producing a jewelled cross*). Wear this upon your breast in token of your sanctified intention. (*He hangs the cross round* JOHN's *neck.*)

JOHN. Diamonds? Good. Silver-gilt. Not so good. Parsimonious, rather.

PANDULPH. Make sure you keep your word. The Pope is a man of honour, he expects his vassals to be likewise.

JOHN. He has evidently little experience of the sort of vassal that I am lumbered with.

1215: a meadow upon the bank of the Thames, between Staines and Windsor: Runnymede.

SCENE THREE

A picture of pavilions, flags, men-at-arms, with a field full of flowers and the river curling round.

CLERKS *arranging a table and a throne, and preparing the apparatus for moulding the royal seal. Copies of the Charter.*

Enter MARSHAL.

JOHN (*to* CLERK). Put that table facing north: I want the light behind me.

MARSHAL. Sire.

JOHN. Marshal.

MARSHAL. It is the nineteenth of June.

JOHN. I do believe it is.

MARSHAL. Your loyal barons, sire, desire to know –

JOHN. My *what*, sir?

MARSHAL. I was endeavouring to apply a correct and decorous courtesy to a situation that is already –

JOHN. But they are not loyal, are they, Marshal?

MARSHAL. No.

JOHN. Then God's Feet, do not call them so! They are in armed rebellion against me, sir, they have captured my castles, they have refused to pay me my taxes, they have colleagued themselves, Marshal, in a treasonable conspiracy and withdrawn their oaths of fealty. A correct courtesy to such runagates is to cut off their testicles. I am very well aware that you are regarded as the ancient arbiter of chivalry in this kingdom, but to be so scrupulous in your terms is to speak with two tongues in one mouth, which is dishonest and I will not have it. Honesty, William, above everything, when conferring with your King. My barons, you were about to say, desire to know – what?

MARSHAL. Whether you intend to confirm the Charter of Liberties you were so gracious as to approve, provisionally, four days ago. I would remind you, sire, that the barons agreed a truce with you until the beginning of this week, and for no longer. It is now Friday.

JOHN. They have more soldiers than I have. They insisted as a condition of truce that I disband my Flemish mercenaries. I suggested in return that as an earnest of good faith they should disband their own levies.

MARSHAL. They have not done so.

JOHN. No. But on the other hand, William, their army has

been raised from the peasants on their estates. It is very nearly harvest time. They will have to let them go home or they will have no food all winter. My men can come back from Flanders any time I care to whistle. Mine is a good policy to employ professionals where possible. They fight better, too.

MARSHAL. This is beside the point, is it not? The barons require an answer.

JOHN. Oh yes. So they do. We are not yet entirely satisfied, Marshal, with the terms of this document. The final clause in it provides for a committee of – let me refresh my memory – (*he picks up a copy of the Charter*) yes, twenty-five barons,

'Who must, with all their might observe, hold, and cause to be observed, the peace and liberties which we have granted by this present Charter.'

And so forth. Now – quis custodiet ipsos custodes? And, even more pertinently, who are to be the ipsos custodes?

MARSHAL. The Archbishop has suggested that a further thirty-eight barons should assist and partly control the twenty-five delegated. As to the composition of the twenty-five themselves, I am afraid –

JOHN. I too am afraid, sir. They will select the most traitorous and self-aggrandizing cormorants out of all their rebellious crew! Eustace de Vesci, Robert Fitzwalter, are they in the list?

MARSHAL. They are, but –

JOHN. And you have a son of your own, Marshal, what about him?

MARSHAL. Sire, my most unworthy headstrong son –

JOHN. Is leagued against his King. He has fallen into bad company, has he not, Marshal? Twenty-five over-kings to control the King of England. Do they desire me to cut my crown into two dozen and more pieces and distribute it among them?

MARSHAL. It was intended as no more than a safeguard, sire.

JOHN. A safeguard against what?

MARSHAL. Bad faith.

> *Enter* ARCHBISHOP. *He bows curtly to* JOHN, *who ignores him.*

JOHN. Whose bad faith? Oh William, I am an old man, grey-headed, fat . . .

MARSHAL. Sire –

JOHN. Not so old as you, of course. That would be difficult. After all, you were, as it were, my father's tutor, if not my grandfather's . . . But none the less, I am old. My memory is failing. So explain to me, my dear and faithful friend – how in the Name of God did all this turbulence begin?

MARSHAL. I suppose it began with the fall of Saucy Castle.

JOHN. And the loss of my French possessions. In order to retain them, I had to make wars. In order to make wars, I needed an army. The provision of such an army is the business of my barons, in return for which they hold their lands. But, as we have discovered, their men must go home to gather in the harvest, so instead I hire mercenaries, and mercenaries must be paid. So I demand from the barons a regular contribution known as the shield-tax, which has been accepted for generations as an adequate substitute for the sending of troops. And by God they refuse it me!

MARSHAL. Your shield-taxes were excessive, sire.

ARCHBISHOP. Not even your brother King Richard, with all the expenses of the Crusade –

JOHN. I am not my brother. (Archbishop, good morning, we are glad to see you here.) Nor is this year last year. And the price of goods and services increases unaccountably. We need a kink in the circle, do we not, Pandulph? Or possibly your immutable geometry does not take into consideration the ups and downs of money. Which are caused by the corn-harvest in Brittany or the wool-trade in Germany or something to do with the Jews – I don't know: do you know?

William here has never even thought about it, have you, William? But my soldiers demand to be paid.

MARSHAL. Your soldiers lost their battles, sire. The battles were in France. The barons of England see but small reason –

JOHN. Why they should be asked to protect the territories of their king. It all amounts to that. A grotesque lack of loyalty. And even defeated soldiers still demand to be paid. I keep to my bargains. Which is more than Richard did. For who holds Jerusalem? He swore that he would liberate it. The infidel is still there. But not for long. Our purpose is declared. It is generally accepted, I think, as being a worthy purpose.

ARCHBISHOP. If the Crusader himself is worthy, his worth is increased by that of his purpose. If he is not worthy –

PANDULPH. Insofar as he is a Crusader, he is to be deemed worthy, my Lord. It is akin to the vocation of a priest. A sacrament administered by a fornicator, for example, is nevertheless a valid endowment of Grace. The point is elementary, but –

ARCHBISHOP. We need not dispute it here. This morning it is not relevant.

JOHN. Oh yes it is.

ARCHBISHOP. Sire, it is not relevant. The barons expect an immediate answer. Are you or are you not prepared to confirm their Charter?

JOHN. As far as it goes, Archbishop, it is a very good Charter.

ARCHBISHOP. I hope so. I drew most of it up myself. I managed to restrain the more unjust of their demands.

JOHN. Indeed you did, and you are very loyal. Some of it is excellent. Listen to this:

'To no-one will we sell, to no-one will we refuse or delay right and justice.'

This clause cuts both ways. *I* have always respected the Laws and the Customs of England, and I have never refused justice. Sometimes the barons have. Now they will

not be able to, nor will anyone else. Good. And this, as well:
'No free man shall be arrested or imprisoned or deprived
of his freehold or outlawed or exiled or in any way destroyed, neither will we set forth against him or send
against him, except by the lawful judgement of his peers
and the law of the land.'
Have I ever attempted to do any of that?

MARSHAL. Sometimes, sire, it has – seemed so.

JOHN. The king in his own kingdom is surely permitted to
seem. Whether what he seems and what he is, are identical,
is quite another matter. If the barons as well as the King
shall pay heed to that clause, this land will be a Paradise for
those that inhabit it. What about this one?
'The City of London shall have all its ancient liberties and
free customs as well by land as by water.'
I have always been most careful to cherish the City of
London – when they built their new bridge across the river
I provided them the architect. How can they walk now from
Thames Street into Southwark without thinking of their
King in shame? And no longer time ago than the beginning
of last month, why, I granted them a Charter!

ARCHBISHOP. You tried to buy them with a Charter.

JOHN. What! Very well, it was a bribe. I needed their loyalty.
Yet such is the gratitude of the commercial classes, that
almost immediately they threw open their gates to the
Baronial Forces. And yet it was, was it not, an idiotic
treachery? The interests of trade and the interests of nobility
have always been disparate.

ARCHBISHOP. Good government under secure law is in the
interests of all classes, my lord.

JOHN. In the interests of all classes with power in their hands,
yes . . . Never mind, never mind it now. I suppose the
Mayor of London may retain his ancient liberties – provided that he tells this garrison to get out. Is he going to tell
them?

ARCHBISHOP. I will tell them, sire. There will be two sides to this agreement.

JOHN. There had better be, I think.

MARSHAL. We must trust to the honour of the barons. They are men of Christian chivalry and I cannot believe –

JOHN. I can. Twenty-five of them, on the evidence of their past history neither Christian nor chivalrous, are to supervise the enforcement of this Charter. We do not like their names and we do not like their intentions. We are not at all sure that we will grant them permission to supervise anything at all. Trust to their honour indeed. I judge men's honour by the standards of my own: and I know how much of the commodity I am able to afford. Will you never learn that a straightforward king is a dead king? You understand about it, don't you, Master Legate – you've seen the orbs and sceptres topple in your time.

PANDULPH. All flesh is grass, certainly.

ARCHBISHOP. But the Laws of God are immutable and the virtuous man –

JOHN. Is nonetheless a free being. And which of us dare predict how or in what direction we are going to sin next? I have a little mistress and last night she deceived me with a cook-boy from my kitchen. If I were the tyrannical Tiberius my loyal barons would have you believe, I would have put out her eyes. Instead, I went to bed with my wife. They are coming here at noon, are they not? I may condescend to receive them, I may even agree with them. On the other hand, perhaps I won't. The King, in fact, will Advise Himself. You must be patient and wait for him . . . (*He is going out, but stops and addresses a* CLERK.) What's your name?

CLERK. Augustine, my Lord.

JOHN. Then you are named after a strange fellow. St Augustine of Hippo. Altogether too penitent. He enjoyed his sins while he committed them: he should have been grateful later for the pleasure he had obtained. It is never too late to give thanks.

Exit JOHN.

MARSHAL. What do you think he intends to do?

ARCHBISHOP. William, he has told you. He intends to advise himself.

MARSHAL. You really believe he has not yet made up his mind?

ARCHBISHOP. I do not believe he has ever made up his mind.

MARSHAL. But surely he cannot repudiate his promises at this stage of the business? He has already sealed a provisional draft of the barons' demands. His honour is committed, Archbishop.

ARCHBISHOP. Yes.

PANDULPH. (*to* CLERK). What are you doing?

CLERK. Making copies of the Charter, sir: and preparing the wax for the seal.

PANDULPH. Upon whose instructions?

CLERK. Upon the King's instructions, sir.

MARSHAL. Surely he would not have ordered these preparations, had he not intended to –

ARCHBISHOP. He has also ordered preparations for undertaking a Crusade.

MARSHAL. Not very serious ones.

ARCHBISHOP. The work of two or three clerks at copying out documents is not necessarily very serious either.

PANDULPH. And yet if he does intend to confirm the Charter, this work will be needed. We should not ignore it. Nor should we ignore the possibility of a Crusade, my Lord Archbishop. The Pope does not ignore it.

ARCHBISHOP. I regret to say the Pope has very little understanding of what goes on in this country, Master Pandulph.

PANDULPH. The Pope had sufficient understanding to appoint you Archbishop, your Grace, at a time when the King had another man in mind and the monks of Canterbury yet another. I did not think that *you* would question the wisdom of His Holiness.

ARCHBISHOP. The wisdom of His Holiness cost England six years of Interdiction. The King, who is a proud man, had to face a humiliating reversal of all that he had striven for, and I myself, despite my Archbishopric, have suffered untold depth of spiritual grief. Despair is a deadly sin. If I have not yet committed it, it is only because my theoretic loyalty to the Vicar of Christ has deterred me. I tell you the truth, Pandulph, because I am a man of God and if God is not truth, God is nothing and my ministry is nothing. The fault of this King is that he has never understood the nature of truth. He has believed that it can be discovered in all worldly manifestations, whether good or bad, with no distinction made between them. It is as though he has looked through a painted church-window and said, 'Here the sky outside is red, here it is green, here it is yellow, and so forth.' Any man of any sense knows that the sky carries one colour only, its own colour, God's colour. God is not a glazier. Glaziers are arbitrary. So is the King.

PANDULPH. Yes. But if the King really thinks he sees all those colours, should not the men who have to deal with the king at least pretend to see them also? To continue your analogy – we put painted windows in our churches to educate and entertain the ignorant: but if we ourselves make too great a parade of our own private contempt for the secrets of the glazier's art, we are in danger of disillusioning our congregation.

MARSHAL. I am not altogether sure what you two gentlemen are talking about. But if the King does not confirm this Charter, the barons will depose him – they may even kill him. Untrustworthy or not, he is still the King of England and I have taken oaths in his service. Upon what does he stick? The Twenty-five Controllers? Would he accept them, do you think, if the barons were to renew their own old oaths of service and keep to those oaths?

ARCHBISHOP. I think that he might. But they have taken

many oaths in the past and they have broken them always.

MARSHAL. Under grave provocation. The King has continually demanded the shield-tax at times when no other king had ever been known to do so. We must be protected by precedent, Archbishop, there are certain precedents and customs governing the duties of the nobility of the realm, and here they are written down –

ARCHBISHOP. Yes, Marshal, yes. I am in agreement with you. Yes. But the King is not predictable. It is necessary to establish more than detailed precedent: we must set forward principles and make him keep to those. I am by no means convinced, Pandulph, that I have your support.

PANDULPH. The only principle which has my support, Your Grace – and it should be the only one to have yours – is the principle of the Supremacy of the Church in spiritual matters. Now the King, being a declared Crusader, has accepted that principle already.

MARSHAL. The King is no more a Crusader than I am a washerwoman. It is completely irrelevant to his quarrel with the barons.

PANDULPH. Do you think so? The leader of the barons has shewn no great love for the Church.

MARSHAL. Indeed, I fear not. Though he chooses to call himself the Marshal of the Army of God. Here he is now. I wonder what angel gives him his battle-orders? My Lord Fitzwalter . . .

    Enter FITZWALTER, DE VESCI, YOUNG MARSHAL *and other Barons, and the* MAYOR OF LONDON.

    FITZWALTER *acknowledges* MARSHAL'S *salutation with a nod.*

FITZWALTER. Ink, parchment, wax, black-beetles in attendance . . . He intends to put his seal? Or does he perhaps not so intend? Archiepiscopal embarrassment . . . Marshal, you have the air of a man whose nose has been tied to the tail of a dog. Where is he?

MARSHAL. The King, do you mean, sir?

FITZWALTER. His soldiers are in Flanders. Mine are across the river. Just over there. I shall allow him one hour. At the end of that time the Army of God will desire to eat its dinner.

ARCHBISHOP. It is unwise of you to call yourselves that.

DE VESCI. The Army of God? Justice belongs to God and we are hungry for justice.

ARCHBISHOP. Hungry. A just word. When your belly is full, the justice will be forgotten.

DE VESCI. I see no reason why you should insult your con-federates in this rebellion. What articles of the Charter will the King not accept?

MARSHAL. Twenty-five over-kings to command the King of England.

FITZWALTER. That article is cardinal.

MARSHAL. I told him so. He will probably agree to it, if there is a second committee to help control the first.

FITZWALTER. He can have that if he wants. I will select it.

ARCHBISHOP. No sir. I will.

FITZWALTER. As you wish. What else?

ARCHBISHOP. The City of London. Whose liberties, you will remember, are to be affirmed in the Charter. Have you asked the Mayor if you may remain within his walls?

FITZWALTER. No, but I'll ask him now. May we, sir, remain within the walls of your city?

MAYOR. Why, you are there already, my Lord. I could not turn you out even if I wanted to. But I suppose you might say our liberties are much the same thing as yours, and your soldiers are needed to keep them. On a question of keeping – what about the king's promises, even if he does put his seal, do you think that he will?

YOUNG MARSHAL. Keep them? No sir.

MARSHAL. The word of your Sovereign is not to be disputed! I had not wished to speak to you. I do not recognize my son as a member of this rebellion.

YOUNG MARSHAL. If the King grants the Charter we will not be a rebellion. Our purposes are lawful, father.

MARSHAL. You have just said he will not grant it.

YOUNG MARSHAL. I said he will not keep to it.

MARSHAL. It is not for the son of the Marshal to doubt the honour of the King!

ARCHBISHOP. Gentlemen, at this present time, there is nothing that is not doubtful. Therefore, in order to shew the king that we at least have truth and justice for our cause, I would like you to subscribe to this small declaration I have concerned myself to draw up. Small but most important. (*He reads from a paper.*)

'Know that we are bound by oaths and homage to our Lord John King of England to protect faithfully his life limbs and worldly honour, against all mortal men, and to guard and defend his rights, the rights of his heirs, and the rights of his realm.'

My Lord Robert Fitzwalter, will you put your seal on this? We can present it to the King.

FITZWALTER. No I will not. He must put his own seal on his own document first.

ARCHBISHOP. My Lord Eustace de Vesci?

DE VESCI. I have taken oaths to the King before. It is not necessary to repeat them.

ARCHBISHOP. It will help to convince the king that –

FITZWALTER (*drawing his sword*). His soldiers are in Flanders. Mine are across the river.

All the BARONS *draw likewise* (*except* YOUNG MARSHAL.)

ARCHBISHOP. Is this your decisive answer?

FITZWALTER. Yes.

ARCHBISHOP. I am afraid that the King is not going to seal the Charter.

DE VESCI. We offered him one hour. It is not yet a quarter gone. We will wait.

The BARONS *sit down, on the ground.*

ARCHBISHOP. Let me endeavour to persuade you once again –

FITZWALTER. No.

MARSHAL. Put away that sword, sir. It is most unseemly to draw your blades in the presence of your Marshal – when he has not drawn his.

DE VESCI. We are the Army of God and we have a Marshal of our own.

MARSHAL. You also have a Charter – there it is, written down, the Word of Law, sir, law, good precedent and good custom, the alternative to blood. Yet here you offer blood as the alternative to law, and I think you would prefer it.

FITZWALTER. Yes, I would too. This is John's Charter, not ours – he has foisted it upon us to withhold his own defeat and by God I do regret that ever we considered it!

ARCHBISHOP. No, Fitzwalter, no, it is not King John's Charter, it is derived from the Charter of King Henry I and according to ancient precedent. Your swords at this moment will devalue it completely. The Marshal is quite right.

FITZWALTER. The Marshal is too old, I have had enough of the Marshal, I am about to give the order to my army to set forward.

YOUNG MARSHAL. Your hour has not expired yet.

FITZWALTER. My hour expired last year. By further prolongation we are being made ridiculous.

> JOHN *enters, behind them, taking them by surprise. They automatically find themselves getting up, leaving their swords on the ground.*

JOHN. Indeed? Please be seated. Do you have the wax ready, Augustine? Good, to work then, to work.

> *The* CLERKS *begin to seal the Charter.*

> JOHN *sits down on the throne.*

Saucy Castle, which was built by my brother King Richard as the principal defence of Normandy, fell eleven years ago, through no fault of its commander: and, as a result, Normandy has ceased to be a possession of the English Crown. The reason why Saucy Castle was so easily captured has been explained as a mistake made by the engineer who planned it. The deep ditch which surrounded the central keep had one small ridge of rock left running across it. This acted as a shelter for King Philip's sappers and miners when they were engaged on the otherwise impossibly dangerous task of damaging the foundations of the great stone wall above. The wall collapsed in due course, and the garrison was, as they put it, reduced. As to why the ridge of rock had been left across the ditch, it would (I think) be unwise to accuse the engineers of any treacherous design. The plans of the castle were largely the work of my brother himself, who had not only no vested interest in the future loss of Normandy, but also was noted as the foremost exponent of the art of fortification in Christendom. Which all goes to shew, does it not, how fallible we are, and equally how fallible is likely to prove the work of our hands.

The sealed Charter is handed to him and he touches it.
This is the work of *my* hand, translate it into the proper formality, I Deliver this my Act and Deed, there you are, Fitzwalter, you may call off your dogs, we intend to hold a Council in the City of Oxford in the middle of next month, we shall be glad of your attendance.

He gets up abruptly and turns away. There is an awkward pause. JOHN *has taken them totally by surprise.*

MARSHAL. The King has spoken, gentlemen.

FITZWALTER. Then there is no more to say. We will meet him at Oxford. In the meantime –

ARCHBISHOP. Copies will be sent at once to every corner of the kingdom. The Sheriffs of each County are to take order that it be read out aloud to the assembled population and displayed in the Cathedrals, so that all men will understand what has been agreed and what has been granted them, what Laws and what Customs have been established, and confirmed, and given under the King's Seal. At this forthcoming Council, each article of the Charter will be examined in detail, and its immediate application conferred upon, and enforced.

MARSHAL. The King gives you leave to depart. God Save the King!

Some of the BARONS *sheepishly join in this invocation. The* BARONS *and the* MAYOR *go out, awkwardly enough.*

JOHN. And you as well, William. Archbishop. Master Pandulph. We are grateful for your duties, so freely carried out ... God's Bones, I am desirous to be left alone!

MARSHAL *and* ARCHBISHOP *go.* PANDULPH *retires to his chair, but does not sit down.*

JOHN *addresses the* CLERKS.

You heard what the Archbishop said. See the document is properly distributed from one end of England to the other. He gave you a schedule, no doubt, of all the copies that are to be made? Let me look at it ... Yes, all these are correct ... And one additional copy, with an explanatory letter. Send it to the Pope.

Exit JOHN.

PANDULPH *comes over to the* CLERK.

PANDULPH. You are astonished?

CLERK. There had been no provision made for a copy to the Pope. But it will not take long to complete. Shall we sent it to Rome, or commit it to you for despatch?

PANDULPH. The King told you to send it. It will get there so much the quicker if you do.

CLERK. I suppose, when you come to think of it, sir, it is only natural that His Holiness should be kept informed. After all –

PANDULPH. After all, the King is now his man. And all the rebellions and coercive conspiracies that may take place against the King, also in a sense take place against the person of the Pope. For which reason his opinion concerning this document may be said to be important. By the end of the summer we in England should have heard it: and also by the

end of the summer the King should have had time to recruit
new troops in Flanders?

As the CLERKS *busy themselves with the parchments,*
PANDULPH *comes downstage.*

Storm breaks in among the perfect circles,
Every day a puff of wind or a rumble of thunder
Declares some vain attempt to declare – what?
Very busy very busy very busy!
Whatever it is, it will be vain,
It will be some broken blunder:
But we who preserve the circles
Preserve their unfaulted music,
And we who are privileged to hear it
Can do no more than wonder
When presumptuous persons, particularly Bishops,
Believe that they with their own false notes can steer it
Into a new tune.
Why, they do not think that God speaks through their
Charter?
This month is the twelve hundredth and fifteenth June
Since God *did* speak.
Who would dare to seek
For the marble fingers of Mount Sinai
Crooked around that serious young man's pen?
Blood bones and water
To be laughed at hereafter
Or brittle glass windows to be broken by broken men.

He rolls up his chart and goes.

Act Two

SCENE ONE

A sealed copy of the Charter hung opposite PANDULPH's *chair.*
A picture of the interior of a Gothic building of some complexity,
with clerks sitting writing at desks.

   Enter PANDULPH *and* CLERK – *the latter carrying an armful*
   of parchments.

PANDULPH. Very busy very busy, yes.

CLERK. Do you think it necessary for copies of these to be
   sent to the Pope?

PANDULPH. I doubt it. His Holiness has been told about the
   sow – he ought to be able to deduce the piglets, surely?

CLERK (*shewing him the parchments*). Chancery Writs for the
   most part, dealing with various personal grievances which
   come within the general terms of the Charter, For example,
   many noblemen have long claimed in vain the possession of
   castles which the King has sequestered for non-payment of
   debt or for failure in loyalty, or, you might say, for no
   reason at all – a simple expression of royal disfavour. They
   are now to be told that the King's action was not in accordance with the Ancient Laws and Customs: and they may
   have their castles back. Thus the Lord de Quenci obtains
   Mountsorrel Castle, the Lord Fitzallen Richmond Castle,
   and the Lord Fitzwalter – to whom I would personally grant
   no more than a six-foot trench of earth – is awarded the
   custody of the castle of Hereford. Eustace de Vesci – to
   whom I would personally grant no more than a six-foot
   trench of earth with quick-lime in it – is permitted once
   again to resume his traditional hunting rights in the County
   of Durham. May he catch a rabbit that has eaten some un-
   wholesome herb and die of it himself. Of course there is no

question but that the King has acted in the past, one might say, illegally. Why not? When unscrupulous men were using the forms of legality to withhold justice, to oppress their people, and to refuse their dutiful services to the household of their sovereign? Why not?

PANDULPH. For the King to amend his own inequitable judgements is a praiseworthy work. But all the judgements he has given are not now accounted inequitable, are they?

CLERK. No, indeed, why should they?

PANDULPH. And he is not yet an old man. Or at least he would not be if he disciplined his appetites. He has many more judgements to give. Can he give them, do you think, from his own free heart and mind as a son of his father anointed by the Oil of God, when twenty-five disloyal barons, unanointed, chosen only by their own self-evident partial word, are to superintend his every act?

CLERK. They can, I suppose, ensure that the King's proceedings do not go too far counter to the promises made at Runnymede – if the King conducts their conduct as carefully as he knows how, they need perhaps no more impede him than ministers or advisers commonly do. Which has not in the past been a very extensive impediment, shall we say?

PANDULPH. In the past maybe, no. But now you will find it different: for these men are pragmatic, they are arbitrary and unpredictable. Of course the King has been accused of being exactly the same himself. But Our Lord once compared the Kingdom of Heaven to an unjust judge: He also told a story of most unsuitable wages offered by an overseer for work in a vineyard, and told it what is more with apparent approval. The afflictions of Job came upon him for no reason; and when the Tower of Siloam fell, the men who were killed by it were in no way outrageous sinners above all who dwelt in Israel. God, by definition, cannot be unjust: therefore, these apparent inequities, when related to the whole of the Divine Wisdom which we are not yet able to perceive, will prove to be by no means as arbitrary as they may seem. Such examples, however, though they may justify the King, can never do so for the barons. Their committee of twenty-five is set up without sanction: it condemns its own self: and you will find it a stumbling-block.

CLERK. Sir, you underestimate the King. He has not yet met the twenty-five. When the Council at Oxford commences –
 Enter JOHN.

JOHN – I think we shall be horrified by some indecent exposure . . . Pandulph, do not dare to say to your most venerable master that I am not an honest man. (*He indicates the parchments.*) Look at all these – silver and gold buttons, jewelled hooks and eyes, snipped from my own garments, my own most personal underwear, and tossed to the disgusting multitude, broadcast largesse like a king in a fairy tale – and for what reason sir? Because I gave my word. My conscience is clear when I enter this Council. I am in process already of abiding by the Charter. But will they be?

Aha, we shall discover.
By the look upon their faces
And their posture in their places,
We shall know what they intend.
God defend
But that I should prove
An easy man to love:
But if hatred is their preference
My own posture at this conference
Will be that of a very hedgehog!

Are we ready, Augustine, are the Barons in Council assembled? Shall we go in?

CLERK. Yes, Your Grace, the Barons attend upon you.

JOHN. The tone of your voice – not very confident . . . why not? Never mind. To business, to business . . .

 PANDULPH *sits down in his chair. The Council is dis-*

*covered – a throne in the centre, two benches for the Coun-
cillors flanking it. These are occupied by all the* BARONS
from Act I, MARSHAL *and the* ARCHBISHOP.
When they see the KING, *the* MARSHAL *and* ARCHBISHOP
rise. The others remain seated.

MARSHAL. My lords, the King's Grace, my lords!

JOHN. Thank you, William: but I have been observed, I
think. Gentlemen, we are making our entrance. Do you not
intend to rise, as a sign of your respect? . . . Very well, you
may be seated. So their postures are relaxed, are they?

He goes and stands by the throne.

A relaxed posture is good for the digestion, I am told. No
doubt you have dined heavily. I am suffering from gout, and
my doctor has not allowed me to eat anything today
except for one inconsiderable collation. I am therefore
hungry, impatient, somewhat irritable, and quite happy to
stand. Despite the pain in my foot. In my right foot,
extreme pain. This Council is declared to be in session, and
as I look at this Council, in session, indeed, as I walk up and
down the hall in which this Council is contained – (*He walks
up and down*) – I come rapidly to the conclusion that there is
only one thing to discuss. Any examination of the detailed
provision of the Charter is entirely redundant, until you
remove your troops from the City of London. Your side of
the agreement, you equivocating whoremongers – are you
going to keep to it or not!

DE VESCI (*leaping to his feet*). Don't you call me a whore-
monger – there are known facts against you –

FITZWALTER (*ditto*). Insults and abuse is not what we have
come here for –

Other BARONS *jump up, shouting –*

BARONS (*generally*). Abide by the Charter – Fulfil your
promises – Why don't you keep your word – etc. etc.

JOHN. Good, you're on your feet. Then I can relieve mine, at

the expense of my buttocks – the gout hasn't reached those
I'm glad to say.

He sits down on the throne. The BARONS *are not quite
decided whether to stand or sit.*

Eustace, now you're up there, you can stay up! You too,
Fitzwalter! That's better . . . Now will you all please sit. So,
having re-established the normal courtesies, let us hear
about these 'known facts'. A little lubricious scandal always
helps to oil the wheels of government. At least when *I'm*
turning the crankshaft it does . . . Go on. then, my bold
cock-a-doodle-dandy – facts, if you please, boy, facts!

DE VESCI. I am a man of unimpeachable nobility. My ancestors –

JOHN. We are not here concerned with your ancestors,
Eustace. We want facts – against *me* – remember?

DE VESCI. You have seduced, contrary to all the regulations of
polite conduct, and the accepted order of society, you have
seduced –

JOHN. Her, her, and her . . . at different intervals of time, and
with different degrees of pleasure. Yes. So have you. Does it
matter?

DE VESCI. I am alluding to ladies of established parentage. I
am alluding to ladies of established matrimonial status. I am
alluding to –

JOHN. You are alluding to your own wife, Eustace – and taking
a very long time to come to the point. So it does matter. She
was yours, and I took her. Have you proof?

DE VESCI. My lords, this is intolerable!

JOHN. It would be, if you had proof, beyond her own word for
it, and women will say anything. So will some men. You
know where the proof will lie – it will lie in the accounts of
the Royal Exchequer, because you know very well that if I
did take your wife it would have been because you yourself
desired me to remit you your taxes. Justifiable taxes. The

King is short of money and will do anything to get it – which is why we are here today. The money is demanded in lieu of levied soldiers, the wife is demanded in lieu of levied money. You don't imagine that an ugly old wineskin like me seduced her by the exercise of my physical charms, do you? God corrode my sweetbreads, de Vesci, did she come to me for nothing! Or did she never come at all? We will not discuss the question of prostitution any further. I mentioned the City of London, I want an answer.

ARCHBISHOP. My Lord –

JOHN. I was really addressing the Marshal of the Army of God, my Lord, who has not yet opened his mouth – at least to any purpose. However, God has another army, happily celibate. You may speak.

ARCHBISHOP. The barons have refused to leave London, my Lord.

JOHN. Why?

ARCHBISHOP. They have a reason. It is not a very good one, in my opinion: but as military men, they justify it thus. Until it becomes manifest that the royal obligations contained in the Charter are to be adhered to, they do not see why they should be compelled to remove a garrison which, again from the point of view of military men, affords them great advantage.

JOHN. So it does. They sit down in London, and they sit down in my Council, and they leave it to me to weary my poor afflicted legs. I know why they sit in London. If they want help from the King of France, all he has to do is to sail up the Thames to them. Which makes them feel so strong they can defy their King to his face, their conciliatory benevolent King, who seeks only to make peace with them. It is absolutely unheard-of that subjects under allegiance can remain seated upon the entry of their monarch: and the only thing that makes them rise is obscenities in the mouth of that monarch. We are amazed . . . Archbishop, if I could kill these fellows here, I would. But at the moment I can't. Can you suggest an alternative?

ARCHBISHOP. Temperance.

JOHN. God help us – for whom?

ARCHBISHOP. For everyone, sire. In order to offer aid to the army in London, any French expedition must somehow pass the Tower. Now, if the Tower were held –

JOHN. By the King? It would be wonderful. But I don't hold it, so why mention it?

ARCHBISHOP. Not by the King, my lord. By me.

JOHN. I was not aware that you were in the possession of troops.

ARCHBISHOP. The Tower garrison is a permanent one, allegedly in your service. But the Constable there has declared for the barons. If he has changed sides once, he can change them again. My Lord Fitzwalter, will you allow this officer to put himself under my orders?

DE VESCI. Can you trust him?

ARCHBISHOP. Can you?

DE VESCI. The Tower is generally recognized as impregnable. So in fact, if he chooses, the fellow inside of it can have the laugh on all of us.

FITZWALTER. We're not giving up the Tower – Holy Virgin, it is impregnable!

DE VESCI. So long as we have an army in London town itself, I think we can give it up.

A BARON. We're not giving up the Tower.

DE VESCI (*beckoning* FITZWALTER *and some others into a huddle*). Come here . . . the Constable at present is our man. There is no doubt about that. Therefore it will do us no harm if he puts himself under the orders of the Archbishop – as a diplomatic fiction, for God's sake. The Constable is not going to stand all-alone-except-for-Jesus at the corner of the city when we occupy the rest of it. (*He jerks his thumb at the* ARCHBISHOP.) *He* can do that sort of thing any time he wants, he's three-quarters of a saint, isn't he? – it's his business. The Constable is a soldier, the business of a soldier is to be on the side that wins, which is either us or King Slapstick, it is certainly not Canterbury. Have I made myself clear? (*He rejoins the main body of the Council.*) My Lord of Canterbury, in the interests of peace, the Army of God is glad to accord to the Clergy of God permission to hold the Tower.

ARCHBISHOP. My Lord Fitzwalter?

FITZWALTER. Eh? Yes, of course, your permission is accorded. Did you not hear him say so?

ARCHBISHOP. Thank you, my Lord.

JOHN. Peace will no doubt be grateful for your concern for her interests, Eustace. She is represented, I believe, in antique statuary, as a beautiful woman, dishevelled, subject to occasional rape. And how long, Archbishop, do you propose to occupy my castle, upon your own volition, while my city next door to it is occupied by these, upon their own volition?

ARCHBISHOP. As a temporary compromise only, my Lord.

JOHN. Then put a term to it, sir.

ARCHBISHOP. The Feast of the Assumption?

FITZWALTER. When is that?

ARCHBISHOP. Really, my Lord . . .

JOHN. Well, when is it? We are not the Diocesan Chapter, you know. (*To* CLERK.) Do you know when is it?

CLERK. The fifteenth of August, my Lord.

JOHN. One month. Very good. You're out of London in one month. Agreed?

FITZWALTER. This can be agreed, yes –

  DE VISCI *whispers in his ear.*

That is to say, provided –

JOHN. Provided what? That the King of France brings in one thousand archers?

FITZWALTER. No. That the King of England brings in none

at all; and that all the nobility, the chief clerisy, the judiciary, in fact the entire apparatus of this kingdom, have taken oaths to accept the Charter. They have not yet done so. Furthermore, they must obey the Charter and in particular the newly-established Council of Twenty-five Barons as represented here. It must be understood that we are the Kingdom of England!

JOHN. God help the English.

JOHN goes out abruptly.

After a moment's confusion the Council disperses, everyone leaving the stage (including PANDULPH*), except the* CLERK*, who remains, sorting out his parchments.*

JOHN re-enters with the ARCHBISHOP *and* MARSHAL.

JOHN. Augustine, shew to these disturbed dignitaries the work you have in hand.

CLERK. These are but a few, my lords, among the enormous number of documents which scriveners of the Household are hastening to complete. They are at their desks night and day –

ARCHBISHOP. Very probably. I have no desire to examine the parchments. If the King states that the provisions of the Charter are being carried out by his servants, it is not for me to put his word to the test. Sire, why did you not declare these letters to the Council? It might have helped to mollify –

JOHN. If you do not presume to put my word to the test, why should they? My word was given at Runnymede: surely I have no need to repeat it.

MARSHAL. All that they require, sire, is an earnest of good faith.

JOHN. Our Seal is upon the Charter, Marshal. Is not that sufficient?

MARSHAL. Sire, I will speak boldly –

JOHN. Will you? You sound overwhelmed by the force of your own intention; I do not know why. There has been, if anything, an excess of bold speaking today. However, do not let yourself be inhibited by your tardy recognition of the atmosphere of the time. Continue, be bold. Sit down, if you wish, and extend your feet before me, omit nothing that will proclaim you to be a man of the mode.

MARSHAL. The mode, sire, disgusts me. But it is a mode that derives from prolonged suspicion and frustration upon both sides of the argument. The barons are aware that although much of the Charter is no more than a recapitulation of previous Charters, – King Henry I, I believe –

ARCHBISHOP. That is correct. King Henry II also made various undertakings, which –

MARSHAL. Quite so. But there is no precedent for the imposition upon the King of the twenty-five Lords Commissioner, or whatever they call themselves. There has always of course been a Council of State to offer advice and it has generally been to the advantage of the commonwealth that such advice should be respected on the part of the King. But a Council with power to forbid a royal enactment – indeed to forbid it under the threat of armed rebellion, which is what the Charter provides for, my Lord Archbishop, and I told you at the time it should never have been framed in precisely those terms –

JOHN. Keep to the point, sir, the whole damned thing should never have been framed . . .

MARSHAL. Such a Council is most dangerous and the more dangerous indeed for being unrepresentative in its members. Had a Parliament been chosen from among *all* your nobility instead of merely from the partisans of Fitzwalter and de Vesci, then perhaps – but in any case, sire: they know as well as we do that their demands are exorbitant, that you cannot be expected to lie down beneath them, and that – well, they are afraid of your reaction and hence behave so badly. I have tried to excuse them: but their conduct is unpardonable, and it's no use trying to blink it.

JOHN. I do not try to blink it – as you have seen.

ARCHBISHOP. I *have* seen it, sire, with abundant sorrow.
  Surely it is obvious that a promise of liberty is worth nothing
  to the liberated unless it can be enforced?

JOHN. Archbishop, it is a promise that has been given by your
  King!

ARCHBISHOP. As the Marshal has just reminded us, you are
  not the first King to have been compelled to give it.

JOHN. Indeed sir, I am, the very first indeed, to have been
  compelled.

ARCHBISHOP. Which only makes it worse. History demon-
  strates and you have admitted that kings have broken faith.
  It is sheer minstrelcraft and rhetoric to pretend otherwise,
  and I for one am not impressed by it.

MARSHAL. My Lord, please, be careful –

ARCHBISHOP. No I will not. I am not now a subject appealing
  to his king, I am a priest of the Lord God reproaching a
  devious man! John, son of Henry, the truth in you has been
  found wanting, too many times.

JOHN (*for a moment it seems as though he is going to strike him*).
  Stephen son of – I don't know who your father was and I am
  surprised you think it appropriate to mention the name of
  mine. He too had difficulties with one of his Archbishops. It
  was more than a word that was broken upon that occasion,
  I remember.

ARCHBISHOP. Words, bones, and hearts – all of them are
  fragile. *My* heart, what about it? (*He points to the Charter.*)
  That work on the wall is the blood of my heart and if in
  defence of it I do have to suffer the fate of Thomas Becket I
  will not turn my hand to the abatement of its meaning! . . .
  But this is foolish, I am sorry, I have only this moment
  described your method of speech as minstrelcraft; and here
  I am parading my own swollen words like any Lancelot or
  Roland in an unreliable romance.

JOHN. Don't be ashamed of yourself, we all enjoy poetry. My
  brother Richard Lionheart even used to compose it, and

when he was taken prisoner it was his minstrel who discovered where. Unfortunately.

ARCHBISHOP. But the poetry that will arise from this cap-
tivity will not be enjoyable. For who can take pleasure when
virtue is in a dungeon and there are none to bring her out?
Yet such will be the song, the lament that will survive you.
It is not only yourself whose sovereignty is committed to
the Charter – your little son Henry, when he becomes king,
and his son, if he has one, and so on into the future to your
uttermost posterity – all these kings and queens will govern
according to custom and justice as set out in that schedule:
or else it is most unlikely that they will ever govern at all.

MARSHAL. Archbishop, this sounds like treason. If they do
not govern, who will?

ARCHBISHOP. The truth, not only of John, but of the House
of Plantagenet, will have been weighed in the balances,
Marshal, and found wanting altogether – 'Mene, mene tekel
upharsin' – their inheritance shall be given over to the Medes
and to the Persians – it is written, upon the wall!

Exit ARCHBISHOP, *weeping.*

JOHN. I suppose he means the French. Is it possible he could
be in league with them and be designing they should invade
this country? Was I unwise perhaps to allow him to command the Tower of London?

MARSHAL. Sire, I cannot believe that –

JOHN. I have always regarded him as honest. But he is a
cleric – consider his history – he is trained to wear two faces.
Here he is again.

The ARCHBISHOP *re-enters.*

MARSHAL (*to* CLERK). What is his history?

CLERK. University of Paris. Scholastic theology.

JOHN. Hardly a hopeful cradle for simply saintly pastors . . .
Well, sir, have you returned? You need not have troubled –
I heard no-one cry 'encore'.

ARCHBISHOP. I am the man responsible for the Charter: I am

the man who persuaded the barons to select from among their multifarious demands only those that could be justified by reference to ancient custom, and to cast away so many others that were selfish and tyrannous. The matter of the twenty-five, I grant you, was clumsily handled: but there had to be something like it, enforcement was essential. I am the man who codified and condensed certain broad, and in my opinion unwise, generalizations which you yourself, sire, suggested – I mean those clauses relating to the refusal of justice and imprisonment without trial. The principle behind them was good, but I think the barons would have preferred them in a more specific form, and I had enough trouble as it was to keep the barons contented, without inserting articles that might one day affect their own private privilege. I am, in fact, the man who has brought the liberty of the subject and the prerogative of the crown to march a little inwards from their palisaded lines, till both have been able to meet, here, on the parchment, in what might have been the place of darkest slaughter in the midst of a stricken field. Is my hard employment, then, to be so readily rejected?

JOHN. No, Stephen, no, it is not. We know you to be a true man, indeed, the truth of Jesus Christ is evident in your mouth – and despite our light and scornful disposition, we can never reject that. Please remember in mitigation that the House of Plantagenet is supposed to be descended from the Devil – we are Christians now, but not always very good ones. Nevertheless, I still do not see how I am going to be able to trust –

MARSHAL. Sire, I will speak boldly, and if you please, this time, do not jeer at me until you have heard me out. When your great predecessor King Arthur found himself at war with Mordred his unhappy son – yes indeed, it is minstrel-craft; but the deeds of the Round Table are an example to all good knights today. Arthur and Mordred brought their armies together on the field of Camlann. With difficulty a trumpet-of-parley was secured, and negotiations began between the chiefs. But alas, a little adder, creeping out of a bracken-bush, came up to one of the King's knights and stung him on the ankle. The knight drew his sword to cut the serpent in two, the drawn sword was observed by the armies on either hand, they took for granted there was treachery at work, and battle was immediately joined, with appalling ferocity. Two men alone survived from that conflict. The King was not one of them.

JOHN. But you were, I suppose. Forgive my frivolity, William; I am as much moved by your plea as by the steadfastness of the Archbishop. If I were to weep in front of you, no doubt you would call me crocodile. Answer me one question. How can I induce the barons to return to their castles? Even had I shewed them proofs of all the vast administration I have been conducting for their benefit, I still do not believe that they would stir their stumps and go. They will be in London long after the Feast of the Assumption. Will they not? Of course they will, and you know it. What are they afraid of, that they keep their army together so long?

MARSHAL. Your own army of Flemings, sire, when you bring them across the Channel.

JOHN. I have no intention whatever of bringing Flemings across the Channel.

ARCHBISHOP. Sire, is that true?

JOHN. Of course it is true. I am not an idiot, Archbishop. I too prefer even a humiliating charter to continued civil war.

MARSHAL. Sire, this is very important. The barons clearly believe that you are recruiting soldiers in Flanders. If I can, in your name, assure them that you are not, I think there is an excellent chance that they will evacuate London.

JOHN. You do? Very well. So listen to this. We are graciously pleased to afford you that assurance, as solemnly as we may. We only desire to levy soldiers from those who have a duty

to supply them: in other words, our loyal barons. Good God,
sir, you do not need me to tell you, the mercenary armies of
Flanders are notorious for uncontrolled brutality, and we
shall be glad to be rid of their help – if it can be so described.
Augustine, write at once to all the recruiting agents in the
Low Countries, with whom we may in past time have been
in communication, and tell them we have no further need
of their services. Write the letters today and let the Marshal
read them through before they are despatched. Sufficient?
Very good.

Exeunt JOHN *and* CLERK.

ARCHBISHOP. The army in London must be disbanded. This
could be a way to do it. I can conceive of no other.

MARSHAL. I am the one to carry this to the barons. If the King
is dishonourable, my name will be marked with the blotch.
Thus I fulfil my duty to the son of Henry Curtmantle and
to the brother of the Lionheart.

Exit MARSHAL.

The ARCHBISHOP *is on the way out by a different door,
when he is met by* PANDULPH *coming in.*

PANDULPH. My Lord, I have often heard His Holiness, when
reminiscent after the evening meal with a few dear companions, refer affectionately to the days that you and he
spent together at the University in Paris.

ARCHBISHOP. I am rejoiced that the Holy Father should so
remember me.

PANDULPH. He has spoken more than once of a course of
lectures you gave upon the Duties of the Episcopal Office.

ARCHBISHOP. They did achieve some small celebrity, in their
theoretic way. But as a guide to the present insensate pre-
dicament, I do not recommend you to study them.

PANDULPH. Did you have anything to say to your students
about the conduct of a bishop in command of a metropolitan
fortress?

ARCHBISHOP. No.

PANDULPH. Not even when the surrounding city is held by a
potentially hostile army?

Exit ARCHBISHOP.

Every additional closely-written line
That tries to fix, determine, and define,
Instead of a hard bright link in an irremovable chain,
Becomes rather the blade of a new hard wedge
Sledged into the tree-trunk to split the protesting grain.

Enter CLERK, *with a letter.*

And here comes one of the hammers.

CLERK. This letter, sir, is addressed by the King to a gentleman of the name of Hugh de Boves, last known to be resident
in the City of Bruges. He is a contractor for the supply of
mercenary soldiers: and will, for a due profit, raise, equip,
and transport entire armies to wherever they may be in
demand. The population of the Low Countries is at present
excessive, so he makes a good living.

PANDULPH. He will make a better one in hell, after he is dead.

CLERK. Precisely so. There is, I believe, a special bailiewick
in the Pit of Lucifer laid apart for stirrers-up of strife . . .
Now, the King is about to send another letter to Sir Hugh
to tell him he has decided to cancel the contract that was
negotiated last month. *This* letter will contradict that letter
and for obvious reasons cannot be sent openly. Therefore
the King would be exceedingly grateful if you, being the
Papal Representative, and therefore, one might say, above
suspicion, could personally take charge of this and despatch
it by your own messenger.

PANDULPH *takes the letter and looks at it dubiously.*

You need not be afraid, it is written in cipher. This may
appear villainous on the part of the King, but whatever the
hopes of the Archbishop, he is certain in his mind that the

leaders of the barons no longer regard the Charter as a satisfactory solution to their various grievances.

PANDULPH. Do they not? Do they not? Then what more do they want?

CLERK. As much as they can take, until the King dies and he is succeeded by a nine-year-old child – and then who will govern England?

PANDULPH. I hope not Sir Hugh de Boves . . . Nevertheless, I will deliver the letter.

CLERK. The King will be most grateful.

Exeunt severally.

SCENE TWO

A view of London river with the Bridge and the Tower.

A table and stools. On the table, wine and flagons, with a dicebox.

Enter DE VESCI, *pours himself a drink, drinks, and plays dice, muttering profanities.*

LADY DE VESCI *enters.*

DE VESCI. I was under the impression, madam, I had ordered you to remain in this lodging. I have just returned from Oxford, you were not here when I came back. Where were you?

LADY DE VESCI. I walked abroad to see the city, my Lord. What is so remarkable about that? The citizens' wives do it every day.

DE VESCI. Very possibly, madam. They have not been forbidden it by their husbands. You have.

LADY DE VESCI. I would be glad to hear the reason.

DE VESCI. You know very well the reason. I will not sully my mouth by repeating it. Why, you are nothing but a navigable river, a sluice, madam.

LADY DE VESCI. Continue.

DE VESCI. What do you mean, continue? I am waiting to hear you defend yourself. Will you please defend yourself, madam!

LADY DE VESCI. It should be easier for you to prove that I have been the King's mistress than for me to prove that I have not.

DE VESCI. I could put you in prison for what you have done to my honour – have you flogged by my knaves. It would not in any way be regarded as outrageous.

LADY DE VESCI. By the terms of the Charter which the King has just granted you, I think it might be regarded as extremely outrageous.

DE VESCI. The Charter, what Charter? It has nothing to do with you!

LADY DE VESCI (*reading from the Charter*). 'No free man shall be arrested or imprisoned or deprived of his freehold . . . except by the lawful judgement of his peers'. I am a free woman, indeed, a noblewoman – if you can establish a court of noble ladies of equivalent rank, I daresay they will be prepared to hear your cause against me, and to pronounce a verdict in accordance with the evidence.

DE VESCI. Evidence – why, I have enough evidence –

LADY DE VESCI. Nonsense, you have none.

DE VESCI. None. Except what is sung at every street corner and whispered in every corridor of every castle in the land . . . and what in the name of the Black Blood of Mahound do you mean by putting that sort of interpretation upon a document which – which does not mean what you think it means. No. The clause that you so amused yourself by quoting at your husband, at your Lord, was specifically intended to prevent men of my class from being hauled before tribunals consisting of persons of inferior rank – commoners and foreigners and God knows who besides. You know very well what the King's been doing with his Law-Courts – French clerks, and so forth, mercenary officers, he has had the impertinence to describe them as his Judges – well, he won't do it any more, we've put the cork in that bottle! And not in such a way as to give free passage for adultery, I hope.

LADY DE VESCI. Adultery with the King.

DE VESCI. He will not protect you here. We are in London now, and fortified.

LADY DE VESCI. Which is more than your Charter is, I'm afraid!

DE VESCI. I do not understand you.

LADY DE VESCI. The interpretation I put upon that clause may well have been unusual, though a lady in danger must grasp at any weapon:

When pursued by strong conquerors
We cannot be pickers and choosers.
For Cleopatra there was a small brown serpent,
For Daphne a green tree:
Sappho, I remember, jumped into the sea,
Penelope with her loom imposed on lechery constraint,
Jezebel spread out her pots of raddle and paint
And her stiff embroidered raiment:
Judith was fortunate – she had a sword.
All that is left for me
Is an ambidextrous word
Scrawled upon dry parchment.
Why should I care if you think it impertinent?

DE VESCI. Ambidextrous, ambidextrous, you say that of a word? A word means what it says and what it is meant to say – are you trying to tell me it can mean anything you want it to mean? Why, if this were found to be true –

LADY DE VESCI. Well, my Lord, if –

Enter FITZWALTER (*shewn in by a* SERVANT).

He helps himself to a drink.

FITZWALTER. The Mayor of London is in the courtyard with a face like a belt-buckle. He wishes to speak to us.

DE VESCI. He can wait. Something has just struck my mind, Robert – you may go, madam – struck it very forcibly –

FITZWALTER. Young Marshal has completed the arrangements for the tournament. We can hold it out at Hounslow, there is a good wide field, and the carpenters have had orders to put the stands up directly. (*He throws a dice and looks at the numbers.*)

Five and a four.

Nine green girls in a dancing line.

Are you going to have a throw?

DE VESCI. The words of the Charter – it has occurred to me suddenly that they are liable to misconstruction.

FITZWALTER. Very probably they are – are you going to throw the dice or not? A word is a word, you can turn it inside out like an old coat as many times as you want to; but victory in war, Eustace, is alone irreversible. Throw if you please.

DE VESCI *throws.* FITZWALTER *checks the score.*

Three and a five

Dead men eight have met their fate.

DE VESCI *passes a coin over.*

Thank you.

DE VESCI. Of course, you are quite right, there is no reason why *we* should be concerned about words . . . What about this war anyway? The old Marshal has solemnly informed me that Landless John has decided to dispense with his landless army. He has written letters to Flanders to say – send no more mercenaries. Are we to believe him?

FITZWALTER. We cannot but believe the old Marshal, he is the very shield and helm of rectitude – but for all that, he is a good man, I was a page in his household when I was a boy, he is an honest man: so therefore the news is true. But whether John's letters are true is quite another matter. Maybe they are. I think he is frightened. He knows that our own recruitment in the northern counties is increasing every week. He does not want a war. It will be very expensive and there is a strong chance he will lose it. (*He throws the dice.*)

DE VESCI (*counting them*).

Three and a two

Five wounds of blood on the Holy Cross of God.

I can do better than that. So, if there is not a war – and it *will* be expensive, I had rather do without it myself – we are committed to a Charter: and, as I have told you already, I am not at all sure that I know what it means.

FITZWALTER. I think we are going to be able to put upon that Charter whatever interpretation we think best. You ought not to be so scrupulous.

DE VESCI. No, I am not scrupulous. I am far-sighted if you like. (*Plays and looks at dice.*)

One, and bloody one

Tiny two, how do you do –

No, I am *not* paying up on that one, my attention was distracted.

LADY DE VESCI. It isn't a game of skill.

DE VESCI. What! Are you still here?

LADY DE VESCI. You can't plead distraction over dice. It is not the same thing as conversation with a lady. If it were, I am sure we would all be most happy to remit you your forfeits, otherwise you would be bankrupt.

DE VESCI. I shall remember this.

FITZWALTER. Which reminds me, young Marshal wants a lady, to be the Queen of Love at the tournament. Whose name should we put forward?

DE VESCI. We don't need a Queen of Love – I thought the purpose of a tournament was to fit ourselves for battle.

FITZWALTER. So it is, but apparently these things are done in Provence and young Marshal thinks he should introduce them here. It will entertain the citizens, and to judge from the expression upon the Mayor's countenance this evening – he is below stairs, I told you – they are in need of entertainment. I suggested your own wife. Have you any objections?

DE VESCI. Are you trying to insult me?

FITZWALTER. It would help you to demonstrate in public that you are not concerned for what was said to you at Oxford. You should take pains to indicate that the lady was seduced against her will and that you bear her no malice for it.

DE VESCI. For what possible reason do you imagine I should bear her no malice?

FITZWALTER. Christian charity. We have the Archbishop to think of, Eustace. If the Archbishop is not with us, I am afraid we will have lost the Mayor of London too. It is necessary for us to be more than a mere faction – I have said so many times.

LADY DE VESCI. I think you had better understand, my Lord Robert, I intend to preside over no tournament, whether for reasons of politics or personal reconciliation.

DE VESCI. She was ordered to go to her private apartment.

FITZWALTER. And yet she defies you. Why don't you take your belt to her?

DE VESCI. Oh yes, I did once, yes, and what happened? You saw very well what happened, at the Council at Oxford. She is encouraged by these damned garlic-mouth poets, there was a herd of them associated with the old black witchcraft queen – you know who I am talking about – Aquitanian Eleanor – *his* mother, that's the one – she brought them into Normandy and then into England, till we don't know where we stand. The fit and proper order laid out in good numbers, one–two–three–four–five it used to be, and no-one contradicted, but it's all over the map of Europe now, five–two–four–three–one or four–two–three–one–five, knees between the elbows and head between the ankles, that's custom and morality today! Seven Devils inside of Maudlin – she's still here and she's grinning – Blood of the Martyrs, Gabriel's Golden Gap, will you go to your room this minute – !

*He grabs his wife and throws her down in fury, then starts
dragging her impotently about the stage.* FITZWALTER *gives
way to laughter.*

Enter YOUNG MARSHAL.

YOUNG MARSHAL. Oh . . . I had not intended . . .

FITZWALTER. She won't go to her room. And he can't get her
to go to her room. By God I have seen a Lombard crossbow
serjeant keep better discipline upon a strumpet of the camp.

DE VESCI (*leaving her and turning upon* YOUNG MARSHAL).
I have a sufficiency of servants: why could they not announce
you?

FITZWALTER. This is indelicate of you, boy. I hope you are
ashamed.

YOUNG MARSHAL. I ask your pardon, Eustace, if I had known
I would have . . . but I have had a message today – from my
father's chaplain – my father himself will have nothing to do
with me – he tells me that the King has written letters to
Flanders –

FITZWALTER. Yes we know, we have heard it.

YOUNG MARSHAL. Then should we not disband our army at
once? It is also a fact that Writs have been issued from the
Royal Chancery confirming all the liberties that were
granted in the Charter.

DE VESCI. All of them?

YOUNG MARSHAL. Most of them.

DE VESCI. It will have to be all of them. And they must all pass
inspection. There is too much latitude in that Charter. I am
highly suspicious of it.

FITZWALTER (*to* YOUNG MARSHAL). I thought that we commissioned you to provide us with some diversion this
evening? Three strong whores from Billingsgate were
spoken of, I believe.

YOUNG MARSHAL (*looking at the lady*). Surely under the circumstances it would be a failure of courtesy to –

DE VESCI. Bring them up, boy. At once! You may oppose your

father in politics, but you have yet over-many of his inherited cobwebs making dismal your social habit. We'll have 'em up, make haste, make haste, young Galahad.

> YOUNG MARSHAL *goes out with an embarrassed bob to the Lady, to whom* DE VESCI *now addresses himself*.

Do you still intend to remain in this apartment?

FITZWALTER. What about the Mayor – we are keeping him waiting?

DE VESCI. He may join us if he wishes . . . Pray be seated, madam, do not on any account put yourself to inconvenience by absenting yourself from our pastime.

> YOUNG MARSHAL *re-enters with three* GIRLS (*one blonde, one dark, and one red-haired*).

YOUNG MARSHAL. Ladies, the Lord Fitzwalter; the Lord de Vesci, whose lodging this is; the Lord de Vesci's –

DE VESCI. Good, let us adjust ourselves. You, you're for this gentleman. Robert, this one's yours: this one (*the blonde*) because she's the fattest, she's a great big pig is this one, *I* am going to take. What's your name, you lovely porker – never mind, no names at all is better, you give no-one your name and they can't put a witchcraft on you: so I intend to baptize you all with names of my own choosing and by these names you shall be known until morning.

> *The* GIRLS *sit down, professionally, and start in on wine and spices.*
>
> DE VESCI *walks round them, appraising them.*

Deadly Nightshade:

Which grows in the dark recesses of the wood:

Serve it to your good friends: they need no further food.

Red Herring:

The dogs in full cry get this one up their nose.

Free may run the quick vixen and the dun deer and his does.

Chop-chop-and-chew-it:

Hot bacon grease runs out of the old man's mouth,

Vinegar settles his stomach, it will never quench his drouth.

Very good. They tell me King Arthur would never drive his teeth into his dinner without he had first heard some wonderful new thing. We'll follow his example. The son of the Marshal is going to sing us a song. A song of the South of France, boy, for the benefit of milady, who would no doubt prefer to be there.

YOUNG MARSHAL. I will attempt one, Eustace, if you wish. For the benefit of my lady, if she will accept it.

LADY DE VESCI. Why yes, she will, why not?

YOUNG MARSHAL (*sings*).

> I send my song to one who cannot hear it:
> In no green garden does her beauty stroll.
> I send a robe of gold, she cannot wear it:
> In bitter sackcloth she her limbs must roll.
> I send a letter, other hands will tear it
> Before its words can ever reach her eyes:
> I send my love to her: yet I do fear it
> That if she ever knows of it, she dies
> > In that close prison where she lies
> > Confined alone
> > In cruel walls of stone
> By one she loved yet now must needs despise.

FITZWALTER. Confined alone by whom?

YOUNG MARSHAL. Her husband.

DE VESCI. Did John send you here to sing that?

YOUNG MARSHAL. Certainly not. It has nothing whatever to do with John. It was written to his mother when Henry Curtmantle had her in gaol for conspiracy. An old lover of hers – a poet from Carcassonne –

DE VESCI (*leaping up suddenly*). They call it the Morpeth Rant: It's a grand stamping dance, I've seen my boors do it in Northumbria – it goes best with the big boots on – the sheep-herders dance it on the hill – there's none of your Provençal adulteries about *this* –

He starts singing, clapping his hands on the beat, then launches into a dance. The others (except YOUNG MARSHAL*), join in one by one. The tune is a reel, but they do not dance it that way – they merely prance round in a circle one after the other, making a great deal of noise.*

Oh *what* will you gie me if I knock you in the teeth, boy,
What will you gie me if I kick your *gut?*
A *knife* in the belly and a club upon the headpiece,
That's what ye're wanting, it's what you'll *get!*

Oh nights are dark and days are cold
And life is short and the world is long
And left is right and right is wrong
And who put the wolf in the *old* sheep fold?

There's only the one set of words, we sing them round and round until we're sick of it –
> *He tries to pull the Lady into the dance, but she evades him and goes out.*
> *As she goes out, she drops her kerchief.* YOUNG MARSHAL *picks it up, but when he offers it her, she makes a gesture refusing it. He puts it quickly in his breast.*

– *She*'s sick of it already, and not before time – come on –
> *The dance continues, until interrupted by voices off.*

1ST VOICE (*off*). No you may not go up, the Barons are in private –

2ND VOICE (*off*). They are taking their pleasure, sir, you are not to disturb them –

> *The* MAYOR *bursts in, despite efforts of some* SERVANTS *to restrain him.*

MAYOR. No man tells the Mayor of London 'not' within the walls of his own city. My Lords, London has her liberties, established, enrolled, and sealed. I am delegate by free choice of our citizens to affirm and to guard the enfranchise of this town.

FITZWALTER. I think you forget yourself, sir.

MAYOR. It may be so, my Lord. It may indeed be very possibly so. The words which I have had occasion to make use of, I made use of, let me in all honesty inform you, as the words of a Gown and Chain, not as the words of a common citizen. The Gown and Chain being susceptible to the corruption (as I believe it is spoken in Scripture) of moth and rust alone: and moth and rust, with due care – that is to say, polishing, oiling, dusting, and the application of camphor – we may very easily inhibit. But as to the corruptions to which the mortal human frame is susceptible, and not only the frame, but the spirit within it, these with naught but grave difficulty are to be avoided. Are they not, young women?

He looks keenly at the BLONDE GIRL.

I knew your father. I knew him for a good man. Poor, but honest, though indeed no more than a fishporter – goes to Mass and pays his dues most regularly. Will I tell him you are here?

BLONDE GIRL. Perhaps he sent me.

MAYOR. No, he did not send you.

DARK GIRL. Didn't he? Trade's poor at the fishmarket.

MAYOR. But there are other markets, are there not? I mean, for the stinking fish – you take my meaning, don't you? And with a town full of soldiers as this town is at present – (*He looks at the* DARK GIRL.) You were whipped two months ago, I recollect it well, at *my* orders from the Bench, for pursuit of that same unchaste market – (*To the* RED HAIRED GIRL.) and I fancy you were too, young lady, weren't you? Or if you weren't you should have been.

DE VESCI. Tell him go and take his market to the bottom of the river – fish market, haddock, cod's head, red herring . . .

FITZWALTER. That will do, Eustace. We are the Mayor of London's guests in London, don't forget: but these little nightingales are *our* guests and we are under no obligation to have them questioned here.

MAYOR. That may be as it may be, my Lord, indeed, very

much it may be, yes. But I had in mind this evening, upon coming here to speak with you, to put down before you, my Lord, in straight cuts with no frayed edges –

YOUNG MARSHAL. Frayed edges – I don't quite –

DE VESCI. The man's a draper – he sells cloth – frayed edges unravel. Well, stop unravelling: talk!

MAYOR. Very good, my Lord: as you put it. There is an established paragraph in the Charter, granting the complete liberties of the City of London. Without frayed edges, my Lord, that paragraph was put in for the purpose of a fair contract. You want a basis to establish your force. We are commercial men here and we enter contract with you to grant you a lease of the walls of this city, and the price is our liberty. Very well, then: tit-for-tat.

FITZWALTER. Tit-for-tat-what?

MAYOR (*indicates* GIRLS). Now take these for a start. It is well understood, and though we may not all confess to such habits, being, as you will very well say, by nature of our trade, as a draper or a goldsmith or a shoemaker or such-like, necessarily sober men and decorously-conducted, and notwithstanding noblemen upon military emergency are commonly granted the sort of pleasures befitting their rank, and certainly not myself nor anyone else would speak a word against it. But the town is full of soldiers, out of all rank and station, and they're all up to the same game, and we'd be better off with the French here, or even the King's Flemings! How long it's going to last, I don't know and nobody does, but the behaviour of your troops is an offence in our nostrils and it was not to cause this that the Charter was drawn up! No, my Lord, no – I speak by Gown and Chain!

DE VESCI. You speak by profit and loss.

FITZWALTER. For you have made commercial contract not only with ourselves but also with the King. Did he not grant to the city of London its own Mayoral Charter not one month before he met us at Runnymede, and was not the purpose of that Mayoral Charter to secure the city to him in the event of civil war, and did not we offer you a higher price in our Charter and beat him at his bargain? You choose to condemn these daughters of your liberty, but what have they done that you have not, Master Mayor?

YOUNG MARSHAL. Do we wish to make a quarrel here with this good man, or what? Sir, I will offer you a cup of wine. Be so good as to drink it. What you speak, you speak seriously – though inhibited perhaps by our superior rank – and therefore you should be listened to. Will you please drink?

MAYOR. I will with pleasure accept your refreshment. I thank you, my Lord ... Grave concern; doubts and hesitations, not only for myself but the Aldermen, the Masters of the City Companies, the entire mercantile body – we are gravely concerned and indeed have taken counsel together. It is not only the matter of the turbulent soldiery for which in regard to my recent outburst of anger I crave pardon – but a serious and deep consideration for our essential purposes at this time. The King has promised to govern his realm with what amounts to justice and restraint. He has taken note –

FITZWALTER. He has been forced to take note.

MAYOR. – of the demands of the nobility, and the church, and also the commercial interests for the first time in history. Forced, yes, my Lord, and forced by your soldiers – that is, the nobility alone. The church, when she was alone in the time of the Interdict, failed to coerce him: and we, as men of commerce, are of course men of peace – we have but our wharves and counting-houses and our profit and loss. Therefore we depend on you: and we depend on your honour. We have let you into London for your manifest advantage: *our* manifest advantage, my Lord, is a complete and equitable enforcement of the entire Charter, no clause of it bated, and with no distortion of its purposes. Are you prepared to grant us that?

FITZWALTER. I was under the impression that you and the Army of God were in a free alliance together to bring down King John. You are remarkably solicitous of the convenience of your enemy, sir. Of course – I had forgotten, he helped you build your bridge.

MAYOR. A bridge is important to us, my Lord, we are a great city with great traffic. Besides, there is a rhyme already current in the ale-houses concerning that same bridge.

To RED HAIRED GIRL *who has laughed.*

I expect *you* know it, don't you?

RED HAIRED GIRL.

As I was going o'er London Bridge
I heard something crack.
Not a man in all England
Can mend a crack like that.

The GIRLS *laugh.*

MAYOR. It is only a probable prophecy – as yet. Do we want it to be true? (*He looks at his wine.*) A very reputable friend of mine imports this, from Gascony. The last shipload to come in, he had had to dodge for three days through the Channel Islands to get it past the pirates. For them it would have been a diversion to catch a cargo of good wine: for him and for his sailormen, my Lords, their life and death – no less! But the point that I would make by the mention of it now is that I would not have you think that I would speak against diversions. I was invited to a tournament – an agreeable diversion, both for me and my family, pageantry of arms, yes, a very gallant spectacle . . . But suppose now that your tournament, upon duly commencing, were never to conclude? That we'd to sit still out at Hounslow for all the rest of the year, all the rest of our lives, and with nothing to do but watch horses and riders in a big field at Hounslow knock each other over? I mean it'd be ridiculous – wouldn't it? We'd get no business done. And what's more to the purpose is that none of the competitors would ever win a prize. Now then: no frayed edges – when are your soldiers going to be removed?

DE VESCI. We never remove soldiers. Not one drunken defaulter. Never remove soldiers.

YOUNG MARSHAL. But I told you – my father's chaplain told me that the King has written letters –

DE VESCI. Oh those letters, that . . . flatfish, mudfish, hake –

MAYOR. My Lord, what letters? Letters to whom?

YOUNG MARSHAL. There are to be no more mercenaries come to the King from Flanders. It is a solemn undertaking. There is absolutely no reason why we should not disband.

MAYOR. Indeed no, there is not – at least if the report is true.

YOUNG MARSHAL. My father has pledged his word that it is.

MAYOR. Then, my Lord, it must be. Why did you not think fit to inform me about these letters, gentlemen? I am asking for an answer.

There is a pause. The GIRLS *are getting restive.*

DARK GIRL. If we're not wanted here, we can always go away.

BLONDE GIRL. We're not short of business, you know, not with all the soldiers in town.

DE VESCI (*rounding upon her*). What did you say!

BLONDE GIRL. Nothing, milord, really, I beg pardon, milord.

YOUNG MARSHAL (*to* GIRLS). Go on, the three of you – out. The porter at the door will give you your money – go on.

The GIRLS *go out.*

MAYOR. I am asking for an answer, and I am still waiting, my Lord.

FITZWALTER. The Feast of the Assumption.

MAYOR. I beg your pardon, my Lord?

FITZWALTER. I do not intend to modify the dispositions of the Army of God until the Feast of the Assumption. It has been agreed at Oxford. You must be satisfied with that.

MAYOR. I cannot pretend I am: and I cannot pretend that the people of London are going to be, either.

FITZWALTER. The ladies who have just left us may not share your opinion.

MAYOR. Conceivably not. However, I will wait upon events. The Feast of the Assumption is not very far away. Good night to you, my Lords.

YOUNG MARSHAL. I will accompany you, sir. I am sure that we can do something to improve the discipline of our troops. I would be glad to discuss it with you. Good night, Eustace. Good night, Robert.

Exeunt MAYOR *and* YOUNG MARSHAL.

DE VESCI (*looking at where the* GIRLS *have sat*). Where did they go to?

FITZWALTER. Who?

DE VESCI. Ah, never mind. They were but a moment's distraction, the old malignant mortification remains. Whether he hires his lances from Flanders or not, whether there is a war or whether there is not: it would be nothing less than lunacy to disband at this moment.

FITZWALTER. I agree. John has always ruled this kingdom as though it were his own private farmyard and we were his pigs, and he is not going to change his habits now, because of words upon a parchment. We can wait until the Assumption.

DE VESCI. And then we can wait until –

FITZWALTER. The next feast-day, or the next. In the meantime my messengers are at the court of the King of France. If we need his help he'll give it, but I hope he won't have to.

DE VESCI. Indeed by God's Bones I hope he won't have to. There is one King too many in this country already.

FITZWALTER. France should be well accustomed to being controlled by his great barons. I anticipate no problem there.

DE VESCI. Where did they go to?

FITZWALTER. Young Marshal sent them fluttering.

DE VESCI. He takes too much upon himself. He is too young to take so much. He is the son of his father. (*He looks vaguely round, as if for his wife.*) And where has the other one gone? By God, she is an ulcer developing under the plaster of wedlock ... How far will you let John gallop you before you send for the King of France?

FITZWALTER. The moment it is clear to everyone, including young Marshal, including his archaic father, including the Archbishop –

DE VESCI. And also the Mayor of London –

FITZWALTER. And also the Mayor of London, that King Softsword as much desires as we do to carve up this useless Charter – straight cuts and no frayed edges – that moment we send word to France. Are you with me?

DE VESCI. Without question. God's Nostrils, where's she got to? She was in here but one minute since ...

He moves drunkenly out.

FITZWALTER *laughs, finishes his wine, and goes out at the opposite door.*

SCENE THREE

Enter PANDULPH.

PANDULPH. Confronted as we are by the apparent spectacle of depravity, treachery and violent self-seeking upon both sides of this miserable dispute, let us not too readily dismiss that aspect of human nature, which, in even the worst of men, contains some yearning for the paths of virtue. Hypocrisy, as exemplified in a Fitzwalter or a de Vesci, nevertheless pays tribute to idealism insofar as it finds it necessary to cloak its evil purposes under the disguise of a worthy cause. The cause, in this instance, I have already shewn to be futile – but never mind: it exists.

As for King John himself – that almost Oriental monster of your history books – do not forget that the records of his Household shew him to have been a tireless administrator, devoted to the pursuit of justice – albeit wrongheadedly, as many would maintain. Day by day, even in the midst of profound political turbulence, he traversed his realm, continually in the saddle, continually hearing causes, receiving petitions, inquiring into abuses . . .

He sits down in his chair.

SCENE FOUR

A picture of an apple orchard, formally drawn, with large fruit on the branches, flowers in the grass, and many birds and little animals.

Enter JOHN, *from riding, together with his travelling-party – the* QUEEN, PRINCE HENRY, LADY DE VESCI, MARSHAL, CLERKS *and other attendants.*

A camp stool is brought for the King, the rest sit down around him on the grass, while a picnic meal is served by the Attendants. Throughout the scene, this meal is being eaten – JOHN *in particular eats a very great deal.*

JOHN. We have travelled far enough this morning – let them serve us with a little food and drink. Here, serve it here . . . I have always been of the opinion that the Southern Counties of England contain the fairest prospects of nature to be found throughout my territory. Observe this agreeable Kentish orchard, where the golden apples on the autumn trees hang waiting for the husbandmen to gather them in to their baskets. An appropriate place, my lords and ladies, for a king in an old legend to sit and dispense justice to his subjects, untroubled by factious discord. Remember what was said of the brave and scholarly King Alfred – that at the end of his reign it was possible for a man to hang golden drinking cups beside a simple wayside fountain, and to have no fear that they would be stolen – or even borrowed. If I in my due time could be laid in a tomb with that epitaph graven over it, I could then regard myself as a fit successor to my famous father. As for my no less famous mother, her beautiful, stubborn, and deceitful spirit has so wound itself into my uncomely body, that not only does my right hand not know what my left hand is doing, – which is indeed recommended in the Holy Gospel – but actual bloody conflict between these two unhappy members prevails every day of my life. Look, the cruel nails of the one dig into the flesh of the other until the white skin is marked with scarlet – a man might believe I was an impoverished smallholder struggling eternally to clear brambles from my land. And even in my domestic affairs old Eleanor still infects me. Here I sit, a Queen on the one side, a mistress on the other . . . or *is* she? At any rate her husband thinks so. And she has happily found ways to escape from his loathsome bed.

LADY DE VESCI. Arduous and surreptitious ways – corruption of servants, melodramatic performances with ropes of knotted sheets hung out of windows, riding on a wild night cloaked and hooded like a highwayman – and not even efficient. I suppose I should at least have brought you some sketch plans of the fortifications of London.

JOHN. God will provide the sketch plans. Saucy Castle fell and Saucy Castle was held by men of great integrity. But you have provided me, my lady, with intelligence of far higher value – a keen description and diagnosis of what is going on inside the muddy mind of my enemies . . . other ladies also have – provided me, in their time. I have no less than five bastards scattered about my dominions, and five legitimate children likewise – (*He puts his arm round* PRINCE HENRY.) – of whom this one here is to become the King of England. You do realise that, my pretty careless boy? It may happen to you quite soon . . . And yet no-one can say that my marital infidelities have detracted any whit from the love I bear my wife.

QUEEN.
When I was but twelve years old

I was betrothed to a lord of France:
But the wild King of England grinned over the garden wall
Where I and my little maidens did dance.

JOHN.

She was as beautiful and delicate a child
As ever I had seen.
And upon that sunlit afternoon
I determined she would be my queen.

QUEEN.

For four years I grew
Through my short ungainly puberty
And at the end of that time
When he knew my woman's beauty
I held him in such thrall
That he lost the whole of Normandy.

JOHN.

It has been alleged
In terms of political scandal
That we took so long time in our tent
On a morning to kiss and fondle
That the battle was lost and broken
And Saucy Castle taken
And yet no man could stir me to rise.
It was more than a scandal
It was in fact a pack of lies.
Yet my mother would say:
If I did not find this story flattering,
By so much the less
Was I truly a king.

> *There is some whispering and shifting about among the
> Attendants – the* CLERK *comes to the King.*

CLERK. My Lord, there are two parties here to a lawsuit – the
plaintiff is anxious that you yourself should give him a
judgement.

JOHN. Certainly not. I am eating my dinner. Have we no

Circuit Courts in the County of Kent? Have we no Justices? Why should they trouble *me* – they invariably trouble *me* – they do not seem to realize that the King cannot personally be expected to handle – and yet, do I not remember saying during the negotiations over the Charter that I never deny right and justice? How long will they have to wait if they wait for the regular Judge?

CLERK. They have been waiting for five years, my Lord – the administrative delays have been –

JOHN. Five years? Intolerable! Inquire into it at once, and see that somebody is punished. Heavily. Punish them with a fine. Always a fine, remember: we have rebellions on hand, we are always in need of money. Very well, the litigants may appear before us, bring them along.

The GOLDSMITH, *his* WIFE *and the* PARSON *are brought in.*

Now then, good people, don't be afraid. I am the King, but I rule under Providence of God, and a small portion at least of His Divine Mercy is ever present in my spirit. Tell me your names and station.

GOLDSMITH. My name is Cuthbert of Dover, sire. I am a goldsmith.

JOHN. In a poor way of business, to judge from your appearance. Are you no good at your trade?

GOLDSMITH. I lay claim to be a master of my trade, my Lord. The pendant that this woman wears is of my own workmanship.

JOHN. Let's have a look at it . . . I know something about jewels . . . A true lovers' knot in gold wire enclosing five garnet stones – why, it is very beautiful, Cuthbert: and so are the breasts upon which it is depending. To whom do they belong?

GOLDSMITH. She is my wife, my Lord.

JOHN. I was asking her, not you. What is your name, sweetheart? Tell it, to your King.

GOLDSMITH'S WIFE. Jennifer, my Lord.

JOHN. Jennifer – what kind of a name is that?

LADY DE VESCI. It is a rustic corruption of Guinevere – King Arthur's adulterous queen.

JOHN. Oh. I hope it isn't catching. And the reverend gentleman over there – who are you?

PARSON. I am the Parish Priest of St Mary in Dover, my Lord: my name is Thomas.

JOHN. Very well. Who's the plaintiff? . . . Cuthbert? Set forward your plea.

GOLDSMITH. This so-called celibate priest, my Lord, five years ago, seduced the affections of my wife and she has cohabited with him in his parsonage ever since. With me she had no children: she has borne him a daughter.

JOHN. Has she indeed? How old are you?

GOLDSMITH. Forty-eight, my Lord.

JOHN. So am I. A middle-aged man with a young wife ought to know how to treat her well enough to prevent her being carried away by the Parson. But precisely what are you asking me for?

GOLDSMITH. Damages, my Lord. I have been made a mock and a scorn among the people of Dover, and my business has greatly suffered as a result. The rude boys in the street replaced my shop-sign only last year with a pair of cow's horns and an upturned chalice. This sort of nonsense has been going on all the time. I shall be ruined if I get no satisfaction.

JOHN. Sir Thomas, come here . . . stout, red-faced, pleasant-looking, young . . . Yes, I can understand it. But this is really an ecclesiastical matter, surely, your Bishop ought to – oh God no, we're in Canterbury's Diocese here, that prelate is concerned with far different business! Lady, what is your opinion?

QUEEN. I think he is entitled to damages. The priest is too handsome. He should never have allowed a body like that to be sequestered by the Church; he must pay some compensation to the World for depriving us of its merits.

JOHN (*to* LADY DE VESCI). And your opinion, madam?

LADY DE VESCI. The child. Is she malformed?

JOHN. Well, is she?

GOLDSMITH'S WIFE. Oh no milord, milady – er milord – no . . .

LADY DE VESCI. Is she beautiful?

GOLDSMITH'S WIFE. *I* think so, yes.

LADY DE VESCI. Then there can be no disgrace in her creation. It is not a fit subject for mockery.

JOHN. Even if she were malformed, it would not be a fit subject for mockery. (*To* GOLDSMITH.) You were unable to provide a child for this woman: the priest has obligingly fulfilled your function for you. How did he succeed in seducing you, Jennifer?

GOLDSMITH'S WIFE. Milord, he plays the mandoline – he sang me ballads in the vestry.

JOHN. Excellent, by God, yes! Have you anything to say, Sir Thomas? Can you deny the accusation? . . . Then you had better not speak at all. Your mandoline has already said far too much. You will pay this good man fifty shillings for the loss of his wife and his reputation, and fifty shillings to me, as a fine for your misconduct. If this were heard in the Archbishop's Court, they'd extort a good deal more, so I warn you not to stand upon the privilege of your cloth. Cuthbert Goldsmith, you likewise will pay me fifty shillings as a fee for my hearing the case and for the interruption of my picnic. That will perhaps teach you to be more tender to young women. Wives are not chattels. I can see by the hang of your nostril that you thought that yours was. However, as the pendant that she is wearing really is extremely beautiful, I shall take order that you be appointed a Craftsman to the Royal Household, and that you shall have the charge of the maintenance of our own jewellery when we are in the Southern Parts. Open that box, Augustine, and take out the little cap badge with the sapphires in it.

The CLERK *finds the badge in a jewel box which the King has had by him.*

One of the stones is working loose from the setting. Will you please repair it for me directly?

GOLDSMITH (*taking the jewel*). With pleasure. my Lord, with great pleasure, indeed it is an honour . . .

JOHN. Off you go now. Augustine, go with them and see that the money is properly transferred . . . Oh, one moment – the woman stays with the priest. Now we are no longer under an Interdict, it is none of my business to interfere with the private lives of clerics. But take heed the Archdeacon doesn't catch you at your games. Good-bye.

Exeunt LITIGANTS, *with* CLERK.

And good riddance . . . What's the matter, William, you are looking upon me with a lack-lustre eye?

MARSHAL. From my limited experience of the Law, sire, I would have thought that your handling of this case was not quite in accordance with precedent.

JOHN. Oh yes, I daresay – but was it not just? In fact, a new precedent has now been established: and all judges in the future – I hope – may understand therefrom that there is no substitute for direct comprehension and even enjoyment of the individual humours of each person brought before them. I have left all three of them satisfied. What more could they want?

YOUNG MARSHAL *enters rapidly, with a drawn sword. He is wearing* LADY DE VESCI's *kerchief in his helmet.*

And Judas' Neckbone – what do *you* want? It was in our mind, young sir, that you were confederate with the body of our enemies at present holding garrison in the City of London! Marshal, put your insensate child under arrest.

YOUNG MARSHAL. I came here with a mounted escort. Do you want a battle? I am ready to oblige – I notice your own escort is considerably smaller – though it might disarrange the ladies.

LADY DE VESCI. That is a noble sentiment, sir. I notice from the favour in your helmet that you are a gentleman of true chivalrous practice – though surely you did not come here solely to proclaim the virtues of your beloved?

YOUNG MARSHAL. No: I did not. I wish that I had. It is a different aspect of knightly honour that has compelled me here today.

MARSHAL. Do you dare to speak of honour in the same voice with which you threaten battle to your King, sir! You shall indeed have your battle – there are more loyal soldiers in this county than you can see at this moment, and I am the commander of them!

YOUNG MARSHAL. Of all of them, father? Including the ones who are to arrive in Dover harbour as soon as the winds are favourable? I fancy they will bring their own general with them – Sir Hugh de Boves, from Flanders.

MARSHAL. What!

YOUNG MARSHAL. The Papal Legate is not the only man who can dispose of an intelligence service across the Channel. We have discovered that a large army of mercenaries is assembled at Antwerp and will sail before Michaelmas. Why else do you think the King's Progress keeps so tightly to the Kentish Coast?

MARSHAL. This must be one of Fitzwalter's lies. It must. Sire, I appeal to you at once to deny this vicious calumny.

JOHN. No. No, I can't deny it, Marshal; it happens to be true. Now, this is going to put your loyalty to quite an extensive test, is it not? But I will demonstrate my justification. This angry Paladin, here, your son, originally joined with Fitzwalter's party because he was of the honest opinion that the Customs of England needed to be codified and clarified under due process of law. I believe in his honesty – he has inherited many virtues from you. And yet, after only a year from his first association with that riotous gang, he storms in upon his King and presents him with the blade of a falchion! Thus you will observe the treason and corruption that still maintains its lair within the walls of London Town. If I bring in no army, I shall be naked in their hands.

MARSHAL. But, sire, the words of the Charter – what about the Charter, sire?

PANDULPH (*coming forward with a letter*). I think I had best explain to everyone the present state of the Charter. I have received a letter from His Holiness Pope Innocent. He writes:

'We have heard that the King of England has been forced to accept an agreement which is not only shameful and base, but also illegal and unjust. We refuse to pass over such shameful presumption; for the Apostolic See would be dishonoured, the King's right injured, the English nation shamed, and the whole plan for the Crusade seriously endangered. Therefore we utterly reject and condemn this settlement and under threat of excommunication we order that the King should not dare to observe it and the Barons and their associates should not insist on its being observed. The Charter itself we declare to be null and void of all validity, for ever.'

JOHN. It would indeed be a pity to endanger my plan for the Crusade.

He pulls the copy of the Charter down and tears it up.

YOUNG MARSHAL. The son of the French King once before laid claim to the Throne of England. If he chooses to renew that claim, in person, at the head of an army, I do not see how the barons in London are to be prevented from supporting him. The liberties of the English people will not be increased by such a procedure.

Exeunt.

Act Three

A large map of England replaces the Charter opposite Pandulph's chair.

    An icon-like illustration of the murder of Becket.

    Enter ARCHBISHOP.

ARCHBISHOP.

Once in the land of Babylon,
Which was then called Babel,
Ingenious and inventive men
Believed themselves able
To erect the greatest tower
That ever had been built.
Architect, mason, carpenter, plumber –
Craftsmen in brick, stone, lead and timber –
For all one year they worked:
And all their work was spilt.
As you will very well remember
It was the Hand of God
That struck them to confusion,
Planting upon their tongues
The discord of His derision,
Making every man's design
Incomprehensible to his neighbour.
No tower was completed,
No wages were paid for all that long labour,
For all that pride there were no rewards,
Nothing but a maze of bewildering words –
And that was far worse than nothing at all.

    PANDULPH *has quietly taken his seat.*

PANDULPH. If you mean to imply, Your Grace, that this

unexpected letter from the Pope is the result of the pride of those overweening barons who corrupted your own good intentions, I will not contradict you. But I would also point out that His Holiness has included you, specifically, in his indictment. He writes, in a second letter –

See how Stephen of Canterbury and his fellow-bishops defy the patrimony of the Roman Church! See how they protect Crusaders!

Indeed, he goes on to say that you are worse than the Saracens, because the Saracens at least are the declared enemies of Christ, while the Bishops of England – I will not grieve your heart further. What do you intend to do?

ARCHBISHOP. If I do not submit to the Pope and obey him, I presume you are empowered to suspend me from my Archbishopric?

PANDULPH. Yes.

ARCHBISHOP. Thomas Becket, when driven out of England by the King, lived for several years the life of a humble brother in a French cloister. I have considered doing the same myself. I have even considered preparing a formal statement of penitence for ever having allowed myself to meddle with the temporal affairs and advocate the liberties of the people of England. But such a self-surrender has never been truly Stephen. I have believed always in the strength of the sword in the hand of Jesus – I mean the sword that will cleave directly through to the betterment of mankind. I do not mean the sword of war – the text is misread if you think so, and you do think so, there are many here that do think so, Simon Peter used that stupid sword in the garden to cut off the ear of a catchpole who was doing no more than earning his daily pay. But we know what happened to the ear that was cut off and we read no more words in the Gospel of the sword that did cut it. No, Pandulph: I will neither submit, nor obey, nor resign. I will carry my sword to Rome and explain to the Pope, who was once my very dear friend, precisely what was meant by the Charter which the King sealed. For my Charter – no, not *my* Charter, the Charter of the English – it is not the Tower of Babel – it will not lie for ever a heap of rain-washed ruin for the donkeys to stale upon and the serpents to breed in the holes of its brickwork – and the Pope must know that it will not.

PANDULPH. But what is the Charter, after all? An up-to-date version of some promises once made by King Henry I? Even taken at best, it has no eternal validity. What is it, what is it?

ARCHBISHOP. Even taken at worst, it is a statement, well-intentioned and futile, if you like – but a precise statement, Pandulph. I thought, in the beginning, it was perhaps no more than a convenient device to hold off for a while the fury of the barons. The King took it as such, and was grateful, he made remarkably little objection to it, under the circumstances. But when I was compelled to admit to myself that (as soon as it had served its original purpose) neither the barons nor the King were likely to take note of it, then I began to realise that the words that it contained, having been said once and having been written down, could no more be blotted out by King, Baron or Pope even, than I can deny the Divinity of My Saviour.

PANDULPH. Aha, I did suspect it. You attribute your own fallible words to the breath of the Holy Spirit. I hope you understand that you are practically in heresy.

ARCHBISHOP. It is nothing whatever to do with heresy, Pandulph. Will you please not endeavour to intimidate me, sir! I am speaking of a document that is the necessary fulfillment of the existing Laws and Customs of this land. Such has not been made before, but we have made it now. The Kings and Lords of England, who will in the future need authority, who will need a definite statement of what they may not do and what may not be done to them – these men will look to it and I believe that they will thank us for it. But not unless the Charter is able to survive. To ensure its survival, I must plead with the Pope. I would not care to accuse the Holy Father of ignorance, but there are nevertheless a few matters concerning England upon which, I suspect, he has been deliberately misinformed.

Exit ARCHBISHOP.

SCENE TWO

Pictures of warfare – men-at-arms fighting, houses burning, refugees, etc.

PANDULPH. Which words – like an ill-directed arrow – do not strike at my heart. Because Pope Innocent III has the most beautiful intellect of any man ever to have occupied the Chair of St Peter: and if he should choose to see England and the affairs of England in a correct proportion relative to the affairs of the entire world, I do not propose to run counter to his opinion. I am a native of Pisa. Archbishop Stephen – the erstwhile Archbishop Stephen – was (I believe) born in the County of Lincoln. There is a difference.

A very short recital of the warfare which followed the papal repudiation of the Charter. I know little about such matters, but I am informed by those who are more expert, that had King John struck directly at London before the barons could receive their reinforcement from France, he might well have succeeded in crushing the rebellion at once. However, he did not.

The first detachment of Flemings to cross the Channel to the King was wrecked in a great storm: the rebels took advantage and occupied Rochester. The King laid siege to Rochester and it surrendered – November 30th, 1215. The greater part of the barons' army – large but ill-organized – remained in London, where they were joined about this time by an inconsiderable body of French. There were pockets of baronial adherents in different parts of the country – particularly the east and north, but disconnected and vulnerable.

He is pointing all this out on the map.

John, balking, as I say, at a decisive attack upon London, determined instead to eliminate the pockets. 'Elimination of pockets' is a craftsmanlike term much employed by those cruel and skilful men who hire out their services from Flanders. It means, of course, the complete destruction of castles, houses, barns, livestock, fishing-boats, windmills, watermills, granaries, the bodies of men, the chastity of women – I speak nothing of children. I would merely remind you that this happened in the months of December and January, and it happened from here –

St Albans on the map.

to *here* –

Berwick-upon-Tweed, on the map.

and back again, in February, *here.*

Suffolk and Essex, on the map.

This happened, in winter, in England, under the orders of a King of England, and at the hands of a foreign army. Many of you, no doubt, will think that I do wrong to lay the responsibility for such wickedness upon the profound and good intentions of Archbishop Stephen Langton. And yet, I do so lay it. His duty to his Church was clear and he denied it. He believed he had been working, in a kind of parenthesis, not for the Church of Christ, but for the amelioration of England – and you have heard the result.

No such belief has attended the deliberations of the King of France. His desire, quite simply, has been to enlarge his boundaries, and to do so, if possible, in an odour of sanctity. I take pains to point out that this will not be possible.

The month of April, 1216: France.

SCENE THREE

The Lilies of France.

Enter PHILIP, LOUIS, BLANCHE.

PANDULPH (*to audience still*). King Philip Augustus; Louis, his eldest son; Blanche, the wife of Louis. The boundaries of King Philip have been in process of enlargement for many years: and for the most part at the expense of England. He has already, in 1212, considered placing an army across the Channel –

He now speaks to Philip.

But in that year, my Lord, King John was excommunicate. Had you put to sea then, you might have flown the Papal Ensign at your masthead and sailed as upon Crusade. Today however, the barbed hook of St Peter sticks in the throat of a different fish.

PHILIP. These reversals of fortune, Master Legate, are the lot of mankind. It would not be seemly to rail against them. But nobility and royalty are not to be put down by such temporary accidents. France is a Catholic Kingdom, and we trust that whether or no the Pope should smile upon our enterprise, God will always continue to do so. He has indeed put into my mind a means of overcoming this present small obstacle. My learned men have elaborated a formula. Listen. King John claims that he handed his crown to the Pope and received it back upon terms of feudal service. But he cannot have done this –

LOUIS. Because it was not his to give.

PANDULPH. Indeed, my Lord? Whose was it?

LOUIS. We'll come to that in a moment. When Richard Lionheart was alive and imprisoned by the Duke of Austria, John laid plots against him –

PHILIP. And consequently, in King Richard's own Court, was adjudged a proven traitor.

LOUIS. That judgement has never been rescinded. Therefore when King Richard Lionheart died –

PHILIP. It was incorrect and illegal for the Lords of England to place John upon his throne. They should have chosen –

LOUIS. Arthur, who was the son of the elder brother of John, and who, alas, unfortunate child that he was –

PHILIP. Was brutally murdered, by John.

LOUIS. France, you will remember, espoused the cause of Arthur at that time. And therefore, Arthur being dead, and the Crown of England usurped, the true heir to England's throne must be sought and found –

PHILIP. Among the surviving progeny of the other brothers and sisters of John. Of whom the most eligible turns out to be the Lady Blanche: here she is, grand-daughter to King Henry Curtmantle of England, and married –

LOUIS. To me.

PANDULPH. Oh happy lady, happy prince, happy King. A jocund family of dynastic lawyers indeed. Would that I could immerse myself, my lords, in chopping your logic with you: there is nothing I enjoy better. But no, I fear not: my instructions are precise. Curt, in fact, to the point of vulgarity. If France invades the realm of England, France will be excommunicate and that is all there is to it.

PHILIP. Master Legate, France is Catholic, and dutiful. Therefore, Prince Louis, as your liege lord and as your Catholic father, we forbid you in the sternest words to offer aid or succour to the irreligious barons of England.

LOUIS (*kneeling*). Sire, as your Catholic vassal and your most submissive son, I humbly accept your necessary orders. But Blanche my wife has a rightful claim to be the Queen of England. You have no power to withhold her from that claim. Neither have you power to withhold me from helping her. (*He gets up again.*) She is but a weak woman and she needs her husband's sword.

BLANCHE (*to* PHILIP). Brother of France, when we achieve

in fact that crown which is already ours in right and title, there shall be no bounds put to the gratitude and friendship which you may demand of us.

PHILIP. We accept with appropriate grace your graceful sentiment, madam: and may the Hand of God confirm your just prosperity.

PANDULPH. The Hand of God has been invoked by a great many people lately. I wonder are we not perhaps in danger of confounding our Divine Redeemer with those obscene idols of the Orient that Crusaders talk of – I mean the ones with six or seven arms growing out of a single body?

Exeunt PHILIP, LOUIS and BLANCHE.

They do not care to listen to my homilies, which is understandable. They are altogether too intelligent not to be aware of what they are doing. God has but two hands. To attempt to dispose of their benefits upon earth without due authority is to court damnation –

SCENE FOUR

A picture of armed soldiers standing in close ranks, with banners etc., and the tops of tents behind them.

Enter JOHN.

PANDULPH. They are courting damnation, my Lord.

JOHN. They are also courting defeat. I have a navy. The coast of England is impregnable.

Enter MARSHAL *and* OFFICERS.

MARSHAL. No, my Lord. God, with the adverse winds at His command, and no doubt for some inscrutable purpose of His own, has scattered your navy; and the French fleet has safely passed the mouth of Pegwell Bay. Prince Louis has established his camp upon the northern coast of Kent, and those rebels whom you thought you had subdued in the winter have once more plucked up their courage. The King of

Scotland has led an army of his own across the Border against you, and far too many of your mercenary soldiers have not received their pay. What is to be done?

JOHN. Not received their pay . . . what is to be done . . . They will get their pay, God's Bread, sir, when they have fulfilled their contract! Let them drive the Frenchmen out. Until they have done that for me, how can I scrabble for money? I have gone into this before – how many times I don't know – that I do not understand, and nobody understands, where the money comes from or where it goes to when it has been spent. If some new Aristotle could develop a science out of that, perhaps we could then know how to govern our people. Had Stephen Langton studied in Paris the pilgrimage of money instead of the pilgrimage of the soul, he might never have needed to frame that destructive Charter, which thank God has ruined him as bitterly as it is ruining me – and yet again, he might . . . Nearly twelve hundred years since Christ gave the Word, and theology knows no more than ever it did – so why should we expect better from any experts in finance? Perhaps some extraordinary taxation, fines for delinquencies, forced loans from the Jews – look into it, Marshal, are they possible, are they?

FIRST OFFICER. Why, your entire kingdom is one black gangrene of warfare – of course they are not possible.

MARSHAL. So what is to be done?

JOHN. Which garrisons are threatened? I mean, which important ones?

SECOND OFFICER (*at map*). Louis controls Kent, Surrey, and Sussex. The Army of God –

MARSHAL. – the excommunicate Army of God –

SECOND OFFICER. – is besieging Windsor and Dover. As before, their principal camp is London. The Scots are besieging Barnard Castle, here, and Durham, here. We still have freedom of manoeuvre in the midlands and south-west.

JOHN. London. The chief city of my realm and the chief city

of my enemies. They have been in London now for over a year. And yet not only their army but the citizens are excommunicated. I know Fitzwalter and de Vesci would not give the snot from their nostrils for the consolations of Holy Church, but I should have thought that to the merchants, to the craft-guilds, to the street-singers and the parish clergy, to the watermen on the Thames – and particularly to their wives, such matters of eternity would be of some importance. They made enough hurly-burly, did they not, when the Interdict was laid upon ourself? And why are they not terrified, when they regard the results of my progress to the north last winter? Let them consider what I did to the Palatinate of Durham and to Berwick-upon-Tweed. Do they want Cheapside and Blackfriars and Ludgate and Aldgate to be dealt with in like manner? The firebrands of my soldiers running under their thatches will only be half as hot, I think, as the torches that Beelzebub is preparing for them below – I suppose Beelzebub has been notified of the excommunication? It were better to leave nothing to chance in these matters.

PANDULPH. I fancy Beelzebub has his own sources of information, my Lord. In the meantime, your army –

JOHN. Is unpaid, disaffected, and not nearly large enough. We will withdraw to the neighbourhood of Devizes and hope to recover our strength.

Exeunt.

SCENE FIVE

View of London River, as before, but this time with the foreground full of men-at-arms drawn oversize, drinking and quarrelling – they wear the French Lilies on their coats.

Enter the DARK GIRL, *and the* RED-HAIRED GIRL, *with a tambourine. The* DARK GIRL *sings, while her companion dances and rattles her instrument, joining in the refrains.*

DARK GIRL (*singing – harshly and loudly*).
  Good people of London
  Come listen to me
  And I'll sing you a song
  Of our free liberty –
    Liberty liberty sign it and seal it
    Liberty liberty who dare repeal it?
  It was wrote out on paper
  What can we want more?
  Who cares for the Frenchmen,
  Who cares for the war?
    (*Refrain.*)
  Who cares for the Pope
  With his horns like old Moses,
  Or the King's hairy legs
  In a garden of roses?
    (*Refrain.*)
  Who cares for the larder
  All empty and bare,
  Who cares for the children
  With lice in their hair?
    (*Refrain.*)
  For they gave us sweet liberty
  To cuddle and love:
  What fairer companion
  Will dance to your grave –
    Liberty liberty sign it and seal it
            Who dare repeal it
            Touch it and feel it
            Meat drink, and fire
            True-lover's desire
    Liberty liberty all in the mire . . .
  Enter the MAYOR *and* YOUNG MARSHAL. *When they see*
  them, the GIRLS *run away.*
MAYOR. Look at them, my Lord, they know what they're up

to – they run away like rats as soon as they see me. It's not only that particular ditty, there's others as well, worse: there's a bad feeling in the streets. And I can't say that I blame them: they've heard enough pious pronouncements about liberty over the last twelve months to make the Fleet-ditch mudlarks vomit. You've uttered some of them yourself. So have I. But what have we got – in practical terms – to shew to the people? What bales of cloth, as it were, to lay upon my counter?

What d'ye lack, then what d'ye lack?
Sheets for your bed or shirts for your back?
Silk and satin, gay brocade
For wedding or for masquerade?

– it's just a little jargon, I made it up myself, my apprentices call it out at the shop-door, you know: it's supposed to attract the quality . . . Silk and satin indeed – it's laughable! I've had nothing in stock since the end of last summer but a hooligan army of drunken Northumbrians – yours.

YOUNG MARSHAL. Not mine, sir. De Vesci's: and most of them have gone.

MAYOR. It makes no great difference. We've been supplied with replacements. French, if you please. I'd call seven out of ten of them pickpockets and the other three pimps. Add to which, the danger.

YOUNG MARSHAL. Danger in defence of liberty –

MAYOR. The King will attack London, sir – as soon as he regroups his forces – and then where will we be with liberty signed and sealed? Where will my wife be, my thirteen-year-old daughter – I keep them locked up at home, which is good enough against the French. But the King has hungry wolves at his back who have had but the one meal, in the winter, and haven't eaten since . . . And the cook who must prepare for them has civic and commercial responsibility as well as his family – he has to weigh in his mind the virtues of freedom against the virtues of an ordered government. Which is what we *may* get from this Prince Louis and his wife. But her claim to the throne is not entirely satisfactory.

YOUNG MARSHAL. If John did in fact usurp his nephew Arthur's crown, then –

MAYOR. But did he? It sticks in my memory he was chosen king by your father and the barons for what seemed at the time sufficient reason. If it was sufficient then, it should be sufficient now. You can't change kings as though they were mats upon the floor, you know: once you call a man a king, you confirm it – with a sacrament. Which brings me to another matter – what about the Pope?

YOUNG MARSHAL. That is unfortunate.

MAYOR. It is more than unfortunate. I've heard it said that by an act of excommunication he has put us, as it were, upon the dark side of the moon, and people think that's uncanny. *I* think it's uncanny: I would prefer to be out of it.

Enter FITZWALTER, *talking with* LOUIS *and* BLANCHE.

FITZWALTER. This is not what you were brought here for.

LOUIS. Those who pay the piper must call the tune, I suppose? But what, my Lord, if the piper is considerably stronger than his audience? King John has proved himself unable to remove my army from your shores – are you likely to do any better? I think not. My wife means to be Queen of England: and if she *is* Queen, she will expect to reward those French Lords that have helped her. You do not imagine they defied excommunication for the mere pleasure of battle?

FITZWALTER (*coming across to* YOUNG MARSHAL). This might have been foreseen – de Vesci no doubt would have foreseen it, himself, if he hadn't decided to go north and help the Scots. But I did not think they would have been quite so direct. Nor so quick neither.

YOUNG MARSHAL. What are you talking about?

FITZWALTER. What do you think? He wants castles, he wants manor-houses, for his serjeants, his pioneers, his camp-cooks, his sutlers – God, he wants the land of England, boy! Do you know what it was told me that he said to his wife there – that he looked upon us as no better than flamboys to light the doorway of his hall for one evening and then be quenched in the cesspool! Why isn't de Vesci here? He's dead – did you know that?

YOUNG MARSHAL. No.

FITZWALTER. Well, he is, you can have his wife now any time you care to ask her, if the King's not got in first . . . He was killed by an arrow at Barnard Castle. And he goes straight to hell as well, that's all in the Pope's bargain. (*To* LOUIS.) I would prefer to discuss this business, Your Grace, when the war is won and not before. By which time, I suppose, there will be no lands left in England capable of supporting a root of wild burdock. (*Exit.*)

BLANCHE (*to* YOUNG MARSHAL). I am sorry your colleague should have taken offence. But surely you must know that whether you choose to serve King Log or King Stork, the pond will be encumbered. Such is the price that little frogs must pay.

   Exeunt BLANCHE *and* LOUIS.

MAYOR. Did you tell me, my Lord, that the Lady Blanche has promised to ratify the Charter – if she becomes Queen?

YOUNG MARSHAL. She did make some, provisional, under-taking – after a fashion, yes.

MAYOR. A French fashion.

YOUNG MARSHAL. Yes . . . Log or Stork, did she say? At any rate the Log has my own father's legs astride of it. Perhaps I had better remember whose subject I was born. Clearly you cannot accompany me to Devizes, but when I have told him your sentiments, I think the King will keep his wildfire out of London.

MAYOR. Goodbye, my Lord – God go with you. It would be an uncouth irony indeed if the very man who built it should be the first one to cry –
'London Bridge is broken down

      broken down
      broken down . . .'
 Exit MAYOR.

SCENE SIX

A picture of lords and ladies feasting in the open air. (This should somewhat resemble the grouping of actors in the beginning of Act II Scene 4.)

YOUNG MARSHAL (*picking up the* MAYOR'S *last words*).

 'London Bridge is broken down
     broken down
 London Bridge is broken down
 Dance over my Lady Lee' . . .

  He walks backwards and forwards about the stage. He is still wearing Lady de Vesci's kerchief.

  Enter LADY DE VESCI.

LADY DE VESCI. Your Lady Lee, if that is what you call her, is astonished that you have so long continued to wear her token, when you have fought all this while upon the adverse party. Do you bring it back to me to tell me you will wear it no longer because you have heard my husband is dead, and therefore your chivalric passion is necessarily blunted?

YOUNG MARSHAL. Madam, I confess that in these wars a knight of true courtesy is not able with confidence to devote his military conduct to the fame of any lady. The wars are dishonourable, being founded upon broken oaths, on both sides broken oaths. But I continue to wear your kerchief, with your permission, in order to shew that I am cognisant of a beautiful ideal over and above the petty treacheries of the time. In any case, I continue to love you in a very correct form – for I believe you to be unattainable. Are you not Caesar's?

  She extends her hand and he kneels to kiss the tips of her fingers.

Enter JOHN *with* MARSHAL *and* OFFICERS.

JOHN. Caesar has indeed put his bridle upon her – his gold chain round her waist, etcetera . . . Are you come to Devizes to win her, or what?

YOUNG MARSHAL. No, my Lord: I am come to offer you my services.

JOHN. Offer? Young man, they are *required!* But never mind, never mind, we are very glad to have you – Marshal, a fatted calf, make it ready, have you got one – every day brings home the foolish prodigals . . . What was the matter then? You found the needles in Blanche's embroidery-box a bit too sharp for your fingers – hey? Well, go on, Marshal, embrace your errant offspring.

MARSHAL. My Lord, he has returned to his allegiance: but he should never have left it. I am pleased to see him here: I am not overjoyed. You may kiss me, my boy. I acknowledge you as mine once more.

A formal kiss between father and son.

JOHN. Affecting – very. Now: here is the situation. (*At map.*) The King of Scots has got to Lincoln, he must never reach London. So we strike eastwards, in between, occupy Cambridge, relieve the siege of Lincoln and, ah, liberate the men of Norfolk. I have my army in good heart at last: I even found some money for them: I have no doubt of victory.

YOUNG MARSHAL. Do you intend to burn London?

JOHN. Of course, of course, of course.

YOUNG MARSHAL. The Londoners, my lord, would declare for you at once, if you promised to spare their city.

JOHN. Oh they would? Are you sure? They are Englishmen after all, then? Well, we must see what we can do. A calculated clemency, Marshal – do you think that it would work?

LADY DE VESCI. Clemency can never be calculated. Like all other virtues, it must arise in full freedom out of the free heart of the man that proposes it – if it does not do that, it is no longer a virtue.

JOHN. Is that a satirical platitude, or is it supposed to be true? By God, do you know – if it were true, we would have to reconsider a great many deeds that have been done, in past time, for the benefit of mankind, and acclaimed, what is more, throughout the Old Testament and the New. What about the Charter? I think you could call that a calculated act of virtue – couldn't you? Couldn't you? . . .

The Liberation of Norfolk, completed in mid-October, 1216, is an item of military history of no great consequence whatever. So off you go – get on with it.

Exeunt MARSHAL *and* YOUNG MARSHAL, *and* OFFICERS.

And although it must take its necessary place in any dramatization of the life and death of me, no doubt we can leave it alone for the moment. It is, after all, in good hands . . .

SCENE SEVEN

No picture – bright lights, possibly house-lights up.

JOHN. There comes a time in any stage-play, when the stage itself, the persons upon it, the persons in front of it, must justify their existence – and I think this is the time now: because on the 18th of October, I have to die, suffering from a surfeit of cider and peaches, which is a great joke of course, for I shall be taken short in the very moment of neither victory nor defeat – my frantic history suspended under circumstances of absolute inconclusion – King John yet again too late to control his situation. A time, I say, must come, when we stand in complete bewilderment as to what we are doing here at all. I mean – what use is this –

He takes off his sword and throws it away, out of sight.

Or this –

Same business with his crown.

Or this –

Same business with his mantle.

– as a means of convincing you of the human importance of what we are talking about? What use am I myself – a bogey-man or ghost seven hundred and fifty years old and still mouldering – set down to prance before you in someone else's body? What in fact have you seen tonight?

A document signed, and nobody knew what for – or at least, nobody knew or could possibly know the ultimate conse-sequences thereof. A document repudiated, and nobody knew what for. A villainous king and his villainous barons sprinkling each other's blood all over the map. A good Archbishop disgraced. A sagacious Pope flung all cack-handed in the Vatican by contradictory letters continually coming in on every post, from an island which he might be pardoned for believing had never been properly converted in the first place. And finally, a few little tit-bits of scandal not even proved to be historically true.

He points to the Lady.

I mean her, for instance. She was a rumour in certain circles in the thirteenth century, to her husband she was a pretext for a grievance: and that's about her lot. Or so you might believe. Because this play concerns Magna Carta, and Magna Carta only. The lady is peripheral. A thoroughly masculine piece of work was Magna Carta – a collaborative effort between brutal military aristocrats and virgin clergy: as you will appreciate, when I read you a certain clause from it.

He finds a scroll of the Charter behind PANDULPH'S *chair.*
Yes: you saw me tear it up at the end of the Second Act, but I kept another copy. I always twist around, you see, I plant one or two careful feet, carefully behind me, in my own footsteps, as I walk . . .

He opens the Charter:
'Paragraph 54:
No-one shall be arrested or imprisoned on the appeal óf a woman for the death of any person except her own hus-band.'

Now this, granted its historical context, may make perfectly good sense. Dr William Sharp McKechnie, in his definitive work upon the subject of the Charter . . .

PANDULPH *enters, hands* JOHN *a book with a page marked, and sits down in his chair, where he busies himself with his papers.*

Ah, thank you. There's nothing peripheral about you, is there? You hieratic analytical rat-nosed porcupine – I am delivering the antidote to all those circles with no kinks in, that you treated us to at the beginning – remember?

He opens the book at the marked page:

Dr McKechnie, to return to the main issue, says that the object of Paragraph 54 was –

'to find a remedy for what the barons evidently considered an unfair advantage enjoyed by women appellants, who were allowed to appoint some champion to act for them in the 'duellum' – or trial by combat – while the accused man had to fight for himself.'

In other words –

Again pointing to the Lady:

– if she had a brother who was murdered by an enemy, and if she believed, sweet innocent, that she could get that enemy done-for by setting-on young Marshal to fight him in the lists with her scarf upon his headpiece – then by God she is in error! The Age of Chivalry is dead – 1215. And so, of course, in 1965, is Paragraph 54. If the whole of the Charter was compiled in that spirit, you would not be here tonight. (I am not going to even try to read you what it says about the Jews, let alone attempt to argue for it. Those of you who may be of that faith and nation would hardly have done worse under Adolf Hitler himself than under the pioneers of liberty who set their hand to this!). But you do see what I mean, – the lady is peripheral, both to the play and to the document.

Yet nevertheless she exists. And the very fact of such

existence is worth taking notice of. If she now stands in the middle of the stage it is not, I assure you, for reasons of fashionable immorality – it could just as well be my Queen here at this moment: but the Queen is in Gloucester, a place of security away from the war, looking after my young son; therefore we have the other woman, and it makes but little difference. For both ladies have been created in the image of God, they are females, of good health and comparative beauty . . . But we are not now discussing sexual attraction. Though of course it can never be entirely eliminated.

Nor should it be – it is part of her manifest corporal mechanism and has been given in a greater or less degree to every creature that walks. I wonder how she does walk? – two legs are common property, but to support a whole body, successfully, without conscious art and effort – did you ever see such a thing as a two-legged stool? And then she has her buttocks, above the legs, to sit on – but also to give pleasure to the eyes and to the touch. She has a womb which has brought forth more than one living child. She has her breasts which have afforded abundant nourishment to those children. She has her bowels and her heart and her lungs, her hands, her arms, her shoulders, her neck. And on her neck – look how it balances! – so small and delicate an egg of bone that I can almost encompass it within my ten fingers, and yet it is quite heavy and contains much that should give us pause. For by means of this egg alone can this creature eat, drink, talk, breathe, smell, see, weep, laugh, hear, and above all, think! Which is essential to her life – but what about the great rope of golden hair that hangs upon the egg? Here is nothing essential – here is decoration and delight – here is pure gratuity. Shave it off and yet she would function as before. Leave it on, comb it loose, braid it up, twist it round, let the wind blow through it, feel it, stroke it, look at it – who does not like to look at it? Yet the body of an eagle or an antelope or a toad could be similarly extolled. How are we to appreciate that she belongs to a unique species? She has a mind: and it has been educated with just that end in view.

LADY DE VESCI. First I was taught how Lucifer rebelled against his God and fell to hell: next how he tempted Eve: next how there is a difference between a mortal and a venial sin: after that there were some details of the life of Our Lord and His Mother, subordinated always to the prime importance of my own hypothetical chastity and how it must be preserved.

JOHN. By whom were you instructed!

LADY DE VESCI. Those who had Authority.

JOHN. Is that what they had? But then you defied your husband, you inspired a genuine if ridiculous devotion in the breast of at least one good-hearted young gentleman, and you became the most favoured subject of your ill-favoured luckless King. She followed in fact the very pattern of this Lucifer she had been warned against when young. Does her uniqueness lie in this then, that she is so easily lost? Much as we would value a diamond or an amethyst which a crack in the floorboards or a thick heap of leaves on the ground could take away from us for ever? If such is her condition she must not remain anonymous. Her name is Margaret, and her father—which will surprise you – was King William the Lion of Scotland. She is illegitimate, of course – but it does fit the picture. Why else has the atrocious Eustace met his death at Barnard Castle in the north, except that he was helping his half-brother-in-law, the present King Alexander, to reduce my own poor royalty? And why else would she be so disinclined to obey his commands?

LADY DE VESCI. I will tell you why else. Because he demanded my obedience. He maintained he had Authority.

JOHN. So he had – you were his wife. Is not that so, Master Legate?

PANDULPH. Yes.

JOHN. A marriage is an oath taken before God – it enjoins obedience upon the inferior party and constant faith upon both parties. So do the oaths taken between kings and their noblemen, and between noblemen and their dependants. Am I right, Pandulph?

PANDULPH. Yes.

JOHN. There is a failure in logic here. Can you put your finger on it?

LADY DE VESCI. Yes, I can. You have condoned my disobedience to Lord Eustace –

JOHN. He laid violent hands upon you –

LADY DE VESCI. That should not have been relevant. You also condoned one or two adulteries on the part of your Queen.

JOHN. I was in love with her.

LADY DE VESCI. But you refused to condone the rebellion of your barons. So far as the doctrine of Authority – either in marriage or statecraft – was convenient to yourself, you insisted upon it: and where it was not, you ignored it.

JOHN. Exactly so! Inconsistent, irregular, unreasonable. And this is our uniqueness. Not in our capacity for damnation or salvation nor yet in our capacity for logical rationality – though both of them are glorious: and both of them, I fear, have distorted our nature. Indeed I am inclined to think, that not only are you unsuited to be a married woman and I to be a king, but that none of us, ever, are suited to be either.

PANDULPH. But you *were* a king, my Lord.

JOHN. God's Teeth, yes, I was, I was – and what did I do with it? I spoiled the Egyptians, Pandulph, that's what I did – I made use of my sacred station for promiscuous enjoyment – not always for myself: look at London Bridge, very useful – and beautiful . . . but, by and large, in this world of constructed Authority which is Egypt of the taskmasters, I played the part of sly escapist Israel – and I nearly got away. Do you want to know the name of Pharaoh? Old hard-heart on his chariot, stuck fast in the quicksand? They call him

Pope Innocent, and you are his servant, and you are also my dupe! Because I do not believe, not one iota, no, in the Authority which you claim, which is claimed in this Charter, and which is claimed by the golden crown I have this very moment doffed!

I do not feel very well.
My bowels are rolling over
Like the first pull on a great bell.
Not only in my kingdom
Are there civil disturbances
The members of my own body
Are bringing forth their grievances . . .

Never mind, it has passed . . . So what have you got to say to me, Egyptian?

PANDULPH. At this late stage, nothing that could be of any use to you. But it is a truth and I know it to be a truth, that the unity of all men is desired by Christ, within Christ: that we are subordinate to Christ and yet will become part of Him: and both the subordination and incorporation are mirrored upon earth. Church, State, and Family are all ordained microcosms of the hierarchy of heaven – just imagine us without them? Where would we be? Choked and lacerated by the brambles of our own appetites – our animal appetites which we share with the eagle, the antelope, and the toad. We would be both barren and over-luxuriant at one and the same time. And yet this can be prevented – a good gardener can prevent it, he can weed, prune and culti-vate, impose in fact Authority. *You* are a dandelion.

JOHN. I am partial to dandelions. Coarse in texture I know, and the scent is undistinguished and they are far too prolific. But powdered across the slope of a green meadow, all those thousand dots of gold – who could want to be rid of them? Even to give place to violets? In any case, despite all your efforts, Pandulph, Authority does not remain as it was – it changes a little, and where it changes it can also be mitigated.

He holds up the Charter.

Authority of the Crown gives way bit by bit to Authority of the Common Law. But even the Law, liberally administered, can one day say to this woman – 'Shave off your hair'. And it will give good reasons: and she will have to do it. What it will never say and can never say, is – 'Here is a cloth-of-gold ribbon, which enhances your hair. Put it on, and I will adore you.' Now, which is better – to have this head shaved by order of the Law, or by the violence of my hand?

PANDULPH. If the Law ordered it, presumably it would have been for the general benefit. If you were to do it by yourself, only you would be satisfied. Obviously the first is better. You are wasting my time.

He turns to his papers and takes little more notice.

JOHN.
Once again my bowels roll over.
What is there inside me I have yet to discover?
Too many women, I think,
Too much food and drink . . .
She will still be bald, whether it is the first or the second! And I have an amorous nature, therefore it is far more likely I would offer her the ribbon. Of course, I have been cruel: but only because the ordained microcosms that you talked about have somehow suffered disruption. Or have they perhaps created disruption by their very existence? Anyhow, it has been because of them that I have had to do the things that made me hated. Had they never been imposed upon the world – but we advance no further, do we? You are not even listening. You are quite right, of course – why should you damned well listen – while the world is as it is, you have the best argument! The lion and the lamb cannot lie down together –

PANDULPH (*a brief glance up and back to his papers*). Until the Second Coming.

JOHN. Which may very well happen before these people here even reach their places of work tomorrow morning! And when it does happen, who will know it? The First Coming was recognized by twelve poor yokels only – and it tormented one of them to the extent of thirty silver pennies and a long rope to hang himself.

> A rope around the neck and
> A rope around the bell:
> Why do they have to give such a
> Terrible strong pull?

Who will be Judas next time? Unpredictable me or Pandulph the microcosmic gardener? But, as we stand now, the lion must be kept in chains and the lamb in a secure sheepfold. I have given thought to both necessities. Consider this clause –

Reading from the Charter:

And no free man shall be arrested or imprisoned . . . except . . .

you have heard it spoken twice already. And also the other one –

To no man will we sell or deny right and justice . . .

No detail, no precision, no temporary or feudal pettifogging that can fix these two clauses in the early thirteenth century or in any other century, yet they can find a home in all. My work, d'you see – not the Archbishop's nor the Marshal's, and certainly not Fitzwalter's. I said: make those clauses general – lax, if you like – because by their very laxity they go some way to admit the existence of dandelions, of disobedient women, and ribbons of cloth-of-gold. Interpret them how you like –

LADY DE VESCI. I tried to interpret one of them –

JOHN. Yes, and you were denied your interpretation: but you were quite right and your husband was wrong. Interpret them how you like, and agreed that they concede the Authority of the Law, not one act of injustice, interpret them how you like, can ever be done, ever that will not be contrary to so general a clause. I gave them to you all, and all of you can use them – against the Barons, or the Bishops, or even the Crown, against the Parliaments, the Scriveners, the Catchpolls, the Beadles and the Bailiffs, the Marshals and their Serjeants – indeed, every single stone, brick, or granule of aggregate that help to build the buttresses which hold up the walls of the Temple of Authority are in peril from these clauses! Every buttress must be made afraid of you – and you must never fear the buttress: because a buttress is a dead thing, inert, fabricated, the result of a delusion – whereas you are men and women – I have shewn you your pattern, here –

He points to the Lady.

– and the pattern for her was God. But I am not capable of talking about God. Pandulph has reconstituted God as if God was a sack of Portland Cement – mix it up with water, it will stand hard for generations, you can chip the bits off, but you cannot remodel it. Never let that be said of this parchment – I warn you! And as you have all come here in some sort of celebratory and congratulatory frame of mind, I will also give a warning to the parchment itself:

'Woe unto you when all men speak well of you.'

He rolls the Charter up.

Pandulph, my throat is dry,
Grey patches are trickling over
The clear pupil of my eye.
I am not very well and I feel a kind of dizziness:
Pandulph have you no answer to my tortuous eloquence?
You consequential nosey-parker
I am waiting for your answer!

PANDULPH. Thou fool, this night thy soul shall be required of thee.

He gathers up his papers and goes.

SCENE EIGHT

A large-scale map of the Wash.
JOHN. The first thing they ever taught you –
LADY DE VESCI. Was how Lucifer invented sin.
JOHN.

As for example, gluttony . . .
I have been the guest, in Norfolk,
Of the loyal citizens of Lynn.
They were not very wise in their good hospitality.
Great vats of stewed peaches and new cider to drink:
The cider was very gassy
And the peaches were too pink.
I don't think you should be here – we have a long march this
morning – keep your bed, be comfortable . . .

*He finds his mantle and sword and assumes them again – not
the crown. He strides about the stage, shouting:*
Come on come on, come on, October the 12th, 1216, past
four o'clock on a filthy wet morning, get your feet on the
floor – bugler, where's the call?

Bugle calls and drums start to beat.
Keep your bed, lady, keep it
Be cosy while you can –
Warm blankets for the warm woman
And a hard horseback for her man.

*He leads the lady off, tenderly kissing her hand: and then
returns to his bustling. He holds the rolled-up Charter in his
left hand rather like a truncheon.*
Colour party, forward! Marshal, where are you? We're on
the move already!

*The stage begins to fill with the confusion of an army breaking
camp – as many persons as can be found, as OFFICERS,
SOLDIERS, WAGGONERS and so forth . . . flags, drums,
kitbags, weapons of all sorts. Practicable wagons are dragged*

on to the stage – they seem very heavy and are being man-handled with difficulty.

MARSHAL *and* YOUNG MARSHAL *enter.*

MARSHAL. I want all the transport over the mudflats before the tide comes in!

YOUNG MARSHAL. Waggoner-serjeant, why aren't those wheels turning? Get on with it, man!

FIRST OFFICER. What time is low water?

SECOND OFFICER. Twelve o'clock by the book – we've got plenty of time.

JOHN. Oh no we have not, we have never got that!

OFFICERS (*generally*). Come on, come on . . . heave, you stupid Dutchmen, heave . . . *etc.*

JOHN. What's holding it up? Why won't that wagon move?
    What began as confused but comparatively purposeful move-ment has now bogged down completely.

A SOLDIER. This mud's more soft than we thought – we can't get a purchase.

JOHN. Late again, late, you are always too late – we are march-ing upon my London –
    I will tolerate no delays!
    My bowels are rolling over
    In seventeen different ways
    Oh peaches and new cider
    And this disgusting muddy river . . .
    There is a flow of water six inches deep pouring over my ankles – *what* time did you say was the tide?

MARSHAL. It should still be running out.

JOHN. Running out? You incompetent antiquity – it's coming in, fast! Ankles, calves, knees – do you want us to be drowned! Clear that wagon – quick!
    In the middle of the stage they are all staggering as though surrounded by swirling water. If possible an effect of shifting eddies should be projected on the map of the Wash behind.

SECOND OFFICER. Jesu Mercy, can the almanack be wrong?

JOHN. Of course it can be wrong. It was written by a bishop!

YOUNG MARSHAL. My Lord, it's no good – these are regular sea waves coming in now, and it's getting deeper every minute.

MARSHAL. We must abandon the wagons, my Lord, get the horses through first.

JOHN. Abandon my wagons – all my jewels are in that wagon – an emerald, a sapphire, a garnet and a topaz, that were sent to me by the Pope, a sapphire and a ruby I would have given to St Edmund but they were too beautiful to leave my hands – my crown and my sceptre – God's Bread, they were my perquisites, the mark of my authority, good God, I was the overseer . . .

He sinks on one knee, and supports himself on his hand.

MARSHAL. Hold up the King. He is falling in the deep mud.

OFFICERS *go to his help.*

SECOND OFFICER. My Lord, it is not the mud, it is mortal sickness that makes him fall.

FIRST OFFICER. He has lost consciousness, my Lord.

He has not in fact lost consciousness, but is now on all fours in the middle of the flood, fighting against it. The men who are helping him have a hard struggle, both against the water and against the weight of his body. MARSHAL *and* YOUNG MARSHAL *stand downstage, as it were upon dry land.* YOUNG MARSHAL *appears to be about to go and assist, but his father checks him quietly.*

MARSHAL. The waters have come over him as the Red Sea came over Pharaoh . . . My son, our new King Henry is not yet ten years old. He has succeeded to a kingdom all but swept away by deluge. I am too near my own grave to be able myself to dredge it up again for him. But one thing must be seen to. At his coronation, whatever the Church may say, he must take oath to observe the Great Charter. There is no other way by which the war can be stopped, the French driven out, and the King's people held together. Let it but

be done, my son, and the commonwealth may continue . . .
Help Landless John back
Onto his own dry land.
Never mind the wagons . . .
Unclench his cold left hand.

The OFFICERS *have brought* JOHN *ashore. One of them takes the scroll, with difficulty, from his hand and gives it to the* MARSHAL. *They carry his body off the stage, and all exeunt, leaving the wagons and gear amid the swirling water.*

Appendix

After I had completed the play, I remembered the legend of the Wise Men of Gotham, and regretted that I failed to insert it in my story. This scene, accordingly, is offered as an alternative to the greater part of Act Two Scene 4. Additional characters are:

A PARSON (of Gotham)

A FARMER

A SMITH

A MILLER.

(The other PARSON, the GOLDSMITH and his Wife, are consequently not used, if this episode is preferred.) Gotham is normally thought to be the Nottinghamshire township of that name. There was however another Gotham in Sussex, and I have the authority of the Oxford Book of Nursery Rhymes for adopting it.

Act Two

SCENE FOUR

A picture of a small hamlet, with church, cottages, and peasants carrying out their harvesting etc.

Enter PARSON, FARMER, SMITH *and* MILLER.

PANDULPH. Therefore, we must take care that the hostility maintained toward the King by both barons and superior clergy is not allowed to outweigh the genuine sentiments of loyalty which no doubt still burn within the breasts of the common people of England. Here, for example, we see the leading inhabitants of some small village, assembled together

with joy to welcome their Sovereign upon his progress. You,
sir, are presumably the Parish Priest – the Parish priest of –
where?

PARSON. Gotham, in the county of Sussex, my Lord. Here is
Robin the Miller, Peter the Blacksmith, and John of the
Manor Farm.

PANDULPH. Very good, very good, continue your preparations . . .

He busies himself with papers at his desk.

PARSON. Certainly he spent the last two days in Lewes.
Where will he come next?

SMITH. My sister Edith whose good man, as you know,
Parson, has a contract for leading the horse dung out of
Lewes Castle stables, she sent word to me by my little
nephew late in the evening that the word is all round Lewes
he's for Pevensey today.

MILLER. He don't have to come through Gotham –

SMITH. He comes where he wants to come. He carries a hawk
on his fist and many of his noblemen do likewise, and he
follows the wild fowl where he rides, taking his needful
journey and the exercise of his sport together. He has the
Queen with him too and great ladies beside. You see the
fine weather – he has time and leisure to diverge his course
into whatsoever downs or meadows take his fancy.

FARMER. Aye or standing crops. We've not got our wheat in
yet. I can't endure to have horsemen riding over that. There's
ever furious ruffians will trample after the King where he
goes – they take no account for nothing and then what will
we do?

PARSON. There's another point to be made out of that, goodman Farmer. It's a matter of Law. Now I don't know and
I've never heard it proved, according to document and
precedent, and I don't hear that it was ever wrote down in
pen and ink: but custom, I am told it is, a Norman custom
brought by old King William, that wheresoever the King

should ride, be it harvest corn or champaine pasture, that very road for ever after becomes a public road – the King's High Road, no less. Now some call that prerogative of royalty. I call it just plain abuse. But how do we prevent it?

MILLER. It should have been prevented in that Charter they made him set his seal to.

PARSON. Not in so many words it wasn't, Miller – I read it, when displayed in Chichester south aisle – it wasn't there.

SMITH. We can't take no chances. We can't let him through.

FARMER. We can't fight him, neither. He's the King, he takes his pleasure and his sport where he wants to, as was said.

PARSON. Suppose, though, upon his journey into Gotham he was to meet with but little pleasure – suppose it seemed a queer-like place for him to come to, and no great comfort for the ladies neither –

SMITH. No great comfort in my poor forge-house, certain: but they won't be wanting to take their dinners inside of there. I don't see how –

PARSON. I didn't mean comfort in the way of cushions and stools, Blacksmith, I meant comfort for the mind. Now a King in a rebellious land with a memory of excommunication – he needs ease for his spirit and for the discourse of his tender ladies. Now, suppose he thought the Devil ruled in Gotham?

FARMER. You mean witchcraft magic, Parson?

PARSON. Jesus Mary no – we'd imperil our immortal souls with that. Something of the nature, though – but gentler, d'you see, and safer, under God. Come here . . .

They get into a huddle and whisper with occasional bursts of laughter.

Enter the CLERK.

CLERK. Is this the village of Gotham? Excuse me, is this the village of Gotham, reverend sir?

PARSON. It is indeed, sir, Christ be with you, sir. Can I be of assistance to you, sir? Can I put you on your road?

CLERK. No no, I am already on it, thank you very much. I am a member of the Royal Household and I am commissioned to inform you that the King's Grace and the Queen's Grace with a considerable retinue intend very shortly to pass the bounds of this parish on their way to Pevensey Castle. No doubt, as the sun is already high in the heavens, the company will desire to eat their noontide meal. You must therefore expect some small levy to be made upon your hen-runs and pig-sties. Sucking-pigs? You have sucking-pigs? Good. The King's falconry has been successful this morning and there will be no shortage of game-birds. But I fancy the services of your good wives will be called upon for plucking and drawing and so forth. Also bread, if you have it, newly-baked. You will of course be paid for your trouble – more or less.

While he is talking to the Parson, the other three have gone off-stage and now return carrying a large wooden bowl or wash-tub, which they manhandle awkwardly, bumping into the CLERK.

CLERK (*cont.*) Might I ask what you think you are doing with that bowl?

SMITH. It's a question, sir, of whether or no the King's Grace is partial to fish?

CLERK. It isn't Friday, is it?

SMITH. Ah sir, we're in Gotham here, all our days is like to be Friday here, sir. On account of the multitude of heavy fish that do befavour the seacoast downalong. We could catch his Grace a powerful draught thereof, if so be he had a taste for it.

CLERK. And how, sir, do you imagine you are going to catch fish in a bowl? I should have thought a net or line would be more appropriate.

MILLER. You think we're daft in Gotham, sir? We have nets and lines galore beside the shingle, sir, but this here bowl, sir, is the vessel we must sail in, for to seek God's fish upon

His waters. When the wind is fresh and lively and we three jolly lads aboard of her, she do heave and she do spin upon the tide most beautiful to be sure.

CLERK. Oh.

FARMER. Would you say the King, sir, was partial to fried fish?

CLERK. But – a boat, surely – you must have a boat?

PARSON. Boats gets wrecked, boats is feeble, frail. This here bowl, with the sacred words we do say over her, she should never wreck nor founder, never, in the service of the King.

CLERK. I fancy the King will confine himself to partridges.

PARSON. Then that being so, sir, there is no need for us to venture. Put it down, good men, and let us take our rakes and set once more to work.

They all collect rakes and go to a corner of the stage.

CLERK. Harvesting, already?

PARSON. No sir, but to rescue the life of a poor female creature in distress. See this dew-pond here, sir. Last night there was a sad discovery.

MILLER. The full moon, sir, out of heaven, we did observe she had fell in, and now by daylight we do rake for her to fetch her out and to restore her to her rightful place. You rake to the north, Peter Smith, and I to the south, and you, John Farmer, to the east, while Parson seeks for her upon the west-hand side. Rake, boys, rake.

They rake, singing 'Rake, boys, rake' in the manner of a chanty.

CLERK. I suppose you would think I was not quite in my right mind if I were to suggest that what you had seen had been no more than the usual reflection?

PARSON. That we would, sir, certain. For all know well enough the moon is insecurely fixed aloft or else why do she turn and turn so changeable every blessed month except as how the wind should waver her and so in wavering, bring her down maybe? Last night it was a stormy night indeed . . .

And when we've done this pond, Rob Miller, you and Edward Carpenter must set about that fencing job around the cuckoo's tree. Rake, boys, rake away . . .

CLERK. You might as well explain to me what is the cuckoo's tree? I am after all a stranger in these parts.

SMITH. So fine a summer as it's been, sir, we can't endure to see the winter come. Now winter comes when cuckoos are flown away, and so we catch our cuckoo here, and set him in a tree and fence him round with good split boards and there he bides according. We're none too soon to do it neither, for cuckoo's tune has changed already. Ah, we're sharp in Gotham, sir: we can watch the devilments of Nature and control them when they come.

CLERK. So it appears. I am not at all sure that the King's Grace will be able to favour your village with his presence after all. It may be necessary for him to push on to Pevensey direct. But he will be informed of the loyal warmth and traditional rustic good sense that obtains among the inhabitants here. Yes indeed. Good morning.

Exit CLERK.

PARSON. Boys, we've done it.

ALL. Arrh . . .

They launch into a dance – a kind of morris dance using their rakes (and if convenient) the bowl: singing . . .

'Rake boys rake, the King is coming to Gotham
Rake boys rake, the King is going away.
Rake boys rake, the bowl is on the ocean
Rake boys rake, the cuckoo's in the tree . . .'

Exeunt dancing.

SCENE FIVE

Picture of apple orchard as in Act Two Scene 4 of original text;
Enter JOHN, QUEEN, LADY DE VESCI, MARSHAL, PRINCE
HENRY, CLERKS *and attendants.*

CLERK. I would not recommend Gotham, my Lord. Either they are up to some sort of dubious magic or else they are all astray in their wits. I fancy the latter. There is a great deal of intermarriage in these rural communities and it sometimes has curious effects.

JOHN. What effects?

CLERK. Three of them intended to put to sea in a bowl.

JOHN. Good God. Of course they might be brewing rebellion ... Possible, do you think?

CLERK. No, my Lord. They are only silly country folk: but if they are indeed imbecile, there might be some unfortunate incident. The modesty of the ladies might perhaps be affronted, if you know what I mean . . .?

JOHN. I doubt if these ladies would mind that very much ... But, eccentricity, though entertaining, is occasionally dangerous. I don't want to stamp it out – indeed I would welcome it – but on the south coast, in this month, in the present state of the kingdom – no, no, there are far too many untoward events taking place as it is. We will not go through Gotham.

QUEEN. But, my Lord, it might prove to be an agreeable and humorous experience.

JOHN. No! No, madam, no! There are plots against my life and against the life of my children. I have a mind to *burn* Gotham.

LADY DE VESCI. My Lord, we have no evidence they are in any conspiracy.

JOHN. Marshal, what do you think? Fire and sword, intimidation?

MARSHAL. Certainly not, my Lord. It would be the clearest contravention of the Charter of Liberties.

JOHN. Why yes, so it would . . . You put me to shame, Marshal. Let us forget about Gotham . . . We have travelled far enough this morning – let them serve us with a little food and drink.

From here on the scene follows the original Act Two Scene 4
until line 26 on page 326.
   (By so much the less
   Was I truly a king)
The ensuing Goldsmith episode is then omitted: and the play
continues as before from the entry of YOUNG MARSHAL on page
330. The only alterations necessary in the retained dialogue of
the original scene are:
   Page 324 line 11: Omit 'Kentish'.
   Page 331 line 25: For 'Kentish Coast' and 'Southern
   Coast'.

Two Autobiographical Plays

The True History of Squire Jonathan and his Unfortunate Treasure

and

The Bagman or *The Impromptu of Muswell Hill*

to RUDI DUTSCHKE:

'I think, therefore I am',
Descartes, in prison, said.
Surrounded by stone walls
He was alone with his own head.

Rudi, being free
In a mobile free society,
Had a wound in *his* head:
But he was not alone:
His walls were made of paper
Not of stone.

He thinks, therefore they followed him about.
He thinks, therefore he scarcely dared go out.
He thinks, therefore they damn well threw him out.

Introductory Note

A SECOND DEDICATION

I dedicate these two plays printed here
To all those nosey-parkers who prefer
To know the poet's life and what he does
Rather than read his words upon the page
Or listen to them spoken on the stage.
Where and with whom he sleeps, and whom he meets –
Bending his knees or turning out his toes –
And what he cooks and how he sits and eats
Is far more interesting to us all
Than any tired old tale he wants to tell.
(Moreover, if the fellow goes and writes a play
You can't get in to see it unless you pay.)

I specially desire this dedication
To warm the hearts of those whose cold devotion
In setting down the facts and piling archives
Within an air-conditioned Institute
Produces, for themselves, a Doctorate:
And for the poet, death – while he still lives.

I also wish my small voice to be heard
By one particular zealous officer
From the Special Branch of Scotland Yard –
He'll know it, if he reads it, he wears a beard
And questioned me for nearly half-an-hour*
In 1969 at the platform-gate
That leads to the Irish boat at Holyhead.

* I think, because I too wore a beard,
I was an Agitator, therefore to be feared.
His own beard, no doubt, was a cute disguise –
He had to watch for dangerous Irishmen:
A growth of hair upon the chin
In such wild company is not unwise.

When I came off the train he lay in wait
And asked me who I was and what I did.
I said
My name was Arden and I was a writer –
His gloomy face did not become much brighter.
Indeed I was most closely interrogated:
What were my politics, for whom had I voted,
Had I ever been arrested, had I ever been convicted?
He made me tell the story of my life.
But, strange, he asked no questions about my wife –
And she is Irish and most radical –
I thought he would have asked, for such as her might well
Keep guns along with love wrapped up in bed . . .
He let me go at last, he shook his head,
He was not satisfied . . . Now he may read
These two short plays Methuen has printed here:
He will discover what he has to fear.

Here I tell all and I hold nothing back:
I stand and wait for the counter-attack.

A Few Historical Facts

(*relating to the background of the plays*):

Facts about 'Squire Jonathan' : About eighteen years ago I was in love with a large blonde beautiful Scot. I told her I wrote plays and poems and such-like. I shewed her a sample or two. She said: 'Oh dear . . . you really mean all this, don't you?' After some length of time I asked her if she would marry me. She said not. I protested that our acquaintance had been of sufficient duration and intimacy as to require her to give reason for her refusal. She said: 'Because you are a poet.' I said I thought that that was not a good reason and that furthermore much of my recent verse had been written in celebration of herself, and she had expressed herself pleased with it. She said that made it worse. Then, as we were stepping into an electric train, a rude man of about sixty pushed out past us, muttering curses under his breath. He had grey hair, becoming bald, a tight ill-tempered mouth, a pair of horn-rimmed spectacles, a briefcase and a black umbrella. He had perhaps had a bad day at the office. I said: 'I suppose you want me to secure a steady job in my regular profession (architecture), and end up like him?' She said: 'But that's how you are going to end up anyway.' Then she gave a gasp of alarm and her eyes went wide: 'Oh my goodness, I really think you *are*!' . . . After that evening there was less of an intimacy between us: and eventually, without telling me what she was up to, she took herself off and married a character in the antique trade – a Turk, was he? Or a Syrian? – who was reputed to have been at one time a smuggler, and who was at least twice my age. I only ever caught one glimpse of him: under artificial light in a coffee bar – he looked like Jack Palance – oh yes, indeed *sinister*, but had Orpheus been able to flash that sort of smile he would have needed no harp to haul Eurydice out of hell. My displacement in his favour occurred at the end of 1956. By 1963, when I wrote the play, I no longer bore anybody any malice.

Facts about 'The Bagman' : This play is in the nature of a dream. Some people think dreams foretell the future. This one in certain respects did. I wrote it in the spring of 1969. Later in the same year I became awkwardly involved with a group of revolutionists, one of whom, a lodger in my house, was arrested for throwing a petrol-bomb at a policeman during a demonstration in front of Ulster House, London. The people of the Bogside, Derry, were at that time beleaguered by an extraordinary body of seventeenth-century Calvinists, wearing uniform, armed with CS gas, and laughably entitled 'The Forces of Law-and-Order'. The Bogsiders repelled their advances with petrol-bombs: the one thrown in front of Ulster House was intended as a reminder to the London Fs of L & O that the Irish Catholics of the Six Counties had a number of friends elsewhere. The boy who threw it deduced correctly that the seventeenth-century Calvinists would not have been so bold if various groups of rich twentieth-century Agnostics on this side of the water had extracted no advantage from their goings-on. It is not only a question of extracting advantage, of course – it's a matter of active encouragement of sectarian strife in order to secure a docile disunited

labour-force in Northern Ireland – James Connolly had it taped
sixty years ago, but it seems an impossible task to make the
British public ever understand that the 'Irish problem' has
always been a 'British problem' and nothing else. The Protes-
tants were *put* into Ireland in the reign of James I for the purpose of consolidating the royal power there, and also for the
purpose of making certain Britons rich. It still goes on. My
lodger wanted to bring, as it were, the battle back home, to the
place from which it receives its continual occult direction. His
strategy was sound: but I was unable to approve the particular
tactic he chose to implement it.

The bomb had hit nothing – neither man nor building – a
policeman had beaten the flames out in a second with a placard
snatched from a lounging demonstrator. But even had a constable been burnt to death the cause would not have been
advanced. Indeed, such a holocaust would only have confirmed
the British public in their habitual blind assumption that all
Irishmen (and their friends) are frantic drunken ruffians to
whom arson is as mother's milk. All this was debated in my
house, day and night, between his remand on bail and his
eventual trial.* (He was sent to prison for several months, which
surprised no one.) I do not think I need go into those intermin-
able debates in detail: except to say that I was described – in a
hostile spirit – as a 'Bourgeois Liberal'. I don't know that this
was correct – to my way of thinking a 'Bourgeois Liberal' is a
man who would have offered his patronizing solidarity to the
comrades, while, at the same time, deploring *on principle* their
use of *violence*. Although I was the Honorary Chairman of
Peace News, I did not raise any such principled objection. The
residents of the Bogside had had little choice but to be violent,
and the sight of their battle on the television had 'stirred my
heart as with a trumpet'. My feelings towards the capitalist/
unionist/protestant Junta in the Six Counties were – and still are
– very violent. But I did feel that this particular bomb had been

* I should point out, by the by, that his bomb business took place some
months *after* the incident at Holyhead Station described in the verses above.
If it had happened before, there might just possibly have been a bit of rhyme
or reason to the detective's questions.

thrown at the wrong time and the wrong target – or rather, at a confused target: was it Ulster House (OK, perhaps); a policeman (why? In contrast to his Derry colleagues, he was unarmed); or, generally, the entire gathering (dreadful!)? – and above all, it had been thrown ineffectively. Further, the young man was trying to maintain a plea of 'not guilty' – he defied the police to prove he had thrown anything. This sort of defence, though permissible in most court cases, seemed oddly unsuitable in the context, and would have deprived him of the opportunity of explaining his action forcefully from the dock. He was, I thought, badly in need of such an opportunity, in view of the type of publicity the bomb had already had in the newspapers.

Of course, I realize that he – and his friends – were angry with me for reasons that had little to do with theoretical ideology. He had the historic distaste of the warrior for the man of words. He had, after all, put himself at risk in a battle – even if the battle had been rather unilateral and not of proven necessity – and I had not. I had been Sitting On The Fence. Under such circumstances, it is no good trying to argue that the only place a writer *can* usefully be is On The Fence, or else how will he be able to see what is going on clearly enough to write about it afterwards? That argument is anyway based on a pretty shifty half-truth. I have no doubt that choleric Norman barons used to bellow at their *jongleurs*: 'Where were *you* in 1066, you Pacifist Idealist, you!' To which, if the *jongleur* was an honest man, the answer would probably have been: 'Hiding in a tent at the back of the camp, scared to death...'

It may perhaps be wondered how, if I was Honorary Chairman of *Peace News*, I did *not* adopt a principled attitude of nonviolence towards the Ulster House Outrage. But just about at that time I resigned from the Honorary Chair. The reason I gave to the Board was that I was about to travel overseas and did not wish to hold such a post when it was not possible for me to attend the monthly meetings. There was another reason, however, which I did not give to the Board, because I did not really give it to myself until a good deal later. A prestige position on a pacifist newspaper was, I came to feel, at any rate for myself, a classic piece of Fence-Sitting. It enabled me to offer pronouncements upon public affairs from a position of safety – I could attack governments and Fs of L & O with enthusiasm, while at the same time avoiding direct action and its consequent peril for myself by pleading my principles. *Non*-violent direct action – often more dangerous than the violent variety – I did not take part in, much, because I was not persuaded of its value at the present time. So altogether I discovered myself in a sufficiently dishonest attitude. So I quit.

I then went to India. In India the war between the fed men and the hungry men, the clothed men and the naked men, the sheltered men and the exposed men, is being waged with great ferocity, compared to which the manifestation outside Ulster House had the appearance of one of those fifteenth-century tourneys where the knights were so heavily armed that they could scarcely ever be seriously hurt, where a wooden barrier between contestants protected even the horses from collision, and where all contestants were of the same social class. (By Indian standards *everyone* in England is of the same social class. The Western proletariat is the oppressive bourgeoisie of the East – the class struggle is now being waged across continental divides instead of 'across the tracks' in one country at a time. To an Indian revolutionist there is no such thing as a Left-wing Western writer. If he is Western he is – by definition – an agent of the Right.)

While in India I had some opportunity to see the non-violence of the late Mahatma Gandhi in action. It did not impress me much. There is also in India a violent movement of Marxist-Leninist derivation known as the Naxalite movement. This includes university intellectuals from the cities and also landless peasants from up-country. I was not, of course, able to meet any of the latter. Even if I had known how to speak their language, or they mine, the very fact of their having conversed with a foreigner would have rendered them under suspicion from the local Fs of L & O. (As usual the authorities there are only too eager to blame all disturbances upon the ubiquitous Outside Agitator.) But I did talk with a few of the university revolutionist element in Delhi and Calcutta. It appeared that they – in contrast with all previous radical movements in India – were making their appeal to the really hungry, naked, exposed men of the sub-continent, the low-caste, out-caste, and often aboriginal peasants – men who had no lands of their own, and who were burdened from their very conception with debts owed to landlords which they could not hope to pay off in their own lifetime, and which therefore condemned them to a servitude such as we have not seen in England since the collapse of the mediaeval feudal system. The Gandhian non-violent workers had for several years been begging the land-owners to give some small proportion of their acreage for the use of the landless masses: but their well-meaning sermons had received little response. Gifts of land had been promised, but the promises had not been kept – or, if kept, the land had turned out to be barren and useless unless much money was to be spent upon irrigation, and who was to provide the money? But now, the growth of Naxalite activity had given the Gandhians a new argument. 'If you will not make over your lands to the poor,' they would say, 'the Naxalites will kill you. You had better listen to us before it is too late.' I did not find this approach particularly high-principled. The Naxalite guerrillas were being used, as it were, as the violent arm of the non-violent movement. And they are indeed a violent arm. They carry out selective murders of landlords and money-lenders, whose severed heads they leave exposed on posts outside their villages. This bloodshed is less cowardly and underhand than it seems. The men they kill are protected by a venal caste-conscious police as well as by private squads of ugly thugs, who will cheerfully burn a peasant's house and all his family if he is so bold as to ask for more than he is already permitted to have. 'Murder' is the wrong word – the Naxalites say 'Execution' or 'An act of war'. I agree with them.

I was unfortunate enough to run up against the Fs of L & O in India. And as a result I spent a few days in the Shillong District Jail. It was a very minor incident, really – the absence of a Foreigner's Permit for the restricted area of Assam: an offence which anyone could commit – so incompetent were the arrangements made by the Government in apprising foreigners of their need to obtain this document – and which does not normally carry with it any worse penalty than expulsion from the area, together with an illegible endorsement on one's passport. But I – or rather, my companion and I – for I rarely stick my neck out unless goaded to it by someone for whose opinion I have respect – had not been too compliant with the police. Questions had been asked about warrants and authority: this had not been liked: it meant – to an Indian policeman, at any rate – that I was a person of 'obvious Communist bent'. (I *am*, now.) So, in order to teach us a lesson, we were slung inside to await trial: instead of being allowed to handle the whole thing over the desk of some courteous official, drinking his tea and puffing at his cigarettes. My belongings were searched and I was found to be in possession of sundry *books* of an 'anti-state nature'. I hadn't written any of these myself, alas. But the dangerous potentialities of literature were, for the first time in my life at first hand, made clear to me. In a country where possession of the works of Mao and Lenin – though this is not exactly *forbidden* – can get a man into prison for an unspecified length of time, the writer begins to take a more encouraging view of the value of his craft than he can normally do in Britain. Also, while I was held in the jail, I had conversation with the other prisoners in my ward. Most of them were there for 'political' reasons. They were awaiting trial like me, but, unlike me, they had no reason to believe that they would ever be brought to court. Some of them had been there for three years. Perhaps one day, when the government decides they are no longer a danger, they will be quietly released. Perhaps that day will never come. They were, in many cases, men of education and wide reading. I talked with them about the Relationship of the Writer to his Public in Times of Social Upheaval: and this typical Western seminar-subject took on an altogether different appearance than it could possibly do in London or even Chicago.

It will be obvious that if I had written *The Bagman* after, instead of before, the events I have here outlined, the play would not have turned out at all in the same way. I considered rewriting the last part of it but I decided against this, because it does reflect fairly enough the state of my mind in the spring of 1969: and I thought it would be better to demonstrate my opinions of 1971 in a new play – which is not yet written. But I should note, for the benefit of the reader, that the attitude of the central character at the end of the story is reprehensible, cowardly, and not to be imitated. The play has, I believe, been praised by some critics apparently on the ground that it deals with an 'Important Modern Dilemma' common to all artists, and so on. . . . Our critics love to be able to write things like that. It gives them a sense of warm communion with the artist. 'After all,' they muse, 'if Poet X and Playwright Y can't sort out their own integrity, why should I worry about mine? Did not the Emperor Nero believe that, were the truth only told, he would be found to be no more perverted than anyone else? These works of art shew that their creators are as cowardly and as time-serving as I am. So I can continue, without qualms, to write my hack-column for this terrible old press-lord – whom, of course, I would cheerfully assassinate if I could . . .' I am not flattered by such persons. Mao Tsetung, that succinct poet, has said, 'Whatever the enemy opposes, we must support: whatever the enemy supports, we must oppose.' Or words to that effect. I hope I have made clear in *The Bagman* (for otherwise I would not have wished it to be published) that I recognize as the enemy the fed man, the clothed man, the sheltered man, whose food, clothes, and house are obtained at the expense of the hunger, the nakedness, and the exposure of so many millions of others: and who will allow anything to be *said*, in books or on the stage, so long as the food, clothes, and house remain undiminished in his possession.

John Arden (1971)

The True History
of Squire Jonathan
and his Unfortunate Treasure

The True History of Squire Jonathan and his Unfortunate Treasure was first performed by the Ambiance Lunch-Hour Theatre Club on June 17 1968, with the following cast:

SQUIRE JONATHAN	Ian Trigger
A BLONDE WOMAN	Jenny Lee
DARK MEN	Richard Stuart
	Bernard Boston

Directed by Ed Berman

The scene is set in wild country several centuries ago.

The interior of a stone tower. One low round-arched door, and a little window with a deep embrasure. A minimum of furniture: but one prominent iron-bound wooden chest. The style of the décor and costumes is what one might call 'Grimm fairy-tale Gothic'. JONATHAN *squats alone in the tower – he is dressed in clothes which have once been quite splendid but are now soiled, threadbare and patched. The room is lit by the glow of a great fire of logs.*

JONATHAN. I am a small man and nothing about me is large. Look at me. My features are small, confined and tight. My hair is red – an unbecoming red – I do not want to hear anybody say it is the colour of the hair of Judas. My teeth are good, hard, yellow, not large, but sharp – as sharp and as dangerous as those of an unreliable dog. When provoked I can bring them together very suddenly indeed and very cruelly. I have in my time taken bites out of the backs of ankles. Malignant ankles. And I am prepared to do so again if my personal convenience is threatened. If I were to remove my clothes – if I were to remove them (which I do not intend to do) – yet – if I were – I say – to remove my clothes, you would be confronted with a body as cadaverous as it is hairy, with ribs like prongs of a garden fork, a navel like an egg-cup full of dust, a ridiculously wrinkled pair of cullions, and a well-loved drooping yard that very badly desires employment. Employment other than that afforded

it periodically by my own unsatisfied fingers. I also have
flat feet. The total aspect of my person would in fact be
absurd and unlikely to give pleasure to any woman save for
the most depraved: unless she were able, by the intensity of
her spirit, to peer right through the flesh of this rotten car-
cass and to discern within it the intensity of *my* spirit, my
small spirit, a bluebottle fly whirring and gyrating in the
prison of a glass jar. That is how I am, myself within
myself, and here is how I am, myself within this tower –
here I live alone. I am descended from kings. These stones
were erected in ancient days, by such kings, for the fortifications of their glory, and the pleasure of their pride. I had in
mind once to decorate my tower, to wash its walls with
snow-white lime and to prick them out with rectilinear
patterns of gold, of blue, and of scarlet. I had in mind also
to rear several pinnacles striped like a barber's pole, and to
hang therefrom clanging banners of beaten copper and
vanes of gilded zinc to revolve in the run of the west wind
and delight my eyes by their rotation and my ears by their
twittering music. All this I have failed to achieve. However.
However . . . I have been compensated. Here is a large black
box.

>Within this box
>Controlled by bolts and locks,
>Not yet available to you
>But known alone to me,
>Lives in its quiet life my true
>Inherited treasure, and my love.
>You shall see.
>Here is the dream that makes my small heart move.

He opens the chest. It is full of treasure, which he shows in hand-
fuls to the audience.

Gold. Basically gold. There are also articles of silver, plati-
num and various other semi-precious metals. Chrys-ele-

phantine work (that is, carved ivory with a golden inlay), enamel work from Limoges, engraved cameos of sardonyx, beryl, malachite and so forth. A great quantity of jewels, cut and uncut, with and without appropriate settings, you see there are brooches, chains, earrings, belts, bangles, finger-rings, toe-rings, nostril-rings, as well as tiaras, crowns, coronets, carcanets, epaulettes and elaborately worked buttons. Also latchets for shoes and fastenings for garters. Here is a necklace. Here is another. Pearls, diamonds, rubies. Emeralds. Emeralds are green. Green as the eyes of a great blonde milky woman. A giantess. A mountain. A green mountain with the warmth of the sunshine turning the clouds about its head to gold. Gold at the top of the mountain. Gold and white silver in the bottom of my box. For fifteen years I have waited for my mountain of a white woman. I have looked out at my small window and watched for her to come to me. Without such a woman all this treasure is worthless. For fifteen years I saw nobody, except the swearing cowherds in their brown coats squelching through the ruts behind their foul-arsed bullocks – and occasionally – across the bog – one or two of the Dark Men who walked deviously with long sticks. Dark Men, in broad tattered hats and wrapped up in tatters against the damp air, they walk with a curious stiffness as though upon stilts – and I know where they come from. They come from the forest at the other side of the bog, and they come around me to spy. They know about my treasure. Or, if they don't know, they suspect it. But my walls are too strong, and they walk around and look up at them from under their broken hat-brims and they sing their filthy jeering songs at me, and then they go back to their uncomfortable camp-fires and burn some more of their damned charcoal (for such is their trade in the forest) and they lay some more plots and they send out more spies – next week will it be? – or most certainly next month – for I tell you they are at it always . . . Listen, do you hear them? Filthy jeering songs. Listen to them. Listen!

DARK MEN (*singing, outside*).

Johnny Johnny Johnny boy
We know you're there
Johnny Johnny Johnny gae and cut your hair:
Cut your hair, boy,
Cut your toes,
Cut your nostrils oot o' your nose –

FIRST DARK MAN. If you're no gaun tae cut them yersel, Johnny, we can come in there and cut them for ye!

SECOND DARK MAN. We've got knives, Johnny, and strong forks.

FIRST DARK MAN. We've got oor spoons tae eat your porridge, Johnny!

They all laugh.

DARK MEN. Hey Johnny Johnny Johnny –

FIRST DARK MAN. Toss us oot a bit o' siller!

SECOND DARK MAN. Toss us oot a gowden cup to drink your health in –

FIRST DARK MAN. Or what about an auld tin jerrycan, Johnny, wi' glintin' diamonds on the handles?

SECOND DARK MAN. What about your piss-pot?

FIRST DARK MAN. What about the wee thin skull frae the top o' your neck-bane, Johnny?

SECOND DARK MAN. What about it, Johnny?

FIRST DARK MAN. What?

SECOND DARK MAN. What?

DARK MEN. What?

They all laugh.'

FIRST DARK MAN. Johnny: we'll be back!

Their laughter recedes into the distance.

JONATHAN. But my walls are too strong for them. They have no weapons but their hatchets: how can such men as these expect to control artillery? And to reach inside of me – to reach deep in to my very mortal core – nothing short of carronades or howitzers can conceivably serve. And handled, moreover, by none but the most experienced of gunlayers . . . Ah yes, you may come back – many times you may come back – but nothing for you, nothing for you, nothing, nothing – nothing!

He is looking out of the window, shouting after them: suddenly he breaks off, rubs his eyes, and looks again.

Aha – aha – no . . . it is a very misty morning, I am deceived by the vapours, I must be hallucinated by the exhalation from the bog – no – no – I am not deceived neither – I can see what I can see. At last, at last, by the mercy of God (God's mercy and the good grace of the Holy Apostles, all twelve of them, twelve) after fifteen years at last – look – I can see her coming! My woman. On horseback . . . Oh, I wonder what her name is? She has a grey horse, and an orange-tawny cloak upon her back, and under the cloak a gown of the brilliant green, and she rides around my inherited property on the other side of the drainage canal . . . if the horse took fright, she might fall off . . . I wonder what might make it take fright? . . . If somebody were to make a rude noise – as it were –

He makes a rude noise.

– or louder perhaps –

He does it again.

– then she might fall off. Oh dear, she has fallen . . . I wonder how that happened? Unexpected. Unfortunate . . . Ah, the horse has run away. She's all covered with mud – what an enormous beautiful woman – huge – golden – green . . .

BLONDE WOMAN (*calls from outside*). Hello –? I've had an accident. Can you let me in?

JONATHAN (*at the window*). Not in here. No.

BLONDE WOMAN. Please let me in.

JONATHAN *steps down from the window.*

JONATHAN (*to himself*). Oh, my my goodness me – no. That wouldn't do at all.

BLONDE WOMAN (*still outside*). Please.

JONATHAN. For suppose she were to prove avaricious, or even larcenous – and lay hands upon my treasure . . .

BLONDE WOMAN (*outside*). Please.

JONATHAN *closes his box and pushes it away.*

JONATHAN. No, of course not, I can't let her – no, it wouldn't do at all . . .

He opens the door and the BLONDE WOMAN *comes in.*

JONATHAN. Madam, do pray enter – accept my hospitality, so poor as it may seem, until you are quite recovered and repaired from the effects of your sad accident . . . yes, I witnessed it from the window, so untoward, so very startling, how could it have occurred? I fear there are malignant persons in this region who would not hesitate to cause distress to a lonely traveller for no better reason than the satisfaction of their own mischief . . . Madam, an unworthy chair – I beg you to be seated. Are you sure you are not hurt? Are you quite sure? Would you like to eat some breakfast? Or at least a cup of wine? Or – yes, there is some whisky – or the remains of my bottled beer – or perhaps a slice of toasted loaf? Sit down, please sit down. May I unfasten your mantle? It is a very heavy mantle, you must be very hot in it, despite the damp and the chill that pervade our dreary marshes. This brooch across your throat is of somewhat pedestrian design –

BLONDE WOMAN. Oh yes, I am afraid it is – had I known you were a connoisseur I would have chosen another one.

JONATHAN. Or would you be offended if I ventured to choose one for you?

He pulls out his box and opens it to take out a jewel.

JONATHAN. What about this? If you like it, it is yours. Do you like it? Do you?

BLONDE WOMAN. You are very kind.

JONATHAN. Look – I'll pin it in for you, then when you resume the mantle, it will provide an unparalleled fastening. There.

BLONDE WOMAN. Good sir, but you are too kind.

JONATHAN. I am looking at the comb in your hair.

BLONDE WOMAN. Tortoise-shell.

JONATHAN (*takes comb out of box*). Ivory. Here is one made of ivory. Let me put it in for you. Or rather, what I'll do is this: I'll fasten your hair, and then I'll put it in. An ivory comb, with a scene of Diana and Acteon carved upon it in relief – standing in the fountain and the water flowing over her . . . See, I'll put it here, and your hair can flow over also, to reinforce the effect of the water. You must not confine your hair. Far better to let it flow. Oh, heavy as the ebb tide – the ninth wave of the ebb tide –

BLONDE WOMAN. I've never had it cut.

JONATHAN. You must be very hot. I keep a large fire going because of the inclement vapours. I have already referred to them. You should take off your gown. Look – let me unfasten it for you . . . This belt you wear – unornamented leather. Would you not prefer a gold one?

BLONDE WOMAN. If I am taking the gown off, I shall not need one at all.

JONATHAN. No. No more you will . . .

Gown off.

You are wearing no necklace or earrings.

BLONDE WOMAN. I have very little money. My great-uncle

may die soon and leave me his fortune, but until such time as he does, I have nothing whatever. My father gives me nothing.

JONATHAN. What about your garters?

BLONDE WOMAN. Cotton.

JONATHAN. Constricting. Prevent the free flow of the blood. Agony. Varicose veins.

Garters off.

BLONDE WOMAN. You are very thoughtful.

JONATHAN. And your stockings are soaking wet where you fell on the wet grass.

Stockings off.

BLONDE WOMAN. You are thoughtful and kind . . . I will not permit you to take off any more.

JONATHAN. Indeed not. Unless you wish me to.

BLONDE WOMAN. Not yet. Shall we say not yet?

JONATHAN. Put on this necklace. Or shall I put it on for you?

BLONDE WOMAN. Whatever you like. I am tired.

JONATHAN. Tired, damp, and indolent . . . you are not unlike my marshes. And the earrings.

BLONDE WOMAN. If you must.

JONATHAN. No, this pair does not suit you. I thought maybe emeralds, but a contrast with the colour of your eyes now appears to me more striking. Here are rubies. Shall you wear them?

BLONDE WOMAN. I have truly no great preference. But you might offer me a mirror.

JONATHAN. Here you are. I apologize for the crack in it.

BLONDE WOMAN. Without a doubt the rubies are far better than the emeralds. Put them on for me. Thank you. You are so kind. You make me look beautiful.

JONATHAN. You must look beautiful all over. I do not approve the cut of this shift.

BLONDE WOMAN. It has no cut to speak of. That is its purpose. It is worn for warmth and decency.

JONATHAN. Ah – modesty . . .

BLONDE WOMAN. Unrevealing.

JONATHAN. Concealing.

BLONDE WOMAN. Not very good material.

JONATHAN. Cheap cotton stuff. Decent indeed: but not too warm, I should have thought.

BLONDE WOMAN. Linen. It is quite chilly.

JONATHAN. Linen of poor quality.

BLONDE WOMAN. Moreover, it is rather old. There are darns and patches in it. Look. I don't like it. Take it off.

Shift off.

Now, here I am. With what do you propose to cover me, instead?

JONATHAN. I am of the opinion that it would be better not to cover you. You have the earrings and the necklace, and the comb. What's this?

He indicates her chastity belt.

BLONDE WOMAN. It is locked. There is no key.

JONATHAN. How can there be no key?

BLONDE WOMAN. It was thrown away, for cruelty, into a deep pit full of rainwater and dead rotten branches.

JONATHAN. I dare say it could be broken.

BLONDE WOMAN. Do you think you have the strength? Your small hands are nervous: but they are not very strong. I am, as it were, chained. I would like some more chains. Golden chains.

JONATHAN. Solid gold.

BLONDE WOMAN. I think hung round my shoulders.

JONATHAN. I could put one around your waist.

BLONDE WOMAN. The belt would be better. You showed it to me earlier. Indeed and indeed you are exceedingly kind to me.

JONATHAN. I have circlets of little bells . . . Here we are . . . listen.

BLONDE WOMAN. You must put them around my ankles. You are nervous but very kind. You shall hear them, when I walk . . . Listen . . .

JONATHAN. Ah, you walk about my tower like a huge embellished elephant.

BLONDE WOMAN. Big enough, certainly.

JONATHAN. But smooth – and much whiter. They tell me the white elephants of the King of Siam are really a kind of blotchy grey.

BLONDE WOMAN. I am white and I am gold.

JONATHAN. You are chrys-elephantine. Carved out of gigantic ivory. Uncut hair all in my fingers – a great cap of beaten gold, chased and engraved, quite covering the quiet nape, and all down your back it falls, heavy, important, dominant, and then the small inlay, delicate, intricate, placed in your three places – here – here – and here – but where is it?

BLONDE WOMAN. Your hands are not strong enough. What about the emeralds?

JONATHAN. One: two.

BLONDE WOMAN. What about the rubies?

JONATHAN. One: two. Three: four. But these are not true rubies. It would be better to call them pearls. I will give you a golden garter.

BLONDE WOMAN. Why not a pair?

JONATHAN. Complete symmetry is not good. Indeed, I find it abhorrent. Ah, you have a rotten tooth at one side of your mouth.

BLONDE WOMAN. It doesn't hurt.

JONATHAN. I'm glad of that. Toothache is most terrifying – I have suffered from it myself only too often, all alone in this grim tower: I could not bear to imagine that you too had known such pain. But it improves your appearance.

BLONDE WOMAN. You do not mean that, surely?

JONATHAN. Why should I not mean it?

BLONDE WOMAN. I have always been ashamed of it and in order to hide it I have frequently distorted my lips. But I was afraid to have it pulled out. In my country they call the torturers in the King's Prisons the Royal Dentists. That is the sort of place I come from.

JONATHAN. No: I have already told you – it improves your appearance. I give you my word, you are *enhanced*. My name is Squire Jonathan: I am descended from Kings. If my forefathers' torturers were the same people as their dentists I am quite sure they would have been dismissed. But one black tooth among thirty-one that gleam so brilliantly is an object of great beauty in itself. Do not distort your lips: for your smile, as it is, is remarkable. Do you know, you smile so warmly?

BLONDE WOMAN. I smile so foolishly.

JONATHAN. Yes, I know: you're not intelligent. Warm you are, certainly, fat slow, with your passive movements – you great bolster, you lurching hay-cart, you vast unfolded circus-tent all a-flap and a-jingle in the buffet of the wind – but you don't use your brains. Now *I* never use anything else.

BLONDE WOMAN. Nothing else – whatever?

JONATHAN. I have no opportunity.

BLONDE WOMAN. Oh, I think you have now. Or if you were strong enough. Or could lay your hand upon a hacksaw.

JONATHAN. No. It is not necessary. It would be bound to be abortive . . . You have only come here to make me into a laughing-stock. You are waiting for the Dark Men.

BLONDE WOMAN. The Dark Men?

JONATHAN. You will wait until they come and call for you and then you will go off with them. You're just filling in the time here, that's all that you are doing! They will bring you back your horse and then you will ride off with them. When they take you to their forest there will be no jewels for you there, you know. They will not undress you there in a warm room with coloured cushions. But a miserable camp fire in the drizzling rain, where your body will be scorched or else it will be wet and cold – or maybe part-wet, part-scorched, burnt arse and frozen tits, and nothing for you to lie down in but the nettles and the black mud. I say no jewels for you there, you arrogant sneering strumpet – the best you can do there is to draw patterns on your skin like a cannibal savage with broken bits of their damned charcoal – for such is their nasty trade, you know. Charcoal burners. Animals. They will violate you among the nettles without offering you any adornment: and they will compel you to wash their abominable garments. Have you ever imagined the crusted filth and half-dried urine in the crutch of a charcoal-burner's trousers? Aha yes, I do disgust you! But I swear it is but a quarter of the disgust I feel for you! ... Where are you going?

BLONDE WOMAN. Away. You have become offensive. Three minutes ago you could have possessed my body: but instead you have tried to take possession of *me*: I am altogether too large for you.

She pulls off all the jewels, etc.

Here, put them back in your box. Comb, chains, garters, necklace, where is my mantle – give it to me –

JONATHAN. Don't take the brooch out of it –

BLONDE WOMAN. Your brooch, not mine. See, I will leave you the mantle with the pin still stuck into it. You can use it to pierce your ears to put in your own earrings – here they are – rubies –

JONATHAN. I shall give her to the Dark Men.
    They have teeth and they have axes:
    Let them cut her up and tear her.
    There is no woman I have ever seen
    With whom I would compare her.
    She is so huge and so white of her body
    She is above all the most selfish and vain lady

I do not love her but I fear her:
She is altogether too enormous.
Let her go, let her go, to the dark charcoal-burners.

BLONDE WOMAN. I don't know who you are talking to, but if you are talking to me I will take you at your word. They are outside, are they not?

JONATHAN. Never mind where they are!

BLONDE WOMAN. Your brooch, not mine, but it still has its uses . . .

Chastity belt unpicked and taken off. JONATHAN *threatens her with a knife.*

BLONDE WOMAN. If you stab me with that blade you will find my cadaver far too heavy for you to lift. And then what will you do? Your situation is impossible. I will leave you to enjoy it.

She goes to the window.

Where are the Dark Men? Where are you, you dirty wanderers? You disconnected fragments of uncoagulated soot – come and catch me – here I am!

DARK MEN (*outside*). Jump for it, lassie – we're here wi' a strang blanket – noo jump for it on the cry – wi' a yan, twa and a *three*!

She jumps out of the window.

We caught her, we held her, my God, when she fell, what a roly-poly wobble – here's a meal for all the people! Johnny, we're right grateful, ye've fulfilled our wames this day!

FIRST DARK MAN. Ah Johnny, you're a grand wee man. Ye hae bestowed us what ye can!

SECOND DARK MAN. Ye're bauld and zealous
Gay and generous,
Here's a cheer frae a' the gang of us!

Their cheers, mixed with laughter, recede into the distance.

JONATHAN. And yet I am not defeated. She has left behind
    her every piece of my jewellery. Or has she? Where's the
    belt I put about her middle? Still about her. Still about her.
        It made creases in her flesh.
        It was scarcely to her advantage.
        She might as well keep it.
        I am not yet defeated.

The Bagman
or
The Impromptu of Muswell Hill

The Bagman or *The Impromptu of Muswell Hill* was first presented as a radio play on BBC Radio 3, on March 27 1970, with the following cast:

NARRATOR	Alan Dobie
OLD WOMAN	Hilda Kriseman
YOUNG WOMAN	Sheila Allen
POPULAR MINISTER	Geoffrey Matthews
UNPOPULAR MINISTER	Hector Ross
AMBASSADOR	Peter Pratt
KING	Austin Trevor
QUEEN	Margaret Wolfit
3 STARVING WOMEN	Hilda Kriseman
	Madi Hedd
	Sonia Fraser
OTHERS	Sean Barrett
	Wilfrid Carter
	John Rye
	David Spenser

Produced by Martin Esslin

Wind, rain, occasional traffic noises.

NARRATOR. Upon a Thursday afternoon, it being half-closing-
day, I set out from my house along Muswell Hill Broadway
in search of an evening newspaper. It was too early for the
street-corner sellers to have set up their little placards, the
newsagents were shut, and a wet north-west wind was
scuttling between the houses.

> Upon the top of Muswell Hill
> I stood alone and felt quite ill
> Without the *Standard* or the *News*
> What could I do of any use?
> No word could I get of peace or war:
> So who was I, where was I,
> What was I for?
> If one had asked of me my name
> I freely could have told the same –
> John Arden (thirty-eight) of ancient family,
> Writer of plays for all the world to see,
> To see, and pay for, and to denigrate:
> Such was my work since 1958.
> I could not boast, like Cicero,
> That I had saved the state,
> Nor yet, like Catiline, that I had tried
> My fiercest best to have it all destroyed.
> If, on this soggy Thursday, I should fall down dead.
> What of my life and death would then be said?
> 'He covered sheets of paper with his babble,

He covered yards of stage-cloth with invented people,
He worked alone for years yet was not able
To chase one little rat from underneath the table.'
The rats would eat the cheese,
The cats would eat the rats,
In convenience and ease:
They would not notice any difference
For Arden's sudden disappearance.
There was no reason why they should.
So I walked alone to Highgate Wood.

Traffic noises recede.

Here in the cold park I wrapped my overcoat about me, sat down upon a bench, and tossed bread crumbs to the squirrels. The dead leaves blew between my feet and the stumps of the trees, the red buses at my back rumbled backwards and forwards out of sight upon the main road, and the children were all at school, so their play-ground was quite empty. As I sat there I fell asleep, and as I slept I dreamed a dream. Or rather it seemed that the dream rose up at me, from out of the rain-darkened sand-pit in the deserted children's playground, it piled itself up so very quickly, in a turbulence of sand and torn scraps of cigarette papers, it had something the shape of a dirty old woman, not quite in her right mind. She was asking me if I would buy from her some white heather or some clothes pegs . . .

OLD WOMAN. White heather . . .

NARRATOR. She was a nuisance there, I didn't want her . . .

OLD WOMAN. Clothes pegs . . .

NARRATOR. Go away, no no no – don't want anything . . . thank you . . .

OLD WOMAN. White heather brings good fortune –

NARRATOR. I've had good fortune, all too soon.

OLD WOMAN.

> And wooden pegs will hold it fast
> So that it will not fly away:
> Peg down the luck you catch today
> And you will have it yet tomorrow.
> Peg down your joy, peg down your sorrow
> Examine them when you have time,
> Weigh the other against the one –
> You will not know what you can do
> Until you know what you have done.

NARRATOR. You're beginning to be tiresome, go, get you gone: Portentous oracular condemnatory old hag . . .

OLD WOMAN. I'll tell you what, how would you like
A beautiful useful canvas bag?
It's yours for ten shillings, with whatever it contains. It's pig-in-a-poke, in fact, all my young gentlemen take great delight to put at risk a few bob on a lucky-bag the like of this. Why, it's only last month I sold just such a one to a courageous lad from overseas, and he opened it up directly and what did he find –?

NARRATOR. Well, what did he find?

OLD WOMAN. He found such an elegant soft young woman, with golden skin like olive oil and black hair down to her sweet haunches as bright as melted bitumen. And she became his private property for evermore without regrets. What do you think to that, then?

NARRATOR. Most improbable.

OLD WOMAN. True.

NARRATOR.

> Whether true or false it was temptation:
> I was in a mood for fornication.
> And also I was, was I not, in a dream
> Where women are always exactly what they seem
> Instead of being no better than they are.
> In any case, I thought, I would not go too far:

> Open the bag, take just a quick peep,
> Put in my hand, make a tentative grope.
> If I did not like her I could quickly shove her back,
> Tie up the strings again round the mouth of the sack –
> For some fresh brief sexuality which might prove very nice
> Ten shillings did not seem to me an inordinate price.
>
> You don't mind a lot of small change?

Sound of money being counted.

OLD WOMAN. Oh no, sir, it's convenient really: there you are, sir, thank you . . .

NARRATOR. So she fluttered away, laughing, and disappeared among the trees, as well-camouflaged by her grime and tatters as were the fidgeting squirrels by their grey fur and rapid movement. Even the reverberation of her laughter through her five or six black teeth was closely akin to the tiny cursing of the squirrels: and I wondered who she was. But even more I was wondering what the devil it was I had bought from her. Surely I could never have been so foolish as to imagine there could really be a complacent greasy concubine stuffed up in this very ordinary kitbag which she had dumped here at my feet? It had the British Army broad-arrow stencilled on it in black and what seemed to be a soldier's number – 22128480. I tried to lift it up, it was heavy enough, certainly. But whatever was inside it was pure deadweight and had neither the shape nor the consistency of living flesh, female, lecherous idiots for the use of. So I gave it a kick. Hurt my foot. Then I tried to unfasten the string. But the rain had soaked it and all I succeeded in doing was to nearly break off a finger-nail. I was about to have a go at it with my penknife and my teeth when I heard foot-steps behind me . . .

Heavy footsteps on leaf-strewn grass.

He had boots on his feet and they crunched the dead leaves, I looked up at him under my armpit, good God, how tall he was, he was hanging right above me the way colliery winding gear would overhang the little streets of West Yorkshire where I was born . . .

PARK-KEEPER. Oy. You.

NARRATOR. On his hat was a small brass badge: he was a park-keeper.

PARK-KEEPER. I said you. What's in that bag, then?

NARRATOR. I don't know.

PARK-KEEPER. Well, get it out of here. It's a Thing.

NARRATOR. Yes.

PARK-KEEPER. It's an Article.

NARRATOR. I suppose so.

PARK-KEEPER. It's an Object of Merchandise. You can't bring it in this park. You are a Vendor.

NARRATOR. No, I'm not.

PARK-KEEPER. And if you aren't, you are a Gipsy or Vagrant: or you are about to use the park for a Purpose of Immorality: and in any case you are in a condition such as is Offensive to Other Members of the Public.

NARRATOR. I most certainly am not. And what other members of the public? There's nobody else here.

PARK-KEEPER. That may well be *your* opinion. If you refuse to comply with the printed and posted regulations of the Greater London Council, I fear I shall have no alternative but to take your Name and Address.

NARRATOR. Yes, but –

PARK-KEEPER. Here is my notebook. Here is my pencil. Right then, we are prepared.

NARRATOR. His pencil was enormous, stuck weapon-wise in his belt, it was the kind that carpenters use, over an inch broad and a third of an inch thick, almost a cubit in length; and his fingers tightened on the shaft of it till the knuckle-bones sprang white beneath the skin. His book was the size

of my grandfather's Family Bible, loaded to the endpapers
with the names and addresses of all those who were accursed
for that they lived in fornication, for that they were covetous
and bore false witness, for that they moved their neighbour's
landmark, for that they –

PARK-KEEPER. Go on, get out of it, and take your dunnage
with you!

NARRATOR. He had lifted up the great stave that he carried
under his swollen elbow, it was a pikestaff shod with steel,
you could have murdered a bull with it, though for him it
was but an implement for the removal of waste paper from
the immaculate greensward. Like the steering oar of the
'Argo' he did poise it in the air, and so drove it with all his
malice into the frayed canvas of my sack.

A squeal like an injured pig.

Oh – don't do that, you cause distress . . .

PARK-KEEPER. Get out of it.

NARRATOR. So I went. He followed me to the gate. I looked
round after I had gone out of the park and there he was
standing, his cruel spike still uplifted in his hand like a sword
of living flame, protecting the fenced garden, and the squirrels, and the birds, and the rabbits, and the prohibited fruit
of the glade, from the nonsense that was in my bag. So the
question arose: what nonsense? I had heard it squeal when it
was poked: but not the squeal of a woman. I was well aware
by now that in that respect I had been deceived. At all events
this bag must hold something that was known to be obnox-
ious to the guardians of the public amenity. So I thought it
would be better not to attempt again to open it until I was
well out of sight of nosey-parkers, bureaucrats, and my
fellow-men in general.

Wind and rain noises continue, together with many bird-calls.

So I heaved it on my shoulder and looked carefully to left

and right in due dread of the passing traffic. But where was the passing traffic? Where indeed was the Muswell Hill Road, which should have run beside the park to the bus-stop and the road-junction and the Northern Line Underground? No road, no cars, no houses? All I could see was a wide heathery brackeny bushy sort of moor with clumps of dark trees here and there, and a trackway across it, a trackway which disappeared towards the south round the shoulder of a wet green hill – Highgate Hill? It might have been Mount Zion for as much as *I* could recognize. Beyond the hill, and several miles away, I could see a cloud of smoke, I supposed hanging over some small inhabited community. It was still raining: and it was cold. Bewildered by these circumstances, and resentful at the weather, I began to walk. South, towards the smoke. Before I did anything else, I must find out where I was. *When* I was. Who else there was, and why.

> This dream of mine
> That I had thought so fine
> Was now becoming burdensome and made
> Me mutter curses underneath my breath.
> It occurred to me it was no dream, but Death.
> If it was Death, why was I not afraid?
> Just mildly curious I was:
> And cross.

A muffled sound of women's voices wailing and croaking, as though from a little distance.

Then I realized that the strange noise that came out of an overgrown hollow towards my left was not being made by birds. I went down between the bushes.

Noise increases.

Here there was a group of women kneeling and crouching

round a man who lay on the grass. He was a long man in a black suit full of holes and covered with clay. He was dead.

FIRST WOMAN (*these women have harsh rasping voices like crows*). He was starved.

SECOND WOMAN. What else with but bad nettles to boil up for his soup?

THIRD WOMAN. Chewing roots.

FOURTH WOMAN. Cramming grass between his teeth till his mouth-water runs all green and his stomach swells out till it was ready to burst.

FIRST WOMAN. And it's burst.

NARRATOR. Who was he?

FIRST WOMAN. How should we know?

SECOND WOMAN. We just found him.

THIRD WOMAN. If we had strength enough, we would dig him his grave.

NARRATOR.

> The man upon the ground was dead.
> Bent down around him every head
> Seemed more than half as dead as his.
> I saw their black and yellow eyes
> Like rat-holes in a river-bank
> Where deep inside the rats will wink
> And blink and grind their savage teeth.
> Four savage women ground their teeth,
> Splintered tent-pegs or such cogs
> As millwrights cut from jagged logs
> They crunched together: then they swung
> Their necks towards me, stared at me long,
> In silence stared and then began
> At once and suddenly to scream and sing:

WOMEN (*in a kind of rhythmic dirge*).

> There he has it
> There he has food in his bag
> Tear it down from him

Tear it and grab it and drag
Rip off his fingers
By root and by sinew
Castrate him and rape him and beat
For what he has got we can eat
Eat eat eat eat eat eat . . .

Their chant becomes a terrifying mob-yell.

NARRATOR (*pleading futilely through their shouts and violent attack*). No no, stop it, God, ladies, give over, no, please – but I didn't even know who you were – I haven't got any food – here, you leave that alone – HELP – oh my God, HELP ME – they've gone mad –!

A growing thunder of horsehoofs and male shouting. The rage of the women turns to screams of fear.

Indeed I had made quite sure that I was already a dead man. The four of them were swarming upon me like four hundred furious bees let loose from an upturned hive. Then suddenly they were gone and the ground all around where they had flung me was bouncing in my ears with the din of great horsehoofs . . .

A silence broken by occasional distant screams and shouts. The horsehoofs recede with these. Then one horse is heard returning. A jingle of harness as the rider reins up.

RIDER. Are you right, boy? Left alive, are you? By Christ, but we came just in time.

NARRATOR. He was a soldier of some sort, well mounted and heavily-accoutred in leather strapwork and brass-buckles, big boots, a thick black club in his hand, six or seven inch-wide moustache across his face, face all but entirely concealed under the wide peak of a black leather helmet. He had half-a-dozen men with him, all equipped in the same style. As I rose to my feet, very vague, very battered, I could see them riding down the hill away from us, waving their truncheons, scattering the tattered women.

> They uttered their blows without remorse
> By heavy stick and hoof of horse.
> Upon one woman's womb they trampled
> She lay in the gorse all bloody and crumpled.
> But I was alive
> And I would thrive.

I am alive. Yes, I think so. I thank you. Good God but what a business. Who were they?

RIDER. They were starving. Didn't they tell you? They have nothing better to do but rake the countryside for food and so near are they to death they care not a scratch for the death of any creature who will come between them and the sustainment of their bellies. This dead fellow on the ground here, had you not interrupted them, they would have eaten him blood and bone.

NARRATOR. But why is this happening? Has there been some disaster? Is there famine in the land?

RIDER. Those who deserve to eat, eat. So what about you? What do *you* deserve? Where are you from?

NARRATOR. I – er – I came from – from over there . . .

RIDER. You seem well-fed, decent class of a man, quiet and unlikely to give trouble to the honest and self-respecting populace. Do you intend to travel far?

NARRATOR. To be frank, I do not know. I don't altogether know anything at all . . .

RIDER. And that is as it should be. A confession of ignorance is more than half-way towards a fulfilled education. With fulfilled education you take a fit place in responsible society. But it's no part of my duty to let you travel around here on your own. As you've seen, it's far from safe. So put up your bag upon the back of my saddle – take a good grasp of my left stirrup – and when the patrol has reassembled, we will escort you into town.

He bellows to his men.

Come along then, let's be having you! You've got 'em all upon the run there, no point in bothering further. You can form yourselves up again upon me, in column of route, and then we can proceed . . .

Sound of the horses trotting.

NARRATOR.
      The road we travelled was not good,
      Rocky and rutted, clogged with mud,
      The land on either side was bare
      With roofless cottages here and there.
      No travellers did we pass or meet,
      Though once I saw the prints of feet,
      Bare feet, in the mud, as though
      Some ragged man who had to go
      Unshod upon this road had seen
      My escort and had fled between
      The thorny bushes out of sight –
      No doubt he crouched there in his fright
      Until we were gone by. And then
      Where three roads met we came upon
      A leafless tree. To the trunk was nailed
      A living man who screamed and railed:
MAN NAILED TO TREE. For the freedom of the people, for the freedom of the people, for the freedom of the people – oh the starving men will live and the well-fed men will rot among the maggots of their own engendering . . .

He stops shouting and whimpers.

For God's sake somebody give me a spoonful of water . . .
RIDER. No no, we ride past him, he's nothing, he don't signify: he'll be dead before tomorrow.
NARRATOR. But who *is* he?

RIDER. Like I told you: he's just nothing . . . Take a look down the road ahead as we cross over this bluff: you'll get your first clear prospect of the town. So what do you think of it? Well-inhabited: and moreover well-protected: and it's my job to keep it so.

NARRATOR.

> There was the town and it was made
> Of wood and thatch. A tall stockade.
> Of sharpened timber rose around
> The huddled houses, and the ground
> Outside of this defence was scraped
> And scooped into a ditch. The moat
> Was dry, there was a drawbridge and a gate.
> The leader of my escort gave a shout:

RIDER. Ho-ho, ho-ho, ho-ho, ho-ho!

NARRATOR.

> The gate swung up, the bridge came down,
> We rode across into the town
> Beside the gate a sentry sprawled
> Loose in the lap of a fat brown girl.
> He wore a flower in his ear,
> He did not seem to take much care
> Upon his duty. In the air
> Above him flapped a worn-out flag
> Of tawdry stripes and patches, rather a rag,
> The whole town could be said to be
> Rather a rag. So slovenly
> Uncared-for were the walls and streets . . .

To the rider. As voices and street-noises become heard.

> And yet the people whom one meets
> Among these slovenly uncared-for streets
> Are fat and greasy, richly-dressed,
> Hung with jewels, their curls well-pressed,

> Their necks and buttocks thick. Why then
> Is all their town untidy and unclean?

RIDER. When everybody is as rich as they are, who is left to do the dirty work?

NARRATOR. You are, are you not?

RIDER. Oh no, we are not. We keep the peace, preserve good order, we have clean clothes and polished gear, our breath don't stink. But then we're different, don't you see?

> We are of the town yet not of it
> In a well-swept corner there we sit –

NARRATOR. He pointed to a sort of compound on a hillock at one extremity of the stockade, fenced off very precisely in isolation from the rest: and there all indeed was neat and trimmed and whitewashed, with living quarters for both men and horses, a smart guard upon the gate, and nothing slovenly at all.

RIDER.

> We are without the town yet not outside:
> Day and night we march and ride,
> Ranging the high ground and the low.
> Where all is desolate we keep it so.
> These people live their scruffy lives because of us:
> We don't converse, we make no fuss.
> They only know that we are here:
> And, knowing that, they know no fear.

SECOND RIDER. Except of us.

THIRD RIDER. Except of us.

FIRST RIDER.

> Except of us. We make no fuss.
> We are quite content with what we do.
> Now, here, I think, is a fit place for *you*.

NARRATOR. And with a sudden twist of his foot he kicked me sprawling through an archway into a large courtyard that opened off the street. He threw my bag after me and then clattered away with his men.

Noise of horses receding. Now is heard the hum of a large crowd and music.

It appeared to be a place of assembly, with benches of rough-hewn timber arranged in tiers upon three sides, while on the fourth side, opposite the entrance, stood a raised platform under the shelter of a long sheet of tarpaulin stretched upon poles. The benches were crowded with people eating and drinking and sweating in the warm sunshine. The rain was over and I had begun to feel very hot. The smell in this courtyard was not at all agreeable and there was a good deal of pushing and shoving. I had hard work to keep hold of my bag, and I had more than a notion that many of those around me were thieves. Upon the platform a pair of dancers were performing for their entertainment. One dancer was a woman – she tinkled little cymbals as she danced, and her long draperies swirled all over the platform. Her partner was a wild-looking bearded man. He wore no more than a red-embroidered breech-clout and a short leather waistcoat. In his hands were two sharp knives with which he cut and tore at the draperies of the woman until she danced entirely naked. The people cheered and cheered at this progressive revelation. For myself, despite my earlier libidinous hopes in regard to the sack, I was more concerned in preventing my feet from being trodden on and my pockets from being picked than I was with the indecent excitement of the exhibition upon the stage. Then I became aware that the two dancers – now prancing arm-in-arm like a pair of yoked chariot-horses – had suddenly broken into song.

Cheers from the crowd as described: then silence for the song, which is accompanied by the cymbals and the stamping of the dancers' feet.

DANCERS (*singing*).

> Pharaoh lived in Egypt
> He dreamed a dream one night
> Seven cows were feeding,
> They were full and fat.
>
> Pharaoh lived in Egypt
> He dreamed another dream
> Seven cows came walking,
> They were long and lean.
>
> The lean cows ate the fat cows up,
> Pharaoh rolled around:
> Pharaoh hid his head then
> Deep in the ground.
>
> 'Joseph Joseph,
> Tell to me my dream.
> If you cannot tell it
> I must groan and scream.
>
> 'Joseph Joseph –
> What does it mean?'
> Joseph said to Pharaoh:
> 'You are dead and gone.'

POPULAR MINISTER (*shouting amid the cheers and applause after the song*). Eat, drink, and be merry: for tomorrow you die!

More cheers and laughter.

NARRATOR. The dancers had moved aside, their place on the platform was now taken by a grey-haired smiling red-cheeked soft-handed dignified benevolent gentleman. He wore a robe like an academic doctor and a chain-of-office round his neck. The people loved him . . .
Who is he?

A VOICE IN THE CROWD. Sh-ssh, he is the King's Chief Minister.

NARRATOR. He seems a very popular minister.

VOICES FROM THE CROWD. The people love him . . . He provides the entertainment, you see, from his own private fortune . . . Just listen to the reception he gets.

NARRATOR. I can hear it. And he enjoys it.

A prolonged ovation for the MINISTER *is now under way.*

A VOICE FROM THE CROWD. Oh he does, yes.

NARRATOR. How did he acquire his own private fortune?

VOICE FROM THE CROWD. How do you think? He inherited it: like everybody else.

NARRATOR. Ah . . .
But now the minister was making a speech . . .

The MINISTER'S *voice is heard in broken fragments against a background of almost continual cheers.*

POPULAR MINISTER. Sugar and spice and all things nice . . . It's a beautiful afternoon, look the sun's come out at last!

NARRATOR. From the way he went on you would think he had brought it out himself . . .

POPULAR MINISTER. Delightful young lady . . . give her a bit of a slap and tickle . . .

Giggles and shrill female laughter.

NARRATOR. This was the female dancer, undulating on the stage there, within two or three inches of the Minister's gesticulating fingers: so he gives a poke to her cheeky plumpness and then more than a poke, he does not spare himself in his indulgence.

A brisk handclap

Then he claps his fat hands and two little girls with big round eyes and many bangles on their wrists came tripping on with baskets. The baskets contained what appeared to be sweets, wrapped up in silver paper, and he tossed them in handfuls to the crowd, and the crowd scrambled.

General excited shouts and scufflings.

Just for toffees – such a scramble?

VOICE FROM THE CROWD. Only some of them are toffees, some of them are pearls and emeralds . . . and some of them are dried beans . . . it's very much a lucky dip.

NARRATOR. Being a stranger I thought it best not to join in the scrambling myself. But the man on my left was unwrapping a real pearl . . .

MAN'S VOICE FROM CROWD. God be praised, God be praised, look at that, sir, there is richness!

NARRATOR. While the woman on my right was unlucky and got no more than a couple of the dried beans.

WOMAN'S VOICE FROM CROWD. Oh the devil, I say to hell with that. God, they were thrown to me on purpose!

NARRATOR. While the scramble was taking place the Minister had gone and the dancers had gone and the little girls had gone too. The platform was now empty.

Boos and jeers from the crowd.

Oh but no, it was not. Here's a tall stooping meagre-featured mean-eyed black-haired hobbling clothes-prop of a spoil-sport and he walks with the aid of a stick. He snarls from the platform as the enraged people snarl at him . . .
Who is he?

VOICE FROM THE CROWD. Ssh-sh, he's the King's Chief Minister.

NARRATOR. But we've just had the King's Chief Minister . . .

VOICE FROM THE CROWD. No no, this is the Other Minister, who is not popular with the people. They always have to have the two of them – stands to reason, when you look at it . . .

UNPOPULAR MINISTER. Oh yes, you may boo and you may

cat-call, and you may make mock of my disabilities: but you know I know the real reason for your pretended scorn! Because I am the one, the only one in all this town to have the courage and the self-respect to inform you of the truth about yourselves, of the perils that do confront you, and of the faults of character through which you will be presently submerged by those same perils, if you do not look sharp about you and pull yourselves together – oh, you improvident dross and floating motes of sad debauchment! Yes, I tell to you the truth: and as truth it is not comfortable: and as teller of it I am hated. Well, do you want it, or do you not? Are you going to let me speak?

The outcry increases for a moment, then dies away.

Thank you. Now listen to this: the horsemen on patrol this afternoon have brought a stranger into town. I don't like the sound of him: and I don't like his looks. If you all turn around, you will see him at the back there – there he is – and if you are half the men I take you for, you won't like him either!

NARRATOR.
It is not at all agreeable.
To be glared at by all the people.
I do not hold that man to be wise
Who desires to be made the cynosure of all eyes.

UNPOPULAR MINISTER. You see, there he stands and his face turns from red to white and from white back to red again. Oh yes, while you were all soaking up the voluptuous depravity so generously provided you by the munificence of my esteemed colleague, you failed to notice, did you not, that someone had crept in, that someone's eyes were popping out at the sight of the private nudities that had been supplied for you alone, that someone at the back there was irregularly experiencing a carnal enjoyment of what was yours and yours alone: and he asked you no permission!

A threatening murmur from the crowd.

Come forward, sir, come forward, and make yourself known to this hospitable assembly. If you have a joke at the back we would all be glad to share it –

NARRATOR. The apologetic smile I was nervously assuming disappeared at once.

UNPOPULAR MINISTER. Or if you have a problem to be solved perhaps we all can solve it for you. Make a gangway for the gentleman; let him set himself up upon the platform. Up beside me, sir, if you please. Now, sir: face the people.

NARRATOR. So I faced them. By God I had no choice: they thrust me up there so violently that I twisted my ankle. And they giggled at me: giggled and whispered. One or two of them threw tomatoes.

Noises from the crowd appropriate to the description.

UNPOPULAR MINISTER. That's enough now, that's enough. Save your applause till the gentleman has performed. You will perform, sir, won't you, you will not disappoint us?

NARRATOR. But I –

UNPOPULAR MINISTER. What's your name?

NARRATOR. John.

UNPOPULAR MINISTER. He says his name is John. Do we think his name is John?

GENERAL SHOUT. No.

UNPOPULAR MINISTER. Oh dear, they don't believe you. So I wonder what your name is. He wears spectacles, does the little gentleman, he must be a gentleman of learning. Do you know what I think he is, I think he is a Professor.

NARRATOR. No, I'm not, I –

UNPOPULAR MINISTER. And just look at his little fingers – he has inkstains on his fingers! Professor Inkspot is his name and a very good name for him too. Shall we sing our little song to him? One: two: three –

CROWD (*sings, led by the* MINISTER).
> Professor Inkspot tell us now
> Why you walk like a pregnant sow
> Why your nose does root and dig
> Into the earth like a grunting pig
> Tell us tell us tell us quick
> Or else he'll whack you with his stick –

UNPOPULAR MINISTER. Or else I'll whack you with my stick! There!

Blow of cane and a cry, repeated.

> There again! Ha: so that's a foretaste. Now explain yourself and smartly. What have you got in that bag? More pens have you got, more bottles of ink?

NARRATOR. I do not know why I should be treated with such disdain.
> From my childhood ever I had felt great fear
> Of a crowd of strange men who would stare at me and jeer:
> But now when confronted by just such a mob
> For a moment indeed of all speech they did me rob:
> But then my sudden courage came out at them in pride–
> I would not be intimidated and my heart I would not hide.

My heart I will not hide from you, nor yet what is in my sack. I am not to be put to shame: and all that I have I am ready to declare.

UNPOPULAR MINISTER. Very well then: what is it?

NARRATOR. Except that I don't know: which is feeble enough, I will agree with you.

UNPOPULAR MINISTER. So open it up for us.

NARRATOR. I can't untie the cord.

UNPOPULAR MINISTER. Feeble-fingered idiot – use this.

NARRATOR. And he handed me a jack-knife and I cut open the bag.

UNPOPULAR MINISTER. Hold it up from the bottom and shake out whatever's in it.

Sound of bag being shaken and objects tumbling out.

NARRATOR. Little men.

UNPOPULAR MINISTER. Little men? You're a little man yourself. So here is a little man with a bag full of little men. How many little men? Will you tell the people, tell them loudly.

NARRATOR. One, two, three –
little men and little women, the largest of them about twelve inches long, made out of wood and carefully jointed and carved. Each one of them dressed in a characteristic costume –
seven, eight, nine – there was a Soldier in a red coat, and a Policeman, and a Doctor with great spectacles, and a pretty little blonde Popsy and a blowsy soot-stained Housewife with a baby at her breast, and a hideous Old Woman, and a Robber with a great sword and bushy whiskers –
thirteen, fourteen, fifteen, sixteen – no, I counted him already – sixteen, seventeen, eighteen –
here were a King and a Queen and a Bishop with a hooked nose –
eighteen, did I say? I must have miscounted, I'll go back again to number twelve –
the funny thing was I couldn't count them at all, my whole notion of numbers seemed to have got muddled-up, so I came to a sort of compromise . . .
I can't count them exactly, it's the sunshine, it's too dazzling, but I suppose it would be fair to say there are something between twenty and thirty of them. Attractive little people, don't you think?
I was still nervous of that stick.

UNPOPULAR MINISTER. But what are they for?

NARRATOR. Ah, yes, what are they for . . .?

I stood upon the platform with the bright sun bang in my eyes, I had a headache, oh God, in this confined courtyard what a stink of overfed and belching bodies – and for what seemed many minutes I stood there in complete silence. A little flurry of wind had set the tarpaulin to rattle and to strain at its cords, and everyone in the crowded place was suddenly as still as death. When I spoke I did not speak with my own voice, nor did it seem to me that I myself had composed the words that I uttered: but it was as though curled up inside my belly a very old and cantankerous dragon was growling and orating: and the sound came through my teeth:

In a strange distorted voice.

> My little people in a row
> Sit on the stage and watch the show.
> The show they watch is rows and rows
> Of people watching them. Who knows
> Which is more alive than which?
> If you fidget, if you twitch,
> Blow your nose or nod your head,
> My little men, though made of wood,
> Can frame a gesture just as good.
> Laugh and leap or shake with terror,
> My little men will be your mirror.
> What you do or what you did
> From little people can't be hid:
> They will know it and reflect
> In strut and jerk your every act –
> Your thoughts expressed in dark of night
> They body forth in broad daylight.
> This Soldier-boy in coat of red
> Is every one of you whose head
> Is turned by dreams of power achieved
> Through violence and the tears of the bereaved:
> This Constable so stiff and straight

Is any man who thinks that Right
Must stamp on Wrong till Wrong can claim
That Right was twice as much to blame:
And see this bright-eyed Girl, her bum
Round as an apple or a plum.
She is any girl who will lie down
Whether for love or half-a-crown,
And rising up again, will say:
'That's enough then for today,
Do not expect as much tomorrow.'
This Mother here, in joy and sorrow
Becomes the mother of you all –
Her Baby from her lap will crawl
And grow to be whichever one
Of you you would he should become.
Who is to say what stories these shall shew you?
You tell me who you are and I will know you:
And then you sit and watch my little men
And you will know yourselves again again again
Again again again again . . .

In his normal voice again.

And no sooner were the words out of my mouth (good
heavens, but I had reminded myself of Adolf Hitler at his
worst, and what were people going to think of me? Even
these appalling people!) – no sooner were they out of my
mouth than all the little men had leapt to their feet, and there
upon the platform, without a moment's pause or hesitation
they had formed themselves up into two opponent groups.
There was a small group of those in rich costumes, and a
large group made up of the ragged and ill-favoured. Straightway the larger party flung themselves with rage upon the
smaller: but were beaten back time and again by the valour
of the Soldier and the brutality of the Constable – there was
also some display of the duplicity of the Bishop and the

cruel faint-heartedness of the King and Queen: but in the end the larger party were compelled to fall to their knees, abase themselves, and sue for mercy. Then the revengeful King decreed various punishments: the leaders of the rebellion were killed in hideous fashion, or flogged and tormented, or locked up in iron cages without food and water. Their cries so worked upon the spirit of their defeated comrades that a new conspiracy was set afoot, the King was assassinated, the Bishop was beaten, the Soldier and the Constable were put to flight, and their overweening Queen was dragged tumultuously through the mire. Such prisoners from the former rebellion as still survived their ill-treatment were released and paraded as heroes, and in fine a Republic was proclaimed and the victors of the civil war rejoiced in their great deliverance. Yet all their efforts in the end were seen to be in vain. No sooner had they prevailed upon their sumptuous enemies than they fell to quarrelling amongst themselves as to which of them should hold the sovereignty. The conclusion was ominous. Hacked and splintered wooden limbs lay everywhere upon the platform, and of those manikins who were not dead only the most crippled and the weakest seemed to have enough voice to bewail their ill-fortune and to call upon the world for redress. None who watched were able to restrain their tears. The more so because all this time an unseen music had been ringing and clanging, stirring the heart and turning the entrails of all that spellbound auditory –

So it has and now it ceases.

– and when at last it fell silent and my little people reassembled themselves, rose once again to their feet, and lifted their right arms in a gesture of courteous dismissal – there came a roar of spontaneous applause that shook the very boards on which we stood.

Applause, as described.

Even the unpopular minister was smiling – in a thin and grudgeful fashion, mind you: but smiling he certainly was.

UNPOPULAR MINISTER. Most impressive. Educational. I am truly amazed, Professor, that upon so short an acquaintance with our community you have been able to diagnose our weaknesses and discover our public perils with such acute perception. How much more salutary than the pabulum served up through the munificence of my esteemed colleague.

POPULAR MINISTER (*voice in crescendo as though he is quickly approaching*). Your esteemed colleague, my dear sir, is entirely of the same opinion as yourself. Professor, I congratulate you. I have never known the people so delighted, so enlivened, so thoroughly stimulated both intellectually and emotionally as they have been this afternoon. Indeed, I think that you and I should have a little talk about some further demonstrations of the same kind, which I trust I may prevail upon you to perform for us very shortly. You will stay with us for some time, of course, we can offer you the very best facilities for the exposition of your strange powers: no expense need be spared. In the meantime –

As crowd starts clapping in slow time.

UNPOPULAR MINISTER. In the meantime, dear colleague, the people are getting impatient. There is business-of-state to be attended to in this Assembly, now that the entertainment is over. Brigands from the outside who were captured by yesterday's patrol have to be brought to trial, sentenced and punished: and there are numerous new regulations for the Security of the City that require to be debated and approved before His Majesty can issue them in form of a Decree.

POPULAR MINISTER. But all this can be dealt with by Junior Members of the Council. The professor here and his

innovation must surely be discussed by you and me, forth-
with.

UNPOPULAR MINISTER. Whatever you wish . . .

He addresses the crowd.

Rabble: be silent! You have not been forgotten. Indeed you
are never forgotten.

POPULAR MINISTER (*addressing the crowd*).

In the midst of jeers and cheers.

The Junior Magistrates will attend to the next business, if
my colleague and I may have your courteous permission to
leave you in their charge . . .

Baying and booing.

Thank you . . . Thank you very much . . . Professor, will you
come this way?

NARRATOR. As they led me from the platform, the meeting
was called to order . . .

*The noise of the crowd recedes. A magistrate is heard appealing
for silence.*

MAGISTRATE. Citizens, if you please, I call this Assembly to
order –

NARRATOR. – by a red-faced loud-voiced Serjeant-Major type
of man who had risen from his seat in the front row and was
greeted by a shower of orange-peel and apple-cores and nut-
shells, for his pains. I had gathered my little men into the
bag and I followed the two Ministers down a corridor into an
ante-chamber.

A door slams, shutting out most of the noise of the crowd.

Here they left me to my own devices with a bottle of wine and
a plate of ginger biscuits. I sat there for say ten minutes. I
could hear their voices in the next room. I am sure I was not

intended to hear, but some holes for ventilation had been left unstoppered up near the ceiling, and their words of necessity came filtering through ...

The MINISTERS' *conversation is heard very indistinctly at first, then by degrees more clearly.*

UNPOPULAR MINISTER. No no no, you are altogether too indulgent. Oh he has these powers, certainly, and considerable skill in their deployment. The question is: how much is him, and how much is his little men? Is it sorcery or conjuring: does he mean to do it or does it happen? We'll not find how to deal with him until we know the answer to that.

POPULAR MINISTER. I do not regard the answer to that as being at all important. Whether it is magical or whether it is calculated, it is perfectly clear to me that the whole performance was informed by the fellow's own personality. So we must act, must we not, as though he intended it all from the very beginning?

UNPOPULAR MINISTER. Very well, let us do so. And precisely *what* did he intend? Subversive encouragement to insurrection and revolution. Setting up the cause of the outlandish men against the citizens. And quite amazingly, the citizens, or the great part of them, applauded.

POPULAR MINISTER. It was exciting, as a narrative, you must grant it that; it had fast movement, confrontation, violent excess of sympathy swinging rapidly to and fro –

UNPOPULAR MINISTER. Sympathy. The audience felt sympathy. Sympathy for the mimic spectacle of their own appalling overthrow. What kind of people *are* they?

POPULAR MINISTER. Very much like any other kind. They know themselves fat because the outlandish men are thin: they suffer now and then in their consciences for this. Either we can help them to forget it, as I do: or else, like this Professor fellow, we can occasionally remind them, let them feel a temporary pang, and their discomfort is assuaged.

Surely this has always been *your* technique. What's wrong with it so suddenly?

UNPOPULAR MINISTER.

> It is altogether one thing to make them afraid
> At rebellion and destruction.
> Quite another to have them urged in open daylight to feel glad
> That such violence can already be conceivably in contemplation.
> Put into their hand a knife with a sharp blade,
> Tell them 'this is for your heart,
> Would you rather have it in your throat,
> Do not forget to offer praise before you die
> For the skill of the knife-grinder
> And the truth of his hand and eye'?
> I ask you: is that politic?
> I tell you, no, it makes me sick.

POPULAR MINISTER. Not altogether as stupid as you would make me out to be. The story concluded after all with the complete failure of the rebellion to consolidate its achievement.

UNPOPULAR MINISTER. I did not consider it a logical development of the plot. And if I did not think so there are likely to be others who would share my opinion.

POPULAR MINISTER. But the fact is they are well-fed and they do not want to be otherwise. Look out of the window, my dear sir, and tell me what is going on.

NARRATOR. I had no window in my room but I could hear sounds from the outside . . .

Screams and cruel laughter, rather faintly heard.

UNPOPULAR MINISTER. Yes. The brigands have been tried and are being put to death in the name of His Majesty. The Assembly is appreciating the act of justice. And so?

POPULAR MINISTER. And so they are appreciating it and their

enjoyment of the execution is in no way diminished by their enjoyment of the recent spectacle, however subversive you may think it has been. In my view the Professor is a young man to be encouraged: though of course we must be careful.

UNPOPULAR MINISTER. Oh, whatever you think best. We can encourage him by all means. And control him.

POPULAR MINISTER. Not control. Suggest directions: that is all . . .

Their voices fade away.

NARRATOR. You will think me very stupid, but the significance of this conversation entirely passed me by. I was so tired, you see, I could hardly keep open my eyes. All I could think of was the power and the splendour of my little men, so newly revealed to me, so manifold in possibility, so outrageously out of proportion to the amount of actual work I had done – they had been absolutely given to me, from where I knew not, and by whom I knew not. But it appeared that they were mine: and I alone was capable of inspiring them into their motions . . . After a little the two ministers returned, they spoke to me in soothing voices, they promised me this, that, and the other –

MINISTERS' VOICES (*through* NARRATOR's *speech*).

Peace and quiet . . . agreeable surroundings . . . appreciative audiences . . . plenty of opportunity for experiment . . . unlimited funds at your disposal . . . and as for any small personal gratifications appropriate to your status amongst us . . . only say the word, my dear fellow, you have only to say the word . . .

NARRATOR. But I think I had already fallen asleep. There was some sensation of being led or carried through one room and then another, and of being laid upon a bed. At any rate there was a bed and I was on it: and I slept.

Yet even asleep I still did keep
The cord that tied my precious bag

Tight in my grasp, lest one should drag
It from me secretly by night.
Mistrustful I was. I was quite right . . .

YOUNG WOMAN (*in a whisper*). What is this cord you grip so tight?

NARRATOR. This cord . . .?

YOUNG WOMAN.

You clench with all your might
Your little fist. I cannot prise
It open. Like a dead man's eyes.

NARRATOR. Hey-up – ho ho – so I've caught you, have I?

YOUNG WOMAN. Let go of my arm, you are hurting me – please!

NARRATOR. No no, you first tell me what you are doing here. Putting out your hand in the dark to grab hold upon my bag: but you grabbed hold upon *me*: and I've got you: so explain yourself and no nonsense.

YOUNG WOMAN. Perfectly happy to explain myself, sir: but keep your voice down. There may be other people awake besides us, late though it is. I came in here as instructed by the Ministers of the King: I am what they call a small personal gratification appropriate to your status – you will have seen me already – I was dancing upon the platform.

NARRATOR. Oh, you were?

YOUNG WOMAN. Yes, I was.

NARRATOR. A most depraved performance.

YOUNG WOMAN. Yes, it was.

NARRATOR. And why should the ministers imagine that I would enjoy your company any further at close quarters?

YOUNG WOMAN. I don't see why you shouldn't – everyone else does.

NARRATOR. Very possibly. But none the less, you had your hand upon my sack.

YOUNG WOMAN. Oh yes, sir, that also was according to instructions.

NARRATOR. Then you'd better get out and be damned to you before I kick you up the –

YOUNG WOMAN. Oh come on, you are half-asleep still. How the devil would you have known I had my hand upon your sack unless I had whispered in your ear that I had, so woke you up?

NARRATOR. And that's a good point . . . Have we not got a light in here – I'd like to have a look at you.

YOUNG WOMAN. We are striking no lights, there are no shutters to the window. What I was told to do I should have done in the dark, if they see a light they will be suspicious. But move over into the moonlight. Now then . . . can you see me?

NARRATOR.

She was not beautiful; but her eyes were big.

Protuberant. They shone like the white of an egg.

The hand by which she held me was wide, hot and strong,

Her lips were thick, her nose was long.

We were quite alone in a narrow plastered room.

Is there anyone listening outside the door?

YOUNG WOMAN. There might be . . . Have a look?

Footsteps on a wooden floor, door opens and shuts.

NARRATOR. Nobody there.

YOUNG WOMAN. Good. Now I am going to tell you what they would kill me for if they heard of it. It will not have escaped your attention that the people of this town live a comfortable life.

NARRATOR. True. And as I take it, you yourself are part of that comfort.

YOUNG WOMAN. Nor yet that the people outside are dying of starvation?

NARRATOR. That's true too. And no one could deny that you have a belly on you like a tub of butter.

YOUNG WOMAN. But you don't know why?

NARRATOR. No.

YOUNG WOMAN.

> So here is the secret:
> Make sure that you keep it.
> By right I should compel you to swear a great oath
> To the burning of your flesh and the shedding of your
>   blood:
> But I do not: so take note –
> It is not possible I should be anything but stark raving
>   mad.
> So being mad, I will begin.
> In the very middle of this town
> Is a deep dark hole struck into the ground,
> Kept well-guarded and closed-in
> By a roof of slate and a wall of stone.
> Day and night selected men
> Descend by ropes to dig and shovel:
> And what they find there as they grovel
> Far underneath us in the dark
> Keeps us as jovial as Midas when
> He touched the door-frame of his but-and-ben
> And turned each rotten timber post
> To what it was he wanted most.
> There is a cave of clay there choked
> With jewels deep in the core of the rock –
> Emeralds, rubies, brooches of gold,
> Every turn of the spade down there will unfold
> A crown or a coronet, a great plate or a goblet
> Or maybe just two or three pearls in a droplet
> Or a thick twist of silver wire for a necklet or armlet.

NARRATOR. And how did it all get there?

YOUNG WOMAN.

> How do you think? It was left there
> By rich men who were frightened, and ran
> From some conqueror or other, in the ancient times.

We are told that these rich men had committed crimes,
Murdered and pillaged – for what other reason
Would they have gathered so much in so short a season?
We call this dirty town the Town of the Murderer's
treasure
And we live on it and live off it,
And we make of it our pleasure.

NARRATOR. So nobody has to do any work.

YOUNG WOMAN. None of the citizens have to do any work.

NARRATOR. And the outlandish men, to whom you deny any
share of your riches?

YOUNG WOMAN. If they work for us, we feed them. But we
don't need very much work.

NARRATOR. Who are they?

YOUNG WOMAN.

Who do you think? You are too slow
To understand what you ought to know.
They are the original murderers who dug the hole and
buried
All that we dig up and all that we inherit.
The citizens came in
One bright year in the season of spring:
They took everything they found
Above and below the ground:
They dwell in a town which they did not build
And they give the name of murderers to the men whom
they killed.

NARRATOR. Is it citizens – *they*? A minute ago you said *we*.
Who are *you*?

YOUNG WOMAN.

I am betwixt and between
Neither the one nor the other
My father was outlandish
He crept in and took theft of my mother

And after that he went back to his old trade as a highway
    robber:
An hereditary enemy of the town where his daughter
    was born.
They let me live and I can feed and survive without
    harm
But I must deserve my protection
By obeying their every instruction
And whatever they do to me
I must have it done to me with charm.

NARRATOR. You are a slave.

YOUNG WOMAN. No more than they are. Because the treasure
that they think is theirs isn't theirs at all. There is a great
King across the water who takes as much of it as he wants,
provides the citizens with the food that ought to be being
grown upon the farms of the outlandish men – if they had
farms, which they once had – he determines his own price
for the treasure that is dug up, he has an ambassador in this
town to supervise the diggings, and he appoints and pays and
administers the horsemen who ride patrol – the ones who
brought you into town. Oh, the whole economy of this
region is entirely ridiculous – you wouldn't credit it if you
met it in real life: but then you are in a dream, and you have
entirely abdicated, have you not, from the regiment of
common-sense?

NARRATOR. I don't know about dreams – I dreamt I had a
young woman in my bag to make love to me, but it wasn't so.
Would you be inclined to make love to me now? I would like
it, if you would?

YOUNG WOMAN. No, take away your fingers from where you
are putting them or I will bite them off this minute – it's not
that kind of dream at all. You have fallen asleep at the wrong
place and the wrong time: and besides I was instructed to
make love to you and I have suddenly turned today into a
mood of rebellion. You know why?

NARRATOR. Why?

YOUNG WOMAN. Because of your little men and the wild memory they dredged up of who my father once was and the strong defiance with which he lived. You send us more remembrances like that, little man, there will be no protection left, no security, no good dinners, nothing but the truth.

Footsteps quickly on the floor, door opens and shuts.

NARRATOR. And at once I was alone in the room without any sign that she had been with me, except for the rancid smell of her breath in the air – such bad breath they all had in this place. For people who lived so voluptuously but in what I now knew to be imminent peril they were extremely indelicate over the detail of their common intercourse. I wished I was back in Muswell Hill – the whole situation was becoming most unpleasant.

> When I fell asleep I had thought my dream would be
> The gulf-weed slowly stroking me on back and side
> The dream of a jellyfish in a warm and waveless sea
> No turbulence to contradict the gentle ebbing of the
> tide:
> I was quite wrong.
> I was not strong.
> I did not think I could survive this kind of sleep.
> I staggered up and down, piercing my feet
> Upon the splinters in the rough-cut floor.

His nervous footsteps.

> I flung open the door –

Sound of door opened.

> Looked out into a passage-way
> And there was no one there.
> I said to myself: I will escape

I will run barefoot upon splinters and stones and thorns
By dint of the pain of it I will surely awake.
This town and its cruel people
Are made only of a vapour
Of falsehood and dirt –
I will awake from them and work
As is my custom without confusion
Upon a clean piece of white paper.
In a clean quiet house with the windows closed
And flowers upon the window-sills elegantly disposed
And my wife between my white sheets
And my children in the green garden
Four children and one sweet wife
Every one of them with the name of Arden.
Let me run, let me run quickly –
Oh God, how the soles of my feet have been torn!

OFFICIAL. Forgive me, but you go no further. I have orders to bring you and your bag directly to a person who is wanting to speak to you.

NARRATOR. Oh . . . I haven't got any shoes on. Let me go back to the room for my shoes.

OFFICIAL. Oh no, that is not possible. Had you been sleeping peacefully I would have woken you with circumspection and let you dress yourself at leisure: but as it is I have run into you in the grey light of dawn apparently in process of making your escape. You are a guest of this city, sir, it is discourteous of you to attempt to evade us: therefore you must come with me, and at once, just as you are. Where is the young woman who was sent to your room to sleep with you?

NARRATOR. I – I sent her away. I did not want her. She was not attractive.

OFFICIAL. You are the first I have heard say so. Come with me, please . . .

NARRATOR. He carried a black wand with a silver knob – some

sort of a tipstaff, no doubt: but there were two men behind
him with clubs, so I could not refuse his invitation. I did put
one nervous question –
Where? To whom? Why?

OFFICIAL. You must not put questions to His Majesty's
Servants.

Footsteps as they go.

NARRATOR. So – ho – it was the King they were taking me to,
was it? But they led me through no glorious forecourts and
tall porticoes of a palace. Down one back-corridor, across a
dingy yard, up another corridor, duck through a storeroom
amongst barrels and boxes, and so at length into a vestibule
about the size of a large tea-chest and here we all four
stopped. There was a four-foot-high door in the whitewashed wall opposite us, and the tipstaff knocked cautiously,
opened it, stuck his head in –

Knock on the door, opening door –

OFFICIAL. Just to check that they're all ready for you. Yes,
they are – in you go.

NARRATOR. And he pushed me in and went out himself and
the door was shut behind me.

Door shuts.

AMBASSADOR. Sit down, there's a stool in the corner.

NARRATOR. A great big man with a face like a bucket of blood.
He sat behind a table in a room surprisingly clean, painted
and gilded, with life-size pictures of soldiers on every panel
of the walls. Each soldier held a different sort of weapon the
blade of every weapon had dark-brown stains upon it, the
faces of the soldiers were like wild animals, with tusks. The
sunrise was coming in through little windows high up near
the ceiling. The great big man was eating eggs. He ate seven
eggs at once and the yolk ran down his chin.

AMBASSADOR. Now then, what's all this, then?

NARRATOR. Your Majesty, I –

AMBASSADOR. Don't call me majesty. Only one majesty in this town, boy, and he's too small.

SECRETARY. You are in the presence, young gentleman, of the Ambassador of the Great King across the water.

NARRATOR. A bespectacled secretary with his face covered with cobwebs, he crouched in the dark behind the door, stabbing flies with his pen-knife. I had not noticed him when I came in.

SECRETARY. You will address the Ambassador as Excellence: because he is.

AMBASSADOR. So you hear who I am.

NARRATOR. Yes, I do – Excellence.

AMBASSADOR. Quiet. I am the enormous Ambassador. I eat eggs and they make me fat. What do you do? Don't tell me. I've been told. You set afoot unauthorized imitations of people you should despise and you blow them out like bull-frogs with the imagination of their strength. *At* the same time, however, you reserve to yourself a sharp pin with which you can at your own convenience prick their distended bellies and explode them into nothing. The first part of your programme, from my point of view, is abhorrent. From the point of view of the underdog people to whom you address yourself, the second part is likewise. Therefore you are very bold, and a man to be objectively admired: or else you are a hedger and a fencesitter, and a contemptible poltroon. I wonder which? In any case you are a man who deserves to be suppressed. But I am not going to suppress you. No: nor am I going to encourage you. I am going to regard you as a challenge and defy you to do your worst. In some sense it may be said that a challenge to us, in this place, is both desirable and requisite . . .

(*In an undertone.*) . . . at least a challenge that we are aware of – for it will attract to its publicity the other, occult,

THE BAGMAN 439

challenges of which at present we have no cognizance, only suspicion . . .

SECRETARY (*likewise in an undertone*). Rather more than suspicion in several cases, Excellence. I am compiling – as you told me – all these dossiers, and there will be certain surprises in the fullness of time –

AMBASSADOR. I don't want to hear them now . . . Boy, you sit there hostile, upon my stool: are you dumbfounded or are you goddamned stubborn? Yes, he's stubborn: yes, he's bold: by God we do admire him. Yes, we lack such men round here. You're going to shake me by the hand!

NARRATOR. His hand had an egg in it. He thought it was funny.

AMBASSADOR *roars with laughter*.

Raw yolk splashed up my sleeve and dribbled between my fingers. Then he threw another egg at the Secretary.

More laughter.

Hit him square upon the spectacles, streaked with white and yellow all the cobwebs across his face.

A strange gravelly noise.

At first I didn't know what the noise was: then I realized it was the Secretary laughing, because the Ambassador was laughing . . . But now I heard this other noise I was not able to account for. Oh God, but it was *me* laughing . . . I suppose I thought it was appropriate and I didn't want to give offence. Never willingly give offence, not me – a disposition always, so I thought, to be both meek and courteous. The next damned egg that the arrogant bastard threw landed right in the middle of my chest.

AMBASSADOR (*still laughing*).

> Eggs are full of gold
> They stink when they are old.
> Scramble boil or poach or fry –

Long and hard oh you may try
You'll never scrape away the stain –
The egg is mine and you are mine.
Go on. Get out. Good-bye . . .

NARRATOR. The Secretary got up, with a sudden and novel politeness he threw open the door for me -- not the small back door by which I had entered: but the proper and painted door of state at the other side of the room, he ushered me out, all deference, into a gallery full of male and female dragon-flies – or so it seemed, so elegant they were, gracefully waving their adorned bodies in this and that inconsequential gesture, one towards the other, and they chewed at little sweetmeats, took discreet sips of little drinks out of thimble-sized crystalware, and buzzed, and then fell silent, and smiled and winked at me as I passed through.

Buzz of conversation, tinkling laughter.

I saw among them the two ministers whom I had seen the previous day but no one else that I recognized. The two ministers were very gracious – smiling at me: but they said nothing. Everyone was looking at my bare feet and my untidy appearance – when all was said this was the audience-chamber of the palace of the King and I was dressed for nothing better than the *Evening Standard* in Muswell Hill – yet there was no malice, there was no scorn, there was a kind of respect about their looks. Just so, I could hear them thinking, comes arrayed the man who holds within his bag the lovely secrets of our lives – so intimate his burden, so abrupt and unmannerly his looks – they found the contrast quite delicious. Then there was a –

Sennet or tucket or fanfare.

– a trumpet, out of Shakespeare, as it were, and the King came in and the Queen, and various other members of the Royal Family, I don't know who they were. Everyone knelt down, except for me – I was a Republican, I said to myself, and I would go on my knees for no man. But I felt a certain embarrassment after standing alone for a long minute, and I began to bend my knees like everybody else, but half-heartedly, in order to show my disapproval of these forms. But the King spoke:

KING. I see you do not kneel.

NARRATOR. I straighten up again, quickly. If he had not noticed my beginning to bend then I might as well appear to be consistent in my disapproval.

No, sir: I do not. I am a Republican, you see.

KING. Yes, you would be. I suppose we all are, these days, are we not? Though you would get a dusty reception in the palace of my cousin, the *Great* King, over the water. But he is a barbarian, really . . . er, his Ambassador's not come in yet?

UNPOPULAR MINISTER. No, Your Majesty, not yet.

KING. Thank goodness for that . . . Very well then, young man – er – Professor, are you called? You may open your bag again and begin. We are yours to command.

NARRATOR. Then they all sat down, put their hands upon their laps, and looked expectantly at me. Somebody clapped –

A small applause, checked by indignant whispers.

– but was immediately shushed. I bowed to them, smiled, opened up the bag, took out the little men, and laid them down upon the polished floorboards in a row, just as before. And just as before the cantankerous dragon inside me began to give tongue . . .

In his distorted voice again.

> My little people in a row
> Sit on the stage and watch the show.
> The show they watch is rows and rows
> Of people watching them . . .

But I felt less at ease than on the previous occasion. I had reminded myself then of Adolf Hitler – Hitler in his prime, at a Nuremburg rally, perhaps – now, if I was Hitler, it was Hitler in the Berlin bunker of 1945, and the boots of the Red Army were stamping above my head. But I got through it and I got on with it and the little people began their story. Not at all the same story. I was amazed at their metamorphosis. They were not even the same sort of people as before. There was a King and a Queen and a Bishop, yes, but the Soldier and the Constable and the Housewife and the ragged men were all gone, their places had been taken by a crowd of posturing exquisites, dolled-up in peacock feathers and waterfalls of gold and silver lace. And there was no fighting in the story. Nothing but extraordinary variations of erotic postures and intrigues, couplings and triplings and quadruplings, men and women together, men and men, women and women, women and men and women – while the audience muttered and laughed and clapped a little and conversed one with another. Some of them walked out. The music was erotic also, but more than a little insipid. At the end, when all the diverse and perverse setting-to-partners had been, in a manner, resolved, there was a courteous but unenthusiastic applause –

Music ends, some clapping etc.

– and I felt ashamed. First because I had not liked the entire narrative from beginning to end, and second, because the audience had not liked it very much either. Or so at least I believed: but when half an hour afterwards I found myself closeted as an honoured guest, in a small and private room with no other than the King and Queen, I began to wonder if I had not been mistaken.

Music playing – a lute.

The King was no more slender than the general run of his subjects: but he was gentle and timorous and kind-hearted.

The Queen was soft and dewy: you could almost call her silly – if she had not been wearing a crown.

KING. So very glad to have this opportunity of speaking to you, my dear Professor.

QUEEN. So different from what we thought you would have been.

KING. But the exhibition itself, the little men – I mean –

QUEEN. Not at all what we expected.

NARRATOR. Oh . . . what did you expect – er – Your Majesty . . .?

KING. Something much more – much more –

QUEEN. Much more flattering, His Majesty means.

KING. We never speak to anybody except flatterers and – and panderers. It was quite a relief to hear the – hear the truth about ourselves.

QUEEN. Yes, it made us squirm.

KING. Indeed, yes . . .

NARRATOR. I did not know whether or not I was expected to say anything . . . Yes, I – er – I try to do my best – Your Majesty . . .

QUEEN. So you do – yes . . .

KING. Yes . . . Tomorrow – at the same time?

NARRATOR. The audience being over, I was shewn to the breakfast room where I ate a huge meal. And the next day at the same time I went through the same performance, and the next day, and the next day, and for days upon days, so it seemed, though there was a kind of odd telescopic effect about the progress of time, and in some way I was not certain but that only a few hours had passed. When I was not employed in demonstrating my powers before the assembled royalty and courtiers, I was left to enjoy myself in the gardens of the palace (for so it was called by everyone, for all that it was no more than a collection of well-decorated summer-houses, cleaner than the town outside but in no sense monumental). Yet gardens it did have, and they were furnished with silver fountains, and marble tables laden with

food and drink, and plenty of sumptuous girls reclining in
their jewels who didn't have anything interesting to say, but
permitted me all manner of familiarity whenever I wanted it.
It was all very indolent and agreeable, and very much beside
the point –

*The lute music has become accompanied by the faraway singing of
a renaissance madrigal, the patter of water from a fountain, the
voices of birds, and the laughter of women. Suddenly this is broken
into by the voice of the* YOUNG WOMAN, *hard and direct. The
music etc., stops abruptly.*

YOUNG WOMAN. And that is a true word. Not only beside the
point – you are entirely beside yourself. Wake up.

NARRATOR. I *am* awake – you are always waking me – it is no
business of yours and in any case I don't believe you have
permission to be in the King's private garden.

YOUNG WOMAN. Private garden?
Turn your sleepy head from left to right
Tell me what you find here in your sight.

NARRATOR.
I turn my head from left to right, right round –
I find myself – on a gravelly patch of ground
Strewn with cinders and old rags,
Rusty buckets, broken jugs.
Where is the fountain, where is the green grass,
Where are the girls whom I dreamed that I did kiss?
Where is the King who spoke to me so kindly?
Can this be his bright palace, all this rubbish piled
around me?

YOUNG WOMAN.
Within your dream you fell asleep again.

NARRATOR.
But when did I fall asleep, when did it go wrong –?

YOUNG WOMAN.
Look at your shirt, boy, look at the yellow stain.

NARRATOR. The egg of the Ambassador – was that the first or second dream?

YOUNG WOMAN. That was the true dream: now I'll show you the true King –

NARRATOR. And stooping through brambles and bits of broken wall and old fences made of useless bedsteads, she brought me secretly by back ways to a derelict shed like a henhouse – you see many such if you go to Dagenham or Romford on the top deck of a London bus, hundreds of them scattered all over the allotments, sordid enough but useful for the men who grow cabbages when not working in the factories. But there was no cabbage-patch here, and the window of the shed was nailed up with creosoted boards. We looked in through a chink between these and it was all dark inside the shed –

A rustling of straw, chink of a chain.

A FEEBLE OLD MAN'S VOICE (*same speaker as the* KING). For the liberty of the people, for the liberty of the people, oh God is there nobody who will give me a drink of water . . .

NARRATOR. Who is it, who have they got in there – is he chained to the wall, or what?

YOUNG WOMAN. Chained to the wall, and has been for twenty years. When they remember, they give him something to eat and drink. That is the King, and this is all that is left of his palace. Now we'd best get out of here before we are caught by the guard.

Heavy footsteps drawing nearer.

S'sst – it's too late, get down among the nettles –

Rustling of undergrowth. Footsteps halt.

GUARD. Stay where you are – who goes! Come out of that and declare yourselves!

YOUNG WOMAN. No no, not yet, not time to declare ourselves yet – put your hand out to the left, what do you find?

NARRATOR. There's an iron ring fixed into a flagstone.

GUARD. I said come out of that – I can see you – all right, then, you want it the hard way –

He blows a whistle and shouts.

Get the dogs, there's two intruders –

More shouts and whistles from a distance. Running feet. The angry yelp of guard-dogs.

YOUNG WOMAN. Pull at it, you fool – it'll come up if you pull strongly, oh for God's sake, look sharp with it!

NARRATOR. It's difficult, the clay all round seems to have set hard – ooh – ugh – aah – I've got it open!

YOUNG WOMAN. Down into it – quick. What the devil are you playing at!

NARRATOR. My bag, I can't leave my bag –

YOUNG WOMAN. God, you'll *have* to leave your bag – you idiot – you –

NARRATOR. No. Aha, I have it. Here we are –

Slam of trapdoor closing, noise of guards instantly shut off.

YOUNG WOMAN. – safe and sound. There's bolts underneath the trap. Shut them.

NARRATOR. Damned rusty . . .

Bolts being dragged.

Do they know about this place? Did they see where we went under?

YOUNG WOMAN. I don't think so – they would have seen us go in among the bushes, and with the dogs they'll soon find the trap. So it can't ever be used again. There was a project, never got anywhere, to rescue the old King this way. Now of course it's finished. But it wasn't any good, the old King's no good to anyone, the fact of the matter is there is nobody any good to anyone, nobody and nothing – except to burn the whole town down. We'll have to do it one of these days –

easy enough, all made of wood: but for some reason nobody wanted to – afraid, I wouldn't wonder, though they *said* they were too humane.

NARRATOR. Where are we?

YOUNG WOMAN. We're in a disused drainpipe. All the old drains in this town are disused. You could tell that from the smell, when you walk about the streets.

NARRATOR. Can we get out anywhere?

YOUNG WOMAN. Not conveniently. It used to lead to the river, but it has been blocked up with dead dogs and so on, there are other trapdoors, we'll find a good one and climb up that way, but we'd better wait till after nightfall. And would you leave that bloody bag behind you – you're going to get stuck in the passageways or goodness knows what – as it is you've already nearly got both of us caught with it!

NARRATOR. I can't leave it. Whatever would I do without it?

YOUNG WOMAN. Just the same as the rest of us – fight.

NARRATOR. Fight . . . but I didn't come here to fight – I was given this bag – to – to – look, I *paid* for this bag: gave all the money I had in my pocket – don't you see that it is all that I have?

YOUNG WOMAN. Which is more than any of the rest of us have. *We* don't need it: *you* don't – get rid of it.

NARRATOR. And who do you think you are talking about – the *rest* of you? – it's the first time I heard –

YOUNG WOMAN. It's the first time you could possibly have heard it – the first time I have ever said it – the first time it has ever happened. This is not just a matter now of little gangs of bold marauders (God rest my father's soul, but that was all that he was) no, it is even *unity*, controlled and organized resistance – we are solidly put together, we are under discipline and we look for power – by God for the first time for how many hundreds of years it is power we are going to get – we are going to get it, in our own hands!

Sudden cheering : cries of 'for the liberty of the people' from many throats, echoing as though in a confined vault.

NARRATOR. And there they all were, crowded in a close dark underground cavern – their emaciated faces lit by flaring torchlight, their fists clenched towards the roof in fantastic ecstasy, their purposeful bodies hung with weapons of every size and variety, from flint axes and bows-and-arrows to great rusty blunderbuss-guns. My young woman, my lascivious dancer, she who had been instructed both to spy upon me and seduce me, now dragged me by force forward into the middle of them all and – without consulting me – proclaimed me to be their brother.

YOUNG WOMAN. He is our brother!

Cheers.

NARRATOR. No; you don't know that at all. And if indeed you are preparing an insurrection in this catacomb, may I tell you that your sense of security leaves a great deal to be desired? As far as you are concerned I'm a complete stranger, yet you bring me into the midst of you and reveal to me your plans. You must be mad.

YOUNG WOMAN. Not at all.

NARRATOR. I could betray you.

YOUNG WOMAN. Not at all. For you are asleep: this is your dream. How can you betray what you have done no more than dream about?

NARRATOR. Oh, very well then, provided that that is clearly understood by all parties.

So: in my dream, I ask of you
To tell me what I am to do.
Outlandish men, who rise in anger
Against the tyrant and oppressor:
What do you want from the lonely stranger –
Beyond that I should share your danger

In, of course, so far as I can?
Lumbered, as I am,
With this most discommodious
But necessary burden –

Generally scornful laughter.

A MAN'S VOICE.
Your burden is no good to us
Throw it down – take up a weapon –
NARRATOR.
This *is* my weapon!
You have your spears and knives:
I have these images of your proud lives.
Here in your secret hold, your dangerous den
I straightway dedicate to you my little men.
So I tore open the sack and tipped them out in front of the
company. I was exalted, my heart burned with zeal – I
was not a fighter, I was no conspirator, I had no power but
this power and I was giving it all to the cause. There was
nothing of Hitler in my voice this time – Savonarola per-
haps, or Oliver Cromwell on the dreich moorland of
Dunbar –
My little people in a row
Sit on the stage and watch the show –

Strange crying voices like birds in a box.

LITTLE MEN. No no, no no, no no, no no –
NARRATOR. I looked down at them in amazement, they were
all clustering and huddling together, some of them struggling
to get back into the bag – they had the appearance of a
whole colony of ants distressed beyond their wits when a
violent boot breaks into their anthill – What are you doing –
why do you not respond to me – you have your business to
perform – for God's sake get on with it – would you put me
to shame before all these men of war?

LITTLE MEN (*one very high thin voice dominant*).
>   Men of war do not require
>   To see themselves in a truthful mirror
>   All that they need to spur them to action
>   Is their own most bloody reflection
>   In the white eyeballs of their foe.
>   We are neat and well-considered little people –
>   If you bring us into battle
>   You bring us only unto grief and woe
>   Fracture and breakage that we cannot repair
>   They will snap our wooden joints
>   And pull out our cotton hair.
>   Please let us please let us get back into the sack
>   When the battle has been won
>   We can peep out again and creep back.

A SUDDEN MAN'S VOICE (*as though running towards them underground*). Comrades, stand to your weapons, we are betrayed, the enemy is upon us – they have got into the tunnels –

YOUNG WOMAN. We are betrayed by this fool with his bag – he has wasted our time and distracted our attention – I warned him, I warned him, he must not bring it here –!

NARRATOR. And in an instant all was blood and death and furious weapons swung at random in the dark.

Great noise of fighting.

The young woman who had brought me there was struck down at the first onslaught – I endeavoured to get between her and the soldier who was beating her to the ground but he thrust me aside with a great backhand blow – I fell down upon my sack and upon the squirming heap of my terrified little men – a huge foot, shod with steel, stamped hard upon my temple. And that was the end of my dream.

>   I awoke upon the platform
>   Of the Highgate Underground Station –

A train was just departing
The passengers thronged in and out
The porter at back of the crowd
Gave his customary shout –

Noises of underground station – 'Mind the doors please' etc ...

I staggered a forsworn traitor,
To the foot of the escalator,
I mounted the moving stair
Came out into the upper air.
In my hand I held a bag
It was a kitbag from the Army,
I looked in it – it was quite empty.
I dropped it in a litter-box
And walked home sideways
Like a slinking fox.
At the corner of Muswell Hill
By the National Provincial Bank
Stood an ancient gipsy beggar-woman
With black hair long and lank.

She spoke to me in an undertone – I make no doubt she was only asking for the price of a bunch of white heather, but the roar of the traffic distorted her voice and all I heard was what she could not possibly have uttered.

OLD WOMAN (*among confused street noises*).

You did not find what you expected
What you found you did not use
What you saw you did not look at
When you looked at it you would not choose!

NARRATOR.

So I pushed past her and went home.
If I had been defeated it was all in a dream.
But the fat men and the thin men
Stood all around me in the street –
I could not carry a fat man's body

Upon a thin man's feet.
It would have been easy it would have been good
To have carried a bag full of solid food
And fed the thin men till they were
As fat as the men who held them in fear
But such is not the nature of these bags
That are given away by old women in rags.
Such is not my nature, nor will be.
All I can do is to look at what I see . . .

Methuen World Classics
include

Jean Anouilh (two volumes)
John Arden (two volumes)
Arden & D'Arcy
Brendan Behan
Aphra Behn
Bertolt Brecht (seven volumes)
Büchner
Bulgakov
Calderón
Čapek
Anton Chekhov
Noël Coward (eight volumes)
Eduardo De Filippo
Max Frisch
John Galsworthy
Gogol
Gorky
Harley Granville Barker
  (two volumes)
Henrik Ibsen (six volumes)
Lorca (three volumes)

Marivaux
Mustapha Matura
David Mercer (two volumes)
Arthur Miller (five volumes)
Molière
Musset
Peter Nichols (two volumes)
Clifford Odets
Joe Orton
A. W. Pinero
Luigi Pirandello
Terence Rattigan
  (two volumes)
W. Somerset Maugham
  (two volumes)
August Strindberg
  (three volumes)
J. M. Synge
Ramón del Valle-Inclán
Frank Wedekind
Oscar Wilde

Methuen Modern Plays
include work by

Methuen Student Editions

Jean Anouilh	*Antigone*
John Arden	*Serjeant Musgrave's Dance*
Alan Ayckbourn	*Confusions*
Aphra Behn	*The Rover*
Edward Bond	*Lear*
Bertolt Brecht	*The Caucasian Chalk Circle*
	Life of Galileo
	Mother Courage and her Children
Anton Chekhov	*The Cherry Orchard*
	The Seagull
Caryl Churchill	*Serious Money*
	Top Girls
Shelagh Delaney	*A Taste of Honey*
Euripides	*Medea*
John Galsworthy	*Strife*
Robert Holman	*Across Oka*
Henrik Ibsen	*A Doll's House*
	Hedda Gabler
Charlotte Keatley	*My Mother Said I Never Should*
Bernard Kops	*Dreams of Anne Frank*
Federico García Lorca	*Blood Wedding*
	The House of Bernarda Alba
	(bilingual edition)
John Marston	*The Malcontent*
Willy Russell	*Blood Brothers*
Wole Soyinka	*Death and the King's Horseman*
August Strindberg	*The Father*
J. M. Synge	*The Playboy of the Western World*
Oscar Wilde	*The Importance of Being Earnest*
Tennessee Williams	*A Streetcar Named Desire*
	The Glass Menagerie
Timberlake Wertenbaker	*Our Country's Good*